REIMAGINING CITIZENSHIP IN POSTWAR EUROPE

REIMAGINING CITIZENSHIP IN POSTWAR EUROPE

Edited by Rachel Chin and Samuel Clowes Huneke

With a Foreword by Anna von der Goltz

CORNELL UNIVERSITY PRESS
Ithaca and London

Copyright © 2025 by Cornell University

This book is freely available in an open access edition through the generous support of George Mason University.

The text of this book is licensed under a Creative Commons Attribution-NonCommercial-NoDerivatives 4.0 International License: https://creativecommons.org/licenses/by-nc-nd/4.0/. To use this book, or parts of this book, in any way not covered by the license, please contact Cornell University Press, Sage House, 512 East State Street, Ithaca, New York 14850. Visit our website at cornellpress.cornell.edu.

First published 2025 by Cornell University Press

Library of Congress Cataloging-in-Publication Data

Names: Chin, Rachel, 1987– editor. | Huneke, Samuel Clowes, editor. | Von der Goltz, Anna, 1978– writer of foreword.
Title: Reimagining citizenship in postwar Europe / edited by Rachel Chin and Samuel Clowes Huneke, with a foreword by Anna von der Goltz.
Description: Ithaca : Cornell University Press, 2025. | Includes bibliographical references and index.
Identifiers: LCCN 2024025095 (print) | LCCN 2024025096 (ebook) | ISBN 9781501779183 (hardcover) | ISBN 9781501779190 (paperback) | ISBN 9781501779206 (epub) | ISBN 9781501779213 (pdf)
Subjects: LCSH: Citizenship—Europe—History—20th century. | Citizenship—Europe—History—21st century.
Classification: LCC JF801 .R42 2025 (print) | LCC JF801 (ebook) | DDC 323.6094/0904—dc23/eng/20240823
LC record available at https://lccn.loc.gov/2024025095
LC ebook record available at https://lccn.loc.gov/2024025096

For Martin and Richard

+

For Edith Sheffer

The confusion in which we live is partly our own work.
—Hannah Arendt, *We Refugees*

The workers, who had once been easily abused nomads drifting from one estate or tin-mine to another, had started to settle down and demand the rights of citizens.
—J. G. Farrell, *The Singapore Grip*

Contents

Foreword: Some Thoughts on Citizenship, Past and Present ANNA VON DER GOLTZ *xi*

Introduction: Citizenship in European History RACHEL CHIN AND SAMUEL CLOWES HUNEKE 1

1. The Stateless Struggle to Belong in the Postwar Period LAURA HILTON 25

2. Women's Suffrage and the Making of the French Union, 1944–1946 EMILY LORD FRANSEE 46

3. Citizenship, Psychiatry, and Gender in Postwar Vienna DAGMAR WERNITZNIG 64

4. Race and Racism in the Citizenship Law and Naturalization Practice of Early West Germany NICHOLAS COURTMAN 85

5. Statelessness and Social Citizenship of Greek Civil War Refugees in Post-1948 Communist Czechoslovakia NIKOLA TOHMA 115

6. Precarious Citizenship in Olivia Manning's *Balkan Trilogy* STANISLAVA DIKOVA 143

7. The Francoist Conception of
   Citizenship in Postwar Spain
   Carlos Domper Lasús   163

8. Gender, Labor, and the Forging
   of Socialist Citizenship in
   East Germany Rachel Weiser   183

9. Compulsory Voting, Gender,
   and Race under the French
   Fourth Republic Zoé Kergomard   201

10. Commercial Sex, Gender, and
    Citizenship in Postwar Poland
    Anna Dobrowolska   224

11. Southern Italian Migrants and
    Contested Social Rights in 1970s
    Italy and West Germany Sarah
    Jacobson   245

12. The Emergence of European
    Citizenship Serhii Lashyn   267

Index 293

Foreword

Some Thoughts on Citizenship, Past and Present

This book, compiled by the historians Rachel Chin and Samuel Clowes Huneke, could hardly be timelier. Debates that touch on the often-contested meanings of citizenship have been omnipresent in recent years, among scholars and the public alike, in Europe and beyond.

In the United States, in 2016, the election of Donald J. Trump, which followed a campaign built on calls for tighter border controls and racist denunciations of immigrants and minorities, put the question of who counted as a full American center-stage. Radical though some of the Republican president's rhetoric and proposed solutions no doubt were, Trumpism stood in a longer line of continuity of a Republican Party ill at ease with the idea of multiracial democracy. Since the 1960s, the American Right had sought different ways to protect the political and economic privileges of a shrinking white majority, with the recent open and sustained assault on voting rights in numerous states offering perhaps the clearest indication that core political rights were at stake.

Europe has been the site of similar conflicts. The Syrian refugee crisis of 2015 challenged ideas of universal human rights and the right to asylum, sparking ongoing debates about immigration, the integration of refugees, and European values. Competing ideas about the meaning of citizenship and national sovereignty were also at the heart of "Brexit"—the British exit from the European Union, which resulted from the British electorate's vote in a national referendum held in June 2016. The figure of the Polish plumber, who was allowed to live and work in the United Kingdom because of his European citizenship (first enshrined in the 1992 Maastricht Treaty) and who allegedly drove ordinary Britons into unemployment, drained public resources, and helped to change the ethnic and linguistic composition of local communities, became a symbol of the Leave campaign's quest to "take back control." Brexit was at least partly the result of a clash between competing visions of citizenship—global or European versus national—and of vastly different understandings of where community was located. In her 2016 Conservative Party Conference speech, the new prime minister Theresa May made this explicit when she said that today "too many people in positions of power behave as though they have more in common with international elites than with the people down the road, the people they employ, the people they pass in the street. But if you believe you are a citizen of the world, you are a citizen of nowhere. You don't understand what the very word 'citizenship' means." Expressing chief complaints from the populist playbook, namely citizens' powerlessness and elite indifference, she called the Brexit referendum a "quiet revolution" in which "millions of our fellow citizens stood up and said they were not prepared to be ignored anymore."[1]

Fast forward a few years, to 2020; the global COVID-19 pandemic thrust questions surrounding citizenship even more directly into the spotlight. Hastily imposed lockdowns and extended travel restrictions to curb the spread of the deadly virus meant that even members of the cosmopolitan elite—May's "citizens of nowhere"—suddenly found that their specific legal citizenship status (and place of residence) still mattered far more than they had grown accustomed to. It determined if and where they were allowed to travel, whether they could see their families abroad, and whether their daily lives came to a complete halt or not. If Brexit and Trump's wall had not yet made it clear, it was now undeniable that borders were back with a vengeance.

The pandemic response, which varied considerably across different countries and localities, also raised countless questions about the civic duties and responsibilities that come with citizenship: the relationship of citizens to one another and their communities. Whose interests and claims to protection were more important—those of the patient with an autoimmune disease or of the business owner fearing financial ruin? What kinds of curbs on individual liberty were justified to help protect one's fellow citizens? In short, what exactly did citizens owe one another? These were weighty and heavily contested questions that reflected and further deepened existing political and cultural cleavages.

While all these issues are as much political as they are cultural, economic concerns, particularly questions related to inequality, have often been at the heart of recent debates surrounding citizenship. In an era

---

1. Theresa May, speech at the Conservative Party Conference, October 5, 2016, available at https://conservativehome.com/2016/10/05/watch-theresa-mays-speech-to-the-conservative-party-conference-in-full/.

of highly globalized economies and international governance, national governments have limited control over many issues affecting their citizens. This has engendered a sense of disempowerment and neglect on the part of many, who have felt left behind and disenfranchised. As the influential work of French economist Thomas Piketty and others has shown, inequality has risen starkly across Europe and in the United States in recent decades—a phenomenon that poses a threat to the very survival of liberal democracy, Piketty has warned.[2] He demonstrated that the years between 1930 and 1975—which include the era that is the focus of this volume—were not the norm from which we have since departed but highly exceptional. This period was the only time since the eighteenth century that the general trend toward higher inequality under capitalism was reversed. Unique circumstances produced this outcome: the destruction of wealth by the Great Depression and Second World War, massive programs of income redistribution introduced in the postwar period, and the immense economic growth that followed meant a rising tide that, for a moment, lifted all boats.

Piketty's findings help to contest T. H. Marshall's Whiggish notion—if it indeed needs further contesting after years of critique—that citizenship rights have expanded in largely linear fashion since the bourgeois revolutions, from legal to political to social rights. Marshall's influential 1949 lectures on the topic identified an equalization of opportunity in the twentieth century that, he argued, went hand in hand with an expansion of citizenship rights.[3] While this equalization did indeed occur, it was only temporary, as Piketty's work showed in great empirical depth. This helps to historicize why the British sociologist might have come to his conclusions in the late 1940s. In the wake of the founding of the National Health Service, the centerpiece of the postwar British welfare state, and in the midst of an unprecedented period of narrowing wealth inequality, his conception of citizenship as ever-expanding made much more sense than it would after the *trente glorieuses* had come to an end and governments began to heed neoliberal economists' calls for cuts to the welfare state. How to reconcile growing economic inequality with the idea of equal citizenship has been at the core of recent political struggles across capitalist liberal democracies.

---

2. Thomas Piketty, *Capital in the Twenty-First Century*, trans. Arthur Goldhammer (Cambridge, MA: Harvard University Press, 2013).

3. T. H. Marshall, *Citizenship and Social Class and Other Essays* (Cambridge: Cambridge University Press, 1950), 46–74.

Other recent developments, which have illustrated that rights can expand but also contract, have further undermined teleological readings of citizenship: the US Supreme Court's *Dobbs v. Jackson Women's Health Organization* decision of 2022 held that, contrary to what had been established in both *Roe v. Wade* (1973) and *Planned Parenthood v. Casey* (1992), the United States Constitution did not confer a right to abortion. In many Republican-led states, women have since lost the right to control their own bodies—a right they had taken for granted for nearly half a century. For British citizens, the contraction of their rights has been palpable since January 31, 2020, the day that the United Kingdom formally left the European Union. After years of benefiting from freedom of movement and much else, Britons lost their European citizenship. Concurrently, European citizens living and working in the UK have faced a host of new requirements and restrictions.

Against this background, it is especially welcome that the authors of this volume have set out to question overly progressive readings of the history of citizenship. Instead of tracing a clear arc that bends toward an extension of rights and greater political inclusion, the authors show in granular detail how exactly citizenship was (re)imagined and put into practice as policy in the postwar period. Rather than understanding the year 1945 as a "zero hour" that saw Europe rise like a phoenix from the ashes, several of the authors write across this caesura. They show that conceptions of citizenship, while recast, often preserved preexisting traditions of exclusionary citizenship, rooted in race, gender, age, or sexuality, or introduced new forms of exclusion. These were expressed in a new key—sometimes in the new idiom of human rights—but in some cases continued older forms of persecution and oppression.

Nicholas Courtman, for instance, shows that even though the Federal Republic of Germany constitutionally banned discrimination on racial grounds, West German officials and legal experts often employed euphemisms that purposefully obscured the fact that they did, in fact, racially discriminate in practice, particularly against Eastern Europeans and nonwhite immigrants. Behind closed doors, they even sometimes still used the language of biological race when crafting citizenship policy. Drawing boundaries of exclusion and inclusion also went hand in hand, as Nikola Tohma shows. While ethnic Germans were stripped of their Czechoslovak citizenship and expelled from the country at the end of the war, communist Greeks who had fought in the Greek Civil War were deemed politically reliable and therefore welcomed as new socialist citizens.

It is worth noting that the editors conceive of postwar European history in terms that are simultaneously broader and deeper than has often been the case in the historiography; the book includes pieces on citizenship in Western liberal democracies, including their (former) colonies, in the new socialist states of Eastern Europe, and in the right-wing, authoritarian state of Spain. At the same time, several authors focus closely on European citizens who were on the margins of their respective societies: Polish sex workers, psychiatric patients in Austria, Southern European migrants, or stateless individuals who lacked any formal legal-political status. The "Europe" that emerges from these pages is one that is quite different from the one we got to know through older surveys that were often much more Western-, elite-, and male-centric.[4]

Finally, the book makes an important contribution in that it helps to illuminate a specific and pivotal moment in the history of a notoriously slippery concept. Whereas in some languages the meaning of this concept is limited to a "thin" political-legal dimension (e.g., the German *Staatsbürgerschaft* or *Staatsangehörigkeit*), the more evocative English term "citizenship" (much like the French *citoyen*) lends itself to a "thicker" understanding, capturing, as it does, a much wider range of phenomena—cultural constructions, self-understandings, and how community members conceive of their mutual ties.[5] While this openness has led to a wealth of interpretations and creative scholarly applications, citizenship has been in danger of losing precision as an analytical tool. If everything is somehow a facet of citizenship, what does the concept ultimately help us explain in any concrete way?

The editors of this fascinating book provide one answer. They suggest that going back to the sources and to the specific historical context of postwar Europe can at least help us understand how present-day notions of citizenship emerged in the way that they did—and what it might take to reshape them to suit our twenty-first-century world. Chin and Huneke write, "It is our claim that returning to a specific time and place in history, in this case the years after World War II in Europe,

---

4. E.g., William Hitchcock, *The Struggle for Europe: The Turbulent History of a Divided Continent, 1945–2002* (New York: Doubleday, 2003).

5. German social scientists indeed often use the English term as an analytical tool. E.g., Jürgen Mackert and Hans-Peter Müller, eds., *Moderne (Staats)Bürgerschaft: Nationale Staatsbürgerschaft und die Debatten der Citizenship Studies* (Wiesbaden: VS Verlag für Sozialwissenschaften, 2007); see further Geoff Eley and Jan Palmowski, "Citizenship and National Identity in Twentieth-Century Germany," in *Citizenship and National Identity in Twentieth-Century Germany*, ed. Geoff Eley and Jan Palmowski (Stanford, CA: Stanford University Press, 2007).

can recoup some precision in our understanding of how citizenship has changed over time and encourage us to once again reimagine what it might mean to belong in the modern world."

This book indeed achieves much of what it set out to do and accomplishes far more than many edited volumes—the contributions here highlight the importance of historical context for thinking about citizenship, stimulate conceptual discussion among scholars, and perhaps even spur European citizens to action.

Anna von der Goltz
Georgetown University

REIMAGINING CITIZENSHIP
IN POSTWAR EUROPE

Introduction

Citizenship in European History

Rachel Chin and Samuel Clowes Huneke

Citizen (si•tizĕn), n.

A member of a state, an enfranchised inhabitant of a country, as opposed to an alien

—*Oxford English Dictionary*, 1st ed., 1893

A legally recognized subject or national of a state, commonwealth, or other polity, either native or naturalized, having certain rights, privileges, or duties

—*Oxford English Dictionary*, 3rd ed., 2014

Is it wrong to begin with destruction? When we consider the factors that have shaped the world we inhabit today, it is difficult not to think of World War II, "the war," the great conflagration. The nearly six years of fighting in Europe were ferocious: cities flattened, whole peoples exterminated or uprooted, diseases rampant, hunger on every street, the specter of death everywhere. Open war in the European theater officially ended in Berlin on May 8, 1945. But reconstruction would take years, even decades, as ordinary individuals—often women—cleared away rubble, governments rationed food, and devastated economies struggled to rebuild. Alongside physical reconstruction, other less tangible shifts were also taking shape. These changes reflected the scale of human displacement that had occurred during the conflict. They spoke to the political divisions that in 1945 were already beginning to solidify into national boundaries, and they grew out of wider debates that had been at the heart of the war. These changes to the continent's social, political, economic, and cultural fabric encompassed a fundamental reimagining of what it meant to be a citizen, of what it meant to belong to a community, a state, a nation, or an empire.

For all that World War II altered, it has been surprisingly easy to think of the postwar period as a restoration, as a return to the liberal, capitalist, democratic principles that even in the first decades of the twenty-first century seemed so smugly self-confident. It has been simple—or at least it was until the political upheavals of 2016—to forget not only the very real ideological challenges that fascism and communism posed to the liberal order, but also the relative openness of the early postwar era.[1] These were years of unprecedented upheaval and renegotiation, both political and social. The axioms of the international order had not yet been established, the constitutions of new states were not yet written, and the norms that would prevail were not yet solidified. The very definition of belonging—of who was a citizen, what citizenship meant, and who could get it—remained in flux.

In recent years, postwar stability has all started to look a little less certain. Brexit, the Syrian refugee crisis, the election of Donald Trump, the growth of the Alternative for Germany, neocolonial violence in Palestine—the consensus that Francis Fukuyama once hailed as "the end of history" has been tottering for some time now.[2] The concept of citizenship is at the heart of the challenges now posed to the liberal, democratic order: who can vote, who can migrate, who can seek asylum, who, in the words of Hannah Arendt, has "the right to have rights."[3] Indeed, as we wrote this introduction, since-sacked British home secretary Suella Braverman challenged the legitimacy of the 1951 Refugee Convention, arguing that multiculturalism has failed in Europe thanks to uncontrolled migration.[4]

These challenges have not emerged from thin air. Many arose directly from institutions, agreements, and understandings that were substantially influenced by the experience of the Second World War and that were solidified in the years that followed. It is the contention of this book that to understand and in turn respond to these challenges, we must first appreciate their historical pedigree. Doing so will shed light on the complex dynamics and the diverse range of actors that played a part in crafting contemporary notions of citizenship and belonging. At the same time, it will create a new opportunity to bring methodological clarity to our understanding of citizenship as a dynamic and malleable concept in history.

---

1. Mark Mazower, *Dark Continent: Europe's Twentieth Century* (New York: Vintage Books, 1998), 3–40.
2. Francis Fukuyama, *The End of History and the Last Man* (New York: Free Press, 1992).
3. Hannah Arendt, *The Origins of Totalitarianism* (New York: Harcourt, 1976), 296.
4. "Braverman's Refugee Speech Sparks UN Human Rights Criticism," BBC, September 26, 2023, https://www.bbc.com/news/live/uk-politics-66922119/page/2.

A Brief Biography of Citizenship

One of the principal difficulties in mapping the evolution of citizenship is that it is both a concept and a practice—and volatile ones at that.[5] Historians, sociologists, political scientists, and legal scholars have all attempted to define what citizenship is and how its meaning has changed over time. At the same time, our understandings of and interactions with citizenship are constantly being shaped and shifted as a result of ongoing contemporary debates. It should therefore come as no surprise that it has proven difficult to pin down a straightforward definition of the term.

The concept of citizenship is an old one. It stretches back to at least the ancient Greek and Roman republics. Yet its ancient roots do not confer definitional rootedness. A century ago, the *Oxford English Dictionary* tells us, the term simply meant the enfranchised national of a given country. But in more recent years, even its dictionary definition has ballooned, taking on new valances. As its meanings have proliferated, some scholars, like Charles Tilly, have clung to normative definitions, asserting that citizenship concerns "duties, obligations, privileges, and rights." Other scholars have slowly given up the hope of pinning it down. The editors of *The Oxford Handbook of Citizenship*, for instance, write that to "articulate a single definition of citizenship" would be "a hopeless task or a sectarian project." Kathleen Canning and Sonya O. Rose have described it as "one of the most porous concepts in contemporary academic parlance."[6]

Citizenship's ambiguity is evident even in its origins. In the Greek polis, which has served as a foil for political philosophers ever since, citizens were—according to the frequently cited Aristotelian model—free adult men equally competent to take part in the governance of the city.[7] But while Arendt termed the politics of the polis a "kind of theater where freedom could appear," it was predicated on the exclusion of

---

5. Frederick Cooper, *Citizenship, Inequality, and Difference* (Princeton, NJ: Princeton University Press), 41.

6. Charles Tilly, "A Primer on Citizenship," *Theory and Society* 26 (1997): 599; Ayelet Schachar et al., "Introduction: Citizenship—*Quo Vadis?*," in *The Oxford Handbook of Citizenship*, ed. Ayelet Schachar, Rainer Bauböck, Irene Bloemraad, and Maarten Vink (Oxford: Oxford University Press, 2017), 5; Kathleen Canning and Sonya O. Rose, "Introduction: Gender, Citizenship and Subjectivity: Some Historical and Theoretical Considerations," *Gender & History* 13, no. 3 (2001): 427.

7. Alain Duplouy, "Pathways to Archaic Citizenship," in *Defining Citizenship in Archaic Greece*, ed. Alain Duplouy and Roger W. Brock (Oxford: Oxford University Press, 2018), 4–6.

women, minors, and enslaved peoples.[8] The early history of citizenship is also inseparable from the history of empire, a fact that underlines its origins beyond the nation-state. Centuries later, Roman intellectuals recognized that citizenship introduced questions of social inclusion, exclusion, and inequality.[9] In Rome itself, only free adult men could participate in the politics of the Republic, although here class distinctions began to creep in, separating plebeian from patrician.[10]

Centuries later, in the corporate politics of the Middle Ages, citizenship was frequently imagined as a quality of free cities, but not of nations or feudal polities.[11] In contrast, starting in the eighteenth century, as modern nation-states took form, beginning with the American and French Revolutions, thinkers once again turned to citizenship as a way of understanding the relationships—and hierarchies of power—among and between individuals, society, and government. In those revolutions of the late eighteenth century, ascendant classes claimed citizenship for themselves as a way of insisting on their right to take part in the political affairs of the nation-state. Drawing on the concepts of both nationality and citizenship, their demands frequently challenged existing feudal and imperial structures.

After 1776, British colonial settlers staked claim to a new American citizenship. It posited free and equal participation in a democratic republic, but it was also predicated on the disenfranchisement of women and the violent suppression of Black and Indigenous peoples. In Europe, in Simon Schama's famous formulation, subjects became French citizens. In the Netherlands, to take Maarten Prak's words, burghers became Dutch citizens.[12]

At this point in history, citizenship, however idealized by Enlightenment philosophers and revolutionary politicians, was little more than a bludgeon by which the nascent bourgeoisie sought to wrest political power from their titled peers.[13] Over the course of the nineteenth

---

8. Hannah Arendt, "Freedom and Politics," *Chicago Review* 14, no. 1 (Spring 1960): 34.

9. Cooper, *Citizenship*, 40–41.

10. Jane F. Gardner, *Being a Roman Citizen* (London: Routledge, 1993), 17.

11. Mack Walker, *German Home Towns: Community, State, and General Estate, 1648–1871* (Ithaca, NY: Cornell University Press, 1971), 204–7.

12. Simon Schama, *Citizens: A Chronicle of the French Revolution* (New York: Vintage Books, 1989), 113; Maarten Prak, "Burghers into Citizens: Urban and National Citizenship in the Netherlands during the Revolutionary Era (c. 1800)," *Theory and Society* 26, no. 4 (August 1997): 403–20.

13. Rousseau, for instance, imagined sovereignty flowing from the assembled "General Will" of free and equal citizens. Jean-Jacques Rousseau, "Of the Social Contract," in *"The*

and into the twentieth century, though, a host of social and political movements sought to expand access to citizenship and thereby increase political participation, social prerogatives, and civil rights.[14] As a result, citizenship came to denote not merely who had a say in politics, but also who could behave in what ways and why, who could travel, own different forms of property, engage in certain sexual acts, or study particular subjects. It is no coincidence that this was the era of the first identitarian movements, from nationalist and feminist movements to socialism and the movement for homosexual rights.

These evolutions took on distinctively national flavors. Different countries imagined the legal belongings conferred by citizenship in different ways. One particularly stark divide lay between those countries that conferred citizenship on those born within their borders (*jus soli*) and those that conferred it only on the offspring of citizens (*jus sanguinis*).[15] These terms, though, often obfuscate as much as they clarify, hiding ideological slippages and paradoxical statuses. The French, for instance, repeatedly insisted that their citizenship was based not on blood or race but rather on republican values—yet still continued to discriminate on the basis of race and to strip women who married foreigners of their French citizenship.[16] The British, for all their high-minded talk of parliamentary democracy, only granted universal suffrage in 1928. And although the postwar Labour government led by Prime Minister Clement Attlee introduced one of the most ambitious modern welfare states after 1945, subjects and citizens of the British empire and commonwealth continued (and continue) to experience undisguised discrimination.[17] Indeed, many of the debates around UK citizenship were rooted in highly racialized arguments over what it meant

---

Social Contract" and Other Later Political Writings, ed. Victor Gourevitch (Cambridge: Cambridge University Press, 1997), 124.

14. Holly Case, *The Age of Questions: Or, A First Attempt at an Aggregate History of the Eastern, Social, Woman, American, Jewish, Polish, Bullion, Tuberculosis, and Many Other Questions over the Nineteenth Century, and Beyond* (Princeton, NJ: Princeton University Press, 2018), 72-95.

15. James Brown Scott, "Jus Soli or Jus Sanguinis," *American Journal of International Law* 24, no. 1 (January 1930): 58-64.

16. Rogers Brubaker, *Citizenship and Nationhood in France and Germany* (Cambridge, MA: Harvard University Press, 1992), 1; Elisa Camiscioli, *Reproducing the French Race: Immigration, Intimacy, and Embodiment in the Early Twentieth Century* (Durham, NC: Duke University Press, 2009). See also Nimisha Barton, *Reproductive Citizens: Gender, Immigration, and the State in Modern France, 1880–1945* (Ithaca, NY: Cornell University Press, 2020).

17. For more on the idea of imperial citizenship and nineteenth-century attempts to establish it see Daniel Gorman, *Imperial Citizenship: Empire and the Question of Belonging* (Manchester: Manchester University Press, 2006); Daniel Gorman, "Wider and Wider Still? Racial Politics, Intra-imperial Immigration and the Absence of an Imperial Citizenship in the British

to be British, and they persist today.[18] In contrast, while still governed as an imperial monarchy in the late nineteenth century, Germany introduced a precocious set of welfare rights and granted universal male suffrage, in part in an attempt to attenuate the shift of political power to the working classes.

By the mid-twentieth century, these uneven expansions of citizenship began to attract the sustained interest of scholars. In 1949, a year we might justifiably consider the pivot of the early Cold War, British sociologist T. H. Marshall delivered his seminal lecture "Citizenship and Social Class" at Cambridge University. Published the following year, the lecture described the gradual expansion of citizenship from a narrow set of civil rights in the eighteenth century to a broader set of democratic political rights in the nineteenth. It concluded with the introduction of social rights in the twentieth century.[19]

Inspired by the emergence of the British welfare state, Marshall's work had a profound influence on scholars. It encouraged researchers to define citizenship as a "thick phenomenon" or a rich web of rights and responsibilities rather than a "thin" set of political privileges.[20] In the years that followed, historians, sociologists, and legal scholars generated a plentiful body of interdisciplinary research. These interrogations into both the historical and the contemporary nature of citizenship have been instrumental in framing debates around the concept and related concepts such as national identity, belonging, migration, and asylum. But Marshall's formulation was not without its critics. By suggesting that citizenship had steadily expanded over time, Marshall implicitly flattened the more complex realities of how and why it had been deployed as a practice in historical time and geographical space. More recently, scholars have questioned his teleological

---

Empire," *Journal of Colonialism and Colonial History* 3, no. 3 (2002): https://doi.org/10.1353/cch.2002.0066.

18. See, for instance, Rieko Karatani and Guy S. Goodwin-Gill, *Defining British Citizenship: Empire, Commonwealth and Modern Britain* (London: Frank Cass, 2003); Wendy Webster, *Englishness and Empire, 1939–1965* (Oxford: Oxford University Press, 2005); Nadine el-Enany, *Bordering Britain: Law, Race and Empire* (Manchester: Manchester University Press, 2020).

19. The rights of the eighteenth century that Marshall identified included "liberty of the person, freedom of speech, thought and faith, the right to own property and to conclude valid contracts, and the right to justice." T. H. Marshall, *Citizenship and Social Class* (Cambridge: Cambridge University Press, 1950), 10.

20. Geoff Eley and Jan Palmowski, "Citizenship and National Identity in Twentieth-Century Germany," in *Citizenship and National Identity in Twentieth-Century Germany*, ed. Geoff Eley and Jan Palmowski (Stanford, CA: Stanford University Press, 2008), 7.

assumption of progress, spurred in particular by neoliberal reforms to the welfare state at the end of the twentieth century.[21]

Regardless of the critiques of Marshall's framework, his conception of citizenship as thick rather than thin persists in scholarship and in practice.[22] This makes the term even more difficult to define conceptually but also reflects the complex and nonlinear fashion in which citizenship has evolved and is still evolving. Today, scholars and practitioners negotiate, construct, and realize a whole range of understandings of citizenship.

One might be tempted to think that legal definitions of citizenship have retained the greatest clarity. Laws create frameworks that, at least in theory, unambiguously delineate who is and who is not a citizen of a given state. But statutes governing citizenship change over time. Individuals can hold multiple and, in some cases, no legal citizenships. States use migration and citizenship law to guard particular (and highly exclusionary) definitions of national identity and belonging. Moreover, citizens who are subject to these laws have historically enjoyed different sets of rights and responsibilities depending on categories such as age, race, ability, sexuality, religion, and gender. Even traditional rights of citizenship, such as the right to vote, have proven malleable. In February 2020, for instance, the Scottish government extended the right to vote in Scottish Parliament and local elections "to all foreign nationals with leave to remain including all those granted refugee status." In the United States, too, certain municipalities have begun to allow noncitizen residents to vote in local elections, sparking a backlash from politicians who want to preserve the franchise for citizens.[23] And across the European Union, resident noncitizens are often enfranchised to vote for members of the European Parliament.[24]

Sociologists and historians have attempted to get around these complex realities by defining citizenship as both "a status and a practice."[25]

---

21. Charles Tilly, "Citizenship, Identity and Social History," *International Review of Social History* 40, no. 3 (1995): 3.

22. This is not to suggest that research and practice are distinct from each other, rather that the relationship between the two is itself complex.

23. "Right to Vote Extended," Scottish Government, February 20, 2020, https://www.gov.scot/news/right-to-vote-extended/; Kira Lerner, "Republicans Lead Charge to Ban Noncitizens from Voting in Local Elections," *Guardian*, December 22, 2022, https://www.theguardian.com/us-news/2022/dec/22/republicans-noncitizen-voting-ban-local-elections.

24. "European Election," Your Europe, https://europa.eu/youreurope/citizens/residence/elections-abroad/european-elections/index_en.htm.

25. See, for instance, Matthew Grant, "Historicizing Citizenship in Post-war Britain," *Historical Journal* 59, no. 4 (2016): 1189; Ruth Lister, *Citizenship: Feminist Perspectives*, 2nd ed.

This view emphasizes its mutable nature while also acknowledging that what we view as formal citizenship is frequently enshrined in a specific set of laws. By acknowledging the formal as well as informal nature of citizenship, scholars have explored how individuals and groups have engaged with and wielded the idea of citizenship in different contexts, using different means, and with different goals. Over the course of the twentieth century, the most private elements of life came to be seen as facets of citizenship. In the watershed of 1960s radicalism, under the slogan "the personal is political," even sexuality was understood as an element of citizenship, something that both limited individuals' access to the full rights and privileges of citizenship and mediated how they experienced and expressed a sense of political, social, and even economic belonging.[26]

Other scholarship has departed yet further from Marshall's tripartite construction in order to focus on citizenship as a relational construct, or a heading under which we understand how individuals engage in political, social, and cultural meaning-making. Margaret Somers argued that Marshall's conception of social citizenship does not recognize that real social relationships are an essential part of the human experience. They are not, as Marshall contends, simply "an outgrowth of civil-political citizenship." Canning, likewise, suggests that "participatory citizenship" offers a better way to understand the expansive ambit of citizenship in the modern era, pointing to individuals' subjective understanding of rights, responsibilities, and belongings that shape their lives in modern states.[27] Viewing citizenship in this way has many advantages. It recognizes that citizenship is not just a formal legal status and instead encompasses intangible and emotive elements such as identity and belonging that are constructed over time.

Still, relational models cannot escape the state entirely. Modern citizenship has required the existence of nation-states. Without a state

---

(Basingstoke, UK: Palgrave Macmillan, 2003). Daniel Gorman similarly argues that citizenship has two sides: (1) rights and responsibilities and (2) social and cultural. Gorman, *Imperial Citizenship*, 205.

26. Samuel Clowes Huneke, *States of Liberation: Gay Men between Dictatorship and Democracy in Cold War Germany* (Toronto: University of Toronto Press, 2022), 122–26; Timothy Scott Brown, *West Germany and the Global Sixties: The Antiauthoritarian Revolt, 1962–1978* (Cambridge: Cambridge University Press, 2013), 286–329.

27. Margaret Somers, *Genealogies of Citizenship: Markets, Statelessness, and the Right to Have Rights* (Cambridge: Cambridge University Press, 2008), 6–7; Cooper, *Citizenship*, 10; Kathleen Canning, "Reflections on the Vocabulary of Citizenship in Twentieth-Century Germany," in *Citizenship and National Identity in Twentieth-Century Germany*, ed. Geoff Eley and Jan Palmowski (Stanford, CA: Stanford University Press, 2008), 223.

that guarantees the "right to have rights," citizenship becomes a rather vacant institution. Indeed, Rogers Brubaker once argued that sociologists and political scientists had neglected this formal side of citizenship. He saw this trend as a mistake, contending that the formalization and codification of citizenship are also important social processes.[28] And formal citizenship, by its very nature, is exclusive. Modern citizenship drew "visible lines between insiders and outsiders," in Charles Tilly's formulation, bringing the entire "coercive power" of government to bear to enforce these lines.[29] Thus, citizenship has come to signify a paradox between the historical expansion of rights and responsibilities, and of forms of governance and community that shape modern life, on the one hand, and the often violent exclusions on which they were predicated, on the other.

Examining the violence inherent to citizenship has also offered a fruitful way to understand the phenomenon's subjective, participatory sides. Interrogating how race, gender, and sexuality both limited individuals' access to citizenship and informed their own subjective sense of citizenship has shaped much of the recent scholarship. Canning's explorations of early twentieth-century German feminism, for instance, underscore not merely the limits that imperial and republican governments placed on their female citizens, but also how female activists generated from their gender "a recognizable language of claims we might call 'citizenship.'" Similarly, Nimisha Barton, Richard Hopkins, and others have demonstrated the practical limitations of Marshall's cascading hierarchy of rights by exploring how, for French women, political and economic rights lagged behind social rights.[30] Intersectional approaches to citizenship, informed by the work of the Black feminist Combahee River Collective and Kimberlé Crenshaw, have likewise underscored the tangled interrelations of identity and citizenship, social belonging and legal status.[31]

---

28. Brubaker, *Citizenship and Nationhood*, 22.
29. Tilly, "Primer on Citizenship," 600.
30. Kathleen Canning, "Class v. Citizenship: Keywords in German Gender History," *Central European History* 37, no. 2 (2005): 242; Nimisha Barton and Richard S. Hopkins, eds., *Practiced Citizenship: Women, Gender, and the State in Modern France* (Lincoln: University of Nebraska Press, 2019).
31. Kimberle Crenshaw, "Mapping the Margins: Intersectionality, Identity Politics, and Violence against Women of Color," *Stanford Law Review* 43, no. 6 (June 1991): 1241-99; Amy L. Brandzel, *Against Citizenship: The Violence of the Normative* (Urbana: University of Illinois Press, 2016), 1-30; Francesca Stella, Yvette Taylor, Tracey Reynolds, and Antoine Rogers, eds., *Sexuality, Citizenship and Belonging: Trans-national and Intersectional Perspectives* (New York: Routledge, 2016).

But if these newer approaches have continued to thicken the concept of citizenship, there is also a sense in which they have made it too mushy, too encompassing, or too omnipresent to actually tell us all that much about what citizenship is or how it has changed over time. It is our claim that returning to a specific time and place in history, in this case the years after World War II in Europe, can recoup some precision in our understanding of how citizenship has changed over time and encourage us to reimagine once again what it might mean to belong in the modern world. This book thus aims to restore a sense of clarity to our understanding of citizenship. To do so, we make two core assertions: one historical and the other theoretical.

First, we argue that the Second World War catalyzed a fundamental shift in understandings of citizenship in Europe. This shift, which was rooted in the wartime years, accelerated and was codified in the decades that followed the war. It was underpinned by the seemingly unprecedented levels of human displacement that the war brought about and which persisted owing to postwar political and social divisions. At the same time, shifts in citizenship were spurred by wider social debates in Europe and in Europe's colonial empires concerning the rights of citizens, subjects, migrants, refugees, and guest workers. Our analysis insists that the wartime and postwar eras comprised a unique moment when citizenship was being fundamentally reshaped. We cannot understand later shifts without first recognizing the significance of this period.

Second, we propose that understandings of citizenship can be mapped onto a two-dimensional framework comprising vertical and temporal dimensions. The vertical dimension of this framework posits that understandings of citizenship are not simply the product of either top-down or bottom-up debates. They are negotiated among and between a range of different actors on a range of different societal and political *rungs*. To capture the complexity of these discussions it is necessary, as the authors of this book have done, to engage with a wide array of sources that can illuminate the stories of those actors.

The temporal dimension of this framework suggests that definitions of citizenship are shaped by understandings of time. This dimension reinforces our first argument, that the postwar period was a critical point in time, during which understandings of citizenship and belonging were under intense study. But, more significantly, it also identifies the constitutive role that temporality plays in practices of citizenship.

The Importance of the Postwar Era

The Second World War transformed prewar structures of citizenship and belonging institutionally and socially. When the fighting ended in the European theater, as many as sixty-five million individuals had been displaced from their homes. In Germany alone there were between eight and eleven million civilians who *officially* qualified as displaced persons (DPs). These included foreign workers, prisoners of war, former concentration camp inmates, and forced laborers.[32] In addition to DPs, who theoretically had homes to return to, there were millions of refugees (both internally and externally displaced) who were presumed to be homeless. It is estimated that twenty-five million people in the Soviet Union and twenty million people in Germany were homeless by the end of the war.[33] Regardless of the reason for displacement, all these individuals experienced an environment in which ideological boundaries were rapidly turning into national borders that shaped resettlement. As Laura Hilton, Dagmar Wernitznig, and Stanislava Dikova underscore in chapters 1, 3, and 6, from common hardship emerged unique refugee experiences that challenged and shaped citizenship in profound ways during and after the war.

The founding of the United Nations Relief and Rehabilitation Administration (UNRRA) in 1943 and the International Refugee Organization (IRO) in 1946 reflected Allied understanding that the scale of displacement caused by the war would be one of the fundamental postwar challenges. But the limitations of such institutions, in terms of scope and manpower, meant that citizenship was being renegotiated from below as much as it was being legislated from above. By the autumn of 1945, officials had returned more than six million DPs to their countries of origin. But efforts to repatriate the remaining DPs soon stalled after 1945. The more than one million DPs who refused to "go home" created a highly vocal minority whose insistence on being resettled elsewhere spoke to a combination of political, economic, and

---

32. Gerard Daniel Cohen, *In War's Wake: Europe's Displaced Persons in the Postwar Order* (Oxford: Oxford University Press, 2011), 5; Laure Humbert, *Reinventing French Aid: The Politics of Humanitarian Relief in French-Occupied Germany, 1945–1952* (Cambridge: Cambridge University Press, 2021), 2; Tara Zahra, *The Lost Children: Reconstructing Europe's Families after World War II* (Cambridge, MA: Harvard University Press, 2011), 7. Qualification as a DP was decided under UNRRA and Allied military directives. Cohen estimates the number of DPs in Germany in 1945 as eight million, while Humbert places the number at eleven million.

33. Tony Judt, *Postwar: A History of Europe since 1945* (New York: Penguin, 2005), 16–17.

psychological factors, all of which placed questions of citizenship front and center.[34]

The global destruction caused by the Second World War also set the stage for an unprecedented series of debates concerning international norms, rights, and integration. The founding of the United Nations at the San Francisco Conference in April 1945 suggested that international cooperation, at least in theory, would play an important role in the postwar era.[35] In December 1946, the UN General Assembly, with the aim of paving the way for an international bill of rights, accepted the principles of international law agreed upon by the Charter of the International Military Tribunal, which convened in Nuremberg from November 1945 to October 1946 to try high-ranking Nazi perpetrators. The UN adopted the Universal Declaration of Human Rights two years later, in December 1948. Two years after that, the newly created Council of Europe drafted the Convention for the Protection of Human Rights and Fundamental Freedoms, which went into effect in 1953. In 1952, the European Coal and Steel Community was established to integrate key industries, thereby binding Western European states closer together. At the same time, as Serhii Lashyn reveals in chapter 12, these agreements raised broader questions about the movement of workers and the idea of European integration. Collectively, these postwar discussions fostered an environment in which questions concerning rights and responsibilities were being considered in a global, humanitarian framework. They created a context in which it was possible to challenge—and expand—the bounds of citizenship.

What these newly recognized rights would look like on the ground, however, varied considerably based on political ideology. On the Iberian Peninsula, fascism kept a tenacious hold for decades to come. As Carlos Domper Lasús highlights in chapter 7, Francisco Franco's government attempted to forge a uniquely fascist citizenship that would nonetheless be compatible with postwar norms of human and civil rights. In Eastern Europe, Soviet satellites developed specifically socialist visions of citizenship, as Nikola Tohma and Rachel Weiser explain in chapters 5 and 8. In these fascist and socialist visions of citizenship, profound challenges endured to the liberal, democratic, and capitalist norms that dominate postwar historiography.

---

34. Cohen, *In War's Wake*, 5.

35. This is not to say that there were not misgivings. See, for instance, Mark Mazower, *Governing the World: The History of an Idea* (London: Penguin, 2012), chap. 7.

The closure of the European theater of war also introduced an intensive period of reconstruction driven by human labor. Although Europe was viewed as being overpopulated at the end of the war, by the 1950s, labor shortages had materialized in many European countries.[36] Guest workers, migrants, and imperial subjects became an important part of postwar economic reconstruction, which Sarah Jacobson interrogates in chapter 11. The arrival of laborers and their families, some of whom would become naturalized citizens, sparked intense debates over the division of rights and responsibilities in individual nation-states and about who truly belonged.

At the same time, women across the continent began to demand greater rights, from enfranchisement (a project only completed in 1990 when the Swiss half-canton Appenzell Innerrhoden finally was forced to grant women's suffrage) to social equality to reproductive health. Spurred by wartime sacrifice, new feminist movements took shape across Europe, eventually culminating in the sexual revolution of the 1960s, which further contested the boundaries of citizenship. Sexuality too became a fulcrum for evolving debates over legal and social citizenship alike. The end of the war saw new homophile associations blossom in major cities, which would eventually give way to radical gay and lesbian liberation movements in the late 1960s and early 1970s. These movements often cited wartime persecution as a principal justification for their demands. As Emily Lord Fransee, Zoé Kergomard, and Anna Dobrowolska highlight in chapters 2, 9, and 10, experiences of war, persecution, and sacrifice lent urgency to novel political projects that interrogated the ways that gender, sex, and sexuality defined the bounds of citizenship.[37]

The geopolitical, social, economic, and legal shifts taking shape in the shadow of the Second World War thus forged a unique environment in which prior assumptions about citizenship and belonging

---

36. Stephen Castles, "Immigration and Asylum: Challenges to European Identities and Citizenship," in *The Oxford Handbook of Postwar European History*, ed. Dan Stone (Oxford: Oxford University Press, 2012), 205.

37. Dagmar Herzog, *Sex after Fascism: Memory and Morality in Twentieth-Century Germany* (Princeton, NJ: Princeton University Press, 2005); Elizabeth Heineman, *What Difference Does a Husband Make? Women and Marital Status in Nazi and Postwar Germany* (Berkeley: University of California Press, 2003); Julian Jackson, *Living in Arcadia: Homosexuality, Politics, and Morality in France from the Liberation to AIDS* (Chicago: University of Chicago Press, 2009); Robert Moeller, *Protecting Motherhood: Women and the Family in the Politics of Postwar West Germany* (Berkeley: University of California Press, 1993); Molly Tambor, *The Lost Wave: Women and Democracy in Postwar Italy* (Oxford: Oxford University Press, 2014).

could be challenged and reimagined. The chapters that constitute this book are rooted in events, debates, and ideas driven by experiences of war. Together, they demonstrate the significance of the postwar era as a distinctly dynamic proving ground for new conceptualizations of citizenship.

The significance this book places on the postwar era, however, should not suggest that it offers a simple story of ever-expanding democratization. While several authors explore the widening of concepts of citizenship, others, such as Nicholas Courtman in chapter 4, trace the perpetuation of older forms of exclusion and prejudice. These exclusions were frequently rooted in differences of race, sexuality, and gender. The scholars assembled here address these challenges through both national and imperial frameworks, thereby demonstrating that questions concerning citizenship, although frequently determined at a national level, often spoke to wider concerns around individual or human rights and the responsibilities of national governments.

Bringing together the research of twelve scholars from a range of disciplines working in different national contexts, the book's chapters span a dozen nations, empires, and superstates. Edited collaboratively in a series of workshops in the winter and spring of 2022, the chapters explore themes that span from the Second World War through to the 1990s. The challenges, discussions, and debates they interrogate each situate the Second World War and early postwar period as key points of reference for how citizenship was reimagined in specific national or transnational contexts. Each chapter deploys a variety of methodologies drawn from disciplines across the humanities and social sciences, including the history of emotions, critical race theory, literary studies, legal history, and gender studies. Looking beyond traditional social and political processes to other realms where individuals and states staked claims to belonging, obligations, and rights, this book encompasses pioneering new approaches to citizenship in order to elucidate how European citizenship changed in the postwar era.

A New Theoretical Framework for Citizenship

To bring a greater sense of methodological clarity to existing "thick" approaches to the study of citizenship, the book conceives a new, two-dimensional framework that preserves the complexity of citizenship as a dynamic concept. At the same time, its vertical and temporal dimensions shed light on the relationships between actors involved in these debates, offering a clearer understanding of how views of citizenship form and shift over time. These dimensions do not exist in isolation from one another. They are in constant tension and dialogue. The benefit of this framework is that it does not limit us to a single definition of citizenship as a legal, political, or social construct. Rather, it understands citizenship as a concept that has been and still is defined and constructed in dynamic ways.

To capture the nuanced ways in which citizenship is conceived as well as the range of actors involved in these processes, the chapters draw from a wide range of source material. Older histories, as well as those within legal studies, often look at the standard sources of political history—laws, regulations, and parliamentary debates—to offer accounts of citizenship that frequently reify its normative dimensions and effects. More recent accounts have sought to "thicken" our understanding of citizenship by analyzing these same documents from the perspectives of marginalized populations.[38]

This book substantially expands the empirical base of these studies. Contributors engage a wide range of sources, including government documents, to unearth the history of marginal figures who are often absent from mainstream narratives. Drawing on official documents to shed light on these marginal actors (and their interactions with more traditional actors) makes sense because it was often through interactions with official bodies that their experiences were documented for later historians. But many of the chapters also rely on unexpected archives that shed light on new figures. They allow us to trace not only the place of individuals denied the full status of belonging but also the policies, customs, behaviors, and events less traditionally associated with citizenship.

In chapter 3, for instance, Dagmar Wernitznig draws on psychiatric files to interrogate what she terms the "para-citizenship" of female refugees deemed "insane" by local authorities. Her work situates the psychiatric ward as a new locus in the study of postwar citizenship. In so doing, she highlights the intersectional nature of psychiatric diagnosis and how it could be used to deny refugees' claims to rights and even citizenship in the chaos of the postwar years. Likewise, in chapter 10, Anna Dobrowolska investigates how the socialist Polish People's Republic regulated women's sexuality, often under the rubric of "sex

---

38. Eley and Palmowski, "Citizenship and National Identity," 5.

work." Employing everything from police files to soft pornography, her chapter reveals how important the "prostitute" became to normative ideals of gender and labor in postwar Poland.

In chapter 11, Sarah Jacobson similarly employs sources from everyday life, including oral histories and squatters' publications, to compare Southern Italian migrants' claims to housing in both northern Italy and West Germany. She uncovers a form of "de-territorialized citizenship." In both countries, and regardless of formal citizenship status, Italian guest workers deployed the language of citizenship and human rights to make claims against local and national governments. They were often allied with other groups of workers, and these alliances generated a localized form of citizenship tied not to nationality but instead to labor, residency, and a shared understanding of common humanity.

Recovering the history of postwar citizenship through lesser-known figures, concepts, events, and institutions thus forces us to reconceptualize the term, not as a hierarchical construct imposed by states or negotiated solely between individuals and states. Instead, it becomes a multifocal paradigm that was constantly being (re)negotiated among individuals, states, societies, economies, and other institutions of social regulation. The following chapters draw our attention away from traditional foci of the citizen-state dyad to reveal that citizenship is not a static relationship between individuals and national governments but rather a dynamic phenomenon—a constantly evolving set of actions, beliefs, and decisions—among a much broader array of actors and institutions.

The Vertical Dimension

Citizenship in the vertical dimension thus considers how citizenship was defined at and between multiple levels of state and society, similar to what Willem Maas has termed "multilevel citizenship."[39] The work of determining what citizenship and belonging meant was not the exclusive preserve of local, national, or supranational governing bodies. Formal and informal citizens played a substantial role in negotiating these meanings.

At the bottom of this spectrum, many of the chapters, like Jacobson's, employ microhistorical approaches to interrogate everyday

---

39. Willem Maas, "The Varieties of Multilevel Citizenship," in *Multilevel Citizenship* (Philadelphia: University of Pennsylvania Press, 2013): 1–22.

interactions among ordinary individuals. Rachel Weiser, in chapter 8, analyzes belonging under state socialism from the vantage of the everyday experiences of female laborers, relying on brigade books penned by these women to interrogate their commitment to the ideals of socialist citizenship. While they did often welcome the gender equality and access to work that the East German government promised, these workers also found greater solidarity in gendered spaces and relationships. These relationships formed a kind of personalized citizenship, Weiser argues, that often undermined state socialism's claims to universality.

In her analysis of communist refugees from the Greek civil war in chapter 5, Nikola Tohma takes both a transnational and a microhistorical view of socialist citizenship. Interrogating the status of Greek refugees within the Eastern bloc, she contends that despite the rhetoric of international brotherhood, state socialism was unable to meet the affective needs satisfied by nationality. Tohma's work points hauntingly to the lingering importance of national belonging even in the wake of genocide and ethnic cleansing.

These accounts question our traditional understanding of citizenship as a nationally situated identity, pointing out how claims to citizenship could diverge from the state to be made at an interpersonal level and through nongovernmental or supragovernmental entities.[40] Many of the privileges that T. H. Marshall first identified as elements of "social citizenship" were tied not only to the national welfare state but also to the emergence of an international paradigm of human rights. While postwar covenants such as the 1948 United Nations Charter of Human Rights understood national citizenship as the bedrock of those rights, it is equally clear that on the ground, individuals and officials alike comprehended the rights and belongings attendant to citizenship in more complex terms.[41]

Laura Hilton, for instance, analyzes IRO files in chapter 1 to uncover the emotional lives of DPs in postwar Central Europe. She focuses on the relationships between IRO officials and stateless persons as well as those between DPs themselves, offering deep readings of refugees' emotional lives and how they understood the rights and burdens of their lack of citizenship. While international organizations continued to see statelessness as a "problem" in need of solving, Hilton argues,

---

40. Linda Bosniak, "Citizenship Denationalized," *Indiana Journal of Global Legal Studies* 7, no. 2 (Spring 2000): 447–509.

41. David Owen, "Citizenship and Human Rights," 250–54, in Schachar et al., *Oxford Handbook of Citizenship*.

many DPs preferred to retain their statelessness for strategic reasons. Like Jacobson and Weiser, Hilton questions the fixedness of both nationality and the state in conceptions of citizenship. She understands it instead as an emergent quality developed through interactions among individuals and officials in a variety of social, economic, and political settings. Viewing citizenship in this way also underlines the importance of individual and personal narratives of citizenship, told and refined over time. These accounts convey a far messier version of citizenship (and its absence) in the early postwar years.

While many of the scholars in this book turn to everyday interactions beyond the nation-state to comprehend citizenship, others approach it from the other direction in order to examine citizenship in supranational organizations. In chapter 12, for example, Serhii Lashyn traces the evolution of European citizenship from antebellum castles in the sky to the 1992 Maastricht Treaty, which codified citizenship in the European Union. As a result, he unearths the idea's long genealogy and highlights how citizenship became de-territorialized in a very different way from that unearthed in Jacobson's microhistory of Italian workers or Tohma's examination of Greek refugees in socialist Czechoslovakia.

These studies exemplify how citizenship developed at different levels of the vertical dimension during the postwar era, as ordinary individuals, states, municipalities, and superstates embraced new ways of belonging and exclusion. This history not only emphasizes that citizenship is a phenomenon that takes place on many different rungs but also highlights how citizenship is more than mere theory. It is a social practice. It is a way for individuals to engage in society, politics, and the economy and to define the obligations that inform their relationships with other citizens and social and state organizations. Thinking about citizenship in this way reflects the movement of people and ideas in postwar Europe, whereby individual rights became "de-territorialized"—no longer linked exclusively to nation-states.

The Temporal Dimension

The second dimension of citizenship that this book posits is temporal. At its most elemental, making time a key factor in our understanding of citizenship acknowledges the importance of historical context in grounding these debates. As historian and resistance fighter Marc Bloch argued, historical time "is the very plasma in which events are immersed, and the field within which they become intelligible."[42] This dimension reinforces our overarching argument regarding the importance of situating these debates in the context of the Second World War and postwar reconstruction. The point is not to uncover precise origins, a task that would prove futile, but rather to assess how particular historical constellations created space within which these debates could take shape.

But this dimension also speaks to how historical actors engaged with what Dan Edelstein, Stefanos Geroulanos, and Natasha Wheatley have defined as "temporal regimes" or "orderings of time and its experience."[43] Just as citizenship has long played a leading role in what Elizabeth Freeman terms the "official time line, [which] effectively shap[es] the contours of a meaningful life," so too time has long inflected understandings of citizenship, from the promise of soon-to-be attained citizenship to what Gary Wilder has referred to in the French imperial context as "a policy of temporal deferral."[44] The timing of one's birth, in conjunction with existing national laws, could decide citizenship status or the right to claim a given citizenship. Tohma, for instance, explores this notion through the changing citizenship laws that governed postwar Greece and which had stripped communist "undesirables" of their Greek citizenship. Many of these individuals chose to wait out time, anticipating the day that they would be repatriated and could regain their Greek citizenship. At the same time, children born of stateless parents grappled with the question of how citizenship, or its lack, is passed through time and across generations.

The length of time spent in a country might also determine an individual's or a family's right to residence and, ultimately, citizenship. The impact of these decisions was also heritable. Many of Tohma's Greek protagonists chose not to claim Czechoslovak citizenship despite the opportunity to do so. But the opposite holds true in chapter 4, where Nicholas Courtman shines a light on West Germany's postwar naturalization practices. For the displaced persons in Courtman's chapter,

---

42. Marc Bloch, *The Historian's Craft* (Manchester: Manchester University Press, 1954), 23.

43. Dan Edelstein, Stefanos Geroulanos, and Natasha Wheatley, "Chronocenosis: An Introduction to Power and Time," in *Power and Time: Temporalities in Conflict and the Making of History*, ed. Dan Edelstein, Stefanos Geroulanos, and Natasha Wheatley (Chicago: University of Chicago Press, 2020), 7.

44. Elizabeth Freeman, "Time Binds, or, Erotohistoriography," *Social Text* 23, nos. 3–4 (Fall-Winter 2005): 58; Gary Wilder, *The French Imperial Nation-State: Negritude and Colonial Humanism between the Two World Wars* (Chicago: University of Chicago Press, 2020), 118.

time spent in Germany did not always translate into citizenship. Regulations did not count time spent in displaced persons camps toward residency requirements. These requirements were also longer and stricter for those of "foreign descent," many of whom were subjected to discriminatory assessments concerning the length of time they needed to properly integrate.

In the postwar period, time also impacted claims to citizenship in the form of age and ability. This is a core feature of Hilton's chapter, which demonstrates that decisions on a stateless person's right to migrate or be granted a new citizenship were influenced by factors such as age. IRO officials viewed young, healthy candidates as "suitable" citizens, while others were deemed "too old to emigrate." In chapters 2 and 9, respectively, Emily Lord Fransee and Zoé Kergomard also address the link between perceived age and the right to vote in metropolitan and imperial France. Debates over the "timeliness" of voting legislation were linked to the perceived political maturity of women.

At the same time, citizenship can sometimes (re)appear as a concept out of time, an unwelcome or untimely apparition. In chapter 6, Stanislava Dikova presents an innovative reading of British writer Olivia Manning's postwar *Balkan Trilogy* to argue that the novels offer a critical view of citizenship. But her chapter also reveals a temporal palimpsest of memory, literature, and critique that informed Manning's conception of citizenship, which in turn responded to postwar concerns in Britain through the lens of her wartime experiences in the Balkans. Citizenship, that is to say, has a temporality all its own that has shaped and continues to shape its deployment in the postwar world.

Bringing the Dimensions Together

Focusing our attention on both the diverse range of actors involved in the processes of defining citizenship and the actual and perceived temporal bounds of these debates does not limit our understanding of citizenship. Rather, it facilitates a rich conversation about the content of the debates that were developing between and among these actors. In other words, by answering the questions of *who* was involved in these debates, *where* they were taking place, and *when* they were imagined, we are better equipped to explore their *what*.

What becomes clear across these chapters is that questions of deservedness and belonging were at the heart of many of these debates about citizenship. Arguments about inclusions and exclusions have formed the backbone of recent studies of modern citizenship, especially in states that understand themselves as liberal democracies, and the chapters in this book substantively develop the intersectional nature of such practices. Dikova's analysis, for instance, informed by both Manning's wartime experiences in Romania and Greece and the Cold War British welfare state, reveals citizenship as an inherently precarious status, riddled with ambiguities, insecurities, and exclusions.

These exclusions often fell along lines of identity and were frequently intersectional in nature. Like Hilton and Wernitznig, who both emphasize the overlapping roles of gender, race, and ability in determining the "deservedness" of citizenship, Courtman reveals that although West Germany's post-Nazi constitution expressly forbade racial discrimination, Eastern Europeans were routinely discriminated against on racial and gendered grounds. At the same time, former Nazi collaborators from Western Europe were given a fast track to citizenship. These explorations extend far beyond the divide between formal systems of *jus soli* and *jus sanguinis* to instead explore overlapping patterns of inclusion and discrimination that defined citizenship after fascism.

Likewise, while voting is often understood as one of the principal rights granted by modern citizenship, by which citizens participate in the governance of a republican nation-state, Fransee and Kergomard both question its place in the evolution of postwar French citizenship. Fransee frames citizenship within a supranational entity, namely the French empire (rechristened the French Union in 1946). Using colonial archives, she highlights the fraught relationship between citizenship and the franchise, underscoring that the two were not synonymous in the minds of either French officials or residents of France's colonies. Instead, Fransee reveals how, in spite of the universalizing rhetoric of French citizenship—and the "civilizing mission" of the French empire—debates over the franchise calcified hierarchies of belonging at the very heart of postwar citizenship. Her work also highlights another key debate of the early postwar years, namely, the future of empire and the rights of imperial subjects as citizens. It demonstrates that these questions concerning inclusion and exclusion took on a global character through the context of empire.

Kergomard too questions the blithe equation of voting with citizenship, interrogating the oft-held assumption that greater enfranchisement equates to greater self-determination. Her work traces efforts to introduce mandatory voting and the anxieties that underlay these disputes. While republican elites hoped that greater participation would bolster the Fourth Republic's legitimacy, they also worried about how new voters—especially women—might vote, again highlighting the tenuous relationship binding franchise, citizenship, and sovereignty in postwar reconstruction.

Carlos Domper Lasús too investigates formal elements of citizenship in Franco's Spain in chapter 7. Looking at the Spanish Charter of Rights (Fuero de los Españoles) promulgated in 1945, Lasús contends that the fascist government envisioned a new kind of corporative, organic citizenship that would elide what it perceived as the decadent liberalism of Western democracies. At the same time, the chapter reveals how this fascist form of citizenship fit comfortably within mainstream Christian-conservative discourses in postwar Europe.

By examining how states drew dividing lines between insiders and outsiders, many of these chapters turn back to the most fundamental, legal totems of citizenship: naturalization, the franchise, and freedom of movement. In so doing, many of them suggest a return to "thin" conceptions of citizenship but interrogated from a "thick" perspective. Kergomard's and Fransee's histories of voting practices and laws, Lashyn's genealogy of European citizenship, and Courtman's investigation of West German naturalization practices all hint that a great deal more is to be gained by reexamining the most basic structures of legal belonging in order to understand who belongs in a given society and how that belonging is construed politically.

These approaches also expose novel, intermediate forms of citizenship, suggesting that the kind of belonging encompassed in the term is not an all-or-nothing proposition. For example, in arguing that psychiatric diagnoses in occupied Vienna performed a sort of citizenship function, Wernitznig contends that refugee women occupied a "paracitizenship" of neither belonging nor nonbelonging. Such ghostly forms of citizenship are apparent in many of the contributions, making clear that liminal figures occupied a tense place within conversations about citizenship, one that helped define the very borders and meanings of belonging.

By making out how postwar states and societies included or excluded certain groups—often continuing wartime persecution through different channels—these chapters also question triumphalist accounts of the postwar period. Fransee, Courtman, Kergomard, Wernitznig, and Lasús all highlight oppressive practices and traditions within the postwar Western European order to contend that forms of persecution, oppression, and exclusion persisted in Western Europe long into the postwar era. Their chapters underscore that such phenomena were not so much liberalism's dark underbelly as they were constitutive of that postwar liberal consensus.

At the same time, work on socialist citizenship highlights the very real challenges posed to liberalism by the people's democracies of Eastern Europe. Tohma, Weiser, and Dobrowolska examine the construction of socialist citizenship in Czechoslovakia, East Germany, and Poland from the perspectives of marginalized citizens—refugees, women, and sex workers. They highlight not only similar contradictions and instabilities in the edifice of communist rule, but also the very appealing nature of the socialist project. Taken together, these twelve chapters thus highlight the instabilities and contradictions at the heart of citizenship as it was renegotiated in the aftermath of the Second World War.

Many of the debates and challenges raised in these chapters enjoy continued salience today. Debates over who is worthy or deserving of citizenship permeate ongoing discussions concerning refugee crises in Europe and North America. States continue to structure citizenship law in ways that exclude some and welcome others. The legacy of wartime and postwar citizenship and migration structures (and their subsequent dismantling) are still being felt today.

Citizenship in the Here and Now

Conceptualizing citizenship through these two dimensions teases out the complexities of the concept while also introducing a level of theoretical clarity that demonstrates how citizenship has been negotiated among and between individual, state, and supranational actors with distinct temporal valences. The chapters do not each speak to only one dimension in this model of citizenship. Rather, they illustrate the interconnectivity between them. Instead of attempting to force the chapters into set themes or dimensions, a decision that would only obscure these interconnections, the book is ordered in rough chronological fashion, proceeding from the DP camps of the immediate postwar era through to the introduction of EU citizenship in 1992.

Doing so offers a sense not only of how citizenship was reimagined in discrete times and places but also how it changed over time across the continent. That is to say, temporality, in a historical study such as this one, is not merely a longed-for promise or a stand-in for how societies conceived of the intersection of age, ability, and deservedness, but rather also the capability to see across years and decades in order to understand how different groups of people succeeded (or failed) at claiming new forms of citizenship. Looking to the future, the book gestures to how many of these same questions continue to shape political, social, and cultural debates in the twenty-first century.

Each chapter represents an episode in the reimagining of citizenship in postwar Europe, each episode illuminating others while also suggesting untrod paths for future research. But this collection not only offers a new, multidimensional model for how to understand citizenship but also insists on the diachronic significance of the postwar period for grasping citizenship today. In the years after World War II, these chapters reveal, citizenships proliferated as individuals made claims of legal, social, political, cultural, and economic belonging in different ways, at different times, in different places, and at different levels of state and society. At the same time, old forms of exclusionary citizenship persisted, rooted in race, gender, ability, age, and sexuality. These exclusions did not simply replicate themselves in this era, however, but instead adapted to new idioms of equality, human rights, and "multi-level" citizenship that took form in these years and continue to pervade our understanding of the concept today.

The diverse scholarship in the following pages spans the vast postwar European continent and methodologically pushes the boundaries of traditional understandings of citizenship, interrogating the concept through lenses of gender, sexuality, emotion, migration, and empire. As a result, it beckons scholars to rethink postwar Europe, to uncover both the enormous potential for individual agency baked into contemporary conceptions of citizenship and the ongoing exclusions and violence that endure, and to find there renewed inspiration to reimagine citizenship today. The tools are ready. The work remains.

Rachel Chin is a lecturer in war studies at the University of Glasgow. She is the author of *War of Words: Britain, France and Discourses of Empire during the Second World War*. Her current research explores the history of Chinese migration to the Caribbean through the lenses of assimilation, integration, and belonging.

Samuel Clowes Huneke is associate professor of history at George Mason University. He is the author of the award-winning *States of Liberation: Gay Men between Dictatorship and Democracy in Cold War Germany* and *A Queer Theory of the State*.

CHAPTER 1

The Stateless Struggle to Belong in the Postwar Period

Laura Hilton

In his memoir, Jonas Mekas reflected on his feelings as a stateless, Lithuanian-born displaced person (DP) after the Second World War. He asked, "Am I a gypsy, a citizen of the world, an eternal DP?"[1] The specter of never possessing citizenship haunted him. Hanna Seckel-Drucker, a Jewish refugee in Scandinavia during the war, also remembered the feeling of being stateless. "Now, you have to understand that all these years, I was citizen of nothing. And it's very, very difficult to move around without citizenship anywhere."[2] Robert Mindelzun, a Polish DP who spent part of the war in a Soviet resettlement center, said he felt as if he was "always the outsider."[3] Max Knight, who fled Vienna to the UK in March of 1938, decided to leave for the "open" city of Shanghai. Reflecting on his precarious situation, he said, "You have to put yourself in the position of a person who was let go into the universe, into nowhere. If for one reason or another something went

---

1. Jonas Mekas, *I Had Nowhere to Go* (New York: Black Thistle, 1991), 328.
2. Hanna Seckel-Drucker, interview by USC Shoah Foundation, March 25, 1998, https://iwitness.usc.edu/testimony/39792.
3. Robert Mindelzun, interview with USC Shoah Foundation, November 2, 2011, https://iwitness.usc.edu/testimony/53150.

wrong on the trip, if in Shanghai they said, 'No, we have enough. We don't want you,' or in between something, there was nowhere to go."[4]

For individuals, being stateless and therefore lacking the protections and rights of formalized citizenship was terrifying. Consequently, in the postwar period, many stateless people sought the protection of a nation state by acquiring new citizenship. At the same time, they feared rejection. Seeking to fit within the world of nation states with its increasing emphasis on citizenship in order to fully belong and be fully human, stateless persons both challenged and ultimately strengthened the system of nation-states.

The existence of stateless persons in Europe in the postwar period and the uncertainty that they represented also haunted policymakers and government officials. Yet this was not a new situation. During the interwar period, hundreds of thousands of stateless persons, escaping conflict in Russia or rendered stateless by the territorial shifts after the First World War, sought asylum, protection, and stability. In response, the League of Nations and legal scholars proposed several solutions, aimed at safeguarding the rights of minority groups within nations rather than forcing states to grant them citizenship, and creating identity documents to protect them.[5] But the idea of this flexible approach, never successfully implemented, vanished just as the scope of the problem exploded following World War II.

After 1945, both practice and policy moved away from the proposed focus on the collective rights of minorities. Instead, they sought to defend national sovereignty, privileging citizenship as the way to guarantee individual rights.[6] Rather than rights being inalienable, nations had denationalized citizens; therefore, the best way to secure rights was to belong to a nation, which conferred citizenship. The hardening of this system left in limbo those who did not possess citizenship, in the process creating a transnational humanitarian crisis. The solution was dependent on the internal politics of states (often states that had

---

4. Max Knight, USHMM oral history interview, March 26, 1991, accession no. 1999. A.0122.771, RG-50.477.0771.

5. Miriam Rürup, "Lives in Limbo," *German Historical Institute Bulletin* 49 (Fall 2011): 122–23.

6. Mark Mazower, *No Enchanted Palace: The End of Empire and the Ideological Origins of the United Nations* (Princeton, NJ: Princeton University Press, 2009), 16–25. Hannah Arendt argued that totalitarianism was the root problem with statelessness. However, some scholars see weakness in this line of argument. See Brad Blitz, "The State and the Stateless," in *Understanding Statelessness*, ed. Tendayi Bloom, Katherine Tonkiss, and Phillip Cole (London: Routledge, 2017), 70–84, 73–74.

denationalized their citizens during or after the war) and controlled by forces that privileged stability over the protection of minority rights.[7] Nikola Tohma's chapter in this volume, for instance, speaks to the ideologically motivated stripping of citizenship from ethnic Germans by the Czechoslovakian government and their embrace of refugees from the Greek Civil War, both in the postwar period.[8]

This chapter examines how stateless persons explained the feeling of statelessness. Their experiences and emotions operated within the system that international agencies, the United Nations Relief and Rehabilitation Administration (UNRRA) and later the International Refugee Organization (IRO), and national governments were strengthening around them. The UNRRA, formed by the United Nations in 1943, organized, cared for, and repatriated DPs in Europe between May 1945 and June 1947. The IRO, with its mandate of resettlement rather than repatriation, operated in Europe from July 1947 until its dissolution in 1952. By focusing on interactions between stateless persons and these agencies as they occurred, scholars can gain insights into how DPs understood and chose their paths within the system to reach their stated aims, be that immigration and securing new citizenship or remaining in place but acquiring protection. It also explores the "aspirational citizenship" of women who claimed the right to belong, even when the legal definitions and policies sought to exclude them.[9] This chapter's approach thus demonstrates the system's fluidity in practice, while also highlighting how entrenched ideas about worthiness to be an immigrant and a potential citizen—tied to gender, age, ethnicity, and ability to work—pervaded it at the same time.[10] In this way, it offers an intersectional approach, one that examines how multiple facets of individual identity operated simultaneously within the system. It also echoes the introduction to this volume, examining how citizenship

---

7. On the post-1945 response to move away from securing minority rights see Nathan Kurz, *Jewish Internationalism and Human Rights after the Holocaust* (Cambridge: Cambridge University Press, 2021), 19–22.

8. Nikola Tohma, "Statelessness and Social Citizenship of Greek Civil War Refugees in Post-1948 Communist Czechoslovakia." in this volume.

9. Anne Epstein and Rachel Fuchs, eds., conclusion in *Gender and Citizenship in Historical and Transnational Perspective* (London: Palgrave, 2017), 232–41.

10. Historians Tara Zahra and Ruth Balint have begun rich conversations about these ideas, using similar methodological approaches: Tara Zahra, *The Lost Children: Reconstructing Europe's Families after World War II* (Cambridge, MA: Harvard University Press, 2011), and Ruth Balint, *Destination Elsewhere: Displaced Persons and Their Quest to Leave Postwar Europe* (Ithaca, NY: Cornell University Press, 2021).

"encompasses intangible and emotive elements such as identity and belonging that are constructed over time."[11]

The experiences of stateless DPs and how the world responded to them cemented two fundamental ideas of the postwar order: each human being must possess a nationality that would guarantee them rights, and nations would prioritize demographic homogenization as a source of stability over the protection of individual rights. Hannah Arendt, for instance, argued in the war's wake that the solution to statelessness was to ignore it by repatriating people to their country of origin.[12] Yet the refusal of hundreds of thousands of DPs to accept repatriation forced the development of the IRO to resettle them. As Arendt argued, the idea that humans need a "right to have rights" developed "only when millions of people emerged who had lost and could not regain these rights because of the new global political situation."[13] Their situation was so precarious because it was at this historical moment that citizenship became wedded to national identity, which left them bereft of both legal protections and a sense of belonging. Rather than impinge on national sovereignty and force nations to re-citizenize people, the system posited stateless people as the problem. At this crucial juncture, when nation states privileged citizenship as a way to restore order, some stateless persons reinvented themselves to secure a place within this system.[14] The irony is that the system then rejected some humans for immigration and potential citizenship on the basis of age, gender, religion, work-preparedness, and ability, thereby perpetuating the existence of stateless persons.

While a top-down approach to statelessness can explain how various governments and intergovernmental institutions administered people, this chapter's methodology is rooted in everyday life, which allows for a more nuanced, bottom-up approach. To explore how stateless persons felt about their situation, I draw on oral history testimonies conducted decades after the war, from both the United States Holocaust Memorial

---

11. Chin and Huneke, introduction to this volume.
12. Hannah Arendt, *On the Origins of Totalitarianism* (Cleveland: Meridian Books, 1958), 279. This emphasis on statelessness as a "problem" to be "solved" continues today. See Katja Swider, "Why End Statelessness?," in Bloom, Tonkiss, and Cole, *Understanding Statelessness*, 191-209, 192-96.
13. Arendt, *Origins of Totalitarianism*, 296-97.
14. Zahra, *Lost Children*, 21-23; Balint, *Destination Elsewhere*, 17-19. Kathleen Canning and Sonya Rose argue that transformations of citizenship are most likely to occur in moments of strife or conflict: see introduction to *Gender, Citizenships and Subjectivity*, ed. Canning and Rose (Oxford: Blackwell, 2001), 7.

Museum (USHMM) and the Shoah Foundation.[15] To examine how they navigated the system, I also use oral history testimonies and documents from the International Tracing Service (ITS) Digital Archive. Once the IRO took it over in 1947, the ITS built on the work done by the Central Tracing Bureau. These records highlight the fluidity of nationality and of citizenship. The sheer volume of Care and Maintenance files and uncertainty about the veracity of the facts contained within these documents complicates the historian's task.[16] In addition, as Silke von der Emde has argued, archival records are replete with feelings: loss, longing, hope, happiness, and trauma. These affective records demonstrate how much the simplified, redemptive narrative of Allied liberation obscures the years-long path to recovery that faced millions of DPs in the postwar era. Such records capture what it felt like to be a DP. Thus, these archival records are not only a fact-based collection but also act as "agents of witnessing."[17]

This rich documentation informs transnational narratives of statelessness in three important ways. First, it illuminates how people felt about their loss of citizenship, and it illustrates how they utilized that loss to make political and social claims. As Kathleen Canning and Sonya Rose contend, citizenship turns humans into subject positions, and "actors in different historical situations appropriate these subject positions in order to challenge, redefine, or honour the boundaries of citizenship."[18] Second, these sources reveal how age and gender intersected with the reality of statelessness, especially in terms of emigration opportunities and potential future citizenship. The chapter thus also draws on Kimberlé Crenshaw's pioneering work on intersectionality, which examines how systems of power inequality operate on multiple levels (age, gender, race) simultaneously.[19] Finally, stateless persons' struggles for stability and recognition highlight the distinctions that

---

15. Documents created in the postwar period and testimonies from subsequent decades reflecting back on these times both provide insights into this reality, but they are distinct kinds of sources, given the medium in which someone created them and the distance from the war.

16. A recent search of only the CM/1 files within the ITS digital files with the parameters of "stateless" for nationality and "female" as gender returns almost two thousand individual records.

17. Silke von der Emde, "Caring for the Dead and the Living," in *Tracing and Documenting Nazi Victims Past and Present*, ed. Henning Borggräfe, Christian Hoschler, and Isabel Panek, Arolsen Research Series, vol. 1 (Oldenbourg: De Gruyter, 2020), 155–72; 155-58, 161.

18. Canning and Rose, *Gender, Citizenships and Subjectivity*, 5.

19. Kimberlé Crenshaw, "Mapping the Margins," *Stanford Law Review* 43, no. 6 (1991): 1241-99.

international law and policies made between refugees (deserving, a moral assessment) and migrants (opportunistic, seeking economic gain). Following the Second World War, citizenship or the lack thereof impacted not only their sense of self-worth but also how others perceived and saw them. Older women became doubly alienated: lack of citizenship meant no state would protect them, and lack of deservedness (i.e., what they could contribute as a laborer and as a citizen) meant the system isolated them. Examining intersectionality and emotions within a system that often saw people as one-dimensional recognizes the agency of stateless persons and captures a more complete spectrum of their responses and experiences. There was not one monolithic way to become, feel, remain, or shed statelessness.

How Statelessness Felt

German poet and botanist Adelbert von Chamisso's 1814 allegorical work *Peter Schlemihl* famously grapples with a sense of not belonging. In the fable, Schlemihl sells the devil his shadow in exchange for a "bottomless" purse. However, as society shuns him for having no shadow, he laments his fate, saying, "for I had no further destination on this earth, no wish, no hope."[20] As the loss of his shadow isolated Schlemihl, so too did stateless persons' loss of citizenship, which accelerated in the interwar period as Nazi persecution intensified. In her testimony, Estelle Laughlin, a Jewish DP born in 1929 in Warsaw, captures this similarity. She recounted, "While freedom is so—it's texture. It's palpable. We were free. But we didn't have a penny in our pockets. We didn't have a home to come back to. We were stateless. There was no state or country to go to."[21] She felt human, deeply so, but knew that her lack of citizenship meant that others saw her still as less than human. Her testimony evinces how central emotions are to understanding statelessness and illustrates how those deprived of citizenship still found possessing it to be meaningful.[22]

The stateless knew the importance of relating the emotions that they felt even prior to the end of the Second World War. In his testimony, Leo Hanin, whose family fled eastward into Asia in 1916, said, "We felt that

---

20. Adelbert von Chamisso, *Peter Schlemihl: The Man Who Sold His Shadow*, trans. Peter Wortsman (New York: Fromm International, 1993), 61.
21. Estelle Laughlin, USHMM oral history interview, July 29, 2008, RG-50.999.0665.
22. Canning and Rose, *Gender, Citizenships and Subjectivity*, 6.

we were being... looked down upon. You see, we were stateless people. We had no passports.... We had no nationality."[23] Sam Ponczak felt similarly, assessing his family's situation as, "We're nothing. We don't have any country behind us."[24] After he emigrated with his parents from France to Argentina, an Argentine university official refused to accept his Polish high school diploma and recommended that he attend school, beginning in the eighth grade, although he was already twenty-five. Reflecting on this experience, he said, "I didn't have a citizenship. I didn't have anything. So, I felt all the doors were closed."[25] Recalling the wait in Shanghai for his visa to the United States, Max Knight says, "This is the trouble with these oral reports, that you can only tell facts, but you cannot tell feelings. You cannot tell what it means to be—to convey the idea, the terror, to sit on a powder keg watching the days slipping by."[26]

Lili Armstrong shared a similar sentiment, struggling to obtain a passport without papers, even though her mother was born in New York. She recalled, "Your space became narrower and narrower. You were sort of emotionally suffocating."[27] When she was able to obtain a stateless passport, she was overjoyed. "A passport I never had.... I was very happy.... A passport with my name. I was there."[28] Her words echoed those of Bertolt Brecht, "The passport is the most noble part of the human being.... When it is good, the passport is also recognized for this quality, whereas a human being, no matter how good, can go unrecognized."[29] Among stateless DPs, these sentiments were common. Estelle Laughlin explained it thusly: "We were nobodies except inside ourselves we were somebody. Everybody is a somebody. We wanted to be somebody. We wanted to have a country. We wanted to have a home."[30] They equated passports with citizenship and citizenship with rights, protection, and belonging, with being fully human.

---

23. Leo Hanin, USHMM interview, June 28, 1989, RG-50.030*0090.
24. Sam Ponczak, USHMM oral history interview, May 17, 2018, RG-50.999.0648.
25. Ponczak interview.
26. Knight interview.
27. Lili Armstrong, USC Shoah Foundation interview 38594, December 2, 1997, Visual History Archive, https://iwitness.usc.edu/testimony/38594.
28. Armstrong interview.
29. Bertolt Brecht, *Flüchtlingsgespräche* (Berlin, 1940), 1.
30. USHMM, "First Person: Conversations with Holocaust Survivors," Estelle Laughlin, July 18, 2018.

Declaring Statelessness and Determining Eligibility

In the early 1950s, Czech diplomat Ivan Kerno penned a report titled "Is Statelessness an Evil?" in which he detailed the complicated nature of the problem. Kerno explained that while statelessness placed humans in brutal and dangerous situations, at other times, people could utilize it to their advantage.[31] The experience of Herbert Lakritz demonstrated the potential benefits of claiming statelessness. His mother, who was born in Poland, had great difficulty emigrating to the United States after the war, since the Polish quota under the 1924 Immigration Act was just 3.6 percent of the total number of immigrants allowed.[32] Yet, as he remembers, "It was easier, actually, for my brother and I because we remained stateless as far as France was concerned. So as stateless, it was [an] easier quota than being under the Polish quota."[33] His gender (male), able-bodied nature, and his age (fourteen) were also factors, illustrating the intersectionality of different facets of his identity within this system, each of which could dictate his future path. Immigration officials and policies valued physically strong, young males over other immigrants, because of their potential labor value. Had Lakritz been mentally or physically disabled or elderly his chances of immigrating and acquiring new citizenship would have been slim.

The irony was that his Polish Jewish parents, who had settled in Germany, lost their nationality in 1938 when the Polish government passed a law denationalizing any citizen who had lived abroad for five consecutive years or more. This policy immediately placed their lives and their livelihoods in jeopardy. It also illustrates the key role played by time (as well as so-called race) in deciding who was worthy of citizenship. But after the war, the boys' ambiguous status provided them and their mother with a better chance to immigrate. Being stateless was more of a continuum rather than a fixed state of unbelonging. It had both positive and negative elements that shifted over time and

---

31. Mira Siegelberg, *Statelessness: A Modern History* (Cambridge, MA: Harvard University Press, 2020), 202–3. When he traveled on behalf of the United Nations, Kerno chose to utilize papers that declared him to be stateless.

32. The annual quota for Polish-born people was just under six thousand. See "Who Was Shut Out? Immigration Quotas, 1925–1927," History Matters, http://historymatters.gmu.edu/d/5078.

33. Herbert Lakritz, USHMM oral history interview, August 7, 1990, accession no. 1999.A.0122.234, RG-50.477.0234. Both his parents were Polish Jews, and the entire family was part of the October 1938 German deportation of Polish Jews. See "October 29" in the 1938 Projekt, https://www.lbi.org/1938projekt/detail/the-expulsion-of-polish-jews/.

were dependent on individual circumstances.[34] This complicated reality is demonstrated by individual decisions to claim statelessness, varying responses to the loss of nationality, and ongoing and necessary negotiations living as stateless persons. At the same time, their stories also elucidate how nation-states exerted increasing control over the movement of people. By examining individual stories of shifting citizenship, or lack thereof, its vertical dimension and the negotiations within multilayered systems become clear.

The testimonies of those stuck between citizenship and noncitizenship often explain the conscious choice they made to renounce their former nationality and become stateless, vividly addressing this exact moment in time. Stephanie Krantz reflected on her family's attempt to flee Europe through Portugal prior to the war. "We sort of resigned our German citizenship," she recalled. "We gave it up. And stateless was more in our favor for getting into the United States. There was a smaller quota in that category."[35] Other DPs lost their citizenship and became stateless upon deliberate denationalization. For example, Lotte Grünfeld Heimann, born in 1918 in Germany to two Polish Jews, found her family threatened in 1938, like Lakritz's family, with denationalization by Poland. This rendered her stateless, and the German government refused to recognize her as a citizen.[36] For Doris Agatston, born in 1925 in Essen, Germany, she recollected her family losing its citizenship, saying, "They took away everybody's German citizenship, even though up to that time, we had been rather proud Germans. But they just took it away and called us stateless."[37] Such denationalization had a serious impact on Jews across Europe, and it happened at varying times, depending on geography and national laws.[38] However, for families such as the Krantzes, the deliberate relinquishing of their citizenship demonstrates their agency and the continuum of experiences of stateless persons.

---

34. Bloom, Tonkiss, and Cole, *Understanding Statelessness*, 3. The authors reiterate the importance of scholars moving beyond positing the stateless as passive victims.

35. Stephanie Krantz, USHMM Holocaust Oral History Project interview, December 1991, accession no. 1999.A.0122.1011, RG Number: RG-50.477.1011.

36. Lotte Grünfeld Heimann, USHMM oral history interview, 1984, accession no. 2016.176.2, RG-50.928.0002. She gained Hungarian citizenship when she married her husband, Kurt Heimann, in 1938.

37. Doris Agatston, USC Shoah Foundation interview, August 4, 1996, https://iwitness.usc.edu/testimony/18161.

38. On the impact upon Jews of losing citizenship within Germany see chap. 2 in Rebecca Boehling and Uta Larkey, *Life and Loss in the Shadow of the Holocaust* (Cambridge, MA: Cambridge University Press, 2011).

After the war, the number of stateless persons in Europe exploded, as many DPs rejected their former nationality and sought to escape antisemitism, the devastation of their former communities, and/or communism. Citing an exact number of stateless persons is not possible, but within Germany they numbered at least in the tens of thousands from the mid-1940s until the early 1950s.[39] One important source for understanding how DPs began to exercise agency in this fraught situation is their responses to an UNRRA survey, conducted in May 1946, to ascertain how many of the DPs then under its care within Germany would accept repatriation. Thousands of DPs listed their nationality as stateless, although the UNRRA informed them this was not a choice.[40] With its mandate to repatriate DPs, the UNRRA rejected "stateless" as a viable answer to this question; yet DPs negotiated within the system to claim this as part of their identity.

For Jewish DPs, many of whose former nations had denationalized them, and other, non-Jewish DPs who feared returning to their places of residence prior to 1939, the idea of repatriation was moot. As one Jewish woman explained, "In a graveyard you can weep, not live."[41] Said another, "We were stateless people and did not dare to go back to Poland."[42] Helen Fagin remembers making this choice while living in a DP camp in Austria. "The first thing that we did, and that was a very determined act," she recalled, "we were told that if we are of a certain nationality, we will be given the opportunity to return to the country of our origin. And if we make that choice, we had to sign up and we would go to our respective countries. The other choice was . . . to declare ourselves stateless." Fagin describes how she felt, saying, "At that moment of our decision, I think we suffered a very tremendous anguish because the decision has to be made on the basis of what is there for us in the future. . . . And it was at that moment, I remember that my thoughts and my feelings ran the gamut; it was a period of feeling tremendous

---

39. Louise Holborn, *The International Refugee Organization: A Specialized Agency of the United Nations; Its History and Work, 1946–1952* (London: Oxford University Press, 1956), 199-202. In 1951 there were still almost sixty thousand stateless foreigners in Germany. See Jacques Vernant, *The Refugee in the Postwar World* (New Haven, CT: Yale University Press, 1953), 145.

40. Laura J. Hilton, "Cultural Nationalism in Exile," *Historian* 71, no. 2 (2009): 280-317, 288-92.

41. A. R. L. Gurland, *Glimpses of Soviet Jewry* (New York: American Jewish Committee, 1948), 61ff.

42. Esther Raab, USHMM interview, April 13, 2010, accession no. 2020.255.2, RG-90.143.0005.

anguish, even despair."[43] Declaring herself to be stateless was a sharp break with her past, and it signaled her commitment to an uncertain future.

Jewish DPs were not alone in their sense of unbelonging. Many other DPs also became stateless, often officially on claims for first UNRRA and later IRO assistance. This deliberate rejection of their former nationalities did not mean that they wanted to remain stateless permanently. Rather, many, but not all, hoped to acquire a new nationality as soon as possible.[44] To do so, they engaged in the creation of "file selves," a version of themselves that survives within bureaucratic files and forms.[45] Some Ukrainians, who sought to avoid involuntary repatriation to the USSR, claimed to be stateless, as did people from the Baltic states (Estonia, Latvia, Lithuania), annexed by the USSR in 1940. Boris T. changed the nationality listed on his temporary foreigners passport from Estonian to stateless after receiving pressure to repatriate from a Soviet repatriation officer.[46] François K. recalled renouncing his nationality because "my mother died when Russians arrested me, my father is deported by Russians and I do not know where he is now, our property was expropriated—there is no freedom—If I had to return in Estonia or in Russia I should be soon deported or processed as traitor."[47] They understood the system and took active steps to negotiate it. As the Cold War intensified, those who rejected a return to a Communist-controlled state by choosing statelessness increased their chances of immigration overseas, thereby shifting themselves in the eyes of Western nations from migrants seeking economic opportunity to refugees, deserving of assistance and resettlement.[48]

---

43. Helen Fagin, USHMM interview, February 21, 1995, accession no. 1995.A.1269.4, RG-50.470.0004.

44. Daniel Cohen refers to this as "therapeutic nationality." See Cohen, *In War's Wake: Europe's Displaced Persons in the Postwar Order* (Oxford: Oxford University Press, 2012), 89.

45. Sheila Fitzpatrick utilizes this phrase in her work on twentieth-century Russia, as does Ruth Balint in her work on DPs in the postwar period. See Balint, *Destination Elsewhere*, 18–19, and Fitzpatrick, *Tear Off the Masks! Identity and Imposture in Twentieth-Century Russia* (Princeton, NJ: Princeton University Press, 2005). There are also important parallels to how people make themselves as they are made by systems of power, as discussed in Canning and Rose, *Gender, Citizenships and Subjectivity*, 7.

46. Boris T., CM/1 file, 3.2.1.1/79831512/ITS Digital Archive, USHMM.

47. François K., CM/1 file, 3.2.1.1/80408567/ITS Digital Archive, USHMM. The Soviets arrested him, interrogated him for eight months, then interned him for years in a forced-labor camp. They sent him to Eastern Europe, where he escaped, burned his documents, and crossed illegally into Italy.

48. Anna Holian, *Between National Socialism and Soviet Communism: Displaced Persons in Postwar Germany* (Ann Arbor: University of Michigan Press, 2011), 99–102.

The Care and Maintenance files (CM/1) and the notes scrawled by IRO officials are key sources to understand the process of determining who was eligible for assistance, and if so, what type (care and maintenance and/or maintenance only and/or resettlement) and how DPs navigated it.[49] Individual files are crucially important for identifying patterns within this shared, lived experience, often obscured within institutional histories.[50] The cover folder for the CM/1 files contained the person's name, birth date, and place of birth and then a section for related/accompanying persons, where it captured information for minors and women.[51] The application for assistance contained multiple sections:

- basic information, including the applicant's nationality, religion, marital status, and that of any accompanying persons
- a list of residences and employment for the previous twelve years
- education level
- languages
- financial resources
- relatives
- assistance from the UNRRA or a voluntary agency
- a list of supporting documents
- present address
- a closing section for remarks / additional information, which included the date of the interview and the signature of the IRO official who conducted it

As Nicholas Courtman explains in his chapter about naturalization processes in the Federal Republic of Germany, systems to determine citizenship often went far beyond one's place of birth and encompassed one's life trajectory and decisions.[52]

On some versions of the form, under nationality, there were then four descriptors: "claimed," "established," "former," "presumed." To

---

49. Holborn, *International Refugee Organization*, 204-7.

50. Dan Stone, "On the Uses and Disadvantages of the Arolsen Archives for History," in Borggräfe, Hoschler, and Panek, *Tracing and Documenting*, 13-36, 18-19.

51. Given the IRO's commitment to maintaining family units, once it determined the eligibility of the head of household (typically a male), all accompanying persons were thusly designated. Holborn, *International Refugee Organization*, 207. See also Balint, *Destination Elsewhere*, 59-76.

52. See chapter 4 in this volume, Nicholas Courtman, "Race and Racism in the Citizenship Law and Naturalization Practice of Early West Germany."

this end, it was one thing for DPs to *assert* their statelessness. But, as Carol Batchelor explains, it was difficult to *prove* statelessness. "The individual must demonstrate something that is *not* there."[53] While IRO historian Louise Holborn states that the policy was to give the applicant the benefit of the doubt, actual records indicate how often officials voiced skepticism, correctly or incorrectly, about each file's complicated narrative. This process—of DPs claiming statelessness, of IRO officials debating the veracity of those claims, of systems pushing for DPs to have citizenship—demonstrates clearly how messy citizenship was in the immediate postwar period. For some versions of the form to have four different categories of nationality (claimed, established, former, and presumed) highlights the vertical and temporal dimensions of citizenship in surprisingly astute terms.

As they decided what to include in their official narratives, some DPs chose to hide aspects of their life experiences.[54] Katherina S. initially lied during her US Army screening in 1946 and again in her initial IRO screening in 1947, "because I was afraid of repatriation to USSR."[55] Nadeshda S. told a story of her mother's response to screening, when they admitted they had held German citizenship (temporarily from January 1945 until 1947) in order to escape forced repatriation to the USSR. Her mother pleaded with the Counter-Intelligence Core (CIC) officer to understand why they had lied, saying, "A bird was once persecuted by a man and an eagle simultaneously. And the bird trew [sic] itself into the hands of the man in order to save its life of [from] the eagle."[56] According to Nadeshda S., this explanation resonated with the official, and he approved their request for emigration. For many DPs, they balanced fear of the unknown against the knowledge that they could not return to their prewar place. They wanted to attain a new citizenship to protect their rights, assure their treatment as equals, and/or enable their resettlement. Others chose to remain stateless if the IRO would accord them rights and protection and if they were free to live, work, and own property within their current country of residence.

---

53. Carol Batchelor, "The 1954 Convention Relating to the Status of Stateless Persons: Implementation within the European Union Member States and Recommendations for Harmonisation," *Refuge* 22, no. 2 (2005): 31-58, 36.

54. Balint discusses the difficulties that IRO officials had in ascertaining the veracity of the documentation and narratives that DPs presented. See *Destination Elsewhere*, esp. pp. 20-40. Louise Holborn also acknowledges this quandary: see Holborn, *International Refugee Organization*, 206-13.

55. Katherina S., CM/1 file, 3.2.1.1/79817310_0_1/ITS Digital Archive, USHMM.

56. Nadeshda S., CM/1 file, 3.2.1.1/79757346_0_5/ITS Digital Archive, USHMM.

Gender, Age, and Statelessness

Not all stateless persons were seen or treated alike. The policies and practices of citizenship reinforced gendered expectations. As Miriam Rürup explains, derivative citizenship determined women's nationality, either that of her husband if married or, for unmarried females, that of her father.[57] As Audrey Macklin explains, this derivative status was rooted in fears of divided loyalty. When a woman married a man from another nation, stripping her of her citizenship was akin to a punishment for her lack of fidelity to the nation.[58] Among some policymakers, restoring "traditional" ideas of women's place within this world and their roles as wives and mothers was as central to reconstruction and stability as demographic homogenization.[59] When the UN assessed the situation of statelessness in 1949, one of its chief recommendations was that nations should stop stripping women of their nationality upon marriage.[60] Individual women's decisions to claim statelessness informed the debates in the UN and among the international community over solutions to stateless persons' lack of citizenship. These women faced roadblocks, challenges, and even occasionally some advantages in acquiring permanent citizenship, as they navigated the system of classification and sought immigration opportunities. As Anne Epstein and Rachel Fuchs have argued, "By appealing to public authorities for fair treatment or equal protection, they laid claim to a modicum of social and cultural citizenship, if not formal civil and political rights and status."[61] By existing—and reminding people that they existed—they exercised power.

Factors such as gender and age also combined with employability and prior citizenship statuses to shape how IRO officials and immigration policies determined an individual's value.[62] In 1948, preparing for

---

57. Rürup, "Lives in Limbo," 119. This remained the status quo until 1957 in terms of international law. For more on how gender impacted policy and practice related to stateless persons see Miriam Rürup, "Das Geschlecht der Staatenlosen," *Journal of Modern European History* 14, no. 3: 411–30. See also Nicholas Courtman's chapter in this volume.

58. Audrey Macklin, "Epilogue," in *Transnational Marriage and Partner Migration*, ed. Anne-Marie S'Aoust (New Brunswick, NJ: Rutgers University Press, 2022), 257–77, 260.

59. Balint, *Destination Elsewhere*, 60–61.

60. UNHCR, *A Study of Statelessness: United Nations, August 1949; Lake Success, New York*, 118–20.

61. Epstein and Fuchs, conclusion in *Gender and Citizenship*, 233. The very act of claiming statelessness and applying for IRO care and resettlement assistance was an act of civic consciousness.

62. IRO officials were often displaced persons themselves. Holborn states that more than half of IRO workers as of December 1950 were refugees. Holborn, *International Refugee Organization*, 308.

resettlement initiatives, the IRO conducted a census, determining that 80 percent of DPs were younger than forty-five, and most of the men had employable skills.[63] For those outside these parameters, prospects for resettlement were slim. On Annetta de G.'s application for assistance from the IRO, her reviewing official wrote, "Subject is too old to emigrate anywhere. Subject is a stateless person.... She is alone in Italy and has not [sic] more relatives at all." Born into a noble Georgian family in Russia in 1878 and trained as classical pianist, she left the USSR in 1925 on a tour and never returned because she "did not want to live any longer under the Bolsheviks, which killed many of her relatives and friends."[64] The official judged her worthy of IRO assistance, validating her claim to be stateless, but in line with most overseas resettlement schemes, denied her immigration assistance because she was seventy-one. Based on her circumstances, she was worthy of material assistance and the IRO's protection; however, based on her age, she was unworthy of resettlement aid.

Sofia A., an ethnic Ukrainian born in 1892 and in poor health, suffered a similar fate after her daughter married an American and emigrated. IRO officials noted under problems "age" and requested her resettlement in a German home for the aged.[65] She was fifty-seven. Although she had worked as a nurse, Eugenia T., stateless from Estonia, found no immigration schemes interested in her, since she was sixty-three.[66] Eugenia possessed skills that were in demand; the British Balt Cygnet scheme specifically recruited Baltic women for employment as nurses.[67] Yet her age precluded her from this opportunity. These individual stories illustrate how the IRO system treated individuals while also bringing a human dimension to the study of statelessness.[68] They are also excellent examples of the emotive character of these records: the DPs felt alone, unwanted, and bereft of family.

---

63. Peter Gatrell, *The Unsettling of Europe: How Migration Reshaped a Continent* (New York: Basic Books, 2019), 47.

64. Annetta G., CM/1 file, 3.2.1.2/80350630_0_2/ITS Digital Archive, USHMM.

65. Sofia A., CM/1 file, 3.2.1.1/78870115_0_1/ITS Digital Archive, USHMM. Most resettlement schemes privileged the young, the unmarried, those without children, and those with specific skills.

66. Eugenia T., CM/1 file, 3.2.1.1/798438554_0_1/ITS Digital Archive, USHMM. Silke von der Emde discusses the copious pleas of two sisters for the IRO to approve their infirm mother for emigration: see Emde, "Caring for the Dead and the Living," 164–65.

67. Kim Salomon, *Refugees in the Cold War* (Lund: Lund University Press, 1991): 201-2.

68. Dan Stone, "On the Uses," 32–33.

Another White Russian (prewar) refugee, Maria D., was also her own head of household. Fleeing Russia in 1921, she spent the interwar period and the war years in Shanghai with her husband until he died in 1942. Traveling from China to Italy with IRO assistance in 1950, she reunited with her daughter. She sought neither assistance nor citizenship but only renewed IRO paperwork that would allow her to remain in Italy indefinitely. The IRO granted her this assistance, and the Italian government gave her a permanent resident visa as a stateless person.[69] Another woman, Welda S. from Estonia, crossed the border illegally from Austria into Italy to be with her daughter. She had fled Estonia in 1941, part of a wave of Balts who moved westward when Soviet forces invaded. She opposed repatriation, saying that her country was "no more a free land and is actually occupied by Russians, who established there by force a communist regime.... Before the war [I was] a rich woman and as a capitalist ... would fear persecutions if returned."[70] The IRO granted Welda S. legal and political protection and recommended that the Italian government provide her with a permanent resident visa. In each of these examples, the IRO decision was likely influenced by the opportunity to allow reunification with existing family and the labeling of DPs from behind the Iron Curtain as "worthy" of assistance, a moral judgment connected to growing Cold War tensions and the USSR's refusal to support the IRO. In addition, since these women were older, this may have also influenced the decision. Their situation, of being permanently stateless, echoes the situation of many of the Greek refugees in Czechoslovakia who chose to not apply for citizenship but for whom residency rights were important.[71]

Upon marriage, women could lose and/or gain citizenship, regardless of their wishes, according to the laws of their husband's land of nationality. For example, when German-born Edith Levy Weinstein married her husband, "I lost my citizen[ship].... My husband made himself stateless. He didn't want to be no Pola** citizen."[72] Rather than gaining his citizenship, she lost hers and became stateless as well. Johanna K., one of the first German employees of the ITS, became stateless when she married her husband, who was a stateless DP.[73] This was

---

69. Maria D., CM/1 file, 3.2.1.2/80537448_0_1-2/ITS Digital Archive, USHMM.

70. Welda S., CM/1 file, 3.2.1.1/80487612/ITS Digital Archive, USHMM.

71. Tohma, "Statelessness and Social Citizenship."

72. Edith Levy Weinstein, USHMM interview, May 18, 2015, accession no. 2015.244.1, RG-50.030*0814.

73. Emde, "Caring for the Dead and the Living," 167.

not uncommon, as evidenced by multiple other files, including that of Irma C., who gained IRO assistance by marrying an IRO-validated DP.[74] Elisabeth B. was a German Jew who gained US citizenship when she married an American in 1948. However, when her husband lost his American citizenship in late July 1948, she became stateless. The IRO granted her discretionary resettlement assistance, perhaps because she was "half Jewish."[75] Else B. was a German woman who married a Polish Jew in 1919; they fled to Palestine illegally in 1935, and she remained there, even after her husband's death in 1941. Poland denied her request for a passport renewal, citing the lapse in time, rendering her stateless. The IRO ruled that since she had left Germany in 1935 she did not fall within their mandate and denied her assistance.[76] These five cases illustrate the continuum of being stateless and the impact on one's status of being female and married, widowed, or divorced. They echo the fragile existence of female DPs unattached to either a father or a husband, existing as noncitizens, as seen in Wernitznig's chapter in this volume.[77]

Contrast the IRO's ruling on Else B. with its decision to grant full assistance to Ann-Maria G., another German woman who married a Polish Jew and had therefore lost citizenship twice (German upon marriage and Polish upon denationalization). The IRO verified that she had remained in Germany during the war and that the Third Reich imprisoned her husband in multiple concentration camps, until he perished. These experiences established her status as the wife of someone persecuted by Germany and therefore considered worthy of assistance.[78] Rosa F., an ethnic German (*Volksdeutsche*) from the Sudetenland, gained IRO protection and resettlement assistance when she married a DP, even though she was German. The IRO official who reviewed her case characterized her as a "quite simple woman" and wrote, "Her husband passed IRO interview on 3/6/48 and has been found eligible therefore

---

74. Irma C., CM/1 file, 3.2.1.1/78999064_0_1-1/ITS Digital Archive, USHMM.
75. Elisabeth B., CM/1 file, 3.2.1.1/78944087_0_4/ITS Digital Archive, USHMM.
76. Else B., CM/1 file, 3.2.1.1/80369158_0_5/ITS Digital Archive, USHMM.
77. Dagmar Wernitznig, "Citizenship, Psychiatry, and Gender in Postwar Vienna," chapter 3 in this volume.
78. Sabina F., CM/1 file, 3.2.1.1/80369158_0_1-2/ITS Digital Archive, USHMM. The file of Else W., a German woman who married a Jewish Pole and converted to Judaism, follows a similar pattern: stateless by marriage, denationalized by Poland, and having suffered the loss of her husband in Auschwitz. See Else W., CM/1 file, 3.2.1.1/79910359_0_1-2/ITS Digital Archive, USHMM.

she follows him in the matter of status."[79] These cases elucidate the importance of intersectionality within this process. IRO officials used a constellation of characteristics and circumstances to determine the fate of stateless persons, and yet their system did not apply these practices consistently across individuals.

The loss of one's citizenship had implications not only in terms of basic protection and the ability to immigrate but also on one's ability to be employed. Reflecting on living in France after the war, Ruth Hagedorn says, "I could not work unless I married a Frenchmen. And a lot of people did it. They paid . . . to get a nationality."[80] Armanda B. lost her Italian citizenship when she married a Polish doctor. But he had renounced his Polish citizenship, fearing retribution for his work as a doctor for the Polish Corps, and moved to London. Their son's health precluded her from living in London, so she was stateless in the country of her own birth and therefore unable to work in Italy. The IRO official reviewing her file noted this, saying, "She is treated now as a stranger and as such can't be employed in Italy."[81] The IRO granted her care and resettlement assistance, but the file does not state what occurred thereafter. Similarly, Giannetta W. lost her Italian citizenship when she married a Polish refugee. Under Italian law, she was not able to work and therefore requested IRO assistance with resettlement overseas.[82] Blanda B. originally held Italian citizenship and then Yugoslavian. She married a stateless Russian to leave Yugoslavia to escape communism, thereby becoming stateless herself. Upon arriving back in Italy, she registered under her maiden name, telling the DP camp officials that "her husband does not consider the marriage as valuable."[83] The IRO granted her legal protection and resettlement assistance for her preferred destination, Canada. Similarly, to the women under discussion in Wernitznig's chapter, the system saw as "surplus" these women who did not fit within the current system and for whom (most alarmingly) they could not envision a future place.[84]

79. Rosa F., CM/1 file, 3.2.1.1/79089899_0_2/ITS Digital Archive, USHMM.
80. Ruth Hagedorn, USC Shoah Foundation interview, August 19, 1996, https://iwitness.usc.edu/testimony/18725.
81. Armanda B., CM/1 file, 3.2.1.2/80327984_0_1/ITS Digital Archive, USHMM.
82. Giannetta W., CM/1 file, 3.2.1.2/80546073_0_1/ITS Digital Archive, USHMM.
83. Blanda B., CM/1 file, 3.2.1.2/80333105_0_1-2/ITS Digital Archive, USHMM. There are several examples of Yugoslavian women married to stateless Russians in the ITS records. See also Danica A., CM/1 file, 3.2.1.2/80305448_0_1-2, and Erzebet G., 3.2.1.2/80380391_0_1/ITS Digital Archive, USHMM.
84. Wernitznig, "Citizenship, Psychiatry, and Gender," 71, 73, 83.

THE STATELESS STRUGGLE TO BELONG 43

Younger women as single heads of households did not fare well within the IRO system. Maria H., a young, unmarried mother of an eighteen-month-old girl, faced skepticism when she applied for IRO assistance in 1949. She listed her nationality as Polish and her citizenship as Ukrainian. Her fiancé, a DP, had emigrated to Canada in 1947 when she was pregnant. In terms of her possibilities for emigration, one IRO official noted that her daughter, Lina, was a "deterring factor." Another typed "unmarried mother" under a section about why resettlement was not possible and noted "chances for resettlement with child so young seem quite unlikely for new future."[85] Their assessment resulted in the resettlement of this young woman within the local German economy, even though she had been a forced laborer under the Nazis. Whether she successfully negotiated the difficult process for Eastern Europeans to gain German citizenship in the Federal Republic, as Courtman explains in this volume, is unknown. However, here too the latitude that individual IRO officials had is evident. They did not deploy a consistent policy toward unwed mothers with small children. Anna P., who had a child with an American soldier in 1946, was also a Ukrainian forced laborer. The IRO assessment was that "her situation is a bad one with the small child" but confirmed her eligibility for IRO assistance.[86] Zofia H., another Ukrainian forced laborer, had a child with a local German man. They did not intend to marry. The IRO assessment stated that "Zofia is a simple but fundamentally honest young woman, who likes any form of agricultural or domestic work and who would most certainly give satisfaction to any employer."[87] They recommended her for resettlement overseas.

There were definitely moments when morality crept into IRO judgments, such as the case of Waberija G., a woman originally from Latvia. She claimed stateless status for herself and her two children. She had married a stateless man in Latvia, but then had a child with another man, a German citizen. She moved to Germany in 1944, lived with the father of her child, and in 1946 they had a second child. She claimed that her husband was missing and that she had been attempting to obtain a divorce. The IRO official who reviewed her request for

---

85. Maria H., CM/1 file, 3.2.1.1/79159596_0_3 and 79159597_0_1/ITS Digital Archive, USHMM. It is likely that she listed her nationality as Polish to avoid forced repatriation to the USSR.
86. Anna P., CM/1 file, 3.2.1.1/79575083_0_1/ITS Digital Archive, USHMM.
87. Zofia H., CM/1 file, 3.2.1.1/79198224_0_1/ITS Digital Archive, USHMM.

immigration wrote, "There is no basis to establish her DP/Ref Status. No documents. No evidence of nationality. Most likely German. Petitioner has no documents. Her Latvian citizenship is not proved.... She is living with the German father of her two children since 1944."[88] It seems likely that this woman was not who she portrayed herself to be, but this also evidences the power that these officials possessed to pass moral and lasting judgments.

Max Knight, who fled Vienna in March 1938, referred to being stateless as "one of the most frightful conditions that you can be in."[89] However, the transnational solution was not to ensure universal human rights but rather to fit as many stateless persons as possible within the system of nation states. As Samuel Moyn explains, "Human rights were already on the edge of the stage in the postwar moment, even before they were pushed off entirely by Cold War politics."[90] This resulting "solution" to statelessness, to reduce it rather than dealing with the reasons why it exploded, perpetuated it. The exploration of statelessness from individual viewpoints demonstrates the complexity of the concept and how individuals negotiated official definitions and policies. How they told their life stories and how IRO officials and potential new countries responded to them highlight the importance of examining their experience while weighing multiple characteristics: age, gender, religion, work-preparedness, and perceived ability. This intersectional approach demonstrates how perceived worthiness and citizenship were wedded. As the stateless explained their lived experience and sought to remedy their temporary existence, some engaged in aspirational citizenship, in an attempt to belong to somewhere once again.[91] They explained how being stateless made them feel, how their age, gender, and other characteristics impacted their futures, and demonstrated that they understood that creating a narrative of being deserving increased their chances for emigration. This is not a story of postwar citizenship as one of welcoming and belonging. Instead, this was a calculated risk-and-reward assessment, driven by factors

---

88. Waberija G., CM/1 file, 3.2.1.1/79112793_0_5/ITS Digital Archive, USHMM.
89. Knight interview.
90. Samuel Moyn, *The Last Utopia: Human Rights in History* (Cambridge, MA: Belknap Press of Harvard University Press, 2010), 46.
91. For more on the idea of aspirational citizenship see Epstein and Fuchs, conclusion in *Gender and Citizenship*, 233.

far beyond the control of the stateless persons themselves, but one in which some of them exercised agency.

Laura Hilton is professor of history at Muskingum University. She received her PhD in history from Ohio State University. She is the co-editor of *Understanding and Teaching the Holocaust*.

CHAPTER 2

Women's Suffrage and the Making of the French Union, 1944–1946

Emily Lord Fransee

In 1948, French-Congolese journalist Jane Vialle formed the Association of French Union Women from Overseas and the Metropole (AFUW) to advocate for the rights of women across a unified French empire.[1] Vialle, who also represented the African territory of Ubangi-Shari in the French legislature, collaborated with her AFUW colleagues to write a founding manifesto that emphasized the centrality of women's rights to the pursuit of global freedom. The statement referenced the "hardships" and "suffering" of the recent war, particularly the "racial methods" of the recently ousted collaborationist Vichy regime.[2] As a member of the French Resistance and a Black French woman, Vialle had very personal experiences of this dynamic, most recently through her capture and imprisonment in the southern

---

1. Sarah Claire Dunstan, "Jane Vialle and the Politics of Representation in Colonial Reform, 1945–1953," *Journal of Contemporary History* 55, no. 3 (2020): 645–65; Annette K. Joseph-Gabriel, *Reimagining Liberation: How Black Women Transformed Citizenship in the French Empire* (Champaign: University of Illinois Press, 2019), chap. 3; and Lorelle Semley, "Women Citizens of the French Union Unite! Jane Vialle's Postwar Crusade," in *Gender and Citizenship in Historical and Transnational Perspective: Agency, Space, Borders*, ed. Anne R. Epstein and Rachel G. Fuchs (London: Palgrave Macmillan, 2017), 186–210.

2. Association des femmes de l'Union Française d'Outre-Mer et de la Métropole, "Statuts," (1948), Fondation Maison des Sciences de l'Homme (Corsica, France), Fonds Marguerite Pichon-Landry, 12 D 1/122.

French Brens women's concentration camp and the Beaumettes women's prison in Marseille.³ To repair such injustices, the AFUW statement both supported and critiqued the French empire, calling on "all women of the French Union" to "unite" their "diverse and original" forms of knowledge and culture to work "all with the same heart" and "restore France to its true face, that of a fair and liberal nation." This meant "putting into practice" the new French administration's postwar promises of democratic reform in the colonies in order "to obtain for all women in the French Union the possibility of living in the dignity required by the human condition, on the level of complete equality as conferred by the rights of the citizen." For the AFUW, the continued marginalization of women's rights in the empire showed that France had yet to reach its "true" potential as a global space of racial and gender equality.

The group was not alone in its concern over women's rights in the French empire, as politicians and activists gave unprecedented attention to the gendered limits of colonial citizenship in the immediate postwar years. In April 1944, the provisional Free French assembly working in exile in Algiers had extended voting rights to women on the "same conditions as men" as part of a larger ordinance to regulate the establishment of its own authority after the anticipated liberation of the metropole.⁴ However, despite repeated assurances that Algeria formed an "integral" part of the national territory, the full provisions of this reform did not automatically apply locally. Given the incoming Republican government's intent to reconcile its identity as both a democracy and an empire, conflict quickly erupted over the best way to address the increasingly conspicuous irregularity of women's political rights in postwar France.⁵

While male suffrage was regularized across the empire immediately after the Second World War, female suffrage fluctuated. This chapter examines this gendered discrepancy as an example of a key "temporal" change established in the introduction to this volume, highlighting the centrality of colonial female suffrage to the formulation of

---

3. Joseph-Gabriel, *Reimagining Liberation*.
4. "Ordonnance du 21 avril 1944," *Journal officiel de la République française (JORF)*, April 22, 1944.
5. René Pleven, Telegram n°1804 to Pierre Cournarie, July 22, 1944, Archives nationales d'outre-mer, Aix-en-Provence, France (ANOM) 1AFFPOL/209; Pleven, Telegram n°1643 to Cournarie, August 18, 1944, ANOM 1AFFPOL/209; Pleven, Telegram n°1239 to André Bayardelle, July 22, 1944, ANOM 1AFFPOL/209.

postwar French citizenship. To understand the temporal dimensions of this shift, it is useful to contextualize the postwar conflict within the intersectional exclusions based on gender and race that had long shaped contingent hierarchies of "Frenchness" and political "capacity" in the empire.[6] In conjunction with discrimination against metropolitan women, colonial law marginalized anyone placed into the nebulous socio-legal category of "the native woman."[7] When postwar debates about the gendered and racialized limits of political rights took new forms (particularly for women in the empire), they were rooted in this history of seemingly permanent crises over the incorporation of "particular" identities within a supposedly universal citizenship across a complicated territorial backdrop.[8]

As voting privileges became attached to or separated from different French citizenship and nationality statuses, gendered voting laws in the colonial context highlighted the contingent role of suffrage within definitions and practices of citizenship. The flexibility of different legal categories allowed members of the metropolitan government to throttle rights when needed to protect centralized imperial power while still maintaining France's identity as a democratic republic. As Zoé Kergomard demonstrates in chapter 9 of this volume, hierarchies of exclusion and articulations of "capacity" could be used strategically in different

---

6. Examples include Jennifer Anne Boittin, Christina Firpo, and Emily Musil Church, "Hierarchies of Race and Gender in the French Colonial Empire, 1914–1946," *Historical Reflections* 37 (2011): 60–90; Mamadou Diouf, "The French Colonial Policy of Assimilation and the Civility of the Originaires of the Four Communes," *Development and Change* 29, no. 4 (1998): 671–96; Claire Fredj and Emmanuelle Sibeud, "Quels citoyens pour l'empire? La citoyenneté française à l'épreuve de la colonisation," *Outre-Mers* 404-5, no. 2 (2019): 5–16; Emmanuelle Saada, *Les enfants de la colonie: Les métis de l'Empire français entre sujétion et citoyenneté* (Paris: Éditions La Découverte, 2007).

7. Marie-Paule Ha, *French Women and the Empire: The Case of Indochina* (New York: Oxford University Press, 2014); Rachel Jean-Baptiste, "'A Black Girl Should Not Be with a White Man': Sex, Race, and African Women's Social and Legal Status in Colonial Gabon, c. 1900–1946," *Journal of Women's History* 22, no. 2 (2010): 56–82; Robin Mitchell, *Vénus Noire: Black Women and Colonial Fantasies in Nineteenth-Century France* (Athens: University of Georgia Press, 2020); and Bibia Pavard, Florence Rochefort, and Michelle Zancarini-Fournel, *Ne nous libérez pas, on s'en charge: Une histoire des féminismes de 1789 à nos jours* (Paris: La Découverte, 2020).

8. On postwar France see Frederick Cooper, *Citizenship between Empire and Nation: Remaking France and French Africa, 1945–1960* (Princeton, NJ: Princeton University Press, 2014); Emily Marker, *Black France, White Europe: Youth, Race, and Belonging in the Postwar Era* (Ithaca, NY: Cornell University Press, 2022); and Minayo Nasiali, *Native to the Republic: Empire, Social Citizenship, and Everyday Life in Marseille since 1945* (Ithaca, NY: Cornell University Press, 2016). On French universalism see Jennifer Anne Boittin and Tyler Stovall, "Who Is French?," *French Historical Studies* 33, no. 3 (2010): 349–56; and Naomi Schor, "The Crisis of French Universalism," *Yale French Studies* 100 (2001): 43–64.

ways across party political lines as well as within broader efforts to establish the democratic legitimacy of the French nation as a whole.[9] In a similar way, the ambiguous definitions of citizenship in the French "republican tradition" illustrate the "vertical" aspects of citizenship in opening up ways for anticolonial activists to seek reforms that better suited their own goals.[10] While metropolitan policies and individuals were important, they did not unilaterally control the ways that the empire was made tangible, maintained, and challenged. Using examples from the Caribbean, Algeria, Senegal, India, Cameroon, Madagascar, Somalia, Syria, Indochina, and New Caledonia, this chapter therefore also highlights the complex juridical patchworks of legal forms and territorial statuses comprised by the French Union. Conflict over the limits of female suffrage in the colonies exposed rapidly changing vulnerabilities of imperial sovereignty, as the franchise became an arena to shore up—or undermine—the postwar French government's desired identity as both a beacon of freedom and a global imperial power.

Making a Government in Exile, 1940–April 1944

Free France was a creature of empire. With the metropole under the control of German occupation forces and the collaborationist Vichy government, the colonies became a contested space where the Resistance could secure an alternative French legitimacy.[11] Félix Éboué, the Black Cayenne-born governor of the French colony of Chad, was the only member of the colonial administration to reject Vichy authority in 1940, prompting Charles de Gaulle to join him in Brazzaville and make francophone central Africa the administrative hub of Free France.[12] In optimistic anticipation of an Allied victory in the autumn of 1943, de Gaulle and his allies converged in recently liberated French Algeria to plan the postwar government by constituting an unelected governing body known as the Provisional Consultative Assembly (PCA).[13]

---

9. Zoé Kergomard, "Compulsory Voting, Gender, and Race under the French Fourth Republic," chapter 9 in this volume.

10. Joseph-Gabriel, *Reimagining Liberation*.

11. Rachel Chin, "Who Speaks for France? Vichy, Free France and the Battle over French Legitimacy: 1940-1942," *British Journal for Military History* 6, no. 3 (2020): 2-22.

12. Eric Jennings, *Free French Africa in World War II: The African Resistance* (Cambridge: Cambridge University Press, 2015).

13. Emmanuel Choisnel, *L'Assemblée Consultative Provisoire (1943–1945)* (Paris: L'Harmattan, 2007); Lamia Benyoussef, "Year of the Typhus: Operation Torch through the Eyes of Tunisian Women," *International Journal of Francophone Studies* 17, no. 1 (2014): 51-75.

PCA delegates emphasized the importance of representative institutions for establishing the legitimacy of their provisional administration. But general agreement over the importance of democratic institutions fractured over conflicting definitions of "the French people" and the way they should be represented in the postwar French state.

The empire was one major point of contention, particularly in the face of escalating crises of French imperial authority in Indochina, Syria, and Lebanon. Elections were risky, and the administration sought ways to reduce opportunities for nationalist candidates while still presenting France as a compelling democratic alternative to separatist movements. PCA delegates asserted that France was particularly well suited to reconcile democratic and imperial forms of government, presenting a French "imperial family" willingly united against fascism and committed to democratic reform. Speakers at the Brazzaville Conference of January 1944 emphasized that France's "progressive and generous colonial policy" was "fully" compatible with the "democratic ideal of the French people."[14] While some representatives pushed for more substantial reform of racist imperial laws, others stressed the need to keep the empire unambiguously "French," with the metropole at the top of a clear power hierarchy. The empire might be a harmonious family, they conceded, but the colonial "children" had not yet come of age. Any expansions of representative institutions needed to be seen as the generous but controlled act of a benevolent world power rather than the desperate floundering of a crumbling empire.

Women played an ambiguous role within this larger effort, as disputes emerged among PCA members about how to address the gendered limits of French democracy in both metropole and colony.[15] Fernand Grenier, a prominent communist supporter of female suffrage, argued that women's right to vote was a pillar of a "broader and more genuine democracy" that would mitigate the risk of establishing an "authoritarian democracy, a 'Vichyism' without Vichy."[16] But the committee drafting the proposed voting law was led by Paul Giacobbi, who, like many of his male peers in the center-left Radical Party, opposed any immediate

---

14. French Ministry of Colonies, *La Conférence africaine française, Brazzaville* (Algiers: Commissaire des Colonies, 1944), 8.

15. Claire Andrieu, "Le programme du CNR dans la dynamique de construction de la nation résistante," *Histoire@Politique* 24 (2014): 5–23; William Guéraiche, *Les femmes et la République* (Paris: Atelier, 1999), 38–39.

16. "10 Novembre 1943," *Journal Officiel de la République Française, Débats de l'Assemblée Consultative Provisoire (JORF: DACP)*, November 13, 1943; and "21 Janvier 1944," *JORF: DACP*, January 27, 1944.

extension of rights to women partly owing to a long-standing fear that female voters would tilt the electorate far to the right.[17] Others in the PCA argued that allowing women to vote before the return of male deportees, soldiers, and prisoners of war would result in a "disequilibrium" of "universal female suffrage" and thereby give a "distorted" or "insincere" representation of the national will.[18] An amendment by Grenier supporting female suffrage gained traction as advocates emphasized women's role in the Resistance to frame suffrage as a reward for service to the nation, suggesting that "wives and daughters" could "replace" missing male relations and vote "in the same spirit as their husbands."[19] While male voters could be universal bearers of national will, even supporters of the suffrage reform restricted women's representative value to standing in for absent male kin.

The PCA removed gender as a formal barrier to the French franchise in April 1944, just as the assembly was also in the midst of drafting the imperial voting regime. When the PCA relocated to Paris after the August 1944 liberation of the mainland, the empire remained an important symbol of both France's Great Power status and its democratic reputation.[20] Concerned that the racist laws that structured the empire might compromise its "democratic" reputation, the government convened a committee in the spring of 1944 to explore the possibility of expanded colonial representation within upcoming elections for a new constitutional assembly.[21] Committee leader (and head of the colonial ministry) René Pleven emphasized that some expansion was "necessary from a national and international point of view," as it would not be taken well if France "denied the chance" for people in the colonies to participate in elections "precisely on the first occasion that the opportunity presents itself."[22] The governor-general of French West Africa wrote to suggest that an extremely limited expansion of rights might "not be very democratic" considering its narrow scope but still "enormously useful to increase the strength of our Empire's constitution"

---

17. Andrieu, "Le programme du CNR"; Pavard, Rochefort, and Zancarini-Fournel, *Ne nous libérez pas*; Karen Offen, *Debating the Woman Question in the French Third Republic, 1870–1920* (Cambridge: Cambridge University Press, 2017).

18. "24 Mars 1944," *JORF: DACP*. March 30, 1944.

19. "24 Mars 1944," *JORF: DACP*, March 30, 1944.

20. Examples include foreign minister Georges Bidault's speech about a "greater France of 110 million inhabitants" as a "member of the family of democratic nations." "21 Novembre 1944," *JORF: DACP*, November 22, 1944.

21. Cooper, *Citizenship between Empire and Nation*, 40–45.

22. Pleven, Telegram n°1306 to Bayardelle, August 3, 1944, ANOM 1AFFPOL/209.

provided it was "adequately enlarged that no criticism could be leveled against us."[23] Other committee members remained reluctant, arguing that any expansion would risk diluting white metropolitan control of the empire.

The issue of colonial women's right to vote thus sat at the intersection of these two major avenues of reform. Members of the administration who supported an expansion of the male colonial electorate expressed far greater objections about the potential inclusion of women within any expanded franchise.[24] Pleven suggested some options for limiting the female vote, noting that it could be simply "set aside" in the colonies or somehow "restricted" through a "formula" that would avoid any overtly racist discrimination.[25] The subsequent conflict over women's suffrage within the colonies highlights how the PCA's attempt to define "greater France" as a unified democracy sat uneasily with the unequal colonial law that held the territory together.

Women in the Colonial Franchise, August 1944–Spring 1945

The legal patchwork of proposed suffrage law to regulate women's right to vote varied between and within different colonies. In territories with the most restricted citizenship rights, such as French Somalia, Oceania, and French Equatorial Africa, very few changes were even discussed.[26] In Madagascar, women were proposed to be made electors "on the same conditions as men," a provision that implied greater gender equality. In fact, it reflected more continuity than change, as the law retained male-majority preconditions like military honors or political titles.[27]

At the same time, the so-called "old colonies"—Guadeloupe, Martinique, Guiana, and Réunion—were in the process of becoming

---

23. Cabinet du Gouverneur General, Letter n°62, August 24, 1944, Archives Nationales du Sénégal (ANS) 20G25.

24. Pleven, Letter n°6954 to Cournarie, June 13, 1944, ANS 20G25; Pleven, Telegram n°1069 to Bayardelle, June 15, 1944, ANOM 1AFFPOL/209; Pleven, Telegram n°400 to Cappagory, June 16, 1944, ANOM 1AFFPOL/210; Pleven, Telegram to Rapenne, June 16, 1944, ANOM 1AFFPOL/209.

25. Pleven, Telegram n°1239, July 22, 1944, ANOM 1AFFPOL/209.

26. Bayardelle, Telegram n°416, August 10, 1944, ANOM 1AFFPOL/209. See also Simon Imbert-Vier, "Devenir citoyen ou national en Côte française des Somalis: Manipuler des catégories," *Outre-Mers* 404-5, no. 2 (2019): 41-62; Isabelle Merle, "Vous avez dit démocratie? L'extension des droits de citoyen en Océanie Française," *Outre-Mers* 404-5, no. 2 (2019): 17-40; Anne-Christine Trémon, "Citoyens indigènes et sujets électeurs: Statut, race et politique dans les Établissements français de l'Océanie (1880-1945)," *Genèses* 91 no. 2 (2013): 28-48.

27. "Décret n°45-268," *JORF*, February 21, 1945.

"overseas departments" whose inhabitants would theoretically have the same rights as citizens living in the metropole.[28] Their administrations agreed that such "complete assimilation" required women be enfranchised on the same terms as in the European mainland. The governor of Réunion also added that the "population would not understand an exception" based on race.[29] This push to assimilate the legal system overrode the more critical governor of Guadeloupe, a "convinced supporter" of female suffrage in the metropole who maintained that "the masses here are too ignorant."[30] In the small enclaves of French India, local administrators also emphasized the "unreadiness" of the local populations, arguing that the participation of "native women" in elections "seems at the very least to be premature."[31] As India's unique political regime meant there were large numbers of Indian women with French citizenship status, the legal deliberations explicitly clarified that all Indian women "citizen or not" be "deprived of the exercise of political rights," as the timing was "inopportune."[32]

As a League of Nations Mandate (and soon to be United Nations Trusteeship) that had once been a German colony, French Cameroon was under particular international scrutiny. Although the colonial ministry hoped that a significant expansion of voting rights could usefully showcase French reform, the governor of Cameroon remained "absolutely adverse," as even the most "evolved natives of Cameroon possess none of the comprehension necessary for international or imperial politics."[33] As far as women were concerned, only the metropolitan-born "female French of Cameroon" should be considered, as they

---

28. Clara Palmiste, *"Le vote féminin et la transformation des colonies françaises d'Amérique en départements en 1946,"* Nuevo Mundo Mundos Nuevos, Colloques (2014); Marie-Christine Touchelay, "La citoyenneté française en Guadeloupe de l'entre-deux-guerres à la départementalisation," *Outre-Mers* 404-5, no. 2 (2019): 119–43.

29. Rapenne, Telegram to Colonies Alger, June 29, 1944, ANOM 1AFFPOL/209; Ponton, Telegram n°481, July 19, 1944, ANOM 1AFFPOL/210; Cappagory, Telegram to Ministry of Colonies, June 29, 1944, ANOM 1AFFPOL/210.

30. Bertaut, Telegram n°337, July 11, 1944, ANOM 1AFFPOL/210.

31. Bonvin, Telegram n°259, July 3, 1944, ANOM Inde-*F//4.

32. "Décret n°45-254," *JORF*, February 18, 1945; "Décret n°45-266," *JORF*, February 21, 1945. Damien Deschamps, "Une citoyenneté différée: Sens civique et assimilation des indigènes dans les Établissements français de l'Inde," *Revue française de science politique* 47, no. 1 (1997): 49-69; Jessica Namakkal, "The Terror of Decolonization: Exploring French India's 'Goonda Raj,'" *Interventions* 19, no. 3 (2017): 338-57.

33. Carras, Telegram n°1885, July 17, 1944, ANOM 1AFFPOL/209; Rose Ndengue, "La citoyenneté au Cameroun au tournant des années 1940-1950," *Outre-Mers* 404-5, no. 2 (2019): 63-82.

"would not understand being refused a right accorded explicitly to female French of the Metropole."[34]

In Algeria, the presence of a large white settler population further complicated any discussion over the limits of the franchise. While "European" women would be able to vote, the larger Muslim population would not. A small exception allowed Muslim Algerian women who "had been residing in continental France continuously" since before the war to vote in municipal elections in the mainland, but it was not clear if this status would accompany the woman if she returned to Algeria.[35] Citizenship status that was limited by gender or race in one territory could acquire additional privileges—such as suffrage—depending on one's physical location within the empire.

In French West Africa and Togo, the local administration advised that suffrage only be extended to "French women from the metropole" who were "temporarily residing" in French West Africa, as an extension to the larger "black and also Muslim" population was "untimely."[36] This recommendation encompassed the subject population of West Africa as well as the citizen *originaires* who lived in the communes of Senegal, four small enclaves (Gorée, Dakar, Rufisque, and Saint-Louis) where all women and men born in the region had automatic French citizenship regardless of race or religion. Despite their status coming under frequent administrative attack, the originaires had a strong tradition of local democratic governance and strategic use of French republican law to defend their citizenship rights.[37] Although originaire women were citizens, the administration decided not to extend them suffrage. While the "equitable character" of female enfranchisement was "obvious when it comes to European or exceptionally evolved African women," the administration in Dakar warned the ministry that it would bring about "not only inconveniences but indeed dangers" if it were to apply to the "whole of indigenous women who have the status of French citizens," making it "absolutely essential" that the vote be withheld.[38]

---

34. Carras, Letter n°538, June 26, 1944, ANOM 1AFFPOL/209.

35. "Ordonnance n°45-403," *JORF*, March 15, 1945; "Décret n°45-405," *JORF*, March 15, 1945; "17 février 1945," *JORF: DACP*, February 28, 1945.

36. Cournarie, Letter to Pleven, June 24, 1944, ANOM 1AFFPOL/209.

37. Hilary Jones, *The Métis of Senegal: Urban Life and Politics in French West Africa* (Bloomington: Indiana University Press, 2013).

38. Mercadier, Letter n°109 to Cournarie, June 22, 1944, ANS 20G15; Cournarie, Letter to Pleven, July 1, 1944, ANS 20G15; Cournarie, Letter to Pleven, August 24, 1944, 1AFFPOL/1072.

When word of the exclusion of female originaires reached Senegal in February 1945, an outraged protest movement formed. Activists seized on the widely circulating language of imperial unity and democratic reform to insist that the government act on its promises.[39] One delegation of female protesters stated, "French Senegalese female citizens benefit from the same rights accorded to our comrades in the French metropole and elsewhere."[40] At one woman's Saint-Louis home, hundreds gathered to declare their "common cause with women of other neighborhoods" to "fight the Public Powers until the very end so that the injustice would be repaired" and that "all female citizens vote without distinction of color."[41] At another public rally, speakers demanded to "reclaim the totality of their citizenship rights ... in accordance with France's long-standing tradition."[42]

Protesters took advantage of the administration's use of republican language and promises of democratic colonial reform. One protester in Dakar argued that "as French, we demand the application of the law for everyone," noting that it was "very easy to say that our women are not yet mature and that they are mostly Muslim, but the Republic is secular and can only be secular; therefore the question of religion will be irrelevant."[43] Veterans' groups offered solidarity in support of women's "legitimate right to vote," emphasizing the "grave diminishment of prestige" that would result if France did not reverse the law.[44] Should the "unhappy lessons" of racism not be fully "uprooted," one group suggested, this would harm the "victims of Vichy" who had "never lost hope in France and its civic virtues." They connected the experience of war to citizenship reform by emphasizing that "at the moment when democracies triumph against Nazism" and "rights and justice seem to overpower force," the exclusion of Senegalese women stood out as a particularly racist holdover.[45]

---

39. Emily Lord Fransee, "'I May Vote Like All Women': Protest, Gender, and Suffrage in French Senegal, 1944–1945," *French Colonial History* 20 (2021): 119–44.
40. Sûreté Générale, "Renseignements," April 4, 1945, ANS 20G25.
41. Sûreté Générale, "Renseignements," March 10, 1945, ANS 20G25.
42. P. Barlet, "Renseignements," March 3, 1945, ANS 20G25.
43. "Extrait d'une lettre avion interceptée to A. Gomis," April 10, 1945, ANS 17G415.
44. Mambaye Tall, Telegram to Guèye, March 2, 1945, ANS 20G25; Sow Telemaque, Telegramme to Gueye n°839, March 2, 1945, ANS 20G25; Seydou N'Daw and Fall Matine, Telegram to Gougal Dakar, March 5, 1945, ANS 20G25.
45. Seydou N'Daw and Joseph Turpin, Telegram to Gougal Dakar, March 5, 1945, ANOM 1AFFPOL/211.

Amid a finger-pointing flurry of telegrams between Paris and Dakar, the governor-general of French West Africa Pierre Cournarie baselessly suggested the protest movement might be due to a "foreign, particularly an American influence" made by "American men of color stationed here" and other "agitators" who had "seized upon the issue" to use as a "weapon against France" by ginning up "accusations of racism against the administration."[46] As the administration's "prestige had already been shaken during Vichy," the growing protests were eroding the population's "attachment to France" and compromising the nation's "very dignity." In desperation, Cournarie suggested the administration consider an "urgent" extension of the right to vote to Senegalese women before "the very principles of our democratic action are called into question." Paul Giacobbi, newly in post as the minister of colonies, tersely informed Cournarie that he would need to "measure the loss of authority that our belated acceptance under popular pressure will necessarily entail" while being sure that "under no circumstances you allow any bloody incidents to repeat themselves."[47] This oblique reference to the brutal French massacre of protesting veterans at Thiaroye emphasized the dire political ramifications that any violent repression would have on France's global image.[48]

Under such pressure, the administration reversed the law, hoping the retraction would avoid further loss of face and "arouse a feeling of sincere gratitude toward France" among the Senegalese originaire population.[49] Minister of Colonies Giacobbi minimized the protest as "some agitation" that "highlights the ardent patriotism of Senegalese citizens." He presented the government's overriding goal as being "to extend this right to all female citizens without distinction of origin" so that "female citizens from Senegal, like French female citizens in other colonies, take their part in public life."[50] The inhabitants of the communes celebrated their victory. A Dakaroise protester named Ange wrote to her "dear husband" stationed as a military physician in Côte d'Ivoire, "We demonstrated in the streets, men and women alike.... I registered to vote, although with much difficulty... but all's well that

---

46. Cournarie, Telegram n°743, March 7, 1945, ANS 20G25; Cournarie, Letter n°1467, March 8, 1945, ANS 20G25.
47. Giacobbi, Telegram n°814, March 10, 1945, ANOM 1AFFPOL/211.
48. Martin Mourre, *Thiaroye 1944: Histoire et mémoire d'un massacre colonial* (Rennes: Presses Universitaires de Rennes, 2017).
49. Cournarie, Telegram n°1119 to Giacobbi, April 12, 1945, ANS 20G25.
50. Giacobbi, Letter n°5507 to Conseil d'État, April 1945, ANOM 1AFFPOL/211.

ends well and on the first of July I may vote like all women."⁵¹ Back in Paris, the ministry noted that the extension of suffrage to women in Senegal now made it "abnormal" and "incomprehensible" that such a right would not also extend to India, where "Hindu women" were now "the only ones not voting."⁵² They overturned the previous ban in India as well, arguing that granting these rights "only to female citizens of metropolitan origin" would be "contrary to the principle of absolute equality which has governed the granting of political rights," as "whether they be of metropolitan origin" or not, "all the French of India vote." Despite such bombastic (and inaccurate) language, the overseas departments, territories, and states remained in an ambiguous position between a centralized and democratic French empire and a racialized hierarchy in which gender continued to play a major role.

Elections and Constitutions, Spring–Fall 1945

Municipal elections in the colonies during the spring and summer of 1945 marked the first test run of female suffrage within a marginally expanded imperial franchise. Across the empire, politicians and parties seized on the new electoral opportunity. Minister of Colonies Giacobbi emphasized the elections' importance for making a "public and lasting testament" of the colonial populations' "absolute preference for France."⁵³ In India, candidates addressed their platforms to "female citizens . . . and sisters" and sought electoral support by taking credit for "the extension of voting rights to women."⁵⁴ Feminists in the Caribbean who had long advocated expanded rights for women took advantage of the new electoral possibilities.⁵⁵ Paulette Nardal's journal *The Woman in the City* and Jeanne Léro's Martinican Women's Union urged women across the Antilles to vote, contributing to such

---

51. Ange, "Extrait d'une lettre avion interceptée," May 18, 1945, ANS 17G415.
52. Ministry of Colonies, "Rapport portant adaptation aux EFI," July 17, 1945, 1AFFPOL/211; Giacobbi, Telegram to Gouverneur Pondichery, July 18, 1945, 1AFFPOL/211.
53. Giacobbi, Letter n°3687, March 23, 1945, ANS 20G15.
54. Gallois-Montrbrun, "Profession de foi," ANF C//10061; Front National et Démocratique de l'Inde Française, "Manifeste," September 30, 1945, ANF C//10061.
55. Myriam Cottias, "Gender and Republican Citizenship in the French West Indies, 1848-1945," *Slavery & Abolition* 26, no. 2 (2005): 233–45; Annie Fitte-Duval, "A l'ombre de la départementalisation: L'émergence de la citoyenneté féminine aux Antilles françaises," in *1946–1996: Cinquante ans de départementalisation outre-mer* (Paris: L'Harmattan, 1997), 216–17; and Clara Palmiste, "Des sociétés féminines de secours mutuels aux premières organisations féminines politisées en Guadeloupe et en Martinique," *Bulletin de la Société d'histoire de la Guadeloupe* 154 (2009): 79-92.

widespread voter registration that women outnumbered men on the registration lists of some communes (including in the capital of Fort-de-France).[56] Candidates solicited support from the new female electorate by highlighting their achievements for "women's issues" while also sternly lecturing women on the seriousness of their electoral duty.[57] In Guadeloupe, politician Gerty Archimède (who would soon be elected to a local council and later to the National Assembly) addressed her fellow female voters about the role they could now play, particularly to promote policies related to family life and improved standards of living.[58]

The municipal voting took place over the course of several rounds in late April and early July 1945, resulting in the election of over ten thousand women to local council seats across the metropolitan mainland, three women "of Malagasy origin" in northern Madagascar, and at least fifty-one women in Martinique.[59] While most of the electoral operations proceeded "without incident," the French administration came under criticism for allowing too short of a window for newly enfranchised women to register, while requiring unobtainable documentation or providing insufficient polling facilities.[60] Breakdowns of electoral infrastructure were particularly egregious in the soon-to-be-overseas departments of Guadeloupe and Guiana, where "reprehensible conditions" and "poor preparation" of electoral lists prevented at least two thousand women from voting, leading to "general discontent" and a popular demand to annul the entire election.[61] A socialist circular in Guadeloupe was particularly forceful in its critique of the state for giving new voters such a "sad image of elections" and called on "the female youth" in particular to "rehabilitate universal suffrage . . . even if they

---

56. Palmiste, "Le vote féminin," 16–17.

57. Palmiste, 17–23.

58. Palmiste, 26; Annette K. Joseph-Gabriel, "Gerty Archimède and the Struggle for Decolonial Citizenship in the French Antilles, 1946-51," in *Black French Women and the Struggle for Equality, 1848–2016* (Lincoln: University of Nebraska Press, 2018).

59. Steven C. Hause, with Anne R. Kenney, *Women's Suffrage and Social Politics in the French Third Republic* (Princeton, NJ: Princeton University Press), 251; Palmiste, "Le vote féminin," 45; Ministry of the Colonies, "Note pour le ministre: Élections municipales à Madagascar" (1945), ANOM 1AFFPOL/211; Saintmart, Telegram to the Ministry of Colonies, July 4, 1945, ANOM 1AFFPOL/211; Gougal Tananarive, Telegram to the Minister of Colonies, July 10, 1945, ANOM 1AFFPOL/211.

60. Palmiste, "Le vote féminin," 14–15.

61. Surlemont, Telegram n°503, July 24, 1945, ANOM 1AFFPOL/210; Governor of Guadeloupe, Letter n°31 to Minister of Colonies, July 31, 1945, ANOM 1AFFPOL/210; Horth, Letter to Ministry of Colonies, August 9, 1945, ANOM 1AFFPOL/210.

must decide to spill blood" to ensure the "expression of popular will on which the Democratic Republic depends."⁶²

In the communes of Senegal, white women abstained almost completely from the summer elections, preferring to stay home rather than share a metaphorical and literal political space with Black female voters. White male and female residents expressed political opposition and racist disgust at the new voting regime, describing it not only as "wrong-headed" but also as "absurd" and even "rather revolting" that African women who had "only become French in recent years, wearing rags, not yet civilized, yet possessing rights" should be able to vote.⁶³ Such commentary made frequent reference to originaire women's supposed "backwardness" and stupidity, which they measured in their supposed ability to speak French and navigate civic bureaucracy. One commentator from Rufisque described how "the women are even voting, the majority of whom don't know how to speak French, read, or write, and probably don't even know their own birthday, all being born in the year 'I-don't-know.' "⁶⁴ For the white inhabitants, the introduction of Black women as voters in a shared franchise compromised the very integrity of the elections and threatened the rights of white women in particular, suggesting how racism intersected with other gendered rights across the empire.

With the local elections complete in late summer of 1945, attention turned to the establishment of a new French constitution through an elected National Constituent Assembly (NCA). Conflict persisted over the place of the empire within the constitution-writing process, including the shape of the electorate and the extent of colonial representation within the upcoming NCA.⁶⁵ A committee formed to provide a recommendation on such questions quickly became bogged down in the irregularity of the legal statuses embedded within colonial law.⁶⁶ Categories included the white "citizens of French status" in Algeria, the "indigenous citizens" of Senegal, the "protégés" of Morocco, the "subjects" of Equatorial Africa, the "French administered populations" of Cameroon, and a host of "partial" categories such as the "noncitizens

---

62. Arvède Kancel, "La fraude électorale et la jeunesse féminine," *La Voix du Peuple de la Guadeloupe*, July 7, 1945, ANF C//10061.

63. Chipot, "Extrait d'une lettre avion interceptée," June 13, 1945, ANS 17G415; "Extrait d'une lettre avion interceptée [Georges Astay]," April 27, 1945, ANS 17G415; R. Gayraud, "Extrait d'une lettre avion interceptée," April 30, 1945, ANS 17G415.

64. Finateu, "Extrait d'une lettre avion interceptée," June 4, 1945, ANS 17G415.

65. Cooper, *Citizenship between Empire and Nation*, chaps. 1 and 2.

66. "Arrete n° 13," March 26, 1945, ANOM 1AFFPOL/215.

electors" of India and the voters of Somalia who would only be able to vote for representatives that matched their own "race."[67] To address this widespread irregularity, the committee recommended that the NCA include increased representation for "all male and female French, citizens, subjects, protégés, or constituents" to better reflect France's "affirmation of the principle of the fundamental equality of all men, of all the races whose union constitutes the great French community." A strongly worded minority statement raised objections, emphasizing the need to protect representation for the minority "French citizens," specifically white metropolitan-born men. While both agreed that the colonies should have representation, they disagreed about who exactly should be represented.

Tensions about France's identity as both a democracy and an empire persisted within the regulations for the empire-wide election for PCA delegates. In reviewing a draft of the new voting law, the French Council of State called attention to a significant discrepancy between its claim to affirm the "fundamental equality" of everyone within "this great French community" and its provisions that limited suffrage to "certain categories of people."[68] Rather than make voting more inclusive, the council suggested that the government remove any assertions of total equality, as "it is better to avoid the proclamation of a principle that is contradicted by the following dispositions." The administration did not take this advice, and retained the contradictory language in the final draft, asserting the "fundamental equality" of the empire and the importance "in principle, of universal suffrage" to introduce a political system that kept the majority of colonial inhabitants disenfranchised.[69] A gap between idealistic front matter and the letter of the law was common in imperial legal codes. The fact that the discrepancy was identified as a problem was, however, unusual, reflecting the growing French preoccupation with the visibility of cracks within its ostensibly democratic empire.

The vote for NCA delegates was scheduled for October 21, 1945, when, as an article in *Le Monde* put it, "for the first time in history, France and the entire empire will participate together in the general

---

67. Commission chargée de l'étude de la représentation des territoires d'outre-mer à la future assemblée constitutante, "Rapport," July 5, 1945, 1AFFPOL/215.

68. Council d'État, "Dossier n°27," August 17, 1945, ANOM 1AFFPOL/1072.

69. "Ordonnance n°45-1874," *JORF*, August 23, 1945; "Ordonnance n°45-2145," *JORF*, September 23, 1945.

elections."[70] The resulting constitutional assembly included thirty-three women, including a widely publicized victory for Eugénie Eboué-Tell in Guadeloupe as the "first female black deputy."[71] In an interview with the journal *Femme Nouvelle*, Eboué-Tell credited other women for her election, as they believed that since "men have not brought much change so far, maybe if we try with a woman, it will be better."[72] At the same time in Congo-Brazzaville—where Eboué-Tell's recently deceased husband Félix Éboué was once the governor-general, registration lists for October 1945 suggest that out of the 1,020 total voters registered, only 26 were women, and almost all were metropolitan-born French women listed as "spouse" of a colonial administrator.[73] The near gender parity within the metropolitan and overseas electorate was not reflected across the empire.

The NCA convened in the fall of 1945 to draft a proposed constitution that would define French governing structures across the empire, including eligible voters and the type and proportionality of representation for each territory.[74] The resulting draft completed in April of 1946 included relatively expanded colonial citizenship provisions and stated the equality of men and women before the law, describing France as an indivisible and democratic republic that formed a "freely consented Union" of overseas territories.[75] All "French nationals and nationals of mainland France and overseas territories" were to "enjoy citizenship rights" (if not necessarily to be citizens) and "exercise their sovereignty through their deputies . . . elected by universal, equal, direct and secret suffrage." This sweeping statement was reined in with an article and series of laws that established ambiguous "conditions," "modalities of application" and other "special dispositions" that would regulate colonial elections.[76] While gender was not explicitly used as a mechanism

---

70. "Les élections générales dans l'empire français," *Le Monde*, October 13, 1945.

71. Joseph-Gabriel, *Reimagining Liberation*; "Une femme noire élue à l'assemblée française," *African Morning Post*, November 22, 1945, ANS 17G140; "Africains élus au parlement français," *Daily Echo*, December 1, 1945, ANS 17G140.

72. Cited in Palmiste, "Le vote féminin," 12.

73. Administrateur-Maire de la Commune Mixte de Brazzaville, "Décision n°228," October 27, 1945, ANF C/10061; Directeur du Service de Santé, "État numérique: Moyen-Congo–Gabon," October 28, 1945, ANF C/10061; Letter n°11 to Monsieur, October 27, 1945, ANF C/10061.

74. Cooper, *Citizenship between Empire and Nation*, chaps. 1–2.

75. "Projet de loi tendant à établir la constitution de la république française (19 avril 1946)," *Journal officiel des établissements française de l'Océanie*, May 4, 1946.

76. Loi n°46-451," *JORF*, March 20, 1946; "Loi n°46-679," *JORF*, April 14, 1946; "Loi n°46-680," *JORF*, April 14, 1946.

of disenfranchisement, these provisions prioritized the older ways that the French colonial state identified potential voters, targeting "assimilated" individuals and elites who were already "known" to the colonial state and overwhelmingly male.[77]

The first constitutional draft failed to pass an empire-wide referendum in May 1946, leading to a scramble to elect a second constituent assembly to create a revised constitutional draft that would ultimately become the constitution of the Fourth Republic. A reshuffling of alliances led to a rightward shift in NCA composition, adding weight to proposals that favored a stronger and more centralized French imperial state that limited colonial citizenship in order to protect white metropolitan interests.[78] The voting laws that accompanied the new constitution also removed an amendment that would have opened up voting rights for "all those who can justify their reading knowledge of French, Arabic, Malagasy or Quoc-ngu," a provision that, while limited, could have potentially applied to more women than the more common male-oriented voting requirements.[79] By relying on prewar laws that primarily identified men as potential political actors, the French Union's promises of expanded democracy remained particularly discriminatory toward women.

In the next few years, debates about the political rights of women in the empire would stall, with little substantial expansion in the female franchise until the early 1950s (and in the case of Muslim women in Algeria, not until 1958).[80] Voting law continued to distinguish a vague array of different legal "types" within the nonmetropolitan population, including "non-Muslim French citizens," "French Muslims," "citizen of French status," "French citizen of native status," "people of French nationality," "French administered citizens," "French nationals," and "French national citizens."[81] The "specific conditions under which" these new citizenship rights could be exercised continued to prioritize

---

77. Cooper, *Citizenship between Empire and Nation*, 91.
78. Cooper, 95–97; "Loi n° 46-2151," *JORF*, October 8, 1946.
79. "Loi n° 46-2151," *JORF*, October 8, 1946; "Décret n° 46-2150," *JORF*, October 6, 1946; "Loi du 19 juillet 1946," *JORF*, July 20, 1946.
80. Elise Franklin, "A Bridge across the Mediterranean: Nafissa Sid Cara and the Politics of Emancipation during the Algerian War," *French Politics, Culture & Society* 36, no. 2 (2018); Ryme Seferdjeli, "French 'Reforms' and Muslim Women's Emancipation during the Algerian War," *Journal of North African Studies* 9, no. 4 (2004): 19–61; and Elizabeth Perego, "Veil as Barrier to Muslim Women's Suffrage in French Algeria, 1944–1954," *Journal of Women of the Middle East and the Islamic World* 11 (2013): 160–86.
81. "Loi n° 46-2151," *JORF*, October 8, 1946; "Loi n° 46-2152," *JORF*, October 8, 1946.

access mostly for men. As voting was not an inherent part of citizenship, suffrage rights could vary widely within the same citizenship status and break down further by gender.

Despite its rechristening as a unified "French Union," the empire remained a complicated administrative mixture of territories, departments, protectorates, trusteeships, settlements, and associated states whose inhabitants had different formal access to rights. The Fourth Republic constitution presented France in democratic and universalist terms but relied on exclusion based on gender and race to shore up centralized authority. While suffrage is often conceptualized as a binary legal status within tidy national borders, the imperial context shows that the question "When did French women get the right to vote?" has a more complicated answer than, "In 1944."

Emily Lord Fransee is assistant professor at the Croft Institute for International Studies and the Department of History at the University of Mississippi. She received her PhD in history from the University of Chicago in 2018.

CHAPTER 3

Citizenship, Psychiatry, and Gender in Postwar Vienna

Dagmar Wernitznig

> Madness is the impasse confronting those whom cultural conditioning has deprived of the very means of protest or self-affirmation.
>
> —Shoshana Felman, "Woman and Madness: The Critical Phallacy"

> These dual images of female insanity—madness as one of the wrongs of woman; madness as the essential feminine nature unveiling itself before scientific male rationality—suggest the two ways that the relationship between women and madness has been perceived.
>
> —Elaine Showalter, *The Female Malady*

In the spring of 1945, toward the end of World War II, Vienna, like so many other devastated and starving cities in Central Europe, was awash in refugees. Since 1943, Allied bombings had reduced many parts of the city to rubble. In April 1945, the Soviet Red Army conquered the city and established sole governance over it until September of that year.[1] Subsequently, Vienna was divided among the four Allied forces—France, Great Britain, the Soviet Union, and the

---

1. This chapter was developed within the EIRENE project (full title: "Post-war Transitions in Gendered Perspective: The Case of the North-Eastern Adriatic Region") funded by the European Research Council under the Horizon 2020 financed Advanced Grant founding scheme (ERC Grant Agreement n. 742683). For more details please see Home—Project EIRENE (project-eirene.eu). All translations from German to English are by the author.

Oliver Rathkolb, "Besatzungspolitik und Besatzungserleben in Ostösterreich vom April bis August 1945," in *Österreich 1945: Ein Ende und viele Anfänge*, ed. Manfried Rauchensteiner and Wolfgang Etschmann (Vienna: Verlag Styria, 1997), 185–206; Evelyn Steinthaler, *Wien 1945* (Vienna: Milena Verlag, 2015); Markus Reisner, *Die Schlacht um Wien 1945: Die Wiener Operation der sowjetischen Streitkräfte im März und April 1945* (Berndorf: Kral-Verlag, 2020).

United States. Its inner city (i.e., the first district) was controlled by all four powers equally and thus mirrored the rest of the country.[2]

Migration, Exile, Identity Politics, and Postwar Nation Building

The living conditions in Austria's biggest urban center at that time could very easily serve as a metaphor for many of its residents' mindsets, whether they were longtime inhabitants or stranded citizens from other countries. With shattered ruins and shortages of food, coal, and other staples, Vienna was Austria's turbulent epicenter as the country made the painful transition out of war. As the capital of a nation that had ceased to exist in 1938 after having been absorbed *Heim ins Reich* (back home) by Hitler's Germany, Vienna symbolized Austria's paradoxical post-1945 status. On the one hand, it was focused on rebuilding a new nation. On the other, it was both haunted by and still flirting with Nazism.[3] Situated between post-Nazi nostalgia and the forging of the Second Republic, Vienna was also an overcrowded transit terminal for refugees, displaced persons, and returning forced laborers or prisoners of death camps. Many of these individuals lacked the option or ability to go anywhere else.

The Allgemeines Krankenhaus (hereafter General Hospital) in the ninth Viennese district, its facilities partially damaged by Allied air raids, became a symbolic site for the war and the postwar chaos. During the war, it was turned into a military hospital with a special bunker, where operations could be performed undisturbed amid bombings. As in numerous other medical institutions after the Anschluss, many forced sterilizations, justified by inhumane Nazi ideology, were carried out at the General Hospital. The victims of these sterilizations were people who were classified as *nicht erbgesund* (genetically tainted) and thus deemed "inferior" in the National Socialist conception of "race hygiene."[4] The General Hospital was emblematic of the post-1945

---

2. Manfried Rauchensteiner, "Kriegsende und Besatzungszeit in Wien 1945-1955," *Wiener Geschichtsblätter* 30, no. 2 (1975): 97-220, and *Stalinplatz 4: Österreich unter alliierter Besatzung* (Vienna: Edition Steinbauer, 2005); Karl Fischer, "Die Vier im Jeep: Die Besatzungszeit in Wien 1945-1955," *Wiener Geschichtsblätter* 40, no. 1 (1985): 1-12. The French districts were 6, 14, 15, 16; the British 3, 5, 11, 12, 13; the Soviet 2, 4, 10, 20, 21; and the American 7, 8, 9, 17, 18, 19.

3. Oliver Rathkolb, *Die paradoxe Republik: Österreich 1945 bis 2015* (Vienna: Paul Zsolnay Verlag, 2015).

4. Claudia Andrea Spring, *Zwischen Krieg und Euthanasie: Zwangssterilisationen in Wien 1940-1945* (Vienna: Böhlau Verlag, 2009); Gabriele Czarnowski, "Österreichs, 'Anschluss' an Nazi-Deutschland und die österreichische Gynäkologie," in *Herausforderungen: 100 Jahre Bayerische*

Austrian landscape, in which citizenship was renegotiated for reasons of convenience and complacency. These renegotiations were inseparable from the context of post-Nazi denials, which combined an Austrian sense of victimization by Hitler's Germany with limited discourses about individual or collective guilt.

This chapter investigates the psychiatric files of female patients at the General Hospital *after* the German defeat, during the period from 1945 to 1948. These documents provide insights into the wider implications of complex dynamics and processes concerning inclusion and exclusion in post-conflict societies. They reflect and elucidate trauma that stemmed from the war and sometimes arose even more forcefully in its wake with new sociopolitical challenges.[5] Postwar Vienna was a city of women, their preponderance due to combat casualties among the male population as well as the absence of prisoners of war still stuck on former front lines. Thus, disproportionately higher numbers of female than male patients were admitted to the General Hospital's psychiatric wing during this time frame. Also, the increased sexual assaults that were predominantly perpetrated by the Red Army in the aftermath of the war, with estimates ranging from 70,000 to 100,000, to up to 240,000, contributed to an influx of female admissions, in comparison to male patients.[6] All in all, around 1,000 women and girls were processed at this psychiatric institution from 1945 to 1948. While their hospitalization was certainly not systemic, it still evidenced an intrinsic Freudian tradition, harking back to a long history of psychoanalysis and psychiatric facilities in that city.

Citizenship for these women and girls with suspected mental conditions remained largely static, gridlocked by bureaucracy inside and outside the asylum walls. The "foreign arrivals" who ended up at the psychiatric institution of the General Hospital faced discrimination, belittlement, and occasionally outright scorn on the basis of gender, race, and class. Diagnosed with "madness," they were excluded from the

---

Gesellschaft für Geburtshilfe und Frauenheilkunde, ed. Christoph Anthuber, Matthias W. Beckmann, Johannes Dietl, Fritz Dross, and Wolfgang Frobenius (Stuttgart: Georg Thieme Verlag, 2012), 141–43; Edith Sheffer, *Asperger's Children: The Origins of Autism in Nazi Vienna* (New York: W. W. Norton, 2018).

5. Maria Sophia Quine, *Population Politics in Twentieth-Century Europe: Fascist Dictatorships and Liberal Democracies* (London: Routledge, 1996); Ann Taylor Allen, *Feminism and Motherhood in Western Europe, 1890–1970: The Maternal Dilemma* (New York: Palgrave Macmillan, 2005).

6. Barbara Stelzl-Marx, *Stalins Soldaten in Österreich: Die Innensicht der sowjetischen Besatzung 1945–1955* (Vienna: Böhlau Verlag, 2012), 411; Marianne Baumgartner, "Vergewaltigungen zwischen Mythos und Realität: Wien und Niederösterreich im Jahr 1945," in *Frauenleben 1945: Kriegsende in Wien. 205. Sonderausstellung des Historischen Museums der Stadt Wien, 21. September bis 19. November 1995*, ed. Peter Eppel (Vienna: Eigenverlag der Museen der Stadt Wien, 1995), 64.

national body politic, deemed "dysfunctional" individuals during an age of state formation and tremendous migratory fluctuation.[7] Their claims to citizenship therefore illustrate a vertical alignment ensuing from social practices, as discussed by the editors in the introduction to this volume. Exposed to the scrutiny of civil servants *as well as* that of medical practitioners, their pursuit of attaining equity and respectability stagnated in a futile verticality. It was a verticality devoid of prospects to become naturalized as an Austrian citizen, especially when evaluated and deflected against their fellow Austrian, nonmigratory inmates at the psychiatric ward and beyond it.

Accordingly, the hospital's clinical charts, which contain narratives of both medics and their female patients through the prism of psychiatry, also provide useful insights into the panorama of everyday life outside the hospital walls, in "normal" or "regular" society.[8] They demonstrate that the medicalization of female patients' previous experiences in this outside world was not free from cultural, economic, and ideological connotations. Such medical discourses become a foil for gendered expectations of "dysfunctionality," as opposed to "conformity." After 1945, the psychiatric wing of the General Hospital was additionally significant in that it admitted female patients from all social strata and national backgrounds, unlike many of Vienna's private clinics.

Using the records of female patients of the General Hospital from approximately September 1945 to August 1948, this study explores the phase of early state building in a post-Nazi Austria when the country was still under Allied occupation. During this era, the medical staff on the General Hospital's psychiatric ward was confronted with waves of "alien" women and girls pouring into the clinic as traumatized refugees and displaced persons. In many instances these women lacked decipherable national backgrounds or family ties. A substantial part of this contribution concerns itself with women and girls who ended up outside the invisible yet powerful confines of sociocultural belonging. In the dichotomy of citizen versus outsider, these women—usually displaced persons without male guardianship or any other family relations—could at best exercise a form of "para-citizenship," hidden behind the

---

7. Ruth Lister, *Citizenship: Feminist Perspectives*, 2nd ed. (Basingstoke, UK: Palgrave Macmillan, 2003), esp. 43–67.

8. Karen Nolte, *Gelebte Hysterie: Erfahrung, Eigensinn und psychiatrische Diskurse im Anstaltsalltag um 1900* (Frankfurt: Campus Verlag, 2003); Sibylle Brändli, Barbara Lüthi, and Gregor Spuhler, eds., *Zum Fall machen, zum Fall werden: Wissensproduktion und Patientenerfahrung in Medizin und Psychiatrie des 19. und 20. Jahrhunderts* (Frankfurt: Campus Verlag, 2009).

walls of a mental clinic.⁹ The term para-citizenship has been chosen to signify women patients' parallel existence as "non-normative" citizens alongside "mainstream" society in the "outside" world. It also entails a legal vacuum, a phenomenon that Nikola Thoma's chapter gravitates around as well, underlining the political whims of governments and states, especially during the Cold War.

Yet this psychiatric clinic was also frequented by ex-Nazi women who instrumentalized it, admitting themselves to psychiatric care in order to avoid prosecution for their actions in the Third Reich. For both groups, citizenship, its entitlements, and its duties turned into a crucible for defining public and private space during the Austrian postwar transition from chauvinist dictatorship to neutral democracy. In the General Hospital of postwar Vienna, the rights and duties of citizenship for the women at the mental ward were never far removed from psychiatric definitions of normality. Their para-citizenship, juxtaposing the agenda of a newly constructed state after totalitarianism and conflict by delineating "alienness," served as a welcome matrix for this very same state and its citizens to craft a new nationhood during the Cold War. Austrian postwar citizenship relied on dualisms that differentiated the "imagined community" of the Second Republic from individuals and entities that were understood as "corrosive."¹⁰ Therefore, concocting an imagery of para-citizens who were doomed to represent the "other"—for example, in terms of ethnicity, gender, or religion—became pertinent to assist the rebirth of "Austrianness." In many ways, the neologism para-citizenship can constitute a helpful blueprint to disentangle the manifold components on the nuanced spectrum of citizenship in any given country or during any given epoch.

The Para-citizenship of "Alien" Women

In the years after World War II, massive numbers of migrants traveled from Eastern Europe westward.¹¹ Vienna, an urban gateway between Eastern and Western Europe, became home to many of these refugees, especially between 1946 and 1948. In that period a large number of

---

9. Andreas Fahrmeir, *Citizenship: The Rise and Fall of a Modern Concept* (New Haven, CT: Yale University Press, 2007).

10. Benedict Anderson, *Imagined Communities: Reflections on the Origin and Spread of Nationalism* (London: Verso, 1983).

11. Peter Gatrell, *The Unsettling of Europe: The Great Migration, 1945 to the Present* (London: Penguin, 2020); David Nasaw, *The Last Million: Europe's Displaced Persons from World War to Cold War* (London: Penguin, 2020).

female inmates, many with unknown nationality, found themselves in the psychiatric clinic of the General Hospital, and almost half of all the aforementioned thousand female admissions had a non-Austrian background.

There was, for example, Marie, a Polish chemist with perfect German who was born in 1922.[12] Viennese authorities sent Marie, a Yugoslav citizen by marriage, back and forth between the General Hospital's mental clinic and the nearby jail. Then there was the arrested laundress Sophia, a Slovenian in her late sixties, whom psychiatrists nonchalantly diagnosed as a "troublemaker" in 1947.[13] Both women were exemplary of many other female refugees confined to the psychiatric ward. They had experienced profound loss and obliteration yet were rarely acknowledged as valuable *Zeitzeugen* or eyewitnesses of the past.[14] Furthermore, female patients who arrived at the psychiatric ward as stateless refugees or displaced persons, mostly from Eastern and Southeastern Europe, faced harsh treatment, the aim of which was to lock them away permanently or deport them across borders in order to make them invisible as noncitizens of the other sex.

From a historiographic and global perspective, the dynamics of citizenship and gender are associated with a multitude of complex factors, such as coverture laws based on the Napoleonic Civil Code or the struggle for equal franchise, to name but two.[15] Postwar transformations of state frameworks and political systems led to additional changes concerning the rights of citizens.[16] Since the concept of citizenship is

---

12. Wiener Stadt- und Landesarchiv [Vienna City and State Archives] (MA 8), Allgemeines Krankenhaus [General Hospital], A56-Psychiatrie [psychiatry]: Krankengeschichten: Frauen [medical histories: women] (hereafter AKH-A56), box 245 (journal no. 35102; protocol no. 1553). For ethical reasons, the patients are anonymized with pseudonyms.

13. AKH-A56, box 246 (journal no. 37730; protocol no. 1672).

14. Simona Mitroiu, "Women's Narratives and the Postmemory of Displacement in Central and Eastern Europe: Introduction," in *Women's Narratives and the Postmemory of Displacement in Central and Eastern Europe*, ed. Simona Mitroiu (Cham, Switzerland: Palgrave Macmillan, 2018), 15–19.

15. See, for instance, Linda K. Kerber, "The Meanings of Citizenship," *Journal of American History* 84, no. 3 (1997): 833–54, https://doi.org/10.2307/2953082; Irma Sulkunen, Seija-Leena Nevala-Nurmi, and Pirjo Markkola, eds., *Suffrage, Gender and Citizenship: International Perspectives on Parliamentary Reforms* (Newcastle upon Tyne: Cambridge Scholars, 2009). See also Kathleen Canning and Sonya O. Rose, "Gender, Citizenship and Subjectivity: Some Historical and Theoretical Considerations," *Gender & History* 13, no. 3 (2001): 427–43, https://doi.org/10.1111/1468-0424.00238.

16. Linda K. Kerber, "May All Our Citizens Be Soldiers and All Our Soldiers Citizens: The Ambiguities of Female Citizenship in the New Nation," in *Women, Militarism, and War: Essays in History, Politics, and Social Theory*, ed. Jean Bethke Elshtain and Sheila Tobias (Savage, MD: Rowman & Littlefield, 1990), 89–103; Fionnuala Ní Aoláin, Dina Francesca Haynes, and Naomi Cahn, eds., *On the Frontlines: Gender, War and the Post-conflict Process* (Oxford: Oxford University Press, 2011); Birgitta Bader-Zaar, "Controversy: War-Related Changes in Gender Relations:

usually bound to gendered notions that tend to reaffirm stereotypes of "masculinities" and "femininities," post-conflict sociopolitical changes tend to affect women and men differently.[17] In conjunction with reconstruction, national ideologies are intertwined with gender identity to a great extent, and women's status in society is frequently determined by their biological function of childbearing.[18] As keepers of the hearth and caretakers of future generations of citizens, they are easily ascribed the roles of "boundary markers" within sociocultural and socioeconomic processes of postwar transitions.[19]

Consequently, statelessness as a lack of determinable nationality or belonging to a "collective" during destabilized postwar times further increased the vulnerability of female patients from Eastern and Southeastern Europe in the charge of Austrian bureaucrats and physicians. By assessing medics' protocols and reports, this chapter aims to unpack the status of para-citizenship assigned to these female and "foreign" residents. More specifically, the diametrical treatment of "alien" and "native" patients corroborated the political status and value of women beyond private spheres when it came to the curtailment or boosting of civil rights. As also teased out in the contributions by Laura Hilton and Nicholas Courtman, for instance, obtaining citizenship could be inherently volatile for those who did not deserve it in the eyes of national and international authorities or officials.

Interestingly, the stateless women and girls at the General Hospital were described in the psychiatric records as intellectually aware, without so much as a hint toward their suffering from moderate mental conditions, much less severe streaks of insanity. This was particularly remarkable, because most of them had to speak German—which was not their native tongue—as psychiatric personnel peppered them with

---

The Issue of Women's Citizenship," 1914–1918-Online. International Encyclopaedia of the First World War (2017).

17. Ursula Vogel, "Is Citizenship Gender-Specific?," in *The Frontiers of Citizenship*, ed. Ursula Vogel and Michael Moran (New York: Palgrave Macmillan, 1991), 58–85; Sylvia Walby, "Is Citizenship Gendered?," *Sociology* 28, no. 2 (1994): 379–95, https://doi.org/10.1177/0038038594028002002; Ronald Inglehart, Pippa Norris, and Christian Welzel, "Gender Equality and Democracy," *Comparative Sociology* 3, no. 4 (2002): 321–45, https://doi.org/10.1163/156913302100418628.

18. Rick Wilford and Robert L. Miller, eds., *Women, Ethnicity and Nationalism: The Politics of Transition* (London: Routledge, 1998); Nira Yuval-Davis and Pnina Werbner, eds., *Women, Citizenship and Difference* (London: Zed Books, 1999).

19. Jan Jindy Pettman, "Boundary Politics: Women, Nationalism and Danger," in *New Frontiers in Women's Studies: Knowledge, Identity and Nationalism*, ed. Mary Maynard and June Purvis (London: Taylor & Francis, 1996), 187–202.

complex questions. These "alien" patients, most of them with rudimentary education, given their social background, were kept in the ward disproportionately longer than fellow patients who were classified as "Austrian," even though the latter sometimes exhibited significant psychological complaints. Alternatively, when these new arrivals could not be "stowed away," either in the psychiatric ward or a nearby jail, they were rapidly moved across the borders of the Iron Curtain, borders that were normally far less porous for "sane" travelers.

Their transfer out of the country as unwanted "surplus" migrants was also aided by the fact that they had all been sent to the clinic by physicians of the individual *Polizeidirektionen* (police departments) in and around Vienna in the first place. In this context, status as "surplus" was attributed to their being perceived by local authorities as "leftover" or "out of place" in society because they had no male guardian. Prior to their being processed via questionable *Leibesvisitationen* (physical examinations) by these doctors, who had no qualification or even basic training in psychiatry, typically these women and girls had been taken off the street more or less at random by police officials. In practices comparable to today's racial profiling, police officers needed only to spot these women in public places, such as the Prater amusement park, in order to arrest them.[20] As "unchaperoned" and "strange-looking" females, they were often suspected of "soliciting," a euphemism for prostitution. The police's stop-and-screen routine echoed earlier Nazi regulation of sex workers.[21] Likewise, it corresponds with Anna Dobrowolska's findings about the female sexuality and prostitution in postwar Poland, which tackled the control of birth rates and morality under the cloak of socialism.

A selection of representative cases of such female patients at the psychiatric ward of the General Hospital provides further insights into the interconnected dynamics of gender and statelessness in postwar Vienna. Emma, for instance, a twenty-year-old stateless refugee with a Jewish background, a self-defined communist, and fluent in several languages, was classified as suspicious by both the police officers who apprehended her and the hospital staff who treated her.[22] She was kept

---

20. For racial profiling see Mathias Risse and Richard Zeckhauser, "Racial Profiling," *Philosophy & Public Affairs* 32, no. 2 (2004): 131–70.

21. Compare Julia Roos, "Backlash against Prostitutes' Rights: Origins and Dynamics of Nazi Prostitution Policies," in *Sexuality and German Fascism*, ed. Dagmar Herzog (New York: Berghahn Books, 2005), 67–94.

22. AKH-A56, box 243 (journal no. 21789; protocol no. 934).

at the clinic for forty-nine days in the spring of 1947, a disproportionately long time compared to the average stay of five to seven days. There she underwent repeated electroconvulsive therapy (ECT), which according to the medics in charge was ineffective, until she died on July 15, 1947. ECT consisted of shocking patients with electrical current applied through electrodes placed on their temples.

Emma's linguistic talent—she had mastered Romanian, French, German, and Hebrew—turned out to be disadvantageous during her stay at the clinic. The physicians on duty disapprovingly classified foreign languages as "gibberish" and equated her polyglotism with logorrhea.[23] Moreover, her outspoken political conviction as a communist did not fit comfortably with the hospital staff's ideological views. After all, they had, until recently, been under fascism's spell. Most personnel continued their employment after 1945. Within the tapestry of the early Cold War and Austria's ambivalent denazification processes, the relatively novel method of ECT became a convenient tool—not simply to sedate but also to silence patients like Emma. Her tragic case demonstrates that ECT was employed much more swiftly and with greater frequency to female "newcomers" from the European east and southeast who were perceived as "racially inferior" than it was to local women.[24]

Unlike Emma, the Polish refugees Marie and Rosa both survived their stays at the clinic.[25] They were speedily moved to an institution, where they could be deposited indefinitely. Personnel of the General Hospital characterized both women as "aware and conscious of time and location." They nevertheless ended up at the long-term psychiatric clinic Am Steinhof, a site that frequently received "suspicious" women from the General Hospital.[26]

Described as "without occupation, without shelter" and possessing an "arrogant personality," Marie had been arrested at the

---

23. AKH-A56, box 243 (journal no. 21789; protocol no. 934), 2.

24. Ever since its original conceptualization in Mussolini's Italy of the 1930s, ECT has been disputed. Ugo Cerletti (1877–1963) and Lucio Bini (1908–1964) count as the godfathers of this treatment; in Rome in 1938 they conducted for the first time what they then decided to name electroshock therapy. For a biography of Cerletti see Roberta Passione, *Cerletti: The History of Electroshock* (Reggio Emilia: Aliberti, 2007).

25. AKH-A56, box 245 (journal no. 35102; protocol no. 1553); AKH-A56, box 247 (journal no. 47258; protocol no. 2006).

26. Designed by Otto Wagner and Franz Berger and founded in 1907 in Penzing, the fourteenth district, Am Steinhof played a major part in euthanasia crimes in the Third Reich. See Susanne Mende, *Die Wiener Heil- und Pflegeanstalt "Am Steinhof" im Nationalsozialismus* (New York: Peter Lang, 2000), and Sophie Ledebur, *Das Wissen der Anstaltspsychiatrie in der Moderne: Zur Geschichte der Heil- und Pflegeanstalten Am Steinhof in Wien* (Vienna: Böhlau Verlag, 2014).

Yugoslavian-Hungarian border on grounds of her multinational (both Polish and Yugoslavian) identity papers in January 1947.[27] The waitress and divorcee Rosa shared the same fate. Expelled from the Auhof refugee camp for "posing a danger to the public" because she demanded more food to nurse her child and criticized the head nurse at Auhof for discriminating against refugees, she was sent to the General Hospital by the police medic in November 1947.[28] Lacking clothing to keep warm, Rosa suffered from a plain cold with fever rather than a psychiatric condition. Nevertheless, she too was locked up at Am Steinhof.

The narratives of stateless and working-class female refugees also exemplify the administrative no-(wo)man's-land of "unchaperoned" or "surplus" females, whose nationality could not be determined and who thus could not be sent "back to where they once belonged."[29] The undernourished deportee Lisa, originally from Brno in Czechoslovakia, lived in the so-called Camp XV, a former Nazi camp for Italian and Greek forced laborers in Vienna.[30] Helena and Eva were both raped by Allied soldiers after the war.[31] "Stored away" at Am Steinhof as the final destination for non-nationals, all three women were part of an endless parade of Eastern European female refugees who experienced othering processes defined by the intersectionality of their gender, race, and class. These experiences happened in conjunction with the loss or denial of citizenship on multiple levels.

As with other female patients from underprivileged backgrounds, their wartime and postwar traumas were unrecognized by the medical community at that time. Rather, their behaviors were belittled as "feminine" hysteria, disconnected from newly formed theories of what had come to be known as "shell shock" after 1918.[32] These women were

---

27. AKH-A56, box 245 (journal no. 35102; protocol no. 1553), "Befund und Gutachten" [diagnosis and expert report] by the police medic Dr. G. Krassel, August 27, 1947, 3.

28. AKH-A56, box 247 (journal no. 47258; protocol no. 2006), "Amtsaerztlicher [sic] Befund und Gutachten" [diagnosis and expert report by the medical officer] by the police physician Dr. Josef Kristovsky, November 20, 1947, 3.

29. Compare Jacqueline Bhabha, "'Get Back to Where You Once Belonged': Identity, Citizenship, and Exclusion in Europe," *Human Rights Quarterly* 20, no. 3 (1998): 592–627, https://doi: 10.1353/HRQ.1998.0023.

30. AKH-A56, box 225 (journal no. 5591; protocol no. 262). See Zwangsarbeiterlager Zinckgasse 12-14—Wien Geschichte Wiki.

31. AKH-A56, box 233 (journal number not given; protocol no. 1150); AKH-A56, box 241 (journal no. 19559; protocol no. 838).

32. For "shell shock" as an acceptable and accepted postwar trauma symptom for army veterans, *not* noncombatants, see Tracey Loughran, "Shell Shock, Trauma, and the First World War: The Making of a Diagnosis and Its Histories," *Journal of the History of Medicine and Allied Sciences* 67, no. 1 (2010): 94–119, https://doi: 10.1093/jhmas/jrq052. See also Hazel

categorized as unwanted aliens from the "less-civilized" east and southeast. They were also a constant reminder of Nazi cruelties committed in these territories, acts that ex-Nazi followers preferred to forget. Thus, arrivals from Eastern and Southeastern Europe ranked decidedly lower in the implicit hospital hierarchy than Austrian patients. They were viewed as single, "unprotected" women without a paterfamilias or any other male provider, frequently stigmatized as prone to promiscuity and as a menace to society. And they were castigated as impoverished, underprivileged women without qualifications or training, whose migratory background was conflated with aspects of class or milieu, ethnicity, and lack of education.[33]

Nationalized and Non-nationalized Citizens

A pivotal point in postwar Austria was the restoration of traditional family parameters with rigorously masculinized and feminized roles. This restoration was mostly accomplished by sending women back to the hearth after the war effort on the home front, to make room for returning veterans in the labor market. Policymakers promoted maternalism in particular because of the decimation of Austria's male population on the battlefields. As many men had fallen on the front or remained in prisoner of war camps, women were encouraged to maintain their patriotic duties as keepers of hearth and home.[34] Thus, Austrian mothers in the psychiatric wing were generally released after short periods so that they could return to childbearing and child-rearing. Equally, Austrian women patients in their roles as wives, fiancées, or girlfriends were denied adequate acknowledgment and treatment as rape victims who had survived attacks by enemy soldiers. As some of their husbands and male partners returned as mentally and physically wounded veterans, addressing these "sexual conquests" by invading armies could have evoked the image of an emasculated and hence denigrated society in

---

Croft, "Emotional Women and Frail Men: Gendered Diagnostics from Shellshock to PTSD, 1914-2010," in *Gender and Conflict since 1914: Historical and Interdisciplinary Perspectives*, ed. Ana Carden-Coyne (Basingstoke, UK: Palgrave Macmillan, 2012), 110-23.

33. For the marginalization of women "standing alone" see especially Elizabeth D. Heineman, *What Difference Does a Husband Make? Women and Marital Status in Nazi and Postwar Germany* (Berkeley: University of California Press, 1999).

34. Irene Bandhauer-Schöffmann and Claire Duchen, eds., *Nach dem Krieg: Frauenleben und Geschlechterkonstruktionen in Europa nach dem Zweiten Weltkrieg* (Herbolzheim: Centaurus, 2000).

the aftermath of war.³⁵ The contrasting experiences of Luisa and Paula showcase this gap between the treatment of local citizens and foreign nationals or stateless women.³⁶

Paula, a forty-two-year-old Roman Catholic, came from Ernsthausen in the Banat, a contested borderland sandwiched between Hungary, Romania, and Serbia. Practically nothing is known about her prewar life, except that she had a husband in Bavaria, a deceased son, and a sixteen-year-old daughter. Toward the end of the war, she was expelled from her farm and put into an unspecified Yugoslavian camp for two years, where she contracted typhus. After the war, she wondered how she had survived when "everyone else around her had died." In conversation with a doctor, she elaborated that at one time "the barrel of a gun was put in her mouth and she was about to be shot." Stranded in Vienna's Camp XV as a stateless refugee after the war, she was picked up by police officials on suspicion of suicidal tendencies. On April 25, 1947, she was inspected by Dr. Eduard Michl, the police medic of Wien XV in Rudolfsheim-Fünfhaus.³⁷

Michl's occupational background was originally in zoology, and in 1925 he had graduated with a medical degree from the University of Vienna. Incarcerated for listening to foreign radio broadcasts in 1940 and for establishing an antifascist, monarchist group in 1943, he was exiled from his home as a noncitizen, like Paula, and fled the Third Reich. After the war ended, he returned to Austria. As the police physician handling Paula, Michl came to the conclusion that "the patient suffers from asthmatic attacks and great physical exhaustion."³⁸ Considering the horrors Paula had lived through, her behavior was understandable. But that did not prevent Michl from referring her to the General Hospital for psychiatric observation, because he labeled her suicidal. There, psychiatrists ascertained that she was "time, place, personally oriented" and had an "orderly flow of thought." Upon further questioning by the

---

35. Compare Jelena Seferović, "Reflection on the (Un)Power of Men in the Context of Post-war Everyday Life of Croatian War Veterans with Mental Disorders from World War I," *Synthesis Philosophica* 69, no. 1 (2020): 25–44, https://doi: 10.21464/sp35102.

36. AKH-A56, box 249 (journal no. 49329; protocol no. 2100); AKH-A56, box 241 (journal no. 17176; protocol no. 740). The old Habsburg town name Ernsthausen (Banatski Despotovac in Serbian) was used on all of Paula's patient sheets. Catholic and German-speaking, she was probably a descendant of the so-called Danube-Swabians settled there by Austria-Hungary in the 1820s as a religious and linguistic enclave. Her expulsion and camp imprisonment in 1945 also cohered with the history of Danube-Swabians in that area.

37. AKH-A56, box 241 (journal no. 17176; protocol no. 740), 2, "Amtsärztlicher Befund und Gutachten" [diagnosis and expert report by the medical officer], April 25, 1947.

38. AKH-A56, box 241 (journal no. 17176; protocol no. 740), 3.

staff, she explained that "the police doctor was very bad to her, told her she had to go back to the Banat, one didn't need sick people in Austria," and that she "has only one wish, to find a quiet spot on this earth and to go to her husband in Bavaria."[39]

But the authorities would not permit her to find her place of tranquility. Instead, from May 1947 onward, her limbo as a stateless and husbandless refugee was perpetuated at the long-term care facility Am Steinhof, owing to the psychiatrist's explanation that she was prone to suicidal tendencies.[40] As a displaced woman, Paula was denied autonomy by a clinical system geared toward the bureaucratic disappearance, or "de-selving," of female refugees.[41] In her case, this loss of agency engendered a secondhand citizenship with diminished rights, closely resembling the precarious situation so aptly presented by Stanislava Dikova in her chapter on Olivia Manning's *Balkan Trilogy*. This precarity or "secondhandedness" undermined the struggle for a fully accessible version of citizenship with dignity, responsibility, and independence. In the end, the supposedly suicidal Paula was denied the right to reunite with her family as an overall "unfit" homemaker.

Compared to Paula, the Austrian mother Luisa was viewed more benevolently at the psychiatric clinic of the General Hospital. Luisa had tried to kill herself and her three-year-old toddler with thirteen veronal tablets, administering three to the minor and swallowing ten herself.[42] Born in 1915 in Baden near Vienna, she was brought to the clinic by her mother-in-law in early December 1947 and released less than three weeks later. Luisa was representative of many mothers and native Austrian citizens who were admitted to this psychiatric ward for suicidal behavior and depression that posed a threat to themselves and their children. For instance, Klara and Hilda both tried to murder their children in the winters of 1945 and 1946, respectively.[43] Luisa spent an exceptionally brief period on the ward and was promptly sent home right

---

39. AKH-A56, box 241 (journal no. 17176; protocol no. 740), 2.
40. Gatrell, *Unsettling of Europe*, 35–50.
41. As defined by Maroussia Hajdukowski-Ahmed, "'De-selving' does not mean a loss of identity and culture, but rather the gradual erosion of *agency* imposed by the organizations, spatial configurations, laws, and relationships they confront in their refugee experience." Hajdukowski-Ahmed, "A Dialogical Approach to Identity: Implications for Refugee Women," in *Not Born a Refugee Woman: Contesting Identities, Rethinking Practices*, ed. Maroussia Hajdukowski-Ahmed, Nazilla Khanlou, and Helene Moussa (New York: Berghahn Books, 2008), 37–38.
42. AKH-A56, box 249 (journal no. 49329; protocol no. 2100).
43. AKH-A56, box 225 (journal no. 2288; protocol no. 110); AKH-A56, box 240 (journal no. 6267; protocol no. 286).

before Christmas as a gesture of goodwill by the hospital chief of staff, Professor Otto Kauders.[44]

When Luisa first arrived at the clinic, she was examined by Dr. Erwin Ringel. She told Ringel the circumstances of her war and postwar existence, which explained her desire to end her and her child's life. She detailed the death of her first child from scarlet fever in 1941, the loss of her husband on the eastern front, and her multiple rapes by Russian soldiers in 1945, an experience she had kept secret out of shame.[45] In Ringel's words, "She could not stand this permanent loneliness, and her second child, who is now 3 years old, could not take away her severe depression, either."[46] Although, as an Austrian citizen, Luisa was given more opportunity than Paula to explain her circumstances, her file is also characterized by omission and neglect. What was prioritized by the medics in her records were her maternal assets and her ability to make a home. She was appropriated by Professor Kauders for his lecture series at the University of Vienna and paraded as the archetypal mother in front of his students. Luisa was showcased as a "rehabilitated specimen" who had been "stitched back together" in the national interest of stabilizing family patterns and reducing welfare costs in critical times. By probing and interrogating her in front of the student audience in the auditorium, with intimate inquiries about her private life, Kauders managed to elicit from her that she even had a potential new partner.[47] This substitute male, stepping into her missing husband's shoes as the head of the family, was also the major reason for Luisa's dangerously premature discharge from the clinic.

---

44. AKH-A56, box 225 (journal no. 2288; protocol no. 110); AKH-A56, box 240 (journal no. 6267; protocol no. 286). Like Eduard Michl, Otto Kauders (1893–1949) was also forced out of Austria by the Nazi regime. After his exile in the United States, where he practiced psychiatry in Buffalo, New York, he returned in 1945 and replaced Otto Pötzl (1877–1962) as head of the psychiatric ward of the General Hospital; Pötzl had led the ward since 1928 and had joined the Nazi Party twice, in 1930 and 1941. See Ernst Klee, *Das Personenlexikon zum Dritten Reich: Wer war was vor und nach 1945*, 2nd ed. (Frankfurt am Main: Fischer-Taschenbuch-Verlag, 2007), 467.

45. AKH-A56, box 249 (journal no. 49329; protocol no. 2100), 2. Then a young medic, Erwin Ringel (1921–1994) moved on to become the foremost psychiatric expert on suicide in Austria and beyond. In 1948, for example, he established the first European suicide prevention center in Vienna, and from 1953 to 1964 he led the women's ward of the General Hospital's psychiatric clinic. His initiative Internationale Vereinigung für Selbstmordverhütung (International Association for Suicide Prevention and Crisis Intervention, or IASP), which he started in 1960, earned him the nickname "Mr. Suicide" in the United States.

46. AKH-A56, box 249 (journal no. 49329; protocol no. 2100), 2.

47. AKH-A56, box 249 (journal no. 49329; protocol no. 2100), 3.

Unlike foreign-born Paula, who was beyond "respectable" childbearing age at that time and whose family was dispersed (her husband's and daughter's whereabouts were unverified), Austrian citizen Luisa was surrounded by a local family structure of in-laws and siblings. After all, it was her mother-in-law who had dropped her off at the General Hospital, and her sister who had collected her from there weeks afterward, vouching that she always had been "unobtrusive." Her boyfriend—the prospective paterfamilias—guaranteed an "intact" and "acceptable" relationship with future possibilities for procreation. As a "substitute" husband and probable patriarch of the family, he also ensured that Luisa, who had been ascribed the status of a "dependent," would be adequately supported.[48] She would not remain a welfare case reliant on social benefits financed by a bankrupted state.[49] Despite the fact that she posed a clear threat to herself and her child, Luisa was allowed to leave the clinic rather swiftly. This arrangement was even more bizarre, since Kauders portrayed her as retaining "total intransigence [i.e., lack of remorse] in the offense against her child."[50] She had spoken about trying to kill her infant on many occasions.

Conversely, Paula had displayed a comparatively moderate depression and understandable physical exhaustion after escaping the Yugoslavian camp and war zone on foot. Yet she was labeled as a graver case and removed from society as a socially disturbed element. As a female outsider without family roots, a living reminder of Austrian war crimes, she was not considered to contribute "efficiently" to the consolidation of Austrian society. Paula's and Luisa's stories thus fit perfectly into the fabric of post-conflict myth-making, which privileged images of maternity and a dichotomy of "feminine" qualities and male virility. Besides race, the negative nexus of age and gender (as Hilton also examines in her chapter) proved detrimental for Paula. Successively, Paula's "otherness" facilitated her removal from postwar society as a para-citizen, highlighting the racial undertones that permeated psychiatric decisions at the General Hospital. These dynamics of race, ageism, and gender shaped Paula's and Luisa's paths, condemning the former

---

48. AKH-A56, box 249 (journal no. 49329; protocol no. 2100), 1.

49. Gisela Bock and Patricia Thane, eds., *Maternity and Gender Policies: Women and the Rise of the European Welfare States, 1880s–1950s* (London: Routledge, 1991); Seth Koven and Sonya Michel, eds., *Mothers of a New World: Maternalist Politics and the Origins of Welfare States* (London: Routledge, 1993); Marian van der Klein, Rebecca Jo Plant, Nichole Sanders, and Lori R. Weintrob, eds., *Maternalism Reconsidered: Motherhood, Welfare and Social Policy in the Twentieth Century* (New York: Berghahn Books, 2012).

50. AKH-A56, box 249 (journal no. 49329; protocol no. 2100), 3.

to unwarranted institutionalization while depriving the latter of much-needed care.

Female Citizens "Playing Mad" after Nazism

The postwar transitions in Vienna specifically and Austria generally also brought to the fore another facet of the previously Nazi-prescribed femininity and domesticity, encapsulated in the slogan "Kinder, Küche, Kirche" (children, kitchen, church). The women's wing of the psychiatric clinic at the General Hospital became another forum for engineered citizenship behind hospital walls, this time realized by female patients themselves. Amid a convoluted phase of denazification and the prosecution of former Austrian Nazis carried out by the occupying Allied Powers, some pro-Hitler women used the obscured space of the psychiatric ward to "sit out" these Allied prosecutions.[51]

As fervent citizens of the previous regime, usually classified as *belastete* (encumbered) citizens, these women readily accepted a stay at this clinic as the lesser evil to potential incarceration. They actively disguised their former "Aryan citizenship" while foregrounding their victimhood, thereby feigning that they were being subjected to unfounded accusations after the fall of the Third Reich. From a pool of a dozen Nazi women who fabricated their own postwar lunacy at the General Hospital, I have selected two representative examples: Elsa and Berta, who both voluntarily showed up at the psychiatric wing after Austria's defeat.

Elsa, who was born in 1875 in Leipzig, walked into the clinic on November 5, 1945, and would stay there until her release on February 16, 1946.[52] An actress by training, she had been employed in a range of variety shows before and during the war. Her family had been well-connected in Nazi Germany. Her son, for instance, was put in charge of an opera house in the Saarland. Extremely loyal to Nazi doctrines, Elsa went as far as denouncing her husband as a homosexual to the authorities. Drawing on her acting skills (even the medics on duty occasionally attested to her "dissimulation tendencies"), Elsa blended into

---

51. Especially the Western Allies, Britain, France, and the United States, less the Soviet forces, pursued such denazification politics, which also became an integral part of Cold War tactics and maneuvers of eliciting "intel" from former members of the Nazi Party. For denazification in Austria see, for instance, Dieter Stiefel, *Entnazifizierung in Österreich* (Vienna: Europaverlag, 1981).

52. AKH-A56, box 225 (journal no. 35506; protocol no. 1395).

the hospital environment almost seamlessly. According to her doctors, many of whom had continued their own careers after 1945 and were sympathetic to her cause, she was "calm, orderly, fully oriented, amiable, approachable, unobtrusive." Purportedly she claimed that she enjoyed her treatment and that she felt "very well . . . at the clinic," by any standards a rather out-of-place statement, considering the general circumstances of institutionalization that others had to withstand.[53]

More than two years later, the Viennese widow Berta, in her interviews with the hospital's psychiatrists, displayed unrepentant pride in being an avid Nazi from the earliest moment and adhering to the party's ideology long after the end of the war. She arrived at the clinic in April 1948 and spent a week there before she was transferred to Am Steinhof. During that time, she expressed her admiration of Hitler, whom she had personally contacted in 1941, and her unshaken belief in a Germanic world order as "a convinced National Socialist." Like Elsa, she was described by her medics as "personally, time, and place oriented with good contact skills."[54] Like Paula from the Banat, she was also placed in Am Steinhof despite her mental lucidity. Unlike Paula, though, Elsa found in Am Steinhof a convenient hideaway. There, in surroundings where most members of staff had seamlessly and inconspicuously transitioned from the Third Reich to the Second Republic, Berta attempted to whitewash her support for the Nazi regime until the Allied denazification processes had run their course and she could resume her life as a citizen. At the same time, displaced women like Paula had to endure a permanently invisible citizenship with little chance of being integrated into Austrian society.

The alternative to Am Steinhof for Berta was bleaker, namely an involuntary stay at one of the two denazification or reeducation camps for women, either the US-run Glasenbach internment camp or the British Wolfsberg internment camp.[55] At either of these institutions she would have had to come to terms with her actions as an ardent Nazi sympathizer, whereas in Am Steinhof she could continue to indulge in her romanticized belonging to an imaginary Anschluss Austria. Significantly, her diagnosis by the physicians who examined her sustained such fascist interpretations of statehood and citizenry. Together with

---

53. AKH-A56, box 225 (journal no. 35506; protocol no. 1395), 3.
54. AKH-A56, box 254 (journal no. 16241; protocol no. 750), 1.
55. Lager Glasenbach was also called Camp Marcus W. Orr (named after the wounded and paralyzed US soldier and later history professor at Memphis State University); the Wolfsberg facility in Carinthia became known as Camp 373.

the steadfast Nazi from Leipzig, Elsa, she was diagnosed as paranoid. This was an exceptionally rare psychiatric classification, which was hardly ever employed in over one thousand medical charts inspected during the course of my research.

Defined as "an alienation from others that has gone beyond a sense of disconnection to one of persecution," paranoia, at least theoretically, could easily be deployed to explain the fascist mindset and fantasies displayed by Elsa and Berta.[56] It also accounted for their perceptions of victimhood after the collapse of Nazi Germany and their loss of privileged citizenship as members of what they believed to be a superior race. Both women stressed their status in the post-1945 democratic Second Republic of Austria as outsiders and persecuted enemies of the state, stripped of the "proper" citizenship that they had possessed under Hitler. More importantly, neither woman received medication or therapy at the psychiatric ward. They were simply monitored until they left of their own free will. Such benign treatment stands out amid drastic measures like ECT used on refugee patients. These practices suggested different logics of care in which citizenship status mattered a great deal and Austrian patients retained a more privileged status. Female patients like Elsa and Berta profited from gendered assumptions about the "weaker, apolitical sex" when it came to active engagement and crimes committed during the Nazi era. For them, psychiatric care and the medicalization of the female mind became an ideal shield against denazification procedures.

Third Women and the Psychiatric Underground

After the Second World War, Vienna became a hot spot for Cold War espionage, a "city of spies," epitomized in the film noir *The Third Man* (1949).[57] In *"The Third Man" and "The Fallen Idol,"* screenwriter Graham Greene explained that "the episode of the Russians kidnapping Anna (a perfectly possible incident in Vienna) was eliminated" as "it threatened to turn the film into a propagandist picture. We had no desire to move

---

56. John Mirowsky and Catherine E. Ross, "Paranoia and the Structure of Powerlessness," *American Sociological Review* 48, no. 2 (1983): 228, https://doi.org/10.2307/2095107.

57. Manfried Rauchensteiner, *Der Sonderfall: Die Besatzungszeit in Österreich 1945 bis 1955* (Vienna: Verlag Styria, 1979); Günter Bischof, *Austria in the First Cold War, 1945–55: The Leverage of the Weak* (Basingstoke, UK: Macmillan, 1999); Erwin A. Schmidl, ed., *Österreich im frühen Kalten Krieg 1945–1958: Spione, Partisanen, Kriegspläne* (Vienna: Böhlau Verlag, 2000); William B. Bader, *Österreich im Spannungsfeld zwischen Ost und West 1945–1955* (Vienna: Braumüller, 2002).

people's political emotions; we wanted to entertain them, to frighten them a little, to make them laugh."[58]

Lynette Carpenter relates the fate of the film's female protagonist Anna Schmidt (a Czechoslovak with a fake passport) to its villain Harry Lime's criminal dealings with tampered penicillin, which caused patients to die or go insane: "By the end of the film, the audience has heard Harry talk about his victims, which Anna has not; the audience knows that Harry betrayed Anna to the Russians, which Anna does not."[59] In *The Third Man*, Anna stays in the dark, a pawn in geopolitics, vanquished by subtle systems of power, like the countless "foreign" female figures in the mental ward of the General Hospital.

In this classic film, Vienna's underground system of canals becomes an archetypal setting for conspiracies, for chasing adversaries "from the other side." This underground, shot in oblique angles, offers more than a simple backdrop to the plotline of intrigue, betrayal, and manufactured identities. It becomes an allegory for the subconscious, the obscured layers of neuroses, paranoias, and obsessive compulsions occasionally surfacing from this sewer. Similarly, while delving into an experimental reservoir and specializing in the dark, untrodden paths of the mind, the staff at the mental clinic of the General Hospital projected standard expectations onto their patients.

By embedding clinical protocols into a wider context of post-1945 migration, refugeedom, and Nazism in Vienna, this chapter has sought to unpack some of the policies that underpinned Austrian reconstruction and postwar state building. The focus of these policies toward the building of a homogeneous nation meant that female refugees or displaced persons who did not fit into the profile of a perceived typical Austrian citizen or belonged to a "different race" were either conveniently placed into the mental asylum—the only asylum they were granted—to conceal them or, alternatively, transferred beyond borders by means of psychiatric diagnoses. In both cases, clinical charts became a meta-text for postwar politics that were intent on constructing a new beginning and a collective identity as a Second Republic. This contrived republic was imagined as a guilt-free country, which, after seven years

---

58. Graham Greene, preface to *"The Third Man" and "The Fallen Idol,"* ed. Graham Greene (London: Heinemann, 1950), 6.

59. Lynette Carpenter, "'I Never Knew the Old Vienna': Cold War Politics and 'The Third Man,'" *Film Criticism* 3, no. 1 (1978): 28.

within the Third Reich, consisted of a purified and monolithic society cleansed of un-Austrian elements.

The treatment of female patients at the General Hospital's mental clinic can be linked to wider sociopolitical and socioeconomic decisions, methods, and motivations. Medical decisions were made during the Austrian *Wiederaufbau* (reconstruction) in the midst of scarce resources, ideological baggage, and shattered buildings and minds. While admittance to psychiatric institutions such as the General Hospital and Am Steinhof was equivalent to a life sentence for those "unfit" to be citizens, like Marie and Rosa, it represented a safe haven for female Nazis like Elsa and Berta to avoid denazification by the Allied authorities. All female patients—whether residing temporarily at the General Hospital like Elsa and Berta in order to "design" a flexible, clean citizenship, or permanently like Marie and Rosa, owing to denied citizenship—turned into the *third*, enigmatic woman, for whom the clinic insides and infrastructures became a psychiatric underground of the mind.

Similar to Germany, Austria's post-1945 quest for statehood and stability emphasized democratization and social cohesion, despite lingering racialization.[60] Alongside race, class, and gender, the desired cohesive canvas of postwar Austrian society further necessitated drawing lines of "normality" to foster a new republic that was partly demarcated by the Iron Curtain. Psychiatric care in that respect became imperative to separate "surplus" citizens—particularly when female and from areas of newly defined Soviet satellite states—whose biographies of trauma alluded to fragmentation rather than social cohesion. As other contributions to this volume show, politics of difference and migrancy after World War II were steeped in racial discrimination and a fixation on statelessness. Dissecting these nationalizing politics of identity through a psychiatric lens sheds light on how undesired individuals were labeled as para-citizens, unable to partake fully in everyday life as a result of being rendered "beyond the norm" in the short twentieth century. With ever more pressing waves of worldwide migration in the twenty-first century, of refugees consigned permanently to camps without prospect of entering society, para-citizenship risks becoming the norm rather than the exception.

---

60. Compare Rita Chin, Heide Fehrenbach, Geoff Eley, and Atina Grossmann, *After the Nazi Racial State: Difference and Democracy in Germany and Europe* (Ann Arbor: University of Michigan Press, 2009), esp. 17–20.

DAGMAR WERNITZNIG

Dagmar Wernitznig is associate professor of history at the University of Ljubljana. She received her PhD in history from the University of Oxford. She is author of *Going Native or Going Naive? White Shamanism and the Neo-noble Savage* and *Europe's Indians, Indians in Europe: European Perceptions and Appropriations of Native American Cultures from Pocahontas to the Present*.

CHAPTER 4

Race and Racism in the Citizenship Law and Naturalization Practice of Early West Germany

Nicholas Courtman

The Nazi Party program of February 1920 proclaimed, "None but members of the German people may be citizens of the state. None but those of German blood, whatever their religion, may be members of the German people. No Jew can therefore be a member of the German people."[1] With this demand, the National Socialist German Workers' Party (NSDAP) not only posited the existence of a German people in the sense of a *Volk* that was bound by a shared set of racial ties. They also, in their denial of the possibility of Jews being members of the German people, insisted that those outside the racially constituted and delineated *Volk* must also remain outside the *Staatsvolk*, the body of German citizens. The implication of this demand was that citizenship law, that bundle of regulations governing legal membership within the political community of the state, had to be subordinated to the protection and production of the (imagined) racial purity of the *Volk*.

During their twelve years in power (1933–1945), the National Socialists translated this idea into legislation and state policy to catastrophic

---

1. "The Program of the National Socialist German Workers' Party: The Twenty-Five Points," in *The Third Reich Sourcebook*, ed. Anson Rabinbach, Sander L. Gilman, and Lilian M. Friedberg (Berkeley: University of California Press, 2013), 52–55. Translation modified by the author.

effect. The most extreme expression of the will to bring *Volk* and *Staatsvolk* into unity was the expulsion of all German Jews from the body of the citizenry,[2] a process that was intimately connected with the expropriation and murder of German Jewry in the Holocaust.[3] Many scholars have argued that the prohibitions on racist discrimination included in the international declarations on human rights of the immediate postwar period were a direct response to the murderous racism of the Nazi regime.[4] As such, the Nazis' racist practices provided the negative foil against which the postwar world, including Europe, tried to define its own antiracist values—as incomplete, partial, and hypocritical as these frequently were.

Similar claims are frequently made about the Grundgesetz, or Basic Law, the founding constitution of the Federal Republic of Germany (FRG, or West Germany) that came into force in May 1949, which is often presented as a repudiation of National Socialism.[5] In a ruling from 2009, for example, the German Federal Constitutional Court stated that the Basic Law was an attempt to learn from the "historical experience" of National Socialism and "to prevent the repetition of such injustice."[6] The Basic Law granted to the FRG's citizens and residents numerous freedoms and protections that had been systematically undone in the twelve years in which the National Socialists tried to create their ideal "racial state."[7] The Basic Law's clearest riposte to such a racial state can be found in Article 3, Paragraph 3, which declared that no one should be discriminated against on the basis of several protected

---

2. David Scott FitzGerald, "The History of Racialized Citizenship," in *The Oxford Handbook of Citizenship*, ed. Ayelet Schachar, Rainer Bauböck, Irene Bloemraad, and Maarten Vink (Oxford: Oxford University Press, 2017), 142.

3. H. G. Adler, *Der verwaltete Mensch: Studien zur Deportation der Juden aus Deutschland* (Tübingen: Mohr, 1974), 491–545; Cornelia Essner, *Die "Nürnberger Gesetze" oder die Verwaltung des Rassenwahns 1933–1945* (Paderborn: Ferdinand Schöningh, 2002), 296–326.

4. Doris Liebscher, *Rasse im Recht—Recht gegen Rassismus: Genealogie einer ambivalenten Kategorie* (Berlin: Suhrkamp, 2021), 272–75; Dieter Gosewinkel, *Struggles for Belonging: Citizenship in Europe, 1900–2020* (Oxford: Oxford University Press, 2021), 251ff.; Cengiz Barskanmaz, "Rasse. Eine interdisziplinäre Einordnung des verfassungsrechtlichen Begriffs," in *Grundgesetz und Rassismus*, ed. Judith Froese and Daniel Thym (Tübingen: Mohr Siebeck, 2022), 99–100.

5. Christoph Möllers, *Das Grundgesetz: Geschichte und Inhalt* (Munich: C. H. Beck, 2009), 17.

6. *Entscheidungen des Bundesverfassungsgerichts* (BVerfGE) 124, 300 (328). Beschluss des Bundesverfassungsgerichts vom 4. November 2009, Akz. 1 BvR 2150/08.

7. See Michael Burleigh and Wolfgang Wippermann, *The Racial State: Germany 1933–1945* (Cambridge: Cambridge University Press, 1993); see also Devin O. Pendas, Mark Roseman, and Richard F. Wetzell, eds., *Beyond the Racial State: Rethinking Nazi Germany* (Cambridge: Cambridge University Press, 2017).

characteristics, including race (*Rasse*) and descent (*Abstammung*). But what effect did this constitutional prohibition of racial discrimination have on the West German government's administration of citizenship? How did the West German government deal with the aftereffects of the Nazi government's thorough racialization of citizenship law, or indeed with the elements of racial discrimination that had been central to the administration of citizenship in Germany even before 1933?

This chapter explores these questions by examining material relating to the administration of West German citizenship law from the first decade of the state's existence. The material, which includes naturalization files, ministerial correspondence, and the records of two specialist commissions, comes largely from the German federal archives and from the state archive of North Rhine–Westphalia (NRW).[8] This chapter illustrates that race continued to play an important role in the administration of citizenship throughout the early years of the Federal Republic and explores how administrative authorities, legal professionals, and governmental officials tried to conceal, justify, and reflect on how they took account of race in their administration of legal belonging within the state.

When processing applications for naturalization, West German states authorities drew numerous factors into consideration, such as applicants' financial status, their past sexual or marital behavior, their criminal history, their actions during the Second World War, their stance regarding communism, and their German-language skills. As we will see, they also took account of the applicants' ethnic background and, in some instances, of what the authorities understood to be their racial difference. Race was unique among these factors, insofar as both the Universal Declaration of Human Rights and, more importantly, the German Basic Law prohibited the use of race as grounds for differentiation or discrimination in state action. This created a conundrum for West German state officials and legal scholars, who had to find ways either to conceal the role played by race in their decision-making practices, or to try to justify how they took race into

---

8. The holdings of the German federal archives on citizenship law leave much to be desired, with whole sets of key files having been lost or destroyed. While it would have been desirable to use material from the archives of other German federal states, this was not possible at the time of writing this chapter. Some states, such as Berlin, have given little to no material relating to citizenship law to their archives. The archives of other states, such as Baden-Württemberg, do not grant access to naturalization files for data protection reasons. Others still, such as Bavaria, were still processing usage requests while this chapter was being written.

account, despite the clear wording of both international and domestic constitutional law.

West Germany's grappling with race vis-à-vis citizenship law and naturalization policy did not occur in a vacuum. Throughout the 1950s many European countries confronted the relevance of race for questions of citizenship law. The years immediately following the Second World War saw the implementation of numerous citizenship law policies across Europe that aimed at producing ethnically homogeneous nation states.[9] By the early 1950s, some states began to question the desirability or legitimacy of such policies, not least in connection with the opposition to racism contained in postwar declarations of universal human rights. In 1953, the French government, for example, altered naturalization guidelines that privileged Western Europeans on the grounds that such preferential treatment constituted "unacceptable racism."[10] This, it would seem, was an example of a liberal democracy making good on the antiracist commitments of the postwar moment. But to what extent did such a move constitute the norm in postwar Europe, let alone in West Germany?

The historiography on race in West Germany has argued that the conceptualization of race and the rules of discourse regarding it underwent a transformation in the early Federal Republic, following both international developments and a set of domestic particularities. This literature has argued that West Germany's political and academic elites, under the influence of the Allies and the international community, came to see the concept of race, especially as expressed in the German term *Rasse*, as tainted through association with the National Socialist regime. For these elites, the historiography argues, the "belief in biologically based, essential differences between groups of people" after 1945 became inextricably tied to the "tarnished notion of *Rasse*," making *Rasse* a concept that "itself had to be officially repudiated in order to transform West Germany into a democratic nation."[11] A central part of this process of repudiation involved rejecting conceptions of difference that emphasized biology in favor of a focus on culture and questions of cultural difference.[12]

---

9. Gosewinkel, *Struggles for Belonging*, 249ff.

10. FitzGerald, "The History of Racialized Citizenship," 145; Gosewinkel, *Struggles for Belonging*, 236.

11. Rita Chin, "Thinking Difference in Postwar Germany: Some Epistemological Obstacles around 'Race,'" in *Migration, Memory and Diversity: Germany from 1945 to the Present*, ed. Cornelia Wilhelm (Oxford: Berghahn Books, 2017), 209.

12. Rita Chin and Heide Fehrenbach, "Introduction: What's Race Got to Do with It? Postwar German History in Context," in *After the Nazi Racial State: Difference and Democracy*

Germany was not the only country in which this turn away from biologically grounded understandings of race in favor of cultural explanations of supposedly essential and immutable differences between groups of people took place in the postwar period. Indeed, both Frantz Fanon and Theodor Adorno remarked on this development in their writings from the mid-1950s as one that affected various parts of the Western world.[13] Scholars writing about the period in the last two decades, however, have noted a set of particularities in the German case, which are connected to the strong association between the term *Rasse* and National Socialist racial science. This association led not only to the banishing of the term from political and social discourse but also to what Rita Chin has described as a particular "symbolic investment" in the term, which meant that the very use of it came to be seen as "tantamount to endorsing a worldview that categorizes and ranks groups of people based on biological differences."[14]

Current historiography has identified only one exception to the banishing of the language of *Rasse* from academia and state policy in West Germany: the treatment of the children born in the postwar years to white German women and Black fathers, who were usually soldiers of the occupying Allied forces. In the 1950s, West German state authorities singled these children out as objects for state and professional observation on the basis of their race—and used the German term *Rasse* when doing so. That the state categorized these children through racial categories but did not do the same with the children of individuals who had been racialized under National Socialism, such as Eastern Europeans or Jews, has been read as evidence of a shift away from earlier German traditions of racialization. Heide Fehrenbach reads this

---

in *Germany and Europe*, ed. Rita Chin, Heide Fehrenbach, Geoff Eley, and Atina Grossmann (Ann Arbor: University of Michigan Press, 2009), 13. Chin and Fehrenbach also underline that biological and cultural understandings of the nature of racial difference tend to coexist alongside one another (14). For more on the impossibility of neatly disentangling biological and cultural racism see Manuela Bojadzijev, *Die windige Internationale: Rassismus und Kämpfe der Migration* (Münster: Westfälisches Dampfboot, 2008), 21-25.

13. See, for example, Frantz Fanon's analysis of this development in relation to the French Empire: Frantz Fanon, "Racisme et Culture," *Présence Africaine* 8, no. 10 (1956): 122-31. Theodor Adorno also took note of this tendency in "Schuld und Abwehr," his 1955 study on the authoritarian personality in West Germany, in which he writes that "fascist nationalism frequently is transformed into a pan-European chauvinism. . . . The noble word 'culture' takes the place of the taboo term 'race,' but remains merely a screen for the brutal claim to domination." Theodor Adorno, *Soziologische Schriften II.2* (Frankfurt am Main: Suhrkamp, 1975), 276-77.

14. Chin, "Thinking Difference," 216.

discrepancy in the state's stance toward children of mixed German and Eastern European parentage as evidence that by the mid-1950s the "perceived threat" of Eastern Europeans to West German "racial integrity was vastly diminished."[15] The current historiography holds that those earlier models of racialization were replaced by an understanding of racial difference modeled on an American understanding of race as centered on a Black/white binary.[16]

This chapter challenges this historiographical narrative by showing that state officials and legal experts continued to use the language of *Rasse* when proposing, formulating, and defending citizenship policy well into the late 1950s. Furthermore, its use was not restricted to discussions of Black people but frequently also included individuals of Eastern European or of non-Black "non-European" descent. The material examined here suggests that while the explicit use of the language of *Rasse* was confined to particular contexts, it went hand in hand with a purposeful deployment of euphemism that allowed authorities to discriminate on the basis of race without using the term *Rasse* itself.[17] This chapter does not address postwar racist discrimination in citizenship law against Jews and Sinti and Roma, the two groups mostly prominently targeted for discrimination and exclusion under National Socialism on the basis of race. The specific forms of discrimination against these groups in postwar citizenship law are complex and cannot be adequately addressed alongside the material analyzed in this chapter.[18] This caveat aside, the files examined here demonstrate that highly influential academic, judicial, and governmental elites continued to

---

15. Heide Fehrenbach, *Race after Hitler: Black Occupation Children in Postwar Germany and America* (Princeton, NJ: Princeton University Press, 2005), 78.

16. See Fehrenbach, *Race after Hitler*, 80, 96; Chin, "Thinking Difference," 209-10.

17. Karen Schönwälder has identified a similar systematic deployment of euphemism to obscure racist discrimination in the West German government's attempts to prevent labor migration from "Afro-Asiatic" countries in the early 1960s. See Karen Schönwälder, *Einwanderung und Ethnische Pluralität: Politische Entscheidungen und öffentliche Debatten in Großbritannien und der Bundesrepublik von den 1950er bis zu den 1970er Jahren* (Essen: Klartext, 2001), 260.

18. German Sinti and Roma faced particular forms of discrimination in citizenship law after 1949, often having their citizenship revoked if they could not provide naturalization certificates for their (often distant) ancestors. There has been some research on this to date, such as Wolfgang Wippermann, "Christine Lehmann and Mazurka Rose: Two 'Gypsies' in the Grip of German Bureaucracy, 1933-1960," in *Confronting the Nazi Past: New Debates on Modern German History*, ed. Michael Burleigh (London: Collins & Brown, 1996), 112-24. I will be publishing further work on antisemitism in German citizenship law. For some first results on this topic see Nicholas Courtman, "Besser spät als nie. Die Mühlen der staatsangehörigkeitsrechtlichen Wiedergutmachung in der BRD seit 1949," *Jalta. Positionen zur jüdischen Gegenwart* 7 (2020): 70-77.

view West Germany as, in a certain sense, a racial state, and that their views had serious consequences for citizenship law and naturalization policy.

Citizenship in the (Pre-)Nazi Racial State

When the Nazis called for a racial reordering of citizenship law in the 1920 foundational program quoted at the beginning of this chapter, the NSDAP was still an insignificant party within the fractured political landscape of the early Weimar Republic. In calling for the expulsion of racial others who possessed German citizenship from the body of the citizenry, their demand went far beyond the racism that already characterized the administration of citizenship in the German Reich. Racism and exclusionary ethno-nationalism had decisively shaped legislative decisions in German citizenship law since at least the late nineteenth century.[19] During the drafting of the Reich and State Citizenship Law of 1913, for example, racist anxieties regarding Eastern Europeans—and especially Eastern European Jews—had been integral in motivating the decision against introducing elements of *jus soli* to German citizenship law, meaning that birth on German territory did not lead to acquisition of German citizenship.[20]

Beyond legislative decisions, racism also determined naturalization practice in pre-Nazi Germany. The naturalization authorities of the Weimar Republic, for example, regularly discriminated against Black people,[21] as well as Eastern Europeans and Eastern European Jews, who were frequently grouped together under the heading of "Eastern European foreigners of foreign descent" (*fremdstämmige Ostausländer*). "Foreigners of foreign descent" were subjected to particularly stringent naturalization requirements. A frequently imposed measure was an extension of the minimum residency period before state authorities would consider applications for naturalization. Prussia, for example,

---

19. See, for example, Olivier Trevisiol, *Die Einbürgerungspraxis im Deutschen Reich 1871-1945* (Göttingen: Vandenhoeck & Ruprecht, 2006), 143-78; Fatima El-Tayeb, "'Blood Is a Very Special Juice': Racialized Bodies and Citizenship in Twentieth-Century Germany," *International Review of Social History* 44 (1999): 149-69; Eli Nathans, *The Politics of Citizenship in Germany: Ethnicity, Utility and Nationalism* (Oxford: Berg, 2002) 146-51, 201-8.

20. Dieter Gosewinkel, *Einbürgern und Ausschließen: Die Nationalisierung der Staatsangehörigkeit vom Deutschen Bund bis zur Bundesrepublik Deutschland* (Göttingen: Vandenhoeck & Ruprecht, 2002), 291-92, 324.

21. See Robbie Aitken and Eve Rosenhaft, *Black Germany: The Making and Unmaking of a Diaspora Community, 1884-1960* (Cambridge: Cambridge University Press, 2013), 72-75.

determined in 1925 that such individuals would need to demonstrate twenty years of residency in Germany before being eligible for naturalization, compared to the ten-year period demanded of foreigners who were not classified as being of foreign descent.[22]

It is important to stress, however, that before the Nazi seizure of power, the acquisition of German citizenship was never *formally* tied to any racial or ethnic criteria. It remained possible for any individual, irrespective of ethnic origin, race, or religious belief, to become a German citizen. Individuals from groups that faced discrimination on the grounds of their claimed or perceived ethnic or racial identities, such as Jews, Eastern Europeans, and people of African descent, could be and were naturalized throughout this period, albeit often not in large numbers. It was only with the Nazis' rise to power in 1933 that racial criteria for the acquisition of German citizenship were legally formalized. This began in 1933 with the introduction of proof of Aryan descent as a requirement for naturalization.[23] The following years saw numerous measures aimed not only at preventing "racially undesirable" individuals from becoming German citizens but also at stripping such "racially undesirable" German citizens of key rights and even of their legal membership in the German state.[24] The Reich Citizenship Law of 1935 established a two-tier system of citizenship in which Jews, Sinti and Roma, and others who were of "foreign blood" were denied full legal rights while retaining their status as German nationals.[25] Later, the Nazis would strip all German Jews of even this remaining legal status.[26]

---

22. Gosewinkel, *Einbürgern und Ausschließen*, 356.
23. Erlass des Preußischen Ministers des Innern vom 9.5.1934, Bundesarchiv Lichterfelde-West, R 1501/213748.
24. For the National Socialists, all individuals who were not of German or related blood were classified as being "racially undesirable." The category of "racially undesirable" was also applied to individuals who were deemed to be carriers of hereditary illnesses according to Nazi eugenics policy, which was often referred to as "racial hygiene." See Burleigh and Wippermann, *Racial State*, chap. 6.
25. The official commentary on the Reich Citizenship Law determined that all European peoples were of "related blood" (*artverwandtes Blut*), with the exceptions of Jews and Sinti and Roma. All non-European peoples did not fulfill this requirement. See Wilhelm Stuckart and Hans Globke, *Kommentare zur deutschen Rassengesetzgebung Band 1* (Berlin: C. H. Beck, 1936), 55–56. See also Gosewinkel, *Einbürgern und Ausschließen*, 383–92.
26. The Eleventh Decree on the Reich Citizenship Law of November 1941 removed German nationality from all Germans who were classified as "Full Jews" according to the Nuremberg racial laws who were living outside the German Reich. The Nazis had already begun stripping many of its political and racial opponents of German nationality on an individual basis in 1933. See Gosewinkel, *Einbürgern und Ausschließen*, 370–80.

Beyond their immediate function within the expropriation of German Jewry,[27] these measures had the symbolic purpose of expelling from the *Staatsvolk* those who did not meet the Nazis' requirements for membership in (what they imagined as the) racially constituted, pre-legally existing *Volk*. But the Nazi use of citizenship law to establish identity between *Volk* and *Staatsvolk* was not limited to acts of exclusion. Between 1938 and 1945, the Nazis bestowed German citizenship on over four million members of the ethnic German minorities in the territories it occupied and annexed.[28] Jews and Sinti and Roma who belonged to these German minorities were excluded on account of their "foreign blood."[29]

After the German defeat, the successor states to the Third Reich thus inherited numerous problems in the field of citizenship law. Almost all of the Nazi mass naturalizations had contravened international law, leaving it unclear whether they had been legally effective. Yet many of these individuals had left or been forced out of their homelands from late 1944 onward. The Allied Powers had approved the expulsion of Germans from Eastern Europe at Potsdam in the summer of 1945. Moreover, they had also determined that Germany should carry responsibility for the displaced Germans.[30] When the members of the West German Parliamentary Council met in 1948 to draft the Basic Law, they had to find a way of meeting this responsibility for the ethnic Germans on West Germany's territory. Many politicians in West Germany refused to recognize the expulsion of ethnic Germans as a finished matter, wanting to keep open the possibility of the displaced Germans returning to their former homelands.[31] In light of this uncertainty, the Parliamentary Council tried to devise a mechanism through which the FRG could provide the displaced ethnic Germans with state

---

27. See fn. 3.
28. An overview of the legal foundations of these mass naturalizations can be found in Franz Maßfeller, *Deutsches Staatsangehörigkeitsrecht von 1870 bis zur Gegenwart* (Frankfurt am Main: Metzner, 1955), 199–302.
29. Gosewinkel, *Struggles for Belonging*, 172–73. It is unclear whether non-Jewish and non-Sinti or Roma individuals who were classified as being totally or partially of "non-European" heritage were excluded from these mass naturalizations. While their exclusion would have been in keeping with Nazi legal definitions of the racial preconditions for recognition as an ethnic German, no explicit mention was made of such individuals in the central legal documents underpinning the mass naturalizations in occupied and annexed Europe.
30. See Pertti Ahonen, *After the Expulsion: West Germany and Eastern Europe 1945–1990* (Oxford: Oxford University Press, 2003), 15–21.
31. Ahonen, 39.

protection, without providing a conclusive answer to the still-contested question of their citizenship.

The Council did this in Paragraph 1 of Article 116 of the Basic Law, which granted displaced ethnic Germans who "found refuge" on German territory the legal status of "Germans according to the Basic Law" (*Deutsche im Sinne des Grundgesetzes*), until the legislature could produce a conclusive answer to the question of their citizenship. This status would in the interim period grant them the same rights as German citizens.[32] In 1955, the West German government passed the Law for the Regulation of Citizenship Issues, which declared almost all of the Nazi mass naturalizations to have been legally effective.[33] It also established numerous provisions for the naturalization of ethnic Germans. These were distinct from the naturalization procedures of the Citizenship Law of 1913 and will not be considered further in this chapter.[34]

Naturalization and "Foreigners of Foreign Descent"

Even after the promulgation of this special legislation, it was still the 1913 Citizenship Law that governed the acquisition, loss, and transmission of German citizenship, including the naturalization of foreign citizens and stateless individuals who were not ethnic Germans. Already in 1945, the occupation government had restored the 1913 Citizenship Law to its pre-Nazi form, which had not possessed any formal racial requirements. This did not, however, mean that the law could not accommodate racist discrimination in its concrete application. Indeed, as mentioned above, pre-Nazi naturalization authorities had regularly discriminated on the basis of race or descent in their interpretation and application of the law, especially with regard to naturalization.

Some of these discriminatory practices had been prescribed in naturalization guidelines drafted by the Reich Ministry of the Interior in 1921. These guidelines preached "caution" when dealing with applicants from "states whose citizens are largely of a culture which is of lesser value than, or entirely foreign to, German culture," and advised

---

32. See Jannis Panagiotidis, *The Unchosen Ones: Diaspora, Nation, and Migration in Israel and Germany* (Bloomington: Indiana University Press, 2019), 36-37.

33. Gesetz zur Regelung von Fragen der Staatsangehörigkeit vom 22.2.1955, *Bundesgesetzblatt*, 65, www.bgbl.de/xaver/bgbl/start.xav?startbk=Bundesanzeiger_BGBl&jumpTo=bgbl15 5s0065.pdf.

34. For an overview of the scope and functioning of this coethnic migration regime, which I will not address further in this chapter, see Panagiotidis, *Unchosen Ones*.

considering naturalizing individuals "of foreign descent" only after long periods of residency in Germany.[35] The guidelines did not, however, spell out which foreigners should be considered to be "of foreign descent," or which cultures were "entirely foreign" to or of "lesser value" than German culture. In practice, Jews and Eastern Europeans were the prime targets for restrictive treatment on these grounds. Non-Jewish Western Europeans, on the other hand, were frequently treated as being both culturally and ancestrally close enough to Germans to be spared such "caution." This differential treatment underlines that in practice, the label of "foreign descent" did not apply to everyone without German ancestry but was rather applied flexibly in line with an unarticulated hierarchy of foreignness.

What became of this pre-Nazi tradition in the Federal Republic of Germany? In the early 1950s, the Federal Ministry of the Interior (Bundesministerium des Innern, or BMI) began working on a new draft of the naturalization guidelines to secure uniformity in naturalization practice between the German federal states, which carried the primary responsibility for executing citizenship law. When it shared its first draft of the new naturalization guidelines with the federal states in November 1950, the ministry took pains in the guidelines' preamble to present its recommendations for a restrictive naturalization policy as a continuation of state policy following the First World War.[36] This explicit linkage with the administrative practice of the early Weimar Republic was likely motivated by the hope that anchoring it outside the Nazi period would lend it greater legitimacy. But how did the ministry deal with those aspects of the administration of naturalization in the Weimar Republic that were hard to reconcile with the new constitution of the West German state, such as the racism and discrimination on the basis of ethnicity and descent that had been ingrained into the naturalization process before 1933? This is a question that we sadly cannot answer with great certainty, given that all of the BMI's own files relating to the drafting and implementation of its naturalization guidelines have been lost or destroyed and are missing from the German federal archives.

---

35. Richtlinien für die Behandlung von Einbürgerungsanträgen vom 20.8.1921, Landesarchiv NRW Abteilung Rheinland (LAV NRW R) BR 2047, Nr. 13.

36. Entwurf der Richtlinien für die Behandlung von Einbürgerungsanträgen des BMI vom 8.11.1950, Berliner Senatsverwaltung für Inneres und Sport, Grundsatzakte Einbürgerungsrichtlinien vol. 1.

Although we cannot reconstruct the BMI's decision-making processes directly, we can use the files of other archives to see what changes were made between the various drafts of the guidelines. The guidelines from November 1950, for example, suggest that the BMI was initially very comfortable with reproducing the type of cultural racism that had characterized the naturalization guidelines in the 1920s. At the beginning of the section on the cultural requirements for naturalization, the BMI writes that "in connection with German naturalization policy from before 1933, all responsible authorities must today strive to keep foreigners who come from an entirely foreign culture [*gänzlich fremden Kulturkreis*] away from German citizenship." Any exceptions to this rule, the guidelines stress, should be dependent on the careful examination of whether the applicants demonstrate the "will and ability to adapt to the German cultural community."[37]

This is a slightly altered reformulation of the section on cultural requirements from the naturalization guidelines of 1921, which underlined that individuals belonging to "a culture that is of lesser value than, or entirely foreign to, German culture" should be treated with "greatest reticence."[38] The guidelines of 1921 and 1950 are both clear examples of cultural racism—individuals are presented on the basis of their national origin as products or adherents of a culture that is presented as being inferior or entirely foreign to German culture, and are on those grounds prima facie identified as ill-suited to becoming German citizens.

While these remarks were still included in the naturalization guidelines that the BMI shared with other federal ministries in May 1952,[39] they had been removed from the new draft of the guidelines the BMI shared with the federal states in December of the same year.[40] This suggests that one of the other ministries of the federal government raised objections to this section of the cultural requirements, leading to its removal. Given the BMI's clear readiness in the early 1950s to connect its own suggestions with restrictive aspects of Weimar naturalization policy, it is somewhat surprising to find that there is no mention of

---

37. Entwurf der Richtlinien vom 8.11.1950, 9.
38. Richtlinien für die Behandlung von Einbürgerungsanträgen vom 20.8.1921, LAV NRW R, BR 2047, Nr. 13.
39. BMI an das Auswärtige Amt und andere Bundesministerien, 3.5.1952, Richtlinien für die Behandlung von Einbürgerungsanträgen, Politisches Archiv des Auswärtigen Amtes (PAAA) B 82/502-V3/499.
40. BMI an die Innenminister/-senatoren der Länder, 8.12.1952, Berliner Senatsverwaltung für Inneres und Sport, Grundsatzakte Einbürgerungsrichtlinien vol. 1.

"foreigners of foreign descent" in any of the drafts of the naturalization guidelines. Should we read this as evidence that the BMI rejected the idea that such individuals deserved differential, particularly harsh treatment? Documents from the NRW state archive suggest otherwise.

In April 1950, the director of Cologne's governmental district wrote to the state's Interior Ministry to report that there had been an increase in the number of former forced laborers applying for German citizenship. Unlike the Greek communist refugees in Czechoslovakia examined in Nikola Tohma's chapter in this volume, who often showed little interest in naturalizing in their new homeland, many of these individuals were already seeking German citizenship by the early 1950s. The director of Cologne's governmental district viewed this development with great concern. He asked NRW's Interior Ministry to propose to the BMI that longer mandatory residency periods for "Eastern European foreigners of foreign descent" be reintroduced to the naturalization guidelines.[41]

The BMI rejected this suggestion, arguing that it seemed inappropriate to single out Eastern Europeans for punitive treatment, given that most of those now living on German territory had been displaced by Nazi Germany and exploited as forced laborers during the Second World War. Despite this, the BMI still closed its letter to NRW's Interior Ministry by encouraging it to "in general treat the naturalization applications of foreigners of foreign descent with caution."[42]

The Federal Ministry seems then to have remained convinced that "foreigners of foreign descent" should be subject to more stringent examination, while refraining from mandating this in its naturalization guidelines. Indeed, other files demonstrate that the ministry continued to view ethnicity as a relevant criterion for naturalization. In 1954, for example, it informed the federal states that it was trying to formalize different residency requirements "in line with the applicants' level of connection with Germany," and that "related or foreign ethnicity [*Volkstum*]" would be among the criteria used to judge that connection.[43] This project was never realized, but as will be demonstrated below, the BMI did continue to approve of variable demands of residency requirements

---

41. Regierungspräsident Köln an den Innenminister NRW, 21.4.1950; Innenminister NRW an den Bundesminister des Innern, 2.5.1950, LAV NRW R, BR 2047, Nr. 13.

42. BMI an den Innenminister NRW, 24.6.1950, ibid.

43. Niederschrift über die Besprechung der Einbürgerungsrichtlinien mit Baden-Württemberg und NRW im BMI am 19.5.1954, Berliner Senatsverwaltung für Inneres und Sport, Grundsatzakte Einbürgerungsrichtlinien vol. 1.

in line with applicants' ethnic background. This points toward a pattern. While the BMI was content with encouraging discrimination on the basis of descent or ethnicity in correspondence pertaining to individual cases, it was wary of mandating such discrimination in formalized documents, such as the naturalization guidelines. This reticence may well have been because the guidelines were shared with all of the country's naturalization authorities and were thereby at greater risk of being leaked beyond state administration.

Racial Discrimination against Eastern Europeans

The BMI's decision against prescribing such practice in its guidelines did not prevent the federal states from implementing such policies themselves. In West Germany, individuals applied for naturalization with their local authority, with their application then being processed by the government of their federal states. All discretionary naturalizations that the federal states wanted to perform needed the final approval of the BMI, which could thereby prevent naturalizations that it judged to be inappropriate.[44] The BMI, however, had no formal power to intervene when federal states decided to reject an application. This meant that federal states could apply requirements in their processing of applications that went beyond those formally prescribed by the BMI. This distribution of decision-making powers along the various levels of local, regional, state, and federal governmental authorities demonstrates that the "vertical" dimension in the constitution of citizenship referenced in the introduction to this volume applies not only to agents positioned at various levels of a social hierarchy but also to various moments within the institutions of government itself.

An examination of naturalization files from NRW indicates that the state continued to subject "foreigners of foreign descent" to harsher requirements. In 1951, the state's Interior Ministry rejected a naturalization application that the government president of Münster had recommended for approval. The ministry used the occasion to formulate instructions for the state's government districts. The applicant in question, Iwan R., had been brought to Germany in 1940 as a prisoner of war, before being exploited as a forced laborer.[45] He applied for

---

44. The legal foundation for this procedure was a decree from 1934 that centralized decision-making powers for naturalization in the Reich Interior Ministry.
45. I am using pseudonyms for all applicants named in this chapter.

naturalization in 1951, as he intended to marry a German woman, who would have automatically lost her German citizenship had she married him before he was naturalized.[46] Iwan had lived in Germany for eleven years, surpassing the general ten-year residency requirement. NRW's Interior Ministry nonetheless rejected his application, reasoning that applicants "from a cultural circle essentially foreign to Germanness" needed to be subject to greater scrutiny before naturalization should be considered.[47]

In 1953, NRW's Interior Ministry formalized this stance in its own naturalization guidelines, which were adapted from those of the BMI. In the section on residency requirements, NRW's Interior Ministry added a section specifying that "special attention" was needed when dealing with applications from "Eastern European foreigners of foreign descent, who often came to Germany as foreign workers during the last war and who lived in Displaced Person camps after the German defeat and took part in attacks on the German population."[48] This statement shows how perceived ethnic difference was fused with narratives about the recent past. Eastern Europeans were simultaneously cast as ethnic others and as aggressors against the German people. The guidelines demanded that such applicants provide stringent documentation of all their places of residence in Germany and underlined that any time spent living in displaced person (DP) camps—like those in which many of the individuals profiled in Laura Hilton's chapter in this volume lived for extended periods—could not be recognized as residency for the purposes of naturalization.

Time spent in DP camps was not the only time that NRW's Interior Ministry refused to recognize as residency. It also occasionally refused to recognize periods that individuals had spent as forced laborers in Germany before the German defeat in 1945. This decision was in one instance justified with the argument that forced laborers had been kept separate from the German population and had thereby been unable to integrate into German life.[49] In another instance, the ministry argued

---

46. Until April 1953, German women automatically lost their German citizenship when marrying a non-German citizen. The only exception to this rule was for women who were marrying stateless men between May 1949 and April 1953, who were asked whether they wished to remain German citizens when they married their husbands.

47. Innenminister NRW an den Regierungspräsidenten in Münster et al., 13.3.1951, LAV NRW R BR 2047, Nr. 13.

48. Richtlinien für die Behandlung von Einbürgerungsanträgen, Regierungspräsident Köln an die Stadt- und Landkreisverwaltungen des Regierungsbezirks, 30.10.1953, ibid.

49. Innenminister NRW an den Regierungspräsidenten Düsseldorf, 2.10.1953, ibid.

that the fact that forced laborers had been held in Germany against their will meant that the period before May 1945 could not count for residency purposes, as it was only following Germany's defeat that the applicants could demonstrate whether "they wanted to belong to the German people as a matter of their _free_ choosing."[50] Regardless of the justification deployed, these policies contravened German federal legislation regarding the treatment of former DPs, which stipulated that any time spent in Germany as a forcibly displaced person during the Second World War had to be recognized as residency in Germany for any relevant legal purposes.[51]

These policies meant that Eastern Europeans brought to Germany as forced laborers were often denied naturalization even after fifteen years of German residency. One example from 1959, relating to a couple, John and Lorena W., demonstrates both the serious personal consequences of such policies, and how any such policy was difficult to reconcile with its purported aim, which was to give state authorities sufficient time to judge whether the applicants were well integrated into German society. In 1942, John had been brought to Germany from Poland as a forced laborer. He remained in Germany after 1945, working as a guard for the British Forces between 1947 and 1951. It was during this time that he met Lorena, a German citizen and single mother of two children. When John and Lorena married in 1950, a misunderstanding at the registry office led to Lorena losing her German citizenship, so that she and her two children became effectively stateless like her husband.[52]

When the family applied for naturalization in 1955, John had lived in Germany for thirteen years and was working as a miner near Baesweiler. His application received strong support from his local community, his current employer, and the employer for whom he had worked as a forced laborer. But NRW's Interior Ministry refused to recognize the years that John had worked as a guard for the British Forces as residency in Germany, arguing that the British Forces had been cold toward Germans and had developed no connections with them. The ministry conveniently sidestepped the fact that John had mixed with the local German population enough during this period to meet and fall in love with Lorena, who was then still a German citizen. After

---

50. Innenminister NRW an den Regierungspräsidenten Detmold, 28.9.1953, LAV NRW R, NW 58, Nr. 386, fol. 74, emphasis in original.

51. See § 7 of the Gesetz über die Rechtsstellung der heimatlosen Ausländer im Bundesgebiet vom 25.04.1951, BGBl. I, 269.

52. See LAV NRW R, BR. 5, Nr. 25520, fol. 138f.

seeking the BMI's opinion on how to proceed, NRW's Interior Ministry decided to naturalize Lorena and her children but refused to consider John's application until 1958.[53] This decision meant that when John and Lorena had a daughter in 1958, she was born stateless. John was eventually naturalized in 1959, seventeen years after arriving in Germany. As Laura Hilton demonstrates in this volume, the experience of statelessness itself could be emotionally distressing. The emotional impact on individuals of their new homeland denying their naturalization and leaving them stateless was likely immense. The naturalization files of men like John contain little evidence that the state officials were aware of the emotional impact of such decisions.

In these examples, the demand for longer residency periods was justified not primarily with the applicants' supposed "foreign descent" but instead through their separation from the German population during their time as forced laborers or in DP camps. How can we then determine whether it was the applicants' supposed "foreign descent" that motivated this harsh treatment, rather than the reasons given by the state authorities? One way to determine this is contrasting the processing of naturalization applications from Eastern Europeans who had fought for Germany during the Second World War as members of the Waffen-SS with those from Western Europeans who had fought in similar units. Throughout the 1950s, the authorities in NRW and the BMI regularly naturalized Western Europeans who had fought in the Waffen-SS, even if they had only lived in Germany for a few months.[54]

One could argue that the preferential treatment given to these men who had fought for Germany during the Second World War stood in a long tradition of rewarding military service with citizenship. The 1913 Citizenship Law, for instance, granted a right to naturalization as a reward for military service, regardless of applicants' ethnicity or religious background. While the Nazis repealed this provision in 1935, they created a provision in 1943 that enabled the naturalization of foreigners

---

53. Innenminister NRW an den Regierungspräsidenten Aachen, 7.8.1956, LAV NRW R, BR 5, Nr. 25520, fol. 178.
54. To give but some examples, the Flemish Waffen-SS volunteer Arnold V. fled to Germany from Belgium in 1955 after being released on probation from prison, where he had been serving a sentence for collaboration with the Germans. He was naturalized after less than six months of residency in Germany. He had never lived in the country before (LAV NRW R, BR 1115 Nr. 3303). A prominent Flemish collaborator, Christian Türcksin, was naturalized less than half a year after fleeing to Germany during temporary release from prison in 1958 (LAV NRW R, NW 58, Nr. 142, fol. 43–48).

"of German stock" who were fighting for Germany.⁵⁵ The principle was thus revived in a racialized form, such that eased access to citizenship was no longer a reward for military service in itself but only for military service in combination with the "right kind" of racial or ethnic background.

When one compares the postwar treatment of Western European Waffen-SS soldiers with that of Eastern Europeans who served in the Waffen-SS, it becomes apparent that it was the Nazis' racially inflected version of the earlier principle that survived after 1949. We can see an example of this in the treatment of Milo S., a Yugoslavian citizen who had joined the Waffen-SS in 1943. After the war, he ended up in a British POW camp, from which he was released in 1947. He remained in Germany and applied for naturalization in 1952 with the support of his local government in Münster. With five years of residency at the time of his application, Milo had lived in Germany much longer than many of the Western European Waffen-SS soldiers who were naturalized in the 1950s. Yet In Milo's instance, NRW's Interior Ministry refused to even consider his application, claiming that the five years he had spent in the country were by no means sufficient for him to "have proven himself as a member of the German people." In their correspondence with the Münster government, the ministry officials underlined the necessity of longer residency requirements for applicants from Eastern Europe, given "the extent of the ethnic difference [*völkischen Verschiedenheit*] of the former residents of Eastern European states" from German people.⁵⁶

While the term "foreigners of foreign descent" stemmed from pre-Nazi administrative traditions, things are less clear-cut with a term like "völkische Verschiedenheit." While it could be read as signaling a form of ethno-cultural difference similar to that associated with the German term *Volkstum*, which does not have any explicit Nazi connotation, the use of the adjectival form *völkisch* evinces a proximity to Nazi racial theory and the type of overt biological racism that had supposedly been delegitimized after 1945. In certain other cases, we find more explicit and unequivocal expressions of biological racism. One such example can be found in the correspondence relating to the 1960 naturalization

---

55. See Sven Devantier, "Der 'Führererlass' zur Einbürgerung 'deutschstämmiger Ausländer' durch die Einwandererzentralstelle," *Zeitschrift für Geschichtswissenschaft* 60, no. 9 (2012): 715-34.

56. NRW Innenministerium an den Regierungspräsidenten Münster, 16.9.1952, LAV NRW R, NW 58, Nr. 93, fol. 43.

application of Wlodomyr S., who had been brought to Germany as a forced laborer in 1941. He remained in Germany after the war and married a German woman in the mid-1950s. When he applied for naturalization, the president of his government district noted that much spoke in his favor, but also identified several reasons speaking against his naturalization. These were his ill health, his poor German language skills, and his "pronounced, typically Slavic facial features."[57]

In the end, Wlodomyr's application was rejected on grounds of ill health. But the very reference to his "Slavic facial features"—which higher authorities did not rebuke—demonstrates the significance of the assumed racial difference of Eastern Europeans within the naturalization process of the 1950s and early 1960s. In most cases, these prejudices were expressed in the relatively innocuous language of "foreign descent." But the slips into the language of National Socialist racial theory or even phrenology indicate that racist convictions regarding biologically grounded difference were still accepted grounds for consideration in the naturalization process, at least to the point that higher authorities did not rebuke lower authorities for making their decisions on those criteria.

Traces of Racist Decision-Making in the Federal Ministry of the Interior

What role did the BMI play within this process? In several of the examples mentioned above, we saw that the BMI approved NRW's requirement of long waiting periods for Eastern Europeans who had spent time in DP camps. The available sources make it difficult for us to determine whether the Federal Ministry actively intervened to impose longer waiting periods, or reject applications outright, on grounds of race or descent. This is because all of the BMI's own discretionary naturalization files for the years 1950–1960 have been lost or destroyed. We do, however, find traces in other archives suggesting that the BMI attempted to prevent or delay naturalizations on assumed racial grounds in at least some cases. In the papers of the German consulate in New York, for example, we find material relating to the naturalization application of Else A., a German citizen who lost German citizenship upon marrying her Syrian husband in 1947. The couple had a daughter in

---

57. Regierungspräsident Arnsberg an den Innenminister NRW, 22.6.1960, LAV NRW R, NW 58, Nr. 392, fol. 44.

1949, before moving to New York City in 1956. A year later, Else applied for renaturalization as a German citizen and for the naturalization of her daughter, with the goal of moving the entire family to Berlin.

The government of Berlin, as Else's last German place of residence, was responsible for processing the application. Berlin approved her application and requested permission to naturalize from the Federal Ministry. But the BMI rejected the application, stating that it doubted that the daughter fulfilled the "cultural requirements" for naturalization, despite the fact that she spoke only German at home.[58] Soon thereafter, the New York consulate wrote to the BMI to request that it change its decision. After stating that he supported Else B.'s naturalization application "most warmly," the consulate official insisted that "despite the fact that the daughter's father is a Syrian citizen, the child is no different in her appearance from other German children, and thereby belongs entirely to the white race."[59]

In the file, nestled behind this letter, is a handwritten note from the consulate official addressed to the director of consular services. In it, the official stresses that he only mentioned the fact "that the child belongs to the white race because the Federal Ministry of the Interior obviously assumes the opposite, and therefore recommended 'caution' in relation to her naturalization."[60] Shortly after this letter, the BMI rescinded its protest and approved the naturalization. Was it the New York consulate's assurances that the daughter belonged to the white race that made the difference?

This is something we cannot establish with certainty, not least because the BMI's own file has been lost or destroyed. Yet even if the file had survived, it may not have provided total clarity on whether racial considerations had been decisive in the BMI's processing of the application. The letter from the consulate suggests that West German state officials by the late 1950s not only sensed that race was an important factor in the decision-making practices of the BMI. It also shows that they harbored the suspicion that systematic euphemism was being used to mask the significance of racial thinking in the ministry's

---

58. BMI an das Auswärtige Amt, 5.8.1957; Besondere Bemerkungen zum Einbürgerungsantrag von Else A., PAAA BAV 172 NEWYGK 17926.

59. Generalkonsulat der Bundesrepublik Deutschland an das Auswärtige Amt, 3.10.1957, ibid. "Obwohl der Vater des Kindes syrischer Staatsangehöriger ist, unterscheidet sich [das Kind] in der äußeren Erscheinung nicht von anderen deutschen Kindern, gehört also völlig der weißen Rasse an."

60. Handwritten note of Reifferscheidt to the general consul of the New York General Consulate, undated, ibid.

decision-making practices, with the evocation of "cultural requirements" serving to mask the fact that assumed racial difference was in fact at stake.

The Racial Constitution of the Federal Republic

While most of these documents evince a deployment of euphemism to mask the consideration of race, other archival material relating to the administration of citizenship law shows that under particular conditions, many West German officials and influential legal scholars were content to continue using explicitly racist language—that is to say, the language of *Rasse*—to discuss government policy. Some of the most interesting material in this regard relates to an expert commission on citizenship law that the BMI established in 1955. It was composed primarily of law professors, as well as judges from two of Germany's federal courts. From 1957 onward, representatives from the interior ministries of Hessen and Bavaria also attended the commission's sessions to observe proceedings for the federal states.[61] While many of the commission's members had been enthusiastic supporters of National Socialism, there were some who had faced persecution under the Nazi regime. The Federal Constitutional Court, for instance, was represented by its first female judge, Erna Scheffler. Scheffler, who had two Jewish grandparents, had lost her position as a judge in 1934 and had suffered persecution on racial grounds, including being prevented from marrying her partner by the Nuremberg racial laws.[62] Frequently recognized for her decisive influence on numerous Constitutional Court judgments that forced the West German government to respect Article 3, Paragraph 2, of the Basic Law, which prescribed the legal equality of men and women, Scheffler is widely credited as an early champion of women's rights in the FRG.[63]

In the commission's earliest sessions, there was little discussion of race. This changed, however, when the commission considered whether elements of *jus soli* should be introduced to German citizenship law, so

---

61. Arbeitsgemeinschaft der Innenministerien der Länder an die Innenministerien der Bundesländer, 12.11.1957, Rheinland-Pfälzisches Landeshauptarchiv Koblenz, Best. 880, Nr. 14755.

62. Marike Hansen, *Erna Scheffler (1893–1983): Erste Richterin am Bundesverfassungsgericht und eine Wegbereiterin einer geschlechtergerechten Gesellschaft* (Tübingen: Mohr Siebeck, 2019), 70–73.

63. Hansen, 142–45, 155–57, 186.

that individuals born on German territory would acquire German citizenship. The commission's response to this proposal, from May 1957, is worth quoting in full:

> The answer to the question was largely no, because such a regulation would lead to an uncontrollable change in the composition of the people [*Staatsvolk*]. . . . The dangers of mixing [*Gefahren der Vermischung*] have to be taken especially seriously, because the ancestral population now only constitutes a fraction of the total population in the German Eastern territories under Polish administration and, to a certain extent, in the Soviet Zone of Occupation and because, if the Eastern states open their borders one day, Germany will have to reckon with a flood of migrants and because, with France belonging to the European federation, we will have to expect a large-scale migration of French citizens from France's territories outside of Europe.[64]

The commission's reasons for opposing introducing *jus soli* centered on the idea that it would lead to unavoidable changes in the composition of the German *Staatsvolk*. While the term *Rasse* is not used explicitly in the written summary minutes of the session, it is clearly the racial composition of the *Staatsvolk* to which commission members were referring. This is indicated by the German phrase "Gefahren der Vermischung," which is likely elliptical for "Gefahren der *Rassen*vermischung"—dangers of *racial* mixing. Both Eastern Europe and France's extra-European territories are identified here as potential sources of danger, indicating that Eastern Europeans as well as North and West Africans were perceived as threats to the imagined racial purity of the *Staatsvolk*.

In the commission's later sessions, members discussed race without even this thin layer of euphemism. In July 1958, as part of a broader discussion on naturalization practice, Hermann Mosler, a professor at the University of Heidelberg, asked the BMI's representative whether "the Executive considers itself permitted to exclude or privilege members of certain nations from naturalization, perhaps on racial grounds." The BMI answered that "accounting for race is a matter of practice," underlining that while the naturalization guidelines did not contain any explicit instructions on this issue, there was in practice a restrictive stance

---

64. Niederschrift der Sitzung der Staatsangehörigkeitskommission am 2–3.5.1957, Bundesarchiv Koblenz (BArch) B 106/73108.

"toward former residents of the Eastern states."⁶⁵ Clearly, the BMI's statement underscores that the government continued to perceive Eastern Europeans as racial others. But it also shows that the BMI not only discriminated on the basis of race in its naturalization decisions—and was aware that the federal states were doing so in their own—but also was aware of a disconnect between this widespread practice and the naturalization guidelines. This suggests that the lack of any mention of "foreign descent" in the naturalization guidelines should be seen within the context of systemic *and* purposefully obscured racist discrimination within the naturalization process.

The issue of race returned in the commission's next meeting in October 1958, in which the experts discussed whether Article 3 of the Basic Law placed legal limits on the decision-making powers of naturalization authorities. Article 3 included both the general declaration that all individuals are equal before the law (Paragraph 1), as well as the prohibition on particular forms of discrimination (Paragraph 3).⁶⁶ If Paragraph 3 were to be accepted as legally binding for naturalization authorities, that would mean that they were not allowed to discriminate on the basis of race, descent, and the other protected characteristics mentioned in the article. Ulrich Scheuner, professor at the University of Bonn, coeditor of an influential early handbook on the fundamental rights of the Basic Law,⁶⁷ and beneficiary of and apologist for the Nazi seizure of power,⁶⁸ responded that "differentiating according to language, race, etc. was appropriate in citizenship law," before asking "with what justification could one reject the naturalization of an Algerian?"⁶⁹ None of the commission members objected to Scheuner's demand for racial discrimination. Instead, Erna Scheffler responded by saying that

---

65. Niederschrift der Sitzung der Staatsangehörigkeitskommission am 11.7.1958, BArch B 106/73109.
66. Niederschrift der Sitzung der Staatsangehörigkeitskommission am 20-21.10.1958, BArch B 106/73109.
67. See Franz L. Neumann, Hans Carl Nipperdey, and Ulrich Scheuner, eds., *Die Grundrechte: Handbuch der Theorie und Praxis der Grundrechte* (Berlin: Duncker & Humboldt, 1958), 3 vols.
68. For an overview of Scheuner's scholarly defense of the Nazi seizure of power and the ways in which he profited under Nazi rule see Dominik Rigoll, *Staatsschutz in Westdeutschland: Von der Entnazifizierung zur Extremistenabwehr* (Göttingen: Wallstein, 2013), 96ff.
69. Algerians presented a particular problem for West German authorities because they possessed French citizenship until Algerian independence in 1962, which made it difficult for West German authorities to discriminate against them when processing applications for labor migration. See Schönwälder, *Einwanderung und ethnische Pluralität*, 267-69.

she would "also like to disable Article 3 Paragraph 3" but did not see an immediate justification for doing so.

Carl Hermann Ule, a professor of public law in Speyer, suggested that a justification could be found in the conceptualization of the state. The Federal Republic of Germany, he argued, was not a "random conglomeration of the individuals who belonged to it" but rather "a real assemblage of the German *Volk* in the form of a state." Hermann Mosler, a professor at the University of Heidelberg, picked up on this idea, offering that the commission could suggest that while the first two paragraphs of Article 3 were legally binding for naturalization authorities, the third paragraph, which forbade discrimination on the basis of race, ancestry, and other characteristics, was not. Scheffler responded to this suggestion favorably, arguing that "language, race, ancestry etc. were characteristics which constituted the German *Volk* and its state, and could therefore be taken into account when dealing with naturalizations."

Other commission members accepted Scheffler's argument, agreeing that the German *Volk* and the Federal Republic, as that *Volk*'s state, were both partially constituted by race. They approved a motion stating that the constitutional prohibitions on discrimination articulated in Article 3, Paragraph 3, of the Basic Law placed no legal limits on the decisions of naturalization authorities. One should note that the idea that the German people and their state were racially constituted had no legally codified foundation in the Basic Law. By accepting that the German people was constituted racially, and that this racial constitution was important enough to countenance ignoring the Basic Law, these experts tacitly concurred that the Federal Republic was, on some level, a racial state. In so doing, they agreed that race stood above the constitution. There is no indication in the minutes that any of the representatives of the BMI or the other federal states present at the session sought to contradict them.

The commission addressed race again in January 1959, when discussing whether West Germany had to recognize people who were naturalized in the German Democratic Republic (the GDR, or East Germany) as German citizens.[70] During the discussion, Scheffler asked

---

70. West Germany claimed that all citizens of the GDR were its own citizens as part of its claim to be the only legitimate German state. For more on this see Sebastian Gehrig, *Legal Entanglements: Law, Rights, and the Battle for Legitimacy in Divided Germany, 1945–1989* (Oxford: Berghahn Books, 2021), chaps. 2 and 4. See also Dieter Wyduckel, "Erwerb der deutschen Staatsangehörigkeit durch Einbürgerung in der DDR?," in *Recht und Staat im sozialen Wandel:*

what would happen if the "population of the Eastern Zone [the GDR] was removed, Chinese people were brought there and then naturalized and later smuggled into West Germany," stating that "Article 3 of the Basic Law is not relevant here," and that "it must be possible to expel such migrants." Scheuner agreed with Scheffler that West Germany should retain the right to expel such individuals from its territory. In the minutes, his justification for doing so is given as follows: "It may well be the case that we differentiate according to race in naturalization [*bei der Einbürgerung Rassenunterschiede machen*] while the Soviet Zone does not. Acts that are foreign to our legal order [*Unserer Rechtsordnung fremdartige Akte*] must not be accepted."[71]

This statement seems to contain a marked radicalization of the commission's position on racist discrimination. The commission's earlier declaration that Article 3, Paragraph 3, of the Basic Law did not bind naturalization authorities had confirmed the state's right to ignore the constitutional limits placed on it with regard to differentiation according to race. Scheuner's statement in the 1959 meeting went beyond this. He implied not only the absence of a prohibition on racist discrimination but rather the existence of an intrinsic imperative to differentiate on the grounds of *Rasse*, to the point that the absence of racist discrimination in matters of naturalization would constitute an administrative act that was so foreign to the FRG's own legal order as to make it irreconcilable with West German law.

It is difficult to determine the direct impact of the commission's deliberations on citizenship law policy and administrative practice. Indeed, one can hardly ascertain when the commission ended its work, let alone identify its direct outcomes. At the end of the second of the two archival files containing the minutes of the commission, we find references to further sessions to be held in the future, as well as descriptions of plans for the commission to publish its recommendations in a memorandum. There are, however, no records in the German Federal Archives relating to the commission after the summer of 1959,[72] and no signs that the commission ever published its findings.

Festschrift für Hans Ulrich Scupin zum 80. Geburtstag, ed. Norbert Achterberg, Werner Krawietz, and Dieter Wyduckel (Berlin: Duncker & Humboldt, 1983), 663–86.

71. Niederschrift der Sitzung der Staatsangehörigkeitskommission am 9.1.1959, BArch B 106/73109.

72. A note sent between *Referate* in the BMI in April 1959 mentions that another meeting was scheduled for July 1959, but there are no minutes for this meeting in the final file relating to the commission. BArch B 106/73109.

The expert commission on citizenship law was not the only high-level deliberative body that harbored concerns regarding the relationship between Article 3 of the Basic Law, citizenship law, and the question of race. Indeed, similar ideas were expressed by the members of the "Ausschuss Inneres," a secret committee composed of top-ranking civil servants from various federal ministries that was established in 1957 to develop ideas for the content of the constitution of a unified German state. This committee had also originally intended to deliver its recommendations in a memorandum for the Bundeskanzler and federal cabinet, but its work ended in 1960 without the memorandum being finalized.[73]

The minutes of the committee's sessions, which were classified as top secret and remained inaccessible to researchers until 2012, show that some of the concerns about race and citizenship expressed by the scholars and judges in the BMI's expert commission were shared by the highest-ranking civil servants of the Federal Republic. During a session held in December 1959, the committee discussed Article 3 of the Basic Law and the place it should have in the future constitution of a unified Germany. Hans Lechner, the director of the sub-department for constitutional law in the BMI, articulated concerns regarding "the danger of Article 3 becoming a gate through which members of colored nations [*Angehörige farbiger Völker*] could force entry into the cultural realm of Central Europe." The minutes do not record Lechner specifying how he imagined "colored" individuals might instrumentalize the constitutional declaration of human equality to do this. One can assume, however, that he was concerned about the article's impact on the executive's ability to discriminate against individuals on the basis of "race" in residency and naturalization law.

This was at least how Lechner's concerns were understood by his colleague Hans Schäfer, who was the director of the BMI's department for Constitutional, Public and Administrative Law. According to the minutes, Schäfer reassured Lechner that the "danger" he described "could be adequately met through an appropriately strict application of naturalization law." This position was confirmed by a representative of the Federal Ministry of Justice, who argued that the legal provisions for naturalization could be formulated in a way that "gave the administrative authorities enough leeway for a justified differential treatment

---

73. Vermerk des Referats I A 1 des BMI über die Arbeiten des Ausschusses Inneres zur Vorbereitung einer gesamtdeutschen Verfassung, 20.7.1963, BArch B 106/202065.

of foreigners of various nationalities," despite the promise of equality formulated in Article 3 of the Basic Law.[74] The other top-level civil servants agreed with this proposition. In doing this, they voiced their support for a process of systemic and purposefully obscured discrimination against members of certain groups, such as those from "colored nations."

Immediately after this, the committee members discussed whether Paragraph 3 of Article 3 should be retained. The minutes record that they agreed "that the prohibition on discrimination on the basis of race was indispensable" and would have to be retained in the constitution of a unified German state. Given that they had just agreed that they should organize naturalization law to allow for the exclusion of individuals from German citizenship on the basis of skin color, their insistence on the indispensability of the ban on racist discrimination seems paradoxical. If one attempts to make sense of it, the most convincing interpretation is that the commission members held the prohibition on racist discrimination to be indispensable as an aesthetic, rather than truly functional, aspect of the constitution—a legal ornament to which the German state could conveniently gesture to underline how it had overcome the horrors of the Nazi past while continuing to discriminate on the basis of race in administrative practice.

At this point, it is worth posing the question: How different is the vision of the relationship between *Volk* and *Staatsvolk* articulated in the deliberations of these two commissions from that advocated by the Nazi Party in their foundational program of 1920? Clearly, the members of these commissions also believed that West Germany was in some way a racial state and that this should have consequences for citizenship law and naturalization policy. The consequences that they envisioned were, however, different from those drawn by the National Socialists.

For the Nazis, the state's racial character demanded not only a blanket ban on individuals from racially "inferior" or "alien" groups from becoming members of the citizenry, but also required the active internal discrimination and disenfranchisement of individuals belonging to those groups who already possessed German citizenship. In the case of German Jews, this later gave way to their expulsion from the body of

---

74. Niederschrift über die Sitzung des "Ausschuss Inneres" am 15.12.1959, BArch B 106/202065.

the citizenry entirely, a process that was intimately connected with the Nazi attempts at their total extermination.

The measures proposed by the commission, and those deployed by naturalization authorities, were more defensive in nature. They aimed at protecting the racial character of the *Staatsvolk* through racist discrimination at the point of entry to citizenship. While they clearly believed that racial criteria should be deployed when determining who was to become a German citizen, they did not advocate stripping existing citizens of their citizenship or systematically denying them central legal rights on racial grounds. The discrimination at the border of entry to citizenship was also not total; indeed, an examination of the archives does show that naturalizations of Black people and other individuals of non-European heritage did take place, albeit not in large numbers.[75] One could thus argue that the policy conclusions these experts and officials derived from their belief in the country's status as a racial state had more in common with the racist citizenship law policies of Imperial and Weimar Germany than with those of the Third Reich.[76]

Yet regardless of whether we determine these racist positions or policies to have their roots in Imperial, Weimar, or Nazi Germany, they remain irreconcilable with both the constitutional order of the Federal Republic and with the widespread understanding of it as a country that had "learned from its past" regarding state racism. Indeed, the deliberations of the expert commission, of the Ausschuss Inneres, and the examples from concrete naturalization practice examined above demonstrate in sobering detail that West German government officials and members of the country's judicial and scholarly elites continued to view

---

75. See, for example, the naturalization in Hamburg in the late 1950s of a Black man who had migrated to Germany from Cameroon in 1912, Staatsarchiv Hamburg, 332-7 B VI 1958, Nr. 187; or the naturalization in the early 1960s of a Black stateless man who had been born in 1931 in Germany to a stateless father of African origin and an African American mother in Cologne, LAV NRW R, NW 208, Nr. 111.

76. This is in line with a general finding of many of the recent large-scale research projects into the continuities between National Socialism and the postwar period in West German federal ministries. These studies have found that many of the difficulties that civil servants experienced in adapting to the liberal democratic state formation of the FRG stemmed not from lingering attachments to National Socialist ideology but often from their attachments to antidemocratic traditions that had their roots in the pre-Nazi period. See Eckart Conze and Annette Weinke, "Krisenhaftes Lernen? Formen der Demokratisierung in deutschen Behörden und Ministerien," in *Demokratisierung der Deutschen: Errungenschaften und Anfechtungen eines Projekts*, ed. Tim Schanetzky et al. (Göttingen: Wallstein, 2020), 95; Stefan Creuzberger and Dominik Geppert, "Die Ämter und ihre Vergangenheit: Eine Zwischenbilanz," in *Die Ämter und ihre Vergangenheit: Ministerien und Behörden im geteilten Deutschland 1949–1972*, ed. Stefan Creuzberger and Dominik Geppert (Bonn: Bundeszentrale für politische Bildung, 2018), 191.

discrimination on the basis of race as permissible and perhaps even necessary in order to conserve the racial purity of the *Staatsvolk* and the racial character of the state itself.

The material examined here suggests that the 1950s were a period of transition as pertains to the coding of racial difference, in which biological and cultural understandings of race coexisted simultaneously. The same can be said for the coexistence of older German modes of racialization (targeting Eastern Europeans, for example) with newer forms influenced by the United States (such as imagining race as a Black/white binary). In both instances, this material complicates the established historiography on the conceptualization and discussion of race in West Germany in the 1950s and 1960s, which has argued that both the language of biological race in the sense of *Rasse*, and the casting of Eastern Europeans as *racial* others, were delegitimized in governmental and academic circles after 1945.

The material also shows, however, that government officials felt the need to obscure the ways in which they "accounted for race," especially in written documents that were intended for broad circulation. The BMI's decisions to elide reference to "foreigners of foreign descent" in the naturalization guidelines while encouraging differentiation on such grounds in practice, and its evocation of "cultural requirements" when it in fact meant race, are evidence of this. Similarly, it is significant that the minutes of both the expert commission and the Ausschuss Inneres were not intended for publication. The minutes of the expert commission were intended only for the internal use of the BMI, while the minutes of the Ausschuss Inneres were only to be made available to those within the federal government with clearance for top secret documents. In both instances, the expectation that the documents would stay within the hands of a select set of civil servants would have certainly played an important role in putting the committees' members at ease to discuss racial discrimination in terms of *Rasse*.

The concerted and purposeful use of euphemism to obscure racist decision-making practices suggests that many officials of the early FRG had a pragmatic, or indeed even cynical, relationship with the constitutional prohibition on racist discrimination. That the members of the Ausschuss Inneres could deliberate on the best ways to legislate so as to surreptitiously enable racist discrimination in residency and naturalization law in one breath, before affirming the indispensability of the constitutional prohibition of racist discrimination in the next, is the most striking example of this cynical relationship. Far from understanding the prohibition as a morally necessary response to National Socialism, which necessarily entailed significant legal restrictions on the decision-making powers of the state, they seem to have viewed it as merely instituting new rules of discourse, by which they had to abide to protect themselves against accusations of racism, while continuing to discriminate on racial grounds in practice.[77] While the language in which it was presented and justified changed, racist discrimination thus remained an integral part of citizenship law policy. In this sense, citizenship law seems not to have been reimagined in the wake of National Socialism and the horrors of its state racism, but in parts simply to have been repackaged.

Nicholas Courtman is the Alfred Landecker Lecturer in the Department of Languages, Literatures and Cultures at King's College London. He received his PhD in German studies from Jesus College at the University of Cambridge in 2021. He is coeditor of *Writing the Economic Subject in Modern Western Europe: Representation, Contestation, Critique*.

---

77. In this, the West German governmental authorities of the 1950s seem to have continued where the Parliamentary Council left off in their discussions of race when drafting Article 3 of the Basic Law. Doris Liebscher notes that much of the council's discussions regarding race centered on how one could justify policies that targeted certain racialized groups, such as Sinti and Roma, if one included a prohibition on racist discrimination. Liebscher states that "one gets the impression that they were less interested in providing the best possible protection against racist discrimination, and more interested in strategies and formulations through which such protection could elegantly be avoided." Liebscher, *Rasse im Recht*, 368.

CHAPTER 5

Statelessness and Social Citizenship of Greek Civil War Refugees in Post-1948 Communist Czechoslovakia

Nikola Tohma

> Nowadays I know that I will be a foreigner there [in Greece] as I am here [in Czechoslovakia]. . . . I didn't do anything to anyone and still I have had no citizenship since I was born. Why?
>
> —Praxitelis Makris, *Děti vyděděnců* (Children of outcasts)

The young protagonist of a 1986 novel by the Czechoslovak author of Greek origin Praxitelis Makris, himself a refugee from the Greek Civil War (1946-1949), acknowledged the stalemate in his life with a genuine sense of injustice, bitterness, and unconcealed frustration. Makris's words make us wonder about the lives of him and other Greek Civil War refugees in communist Czechoslovakia (1948-1989), later the Czech Republic, and their coping strategies in such an adverse situation.

The memoirs, novels, and popular histories of these refugees, as well as numerous interviews with them, abound with references to their legal citizenship, national identity, and sense of belonging. Even the titles of their books, such as *Children of Hellas*; *Foreigners without Passports*; and *Children of Outcasts*; as well as more abstract ones like *Stolen Sun*; *Children of the Storm*; and *Olive Trees Do Not Blossom in Moravia*, suggest their sense of loss and uprootedness.[1] They left Greece in the late 1940s, escaping

---

1. Petros Cironis, *Děti Helady* [Children of Hellas] (Západočeské nakladatelství, 1976); Petros Cironis, *Cizinci bez pasů* [Foreigners without passports] (Rokycany: Faros, 1994); Praxitelis Makris, *Děti vyděděnců* [Children of outcasts] (Ostrava: Profil, 1986); Georgis Karadzos, *Ukradené slunce* [Stolen sun] (Lomnice nad Popelkou: Studio JB, 2004); Lysimachos Chr. Papadopulos, *Pedia tis thyellas / Děti bouře* [Children of the storm] (Prague, 1998); George

from one of the major military conflicts of the early Cold War. The conflict between the US-supported monarchy and Soviet-backed Greek communists was characterized by prolonged ground warfare, heavy bombardment by the pro-government forces, and countless atrocities carried out by both sides.² As adherents of the defeated communist Democratic Army of Greece (DSE)—most of them partisans, their families, and orphaned children—the refugees had been exposed to persistent political persecution in Greece. For these reasons, they collectively qualified for large-scale humanitarian aid in Eastern bloc countries, organized transnationally by the coordinated action of several communist states under the USSR's aegis.³

As one of the receiving countries, Czechoslovakia welcomed about 12,100 refugees from Greece, out of approximately 56,200 refugees who found homes across the Eastern bloc.⁴ After their arrival, the refugees were provided with food, clothing, accommodations, and medical aid. Within months, adult refugees attained professional training and gradually entered workplaces, receiving equal access to the country's social security system. Children, mostly separated from their parents, were placed in child-care institutions to obtain education in a socially and economically stable yet deeply ideologized environment.⁵ Despite the state's inclusive approach, the legal status of these refugees remained unclear for years and, in many cases, even decades. In retribution for their participation in the civil war and based on the principle of collective

---

Agathonikiadis, *Na Moravě nekvetou olivy* [Olive trees do not blossom in Moravia] (Prague: Česká citadela, 2019).

2. For example, André Gerolymatos, *An International Civil War: Greece 1943–1949* (New Haven, CT: Yale University Press, 2016); David Brewer, *Greece, the Decade of War: Occupation, Resistance and Civil War* (London: I. B. Tauris, 2016).

3. For general overview see Ilios Giannakakis, "Ta opla para poda: I egkatastasi ton prosfygon stis sosialistikes chores" [Ground arms: The settlement of refugees in socialist countries], in *To oplo para poda. Oi politikoi prosfyges tou ellinikou emfyliou polemou stin Anatoliki Evropi* [Ground arms: The political refugees of the Greek Civil War in Eastern Europe], ed. E. Voutyra, V. Dalkavoukis, N. Marantzidis, and M. Bontila (Thessaloniki: Ekdoseis Panepistimiou Makedonias, 2005), 3–18, and for individual countries, for instance, Katerina Tsekou, "The Greek Political Refugees in the People's Republic of Bulgaria," *Acta Universitatis Carolinae—Studia Territorialia Supplementum* 1, no. 1 (2010): 77–93; or Milan Ristović, *A Long Journey Home: Greek Refugee Children in Yugoslavia, 1948–1960* (Thessaloniki: Institute for Balkan Studies, 2000).

4. National Archives of the Czech Republic (NACR) 1261/2 KSČ ÚV 100/3 Sv. 140, a. j. 547, sv. 2; see also Kateřina Králová and Konstantinos Tsivos, eds., *Vyschly nám slzy. Řečtí uprchlíci v Československu* [Our tears dried up: Greek refugees in Czechoslovakia] (Prague: Dokořán, 2012), 42; Katerina Tsekou, *Ellines politikoi prosfyges stin Anatoliki Europi, 1945–1989* [Greek political refugees in Eastern Europe, 1945–1989] (Athina: Alexandreia, 2013), 188.

5. Frank Henschel, "All Children Are Ours—Children's Homes in Socialist Czechoslovakia as Laboratories of Social Engineering," *Bohemia* 56, no. 1 (2016): 122–44.

guilt, the Greek state revoked the Greek citizenship of a large number of the political refugees, aiming to prevent their future repatriation. Even in cases when they were not made stateless, many were not able, for a long time, to return to their country, for fear that they would face political persecution.[6] Thus, many continued to live in a legal vacuum between the two countries, a vacuum sustained by the ongoing Cold War.

This chapter takes the case of Greek Civil War refugees in order to interrogate how their citizenship was (re)negotiated in postwar anticommunist Greece and communist Czechoslovakia, both in national and transnational contexts. Examining the state, party, public, and refugees' perspectives, this case study focuses on the modifications of citizenship under state socialism in terms of formal and informal understandings over the *longue durée*.

The chapter is divided into three sections. Its initial analysis contributes to the transnational history of citizenship, developing along two research axes: First, it investigates the question of statelessness, assessing how Czechoslovakia handled the arrival of stateless refugees from Greece, while at the same time looking into the statelessness of the country's ethnic German population, whose citizenship Czechoslovakia revoked after the war. The expulsion of Germans as alleged traitors and collaborators and the reception of Greek Civil War refugees as presumed loyal comrades (and even the spatial replacement of one by the other) were symptomatic of postwar Czechoslovakia's ideological transformation as a communist state, realized in the takeover of power by the Communist Party of Czechoslovakia (KSČ) in February 1948.[7] The second axis focuses on how Greece and Czechoslovakia, standing on opposing sides of the Iron Curtain, instrumentalized the citizenship of Greek Civil War refugees as a political tool. Enforcing political loyalty, whether nationally or ideologically defined, shaped citizenship in both countries, turning questions of solidarity, asylum, and citizenship granting into a matter of purely political, rather than legal, character.[8]

---

6. Kateřina Králová and Karin Hofmeisterová, "The Voices of Greek Child Refugees in Czechoslovakia," *Journal of Modern Greek Studies* 38, no. 1 (2020): 148–49.

7. The framing of Czechoslovak Germans as traitors and collaborators formed the legal basis for the expulsion on the grounds of the Constitutional Decree of the President of the Republic of August 2, 1945, on the regulation of Czechoslovak citizenship of persons of German and Hungarian nationality (Ústavní dekret presidenta republiky ze dne 2. srpna 1945 o úpravě československého státního občanství osob národnosti německé a maďarské), no. 33/1945, Art. 1.

8. For similar observations related to Greece compare Loring M. Danforth and Riki Van Boeschoten, *Children of the Greek Civil War: Refugees and the Politics of Memory* (Chicago: University of Chicago Press, 2012), 31, 82, 125.

The chapter's second part delves into the political reasoning behind "asylum" as a form of protection that Czechoslovakia granted to refugees from Greece. It exposed refugees' vulnerability in a legal sense, which contrasted starkly with the communist heroization of political refugees as a deserving category of migrants. As a result, the social status of Greek Civil War refugees oscillated between a seemingly privileged echelon of the communist establishment and an unremarkable group of foreign nationals or stateless persons, unable to rely on the support of any independent institution.

The chapter's final section contributes to the existing research on socialist citizenship, transcending the limitations of more traditional legal analyses.[9] As Czech historian and lawyer Andrea Baršová has emphasized with regard to the evolution of Czech(oslovak) citizenship policies, "Both in the communist ideology and in legal theory, citizenship meant not only legal but also factual bonds between a citizen and the society."[10] She quotes a 1963 Czechoslovak legal textbook that additionally characterizes socialist citizenship as "belonging to a community of working people, who participate in the building of socialist (communist) society and in the building and defense of the socialist state" and "belonging to the community connected by shared dreams and ideals."[11] This chapter goes even further by claiming that the universal access to social rights challenged the importance of legal citizenship in state socialism. Czechoslovakia distributed social rights equally among those who demonstrated political loyalty, consistent with the ideal of "a new socialist man" as the "builder of socialism."[12] Labor integration, an absolute precondition to social inclusion, was enforced

---

9. See esp. Igor Štiks, *Nations and Citizens in Yugoslavia and the Post-Yugoslav States: One Hundred Years of Citizenship* (London: Bloomsbury Academic, 2015), 11–17; André Liebich, Daniel Warner, and Jasna Dragovic, eds., *Citizenship East and West* (London: Kegan Paul, 1995); Ben Herzog, "The Paradoxes of Citizenship Removal: Soviet and Post-Soviet Citizenship," *East European Politics and Societies* 26, no. 4 (2012): 792–810; Krista A. Goff, "Why Not Love Our Language and Our Culture? National Rights and Citizenship in Khrushchev's Soviet Union," *Nationalities papers* 43, no. 1 (2015): 27–44; Hang B. Duong and Le-Ha Phan, "Socialist Citizenship in the Post-socialist Era across Time and Space: A Closer Look at Cuba and Vietnam," in *The Palgrave Handbook of Citizenship and Education*, ed. A. Peterson, G. Stahl, and H. Soong (Cham, Switzerland: Palgrave Macmillan, 2020).

10. Andrea Baršová, "Czech Citizenship Legislation between Past and Future," in *Citizenship Policies in the New Europe*, ed. Rainer Bauböck, Bernhard Perchinig, and Wiebke Sievers (Amsterdam: Amsterdam University Press, 2009), 250.

11. Jan Černý and Václav Červenka, *Státní občanství ČSSR* [State citizenship of the Czechoslovak Socialist Republic] (Prague: Orbis, 1963), 19.

12. Denisa Nečasová, *Nový socialistický člověk: Československo 1948–1956* [New socialist man: Czechoslovakia 1948–1956] (Brno: Host, 2018).

by a general right and duty to work. In this volume, for instance, Rachel Weiser elaborates on the impact of gender on the postwar citizenship of working women in the GDR, while Anna Dobrowolska investigates the interconnections between prostitution, gender, and citizenship in socialist Poland, to once again emphasize the importance of women's labor for their status in state socialism, both in the sense of work and reproduction. Adding to this gendered perspective, the case of Greek Civil War refugees in Czechoslovakia points to the role of labor integration as a tool for constructing a socialist society in which representatives of various nationalities are made equal to the Czechoslovak state-building nation. Thus, labor was socially integrative in service of the state's broader internationalist political mission.

The accessibility of social rights in the context of socialist citizenship enabled refugees to maintain their statelessness rather than seek formal Czechoslovak citizenship. They resented statelessness with a sense of injustice and grievance and experienced it through emotions comparable to those of postwar DPs considered in Laura Hilton's chapter. Yet, in practical terms, they succeeded in turning statelessness into a resource, subverting typical understandings of this status as precarious or imposed, an ironic use of statelessness that Dagmar Wernitznig also explores earlier in this volume. For decades, the civil war refugees kept their options open while awaiting a fundamental political change in Greece. Thus, the refugees' social integration into Czechoslovak society did not erase their self-identification with the Greek nation and, eventually, failed to establish a long-term sense of belonging, suggesting the limits of citizenship divorced from nationality.

On Disloyalty and Statelessness

On December 7, 1947, the Greek government led by Themistoklis Sofoulis issued Resolution no. 37 on the revocation of citizenship (*ithageneia*). It concerned those "Greek citizens, living temporarily or permanently abroad, who during the current rebellion acted provably in an antinational way or supported in any manner the bandit war against the state."[13] The measure was part of other exceptional legislation approved

---

13. Resolution 37/1947 on the "Revocation of the Greek citizenship from Persons That Are Acting in an Antinational Way Abroad" (Psifisma LZ' Peri aposteriseos tis Ellinikis ithageneias prosopon antethnikos dronton eis to exoterikon, 07/12/1947), FEK 267/1947, 1451.

in response to the ongoing civil war, in which the Athens-based monarchist regime clashed with partisan units of the DSE. The legislation, adopted without authorization from the Hellenic Parliament, curbed left-wing activities by banning their presses, outlawing strikes, and confiscating the property of communist sympathizers.[14] The vaguely formulated Resolution no. 37 itself enabled the government to strip Greek citizenship from those who had engaged in undefined "antinational activities" and lived abroad.

The triumphs of the left-wing resistance to Axis occupation during World War II and the subsequent civil war had catalyzed this anticommunist campaign in Greece. Yet its roots stretched into the interwar period when Greek liberals and conservatives—as elsewhere in Europe—perceived the Communist Party of Greece (KKE), not quite inaccurately, as the USSR's fifth column and thus a threat to the country's sovereignty.[15] Since the far-right Metaxas dictatorship (1936–1941), the Greek population had witnessed the social exclusion of left-wing citizens, justified by the ideological principle of "national mindedness" (*ethnikofrosyni*) or, in other terms, "patriotic soundness."[16] The public sphere saw the introduction of "civic-mindedness" certificates as proof of political loyalty and a prerequisite for employment in the state-affiliated sectors.[17] Following the civil war, American influence in the era of McCarthyism further intensified this process, as the government set out to "purge" the state apparatus and public organizations of "noncompliant" citizens.[18]

The language of anticommunist propaganda deliberately aimed to "denationalize" left-wing sympathizers in an ethno-national sense to prepare grounds for their denationalization in a legal sense.

---

14. Nikola Karasová, "Řecký antikomunismus z pohledu protikomunistické legislativy (1917–1967)" [Greek anticommunism from the legislative perspective], *Neograeca Bohemica* 19 (2019): 60.

15. Compare Anastasia I. Mitsopoulou, *O ellinikos antikommounismos ston "syntomo 20o aiona": Opseis tou dimosiou logou stin politiki, stin ekpaideusi kai sti logotechnia* [Greek anticommunism in the "short 20th century": Aspects of the public speech in politics, education and literature] (Thessaloniki: Epikentro, 2014).

16. David H. Close, "The Reconstruction of a Right-Wing State," in *The Greek Civil War: Studies of Polarization*, ed. David H. Close (London: Routledge, 1993), 158.

17. Compulsory Law 1075/1938, "On Security Measures of the Social System and Citizen's Protection" (Anagkastikos Nomos yp' arith. 1075 Peri metron asfaleias tou koinonikou kathestotos kai prostasias ton politon, 11/02/1938), FEK 45/1938, 237–40.

18. Minas Samatas, "Greek McCarthyism: A Comparative Assessment of Greek Post-Civil War Repressive Anticommunism and the U.S. Truman-McCarthy Era," *Journal of the Hellenic Diaspora* 13, no. 3-4 (1986): 5–75.

Government sources commonly referred to the civil war (the term itself was banned) as "a rebellion," a "war of gangsters," or a "war of rebels." The KKE's sympathizers were characterized as antinational and anti-Greek. Instead, they were portrayed as "Slavs," "external enemies," "traitors," "criminals," and "infidel barbarians," the latter highlighting Greek Orthodoxy as an essential feature of modern Greek identity.[19] Thus, according to Greek historian Tasos Kostopoulos, the "concept of national mindedness . . . could be used on the basis of purely political criteria."[20] While Resolution no. 37, being an exceptional measure, was only applicable to the civil war period, it became an instrument of persecution in the 1950s and the early 1960s, targeting en masse the refugees of the Greek Civil War dispersed across East Central and Southeastern Europe. Further contradicting the law, which required assessments to be made on a case-by-case basis, the authorities applied the revocation of citizenship collectively in retribution for the civil war.[21]

Thus, a total of 22,266 people (out of about 56,200 refugees in the Eastern bloc) lost their Greek citizenship by royal decrees issued between 1948 and 1963 (see table 5.1). Only 124 cases were decided during the civil war and 289 cases before the declaration of the Constitution

---

19. For example see Despina Papadimitriou, *Apo ton lao ton nomimofronon sto ethnos ton ethnikofronon: I syntiritiki skepsi stin Ellada, 1922–1967* [From the law-abiding people to the nation of the nationally minded: Conservative thought in Greece, 1922-1967] (Athina: Savvalas, 2006), 178-87; Eleni Paschaloudi, *Enas polemos choris telos: I dekaetia tou 1940 ston politiko logo, 1950–1967* [A war without an end: The decade of the 1940s in the political speech, 1950-1967] (Thessaloniki: Epikentro, 2010), 43-44; Stratis Bournazos, "To kratos ton ethnikofronon: Antikommounistikos logos kai praktikes" [The state of nationally minded: Anticommunist speech and practice], in *Archeiotaxio* 16 (2014): 17-19; Zinovia Lialiouti, "Contesting the Antitotalitarian Consensus: The Concept of National Independence, the Memory of the Second World War and the Ideological Cleavages in Post-war Greece," in *National Identities* 18, no. 2 (2016): 108.

20. Tasos Kostopoulos, "Afaireseis ithageneias. I skoteini pleura tis neoellinikis istorias" [Denationalizations. The dark side of the modern Greek history], *elaliberta.gr*, February 3, 2019, https://www.elaliberta.gr/.

21. According to Article 2 of Resolution no. 37/1947, citizenship could be revoked upon the publication of a royal decree following the suggestion of the minister of interior and the minister of justice and based on the recommendation of the Council of Citizenship at the Ministry of Interior. A special advisory committee, composed of high representatives of the State Council, the Supreme Court, the Ministry of Foreign Affairs, and the police, was made responsible for compiling information files on the suspected individuals. The length of the administrative process was set for maximally one month. Greek citizens whose citizenship had been revoked were perceived as foreign nationals and were banned from reentering Greece. See Resolution 37/1947 on the "Revocation of the Greek Citizenship from Persons That Are Acting in an Antinational Way Abroad" (Psifisma LZ' Peri aposteriseos tis Ellinikis ithageneias prosopon antethnikos dronton eis to exoterikon, 07/12/1947), FEK 267/1947, 1451, Art. 2.

Table 5.1 Revocation of citizenship (*ithageneia*) for political reasons, 1948–1963

YEAR	NO. OF DECREES OR DECISIONS	NO. OF CONCERNED PERSONS
1948	1	92
1949	2	32
1950	2	93
1951	3	72
1952	27	796
1953	5	133
1954	13	1,230
1955	13	3,967
1956	16	3,697
1957	18	5,521
1958	11	2,115
1959	11	2,997
1960	3	456
1961	3	290
1962	5	377
1963	2	398
Total	135	22,266

Source: Nikos Alivizatos, *Oi politikoi thesmoi se krisi 1922–1974. Opseis tis ellinikis embirias* [Political institutions in crisis 1922-1974. Perspectives of the Greek experience] (Athina: Themelio, 1983), 491.

of 1952. A majority were thus stripped of their citizenship after the country had restored its constitutional order.[22] Furthermore, the revocation of citizenship concerned children born after the date when their parents lost Greek citizenship.[23] By revoking the citizenship of entire families and local communities and, additionally, expropriating their property, Greece temporarily prevented its "politically disloyal" population from repatriating.[24] And as Macedonian repatriates were particularly unwelcome, the government decided to repopulate the formerly Slavic villages of northwestern Greece.[25] In 1962, legislative decree no. 4234 specified that even those whose citizenship was not

---

22. Nikos Alivizatos, *Oi politikoi thesmoi se krisi 1922–1974. Opseis tis ellinikis embirias* [Political institutions in crisis 1922-1974. Perspectives of the Greek experience] (Athina: Themelio, 1983), 488–91.

23. Tsekou, *Ellines politikoi prosfyges*, 188.

24. Resolution no. 40 of January 21, 1949, enabled the expropriation of property of the communist civil war fighters and the partial expropriation of property of their spouses. Resolution 40/1948 on the "Confiscation of the Property from the Participants of the Bandit War" (Psifisma M' Peri dimevseos ton periousion ton symmetechonton eis ton symmoriakon agona, 21/01/1948), FEK A 17/1948, 1–2.

25. Legislative decree no. 2536/1953 on the "Repopulation of the Borderland Areas and the Strengthening of Their Population" (Nomothetiko diatagma Peri epanepoikismou

revoked but who had stayed abroad without a valid passport could not return to the country.[26] Besides some limited repatriation negotiated between Greece and Czechoslovakia in the mid-1950s and mid-1960s, the hostile political situation in Greece and the ongoing risk of persecution forced refugees to stay abroad much longer than they had originally anticipated. Thus, what was initially planned as a temporary shelter until the DSE could resume its military operations in Greece and install a communist regime turned into long-term residence within the Eastern bloc.

From an ideological perspective, the reception of refugees from Greece in the Eastern bloc was understood as an act of communist solidarity, an ideal display of mutual aid between comrades regardless of ethnic or racial differences in their common struggle against capitalist imperialism. Portrayed as "martyrs" and "victims" of American interests in Europe, they received protection and material support based on a shared political struggle, demonstrated by loyalty to Soviet doctrine.[27] In exchange, the refugees were expected to actively contribute to the political and economic development of the emerging socialist societies of Eastern Europe. Their professional integration was essential, as the Eastern bloc's weakened postwar economies could not support them in the long term.[28] But there were also ideological reasons for their socioeconomic integration. A report from a December 1950 conference of KKE functionaries in Czechoslovakia highlighted this mission: "No Greek emigrant capable of work must stay idle here, especially not a KKE member. No party members shall work below the norm; otherwise, they can no longer be party members. All KKE members need to realize that only the best of the best—Stakhanovites—can be admitted to the KSČ, and to be worthy of such honor, they must take care of their professional training and use all possibilities and opportunities for political and specialized education."[29] The refugees perceived

---

ton paramethorion periochon kai enyschiseos tou plythysmou auton, 23/08/1953), FEK A 225/1953, 1496–1500.

26. Legislative decree no. 4234/1962 on the "Regulation of Issues Related to the Country's Safety" (Nomothetiko diatagma Peri rythmiseos thematon aforonton tin asfaleian tis choras, 23/07/1962), FEK A 116/1962, 897–99.

27. Milan Bárta, "Právo azylu. Vznik politické emigrace v Československu po roce 1948" [The right of asylum. The emergence of political emigration in Czechoslovakia after 1948], Paměť a dějiny 1 (2011): 16.

28. Tsekou, Ellines politikoi prosfyges, 117–18.

29. NACR 1261/2 KSČ-ÚV-100/3 Sv. 132, a.j. 520, Report on the conference of functionaries of the basic organizations of the KKE in Jeseník on December 3, 1950]. However, the KSČ never agreed to admitting foreign nationals as members.

work as a means of subsistence but also as an expression of their moral commitment to building socialism.[30] Through their labor and given their refugee status, they believed to contribute to the political (and not simply economic) development of the society. As one Greek refugee in Poland said, "We were proud of our mission as political refugees and not immigrants; it was a mission to serve ideas and not to gain material benefits."[31]

The arrival of the refugees occurred alongside the abrupt imposition of Soviet-style dictatorships in the region. Welcoming them also served to legitimize the new state socialist governments, thus offering yet another example of the Eastern bloc's perceived role as a human rights defender and a competitor in political affairs with global outreach.[32] In Czechoslovakia, the KSČ acted as the main driving force behind Greek aid even before it consolidated power in February 1948. Having won the first postwar election in 1946, the party gradually solidified its position by occupying prominent posts in the state administration. Among them, the Ministry of Information gave the party political control of the media.[33] The KSČ also established a formally nongovernmental agency, the Czechoslovak-Greek Society, which helped foster a positive image of Greek partisans. Lashing out at "bloodthirsty" US imperialism and "monarcho-fascist" Greece, the left-wing newspaper *Právo lidu* claimed in June 1948 that the Greek government "gave up on all principles of humanity and exposed its true nature of a bestial murderer, who follows the example of their teachers-Nazis to murder innocent civilian population."[34] Following the Soviet example, these narratives were instrumental in preparing the ground for the positive response

---

30. Ioanna Papathanasiou, "Prosfyges stis nees patrides: I elliniki diaspora stis chores tou yparktou sosialismou" [The refugees in new homelands: The Greek diaspora in the countries of real socialism], in *Praktika Imeridas. Ellines Politikoi Prosfyges Stin Anatoliki Evropi*, ed. Anna Karapanou (Athina: Idryma tis Voulis ton Ellinon, 2017), 21.

31. Filippos Fylaktos, *Pos ezisa stin politiki mou prosfygia* [How I lived in political exile] (Athina, 1990), 617.

32. Compare Ned Richardson-Little, *The Human Rights Dictatorship: Socialism, Global Solidarity and Revolution in East Germany* (Cambridge: Cambridge University Press, 2020), and James Mark and Paul Betts, eds., *Socialism Goes Global: The Soviet Union and Eastern Europe in the Age of Decolonisation* (Oxford: Oxford University Press, 2022).

33. Katarína Zavacká, "Cenzúra v Československu v rokoch 1945–1948" [Censorship in Czechoslovakia between 1945 and 1948], in *Evropa mezi Německem a Ruskem* [Europe between Germany and Russia], ed. Miroslav Šesták and Emil Vondráček (Prague: Historický ústav AV ČR, 2000), 555–65.

34. "Pro pomoc demokratickému Řecku a proti běsnění monarchofašistické vlády" [For aid to a democratic Greece and against the rage of the monarch-fascist government], *Právo lidu*, June 18, 1948.

to refugees by the Czechoslovak public. They also illustrate how early understandings of the "political refugee" in the Eastern bloc built upon the myth of a continuous antifascist struggle.[35]

In line with this trend, postwar Czechoslovakia accentuated the importance of its wider population's political loyalty. After liberation in May 1945, the country violently expelled its indigenous German-speaking population, assigning them collective responsibility for assisting Nazi Germany. With the full knowledge of the authorities and the complicity of the armed forces, but without formal approval from the Allied Powers, Czechoslovak Germans became refugees after being the target of massacres by civilians and widespread persecution in the initial violent stage of the expulsion from May to September 1945.[36] Continued as an "organized" transfer from January to October 1946, in line with the decision of the Allied Powers at the Potsdam conference, the expulsion eventually encompassed nearly three million German civilians. Only about three hundred thousand people of German ethnicity remained in the country, often allowed to stay because of their role in the local economy.[37] A much smaller share of Czechoslovakia's Hungarian minority was also deported. The Potsdam conference did not support their mass expulsion.[38]

Before their expulsion, local Germans were Czechoslovak citizens. Although they gained German citizenship after the annexation of the Czechoslovak borderland by Nazi Germany in 1938, they were recognized as Czechoslovak citizens after the war on the grounds of the previously declared nullity of the Munich agreement, recognized by Allied

---

35. Nikola Tohma and Julia Reinke, "Like We Would Help Brothers or Sisters"? Practising Solidarity with Greek Civil War Refugees in Socialist Czechoslovakia and the GDR in the Shadow of World War II," *International Review of Social History* 69, S32 (2024): 13–41, https://doi.org/10.1017/S0020859024000063.

36. Compare R. M. Douglas, *Orderly and Humane: The Expulsion of the Germans after the Second World War* (New Haven, CT: Yale University Press, 2013); Philipp Ther and Ana Siljak, eds., *Redrawing Nations: Ethnic Cleansing in East-Central Europe, 1944–1948* (Lanham, MD: Rowman & Littlefield, 2001); Eagle Glassheim, *Cleansing the Czechoslovak Borderlands: Migration, Environment, and Health in the Former Sudetenland* (Pittsburgh: University of Pittsburgh Press, 2016).

37. Kateřina Čapková, "Between Expulsion and Rescue: The Transports for German-Speaking Jews of Czechoslovakia in 1946," *Holocaust and Genocide Studies* 32, no. 1 (April 2018): 69, https://doi.org/10.1093/hgs/dcy005.

38. About 40,000 out of 650,000 Czechoslovak Hungarians were forced to flee or were transported after the war in relation to their wartime deeds; 75,000 Hungarians left the country based on the Hungarian-Czechoslovak population exchange; and 50,000 of them were subject to internal forced displacement. Jan Křen, *Dvě století střední Evropy* [Two centuries of Central Europe] (Prague: Argo, 2019), 544.

Powers.³⁹ To provide a legal framework for their denaturalization, the (noncommunist) Czechoslovak president Edvard Beneš issued a series of decrees, in particular decree no. 33/1945 on the revocation of citizenship, which was enacted in early August 1945. Czechoslovak citizens of German and Hungarian ethnicity who had gained German or Hungarian nationality from the occupying powers lost their Czechoslovak citizenship immediately, while others were stripped of it on August 10, 1945, when the decree came into force.⁴⁰ The decree exempted only those who "remained loyal to the Czechoslovak republic, have never committed any offenses against the Czech and Slovak nations and either actively participated in the struggle for its liberation or suffered under Nazi or fascist terror," while also imposing the burden of proof on those affected.⁴¹ The decree, as Polish historian Piotr M. Majewski emphasizes, turned these formerly Czechoslovak citizens into "undesirable citizens of another state," formally legalizing their expulsion.⁴² Further presidential decrees enforced the nationalization of agricultural land belonging to "Germans, Hungarians as well as traitors and enemies of the Czech and Slovak nations," the introduction of work duty, expropriation of large businesses and industrial plants, and the confiscation of movable and immovable assets.⁴³

Assessing the reception of Greek Civil War refugees by Czechoslovakia in the context of the population expulsions from Greece and Czechoslovakia is important for two reasons. First, the two cases illustrate the postwar shifting of focus from ethnically to ideologically conditioned loyalty, required from its population by Czechoslovakia, turning communist, and Greece solidifying as an anticommunist state. This reconceptualization then impacted the understanding of citizenship in both countries as reserved to ideologically "reliable" groups of

---

39. Detlef Brandes, *Cesta k vyhnání 1938–1945: Plány a rozhodnutí o "transferu" Němců z Československa a z Polska* [The road to expulsion 1938-1945: Plans and decisions on the "transfer" of Germans from Czechoslovakia and Poland] (Prague: Prostor, 2002), 125–41.

40. Constitutional Decree no. 33/1945, Art. 1. Although the decree relied on ethnic criteria, its authors avoided a clearer definition for the sake of greater flexibility regarding the ethnically mixed population in the borderland. Dieter Gosewinkel and Matěj Spurný, "Citoyenneté et expropriation en Tchécoslovaquie au lendemain des deux guerres mondiales," *Revue d'histoire moderne & contemporaine* 61, no. 1 (2014): 46–47.

41. Constitutional decree no. 33/1945, Art. 2.

42. Piotr Maciej Majewski, *Sudetští Němci: 1848–1948. Dějiny jednoho nacionalismu* [Sudeten Germans: 1848-1948. A history of one nationalism] (Brno: Conditio Humana, 2014), 420.

43. See the series of presidential decrees on confiscation and redistribution of property and labour duty: no. 12/1945; no. 71/1945; no. 108/1945; as well as nationalization decrees no. 100–104/1945.

people. Even the ethnic cleansing of Czechoslovak Germans gradually acquired ideological overtones, being fully endorsed by the KSČ, whose leadership played the antifascist card while enforcing nationalist policies. Thus, second, the subsequent spatial replacement of the unwanted Czechoslovak Germans by communist refugees from Greece became symbolic as the latter assisted Czechoslovakia in the "(re)colonization" of the vacated borderlands, keeping it clear from disloyal residents.[44]

To provide a few examples, upon their arrival in Czechoslovakia, the Greek Civil War refugees were first quarantined in reception centers while waiting for resettlement. One of these facilities, the Svatobořice refugee camp, had previously accommodated German refugees until September 1949.[45] In some cases, the newcomers from Greece received personal belongings taken from Germans, such as clothing, stocked in the reserves of the Ministry of Interior or directly distributed within the camp from the estates of deceased Germans.[46] The Greek Civil War refugees later settled in villages and houses formerly occupied by Germans. Thus, the expropriated German property was turned into humanitarian relief for refugees from Greece.[47] As the latter were moving into the formerly German-inhabited areas, the remaining German residents had to relocate to provide space.[48]

Although, on a larger scale, the German population, facing the arrival of Czechoslovak colonizers, had started retreating earlier,[49] the settlement of civil war refugees exposed the logic of these population transfers even more clearly. The Czechoslovak aid to these refugees and the expulsions of Germans happened in parallel to represent two sides of the same coin: they not only testified to the redefinition of who were (un)wanted citizens in postwar Czechoslovakia, but also offered a more

---

44. Compare David Gerlach, "Beyond Expulsion: The Emergence of 'Unwanted Elements' in the Postwar Czech Borderlands, 1945–1950," *East European Politics and Societies* 24, no. 2 (May 2010): 269–93; Matěj Spurný, *Nejsou jako my: Česká společnost a menšiny v pohraničí (1945–1960)* [They are not like us: Czech society and minorities in the borderlands] (Prague: Antikomplex, 2011), 30–81.

45. Moravian Provincial Archive (MZA) B 293, karton 13, Report on the dissolution of the Svatobořice camp, 1950.

46. Security Services Archives (ABS) E 6 inv. j. 77, Report, May 3, 1948; MZA B 293, karton 13, List of items from the belongings of deceased Germans distributed in the medical center in Svatobořice, March 29, 1950.

47. NACR 1261/2 KSČ ÚV 100/3 Sv. 143, a. j. 559, Minutes of the meeting from September 7, 1949.

48. NACR 1261/2 KSČ ÚV 100/3 Sv. 140, a. j. 547, Report from the refugee settlements in Žamberk, Jeseník a Krnov districts between September 26 and 28, 1949.

49. Spurný, *Nejsou jako my*, 48–61.

general observation about citizenship that the inclusion of one group often entails the exclusion of the other.

Asylum or Hospitality? Between Political Refugees and Foreign Nationals

The politicization of civil war refugees as "loyal" comrades who could replace German "traitors" also influenced their putative legal status in the country. Rather than determined by law, their residency rights as stateless persons were dictated by the political interests of the communist leadership. The refugees featured in administrative documents, political speeches, and media outlets across the Eastern bloc as "political emigration," "freedom fighters," and "Democratic Greeks."[50] Rhetorically, they were endowed with a strongly symbolic status, entitling them not solely to humanitarian aid but also to vaguely defined "political asylum." This section offers a closer look at the meaning of this term and its practical implications for the legal and social status of its holders. The argument that the refugee protection in communist Czechoslovakia was politically arbitrary and oriented at providing full material support without any legal guarantees adds to this chapter's understanding of socialist citizenship primarily as an ideologically conditioned and politically volatile grant of social rights.

Most Eastern bloc countries granted asylum under their post-1945 "Sovietized" constitutions, following the example of the 1936 Constitution of the USSR.[51] Yet Czechoslovakia only included asylum in its constitution of July 11, 1960.[52] Until then, the right of asylum was regulated neither constitutionally nor under ordinary law. Instead, it was rooted in interwar administrative practices, consisting mostly of granted residence rights and domicile (*Heimatrecht*).[53] After 1948, Czechoslovakia continued using "asylum" as an administrative

---

50. The term "Democratic Greeks" refers to Greek Civil War refugees as related to the DSE and in juxtaposition to the presumably nondemocratic Greece.

51. According to it, "the USSR grants the right of asylum to foreign citizens persecuted for defending the interests of workers, or scientific activity, or the national liberation struggle," Constitution of the USSR, December 5, 1936, Ch. 10, Art. 129.

52. According to it, "the Czechoslovak Socialist Republic shall grant the right of asylum to citizens of a foreign state persecuted for defending the interests of the working people, for participating in the national liberation movement, for scientific or artistic work, or for activity in defence of peace." Constitution of Czechoslovakia of July 11, 1960, Art. 33.

53. David Kryska, "Právo azylu v Listině základních práv a svobod v historické perspektivě" [The right of asylum in the Charter of Fundamental Rights and Freedoms in historical perspective], *Správní právo* 48, no. 3 (2015): 133, 144–45, 147.

measure, providing residential rights or citizenship of "asylum" seekers. Analogous to Soviet practice, "asylum" had a purely political character. This character influenced the reasons for which asylum was granted, cementing its role as a tool of domestic and foreign policy.[54] In December 1948, the Ministry of Interior indicated that asylum could be granted to "foreigners who fled from a country that persecuted them for their communist, socialist, and antifascist convictions."[55]

In March 1953, the Social Department of the Czechoslovak Red Cross, a semi-independent organization responsible for administering the personal agenda of political refugees, including their representation in communication with state authorities, interpreted the absence of a sufficient legal basis for "asylum" as a deficiency, leading to "political refugees being legally put on a par with other foreigners although it is desirable for the people's democratic republic to differentiate their status."[56] That is, the organization captured the discrepancy between the politically desirable status of a refugee and its absence in the law. That starkly contrasted with the situation of foreign nationals who did not have any social privileges but whose legal status was determined by their foreign citizenship. Indeed, in the same year, the Ministry of Interior proposed a draft resolution that would introduce political asylum into the legal system.[57] Yet the issue remained unresolved until the constitutional change of 1960.

The use of the term "political asylum" in the Eastern bloc, Czechoslovakia included, also played a role in local propaganda. Although not signatories of the 1951 Refugee Convention, the Eastern bloc countries contributed to the emergence of an alternative refugee regime. They introduced a contrasting model, which welcomed political refugees from the West and challenged the idea that political refugees were fleeing solely from communism. The aim of this propaganda was to discredit Western countries and associated concepts of liberal democracy and freedom. The term "political refugee" was used to emphasize the joint mission of the Eastern bloc countries to protect communist refugees from capitalist countries. The Czechoslovak authorities thus described

---

54. Kryska, "Právo azylu," 141.
55. NACR 1261/2 KSČ-ÚV-100/3 Sv. 2, a. j. 6, Report on illegal border crossings, December 14, 1948.
56. Antula Botu and Milan Konečný, *Řečtí uprchlíci: Kronika řeckého lidu v Čechách, na Moravě a ve Slezsku 1948–1989* [Greek refugees: Chronicle of the Greek people in Bohemia, Moravia, and Silesia 1948–1989] (Prague: Řecká obec Praha, 2005), 356.
57. NACR 1169 ČSČK k. 26, Granting of asylum to political emigrants.

their treatment of refugees—who were "invited" (*pozvání*)—as an act of "hospitality" (*pohostinství*).⁵⁸ This selection of words emphasized the planned rather than spontaneous character of the refugee reception, as well as the expected temporality of their stay. In contrast, the term "shelter" (*přístřeší*) was employed for child refugees, as it better suited the usual understanding of children as particularly vulnerable victims of the "barbarian" West.⁵⁹

Most refugees from Greece reached Czechoslovakia without documents, making it difficult to confirm their identities. This data collection was particularly complicated in the case of refugee children, given their low age and the frequent absence of accompanying parents. Even those arriving with their families often struggled to provide official documentation. For instance, Georgios Karadzos (1941-2015) did not know his exact date of birth when he arrived in Czechoslovakia, as his documents had been burned during the Greek Civil War. He only settled the issue with the Hellenic Red Cross after 1989.⁶⁰ One of his brothers, born on a ship that evacuated the refugees from Albania to Poland, for many years gave the Mediterranean Sea as the place of his birth, realizing only later that, being born on a Polish ship, his actual place of birth should be Poland. Nevertheless, he never established the data as officially recognized by the authorities.⁶¹ Unlike their parents and grandparents, children were particularly vulnerable concerning their statelessness.⁶² They lacked personal experience of stable citizenship and frequently remained stateless until adulthood or even for the duration of their lives. While Ilios Yannakakis (1931-2017) spoke of a "great psychological rift" in the first generation of refugees, who "hoped for a return to Greece but realized it was not possible,"⁶³ Praxitelis Makris

---

58. Konstantinos Tsivos, *Řecká emigrace v Československu (1948–1968)—od jednoho rozštěpení ke druhému* [Greek emigration in Czechoslovakia (1948-1968): In between two splits] (Prague: FSV UK: Dokořán, 2012), 161.

59. "2000 řeckých dětí přijede do ČSR" [2,000 Greek children will arrive in Czechoslovakia], *Rudé Právo*, April 3, 1948; see also Monika Janfelt, "War in the Twentieth Century," in *Encyclopedia of Children and Childhood in History and Society*, ed. Paula S. Fass (New York: Thomson Gale, 2004), 875.

60. Paměť národa, "Sixty Years After" Collection, interview with Georgios Karadzos by Kateřina Králová, Semily, May 22, 2010.

61. Karadzos, *Ukradené slunce*, 25.

62. Tara Zahra, *The Lost Children: Reconstructing Europe's Families after World War II* (Cambridge, MA: Harvard University Press, 2011).

63. Paměť národa, "Sixty Years After" Collection, interview with Ilios Yannakakis by Tereza Vorlová, Prague, December 3, 2010.

(born in 1953) described his peers in his 1986 novel as "a generation of lifelong outcasts" who spent decades living "in a vacuum."[64]

Alongside their ethnicity and other personal information, refugees' statelessness, literally "homelessness" (*bezdomovectví*) in the Czechoslovak state's bureaucratese,[65] was listed in gray-colored interim identity cards that the National Security Corps, the Czechoslovak national police, issued shortly after their arrival. These cards entitled their holders to residency in Czechoslovakia and were valid for up to two years, after which it was necessary to reapply.[66] Children below fifteen years of age were provided with a red-colored variant, subject to regional child welfare authorities.[67] The declared status of adult refugees as "political asylees" provided the official justification for their stay in the Czechoslovak territory and constituted a prerequisite for future granting of residence permits.[68]

The fact that both the International Department of the Central Committee of the KSČ and the KKE's leadership had a major say in this administrative procedure put the refugees into a vulnerable position. They relied on the goodwill of the political elite without having access to credible legal protection.[69] In an authoritarian climate, where the secret police monitored citizens and foreigners alike, refugees' political protection was often arbitrary, even used to justify internal party purges.[70] Indeed, Czechoslovak authorities effectively revoked the political "asylum" of some factionists, whom they blamed for undermining communist unity, by expelling them from the country.[71] At any moment they might face extradition and political persecution in Greece. Like the rest of the Eastern bloc, Czechoslovakia was not among the signatories of the 1951 Refugee Convention, which together with its

---

64. Makris, *Děti vyděděnců*, 114.
65. According to the order no. 28 of the Ministry for National Security from June 9, 1953, a "homeless" person was defined as "a person who is neither a Czechoslovak citizen, nor can prove to be a foreign national by presenting a valid passport."
66. Security Services Archive (ABS), B 7_9-2 inv. j. 89, Temporary identity card for stateless persons.
67. ABS, B 5_5-1 inv. j. 11. Temporary identity card for children from Greece.
68. Compare Zákon č. 52/1949 Sb., o hlášení obyvatelstva a o povolování pobytu cizincům [Act no. 52/1949 about population registry and residence permits for foreigners].
69. Milan Bárta, "Politická emigrace v Československu po únoru 1948," in *Únor 1948 v Československu: Nástup komunistické totality a proměny společnosti* (Prague: ÚSD AV ČR, 2011), 177.
70. Ondřej Vojtěchovský, *Z Prahy proti Titovi! Jugoslávská prosovětská emigrace v Československu* (Prague: FF UK, 2012), 111. Also, Kryska, "Právo azylu," 147.
71. For instance, ABS A 2/2, II. díl, i.j. 249, Fractionism of Greek political emigration; and i.j. 928 Resolution of the Bureau of the CC KSČ from June 9, 1964.

1967 Protocol was a groundbreaking achievement in defining who a refugee is and stipulating the rights of asylees and the responsibilities of nations toward them.[72] Its legal system thus also did not follow the principle of non-refoulement.[73] Furthermore, the Ministry of Interior could revoke or refuse residency permits and Czechoslovak citizenship.[74] Refugees were entirely dependent on the political whims of the Czechoslovak state.

Apart from communist renegades, Czechoslovakia also expelled at least forty-three out of several hundred POWs of the Greek royalist army, forcibly taken to the Eastern bloc countries together with the evacuating DSE.[75] Even later, in the more settled 1960s, the Czechoslovak secret police perceived any independent communication with the Greek Embassy as a potential threat to national security.[76] At the same time, Czechoslovakia was responsive to visa requests from family members of refugees and enabled family reunifications. Unsurprisingly, the government assessed their applications on political criteria in order to ensure their reliability.[77]

Stateless refugees faced other bureaucratic obstacles while dealing with personal and family issues. Stripped of their right of domicile in Greece, they could not contact Greek authorities to obtain copies of missing documents, such as birth and marriage certificates. After multiple interventions by the Central Greek Administration, a formally self-governing body operating under the KKE's control, and the Czechoslovak Red Cross, Czechoslovak authorities gradually adapted to this everyday reality of the refugees, exempting the refugees from

---

72. Gilad Ben-Nun, "From *Ad Hoc* to Universal: The International Refugee Regime from Fragmentation to Unity 1922–1954," *Refugee Survey Quarterly* 34, no. 2 (2015): 23–44.

73. This principle "prohibits states from transferring or removing individuals from their jurisdiction or effective control when there are substantial grounds for believing that the person would be at risk of irreparable harm upon return, including persecution, torture, ill treatment or other serious human rights violations." Compare "The Principle of Non-refoulement under International Human Rights Law," OHCHR, https://www.ohchr.org/sites/default/files/Documents/Issues/Migration/GlobalCompactMigration/ThePrinciple Non-RefoulementUnderInternationalHumanRightsLaw.pdf.

74. Kryska, "Právo azylu," 147–48.

75. ABS A 2/1, I. díl, i. j. 1392, Greek monarchofacists"; also i. j. 1451, Imposition of detention for eighty-three Greek nationals. See also Ondřej Hladík, "Georgios Papanikas—Řek, kterého nechala StB zmizet" [Georgios Papanikas—The Greek whom the StB made disappear], *Paměť a Dějiny* 3 (2016): 47–56.

76. ABS A 9 inv. j. 269, Report on attempts of Greek political emigrants to leave from Czechoslovakia.

77. ABS A 2-2, II. díl, i.j. 516, Reunification of families of Greek emigration.

submitting certain usual documents to lessen their burden.[78] Despite that, there were numerous cases of unofficial or unrecognized marriages and children born out of them as well as protracted divorces, which took many years to settle.[79]

Although civil war refugees were granted residency in Czechoslovakia, the government largely ignored the issue of their statelessness. Legislatively, it prioritized returning Czechoslovak citizenship to Hungarians and Germans who continued to reside on Czechoslovak soil. They achieved this with laws passed in October 1948 and April 1953. Czechoslovak authorities perceived this step as a way to increase political influence on these groups and "educate [them], in the spirit of proletarian internationalism, [as] loyal citizens of our people's democratic state."[80]

In November 1952, refugees from Greece were neither included in Czechoslovak statistics that recorded the presence of approximately fifty-two thousand stateless persons in the country, nor mentioned in the categories of individual stateless groups.[81] The 1962/63 survey by the Czechoslovak Red Cross then indicated that the refugees themselves continued reporting Greek nationality regardless of most of them being stateless. While 8,452 out of 8,574 adult participants claimed Greek citizenship, 116 refugees had been granted Czechoslovak citizenship. Only six refugees stated no citizenship.[82] These two pieces of evidence suggest that the refugees themselves largely preferred to be treated as temporary residents in the country, and the Czechoslovak state understood it this way. The refugees put any resolution of their citizenship on hold, instead waiting for the political winds to change in Greece. After all, statelessness did not hinder them from living normal lives in Czechoslovakia. As this section has shown, the legal parameters of the refugees' stay in Czechoslovakia were of lesser importance to both the state and the refugees. Indeed, it took decades for many of them to formally define their legal status in the country or even to establish their correct personal data in identity documents. The ideological justification of their stay as political refugees overshadowed any such technical debates. But the political support of refugees by the authoritarian state

---

78. NACR 850/1 MV II-T sign. T-C 223 k. 13, Marriages of Greeks.
79. Botu and Konečný, *Řečtí uprchlíci*, 267.
80. NACR 850/1 MV II-T sign. 465 k. 216, Minutes of the meeting at the Ministry of Interior on February 13, 1952, on labor duty of stateless persons.
81. NACR 850/1 MV II-T sign. 465 k. 216, New legislative regulation of state-citizenship relations, November 8, 1952.
82. Tsivos, *Řecká emigrace*, 130.

proved capricious, at times leading to the arbitrary withdrawal of the state protection of individuals whose political loyalty was called into question.

Between Legal and Social Citizenship

This final section sheds light on the ways the refugees from Greece straddled legal citizenship and informal social citizenship. Using the latter, the refugees could transform their statelessness to become less of a burden and more of a resource to be used in the future renegotiation of their legal citizenship in Greece. Similar to foreign nationals, the civil war refugees could apply for Czechoslovak citizenship after a minimum residency of five years.[83] Among the main criteria, the review process considered the applicants' criminal record, political profile, and class origin. Authorities would delve into the applicant's personal views toward building socialism, past political affiliations, and their attitudes regarding the Nazi occupation of Czechoslovakia during World War II.[84]

In contrast to ethnically defined political loyalty enforced by the Greek and Czechoslovak governments in their postwar revocations of citizenship, Czechoslovakia came to define loyalty as ideologically rooted, characterized by communist solidarity. Serbian anthropologist Jelena Vasiljević, who investigated connections between solidarity and citizenship in socialist Yugoslavia, claims that "the former usually operates as the 'social glue' for the latter, holding together its formal components such as rights, duties, and membership criteria."[85] She highlights the principle of "brotherhood and unity" and solidarity with "all our working people" as the cornerstones of socialist Yugoslav citizenship. She claims that "the question of with whom we should be solidary and why . . . has a functional role in maintaining citizenship agendas and changes to support and enable shifts in those agendas."[86]

---

83. Zákon č. 194/1949 Sb. o nabývání a pozbývání československého státního občanství [Act No. 194/1949 Coll. on the acquisition and loss of Czechoslovak citizenship].

84. NACR 850/1 MV II-T sign. 213 k. 192 Directive for processing applications of foreigners for Czechoslovak citizenship employed in enterprises important for the defense of the state pursuant to Act No. 131/36 Coll. 6, par. 22 on the defense of the state.

85. Jelena Vasiljević, "Solidarity Reasoning and Citizenship Agendas: From Socialist Yugoslavia to Neoliberal Serbia," *East European Politics and Societies: And Cultures* 35, no. 2 (May 2021): 272, https://doi.org/10.1177/0888325420923023.

86. Vasiljević, "Solidarity Reasoning."

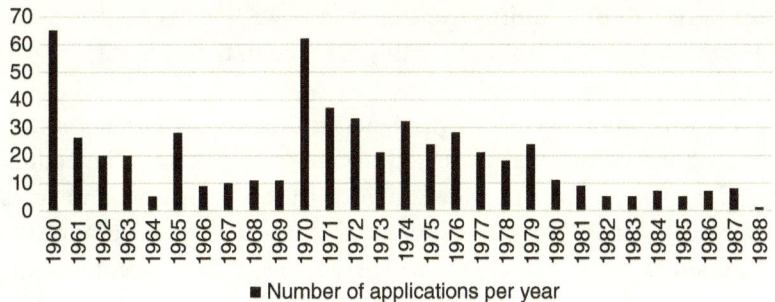

FIGURE 5.1 Granting of Czechoslovak citizenship to refugees from Greece, 1960–1988.

Yet while the principle of solidarity could have eased the refugees' legal status in Czechoslovakia, very few of them ever applied for Czechoslovak citizenship. Citizenship requests were only first recorded in 1960; between then and 1988, only 522 refugees from Greece received Czechoslovak citizenship (see figure 5.1). The number of mixed marriages over a similar period was about three times higher—1,574 between 1958 and 1991,[87] showing that even marriage with a Czechoslovak citizen was not sufficient motivation to opt for local citizenship. The higher numbers of applications for Czechoslovak citizenship during the years of the anticommunist junta in Greece (1967–1974) suggest that the worsening political situation was leaving some of the refugees helpless.

The majority of the refugees nevertheless aimed to return to Greece in the future. Since the Czechoslovak law forbade dual citizenship, they feared that relinquishing their right to Greek citizenship could thwart their return and their ability to reclaim confiscated property. Therefore, they largely opted to preserve their status quo until their repatriation was made possible by political changes in Greece in the 1970s and the 1980s. As the memory of the Greek refugee Tanasis Avukatos illustrates, rather than being purely pragmatic, their choice was an expression of a deeply rooted sense of national belonging: "We were raised to leave one day. Everyone wanted to return [to Greece]. Although Czechia was our second homeland, still, we were foreigners. . . . We were not Czechs, and even if we were integrated . . ., we refused to become Czechs as we expected to leave one day."[88] While the refugees' positive sentiment about Greece was rooted in their identification with an imagined

---

87. Botu and Konečný, *Řečtí uprchlíci*, 370–71.
88. Paměť národa, "Sixty Years After" Collection, interview with Tanasis Avukatos by Karin Hofmeisterová, Prague, January 6, 2011.

Greek national community, their long-term dwelling in Czechoslovakia and their sense of gratitude inevitably resulted in their identifying with their "second home" as well.

Even without citizenship, residency rights entitled refugees to a wide range of social benefits. In addition to free health care and education, the socialist state provided them with jobs, housing, and access to social security.[89] Work represented not only a duty but also a right accompanied with entitlement to leisure time, paid leave, maternity support, child care, and pension.[90] In its July 1950 statement, the Ministry of Labor and Social Care underlined the importance of providing refugees with unconditional access to such rights by calling it "not a [mere] administrative measure but a political task by which Greeks are made equal to Czech citizens."[91] In stark contrast with the conception of citizenship in the Western world, socialist citizenship thus distinguished less between formal citizens and mere residents, allowing for more seamless social and economic inclusion.

Despite their open-ended status, refugees enjoyed unprecedented social stability, especially compared to Western Europe and the United States. They could rely—as Karadzos emphasizes—on "the certainty of working hours, meaning 8 hours at work, after which everyone could do whatever they wanted, had a certain salary . . . and everyone had more or less the same."[92] Under state socialism, the importance of access to social benefits often stood higher than formal citizenship. Expressing gratitude to his host country, refugee Agorastos Dimoschakis exclaimed, "They gave us a job, they gave us a flat, they gave us everything. How can we forget?"[93] In contrast, he evaluated the situation of returnees to Greece in a negative light: "Did you know how many of us committed suicide after they returned to Greece? The Greek state did not take care of them. They had no radio, no electricity, no care. They were capitalist there."[94] This quote illustrates the vast gap between the

---

89. Jan Kuklík, *Czech Law in Historical Contexts* (Prague: Karolinum, 2015), 180–82.

90. Mark B. Smith, "Social Rights in the Soviet Dictatorship: The Constitutional Right to Welfare from Stalin to Brezhnev," *Humanity* 3, no. 3 (2012): 387–88.

91. NACR 1261/2 KSČ ÚV 100/3 Sv. 143, a. j. 559, Minutes of the meeting held on June 2, 1950, in Krnov in the presence of representatives of the Ministry of Labor and Social Care, Greek self-government and district commissioners].

92. Paměť národa, "Sixty Years After" Collection, interview with Georgios Karadzos by Kateřina Králová, Semily, May 22, 2010.

93. Paměť národa, "Sixty Years After" Collection, interview with Agorastos a Eleni Dimoschaki by Janis Koreček, Šumperk, October 22, 2010.

94. Agorastos and Eleni Dimoschaki interview.

conceptions of citizenship in socialist and capitalist countries, highlighting that noncitizens in socialist countries possessed more social rights and interrelated responsibilities than did citizens in capitalist countries.

In Czechoslovakia, refugees derived access to these benefits from their contribution to the building of socialism through political, intellectual, and physical labor. As numerous scholars note, the collective right and duty to work was central to the socialist conception of citizenship. Analyzing the case of Romani rights in postwar Czechoslovakia, Celia Donert theorized this social citizenship as an Eastern alternative to Western understandings of social rights as "legal or moral abstractions protecting individual citizens from the state." Drawing on Marxism, socialist regimes conceived rights as state-guaranteed entitlement to "material" benefits—an "access to goods and services—such as health care, education, food, or housing—provided by the state in return for citizens fulfilling their collective duty to work."[95]

Eastern bloc countries imposed social rights from above on a collective basis, ranking the political loyalty and class origin of their recipients over their economic impact. Mark B. Smith links the right to work in the USSR to "the right to access a universe of welfare and a certain standard of living."[96] According to him, welfare in the Soviet Union represented both a paternalistic grant from the authorities and a vulnerable right pledged by the constitution. But it was not guaranteed by any independent institution.[97]

Whereas T. H. Marshall identified rights as civil, political, and social in postwar, capitalist England, in socialist countries social rights thus constituted the core of citizenship.[98] Researching citizenship in socialist Yugoslavia, Igor Štiks, for instance, shows how the regime did little to guarantee civil and political rights but did enforce social and cultural rights, in particular women's rights.[99] In Czechoslovakia, refugees enjoyed not only social rights equal to those of Czechoslovak citizens but were also provided with considerable cultural autonomy and offered

---

95. Celia Donert, *The Rights of the Roma: The Struggle for Citizenship in Postwar Czechoslovakia* (Cambridge: Cambridge University Press, 2020), 6.
96. Smith, "Social Rights," 385.
97. Smith, 386.
98. Thomas H. Marshall, *Citizenship and Social Class and Other Essays* (Cambridge: Cambridge University Press, 1950), 10–14.
99. Štiks, *Nations and Citizens*, 14–15.

education both in Czech and their mother tongues.[100] The country also strove to challenge patriarchal structures within the Greek community by supporting the emancipation of refugee women.[101]

Yet, as Štiks contends, the experience of rights in real life (rather than their mere formal possession) is what actually mattered. The reality of living under an authoritarian regime limited political participation.[102] In socialist states, the practices of political inclusion and exclusion were directly related to one's membership in the domestic Communist Party and participation in mass organizations. In this sense, the social citizenship granted to refugees failed to provide them with full access to the Czechoslovak national community. While being able to organize politically in workplaces and public associations, as noncitizens refugees were denied the right to vote, to be elected, and to become members of domestic political parties. Unlike in other Eastern bloc countries (but as in the USSR), the KSČ did not allow membership of foreign nationals, although the KKE repeatedly yet unsuccessfully requested that its members be accepted.[103] The refugees could join the local organization of the KKE, but because it was not a legally registered political party, it had practically no say on issues outside the Greek community.[104]

The civil war refugees were not subject to the obligation of military service. The fact that this was probably perceived as an advantage can be illustrated by the argument made by the Czechoslovak Ministry of Interior in 1952 on behalf of stateless Germans and their reluctance to apply for citizenship: "All homeless [stateless] persons agree that they would not acquire much by being granted Czechoslovak citizenship because even without it, they enjoy, all in all, the same benefits as our citizens: jobs, wages, medical treatment, vacation, provisions, and others, but they do not share equal duties, the obligation of military service, in the first place."[105] This quote illustrates how some authorities understood the rights and duties of citizenship under socialism.

---

100. Miloš Hájek and Olga Stašková, *Národnostní otázka v lidově demokratickém Československu* [Ethnic issues in the People's Democratic Czechoslovakia] (Prague: SNPL, 1956), 39–42.

101. Antula Botu, "Řecká etnická skupina v Československu" [Greek ethnic group in Czechoslovakia], *Český Lid* 69, no. 1 (1982): 49.

102. Štiks, *Nations and Citizens*, 5–6.

103. NACR 1261/2 KSČ ÚV 100/3 Sv. 146, a.j. 572, Information on requests of the KKE suggested by its Politburo members], January 19, 1951; Sv. 143, a.j. 554, Debate with comrade Bardzodas, March 28, 1952.

104. Králová and Tsivos, *Vyschly nám slzy*, 201.

105. NACR 850/1 MV II-T sign. 465 k. 216 Minutes of the meeting held in the Ministry of the Interior on February 13, 1952, on keeping stateless persons, permanently settled in the territory of Czechoslovakia, on working duty.

The absence of references to obligatory military service by civil war refugees indicates that their exclusion from this duty was not perceived as a hardship.

On the contrary, refugees resented the existing travel restrictions, which were imposed on Czechoslovak citizens as well. The refugees could, theoretically, apply for a Greek passport, as Greek nationality law was based on the principle of *jus sanguinis*, citizenship by bloodline. Yet the Greek Embassy would only issue passports to "desirable" applicants, that is, to noncommunists and those of Greek (and not Macedonian, that is Slavic) origin, as well as those perceived as economically beneficial.[106] Its representatives often resorted to humiliating, discriminatory practices, demanding that applicants renounce their communist stances in signed "declarations of repentance" (*diloseis metanoias*), which could then be used to discredit them.[107]

Czechoslovakia, in contrast, would issue a travel identity document to substitute for the passports of foreign nationals or stateless persons, provided that they were granted the status of political "asylees."[108] The use of such passports was, however, limited by possible destinations and clearly defined purposes. Group (and not individual) passports were initially issued for travel within the Eastern bloc, mostly within the framework of family visits and reunifications. Visits to Greece, made possible especially in the 1970s and 1980s, were organized and administered for entire groups of travelers. For reasons of "security," meaning defection to a capitalist country, the participants, supervised by an accompanying guide, were usually not in direct possession of their passports. Most importantly, the refugees were required to obtain an exit permit (*výjezdní doložka*), without which they—the same as Czechoslovak citizens—were not allowed to leave the country without being accused of attempting to illegally cross the Czechoslovak border. They had to acquire this permit even after they received a Greek passport. The Czechoslovak authorities argued that their "asylum" made refugees subject to domestic legislative regulations. By this logic, the protection of asylum resulted in asylees being trapped behind the barbed-wire borders.[109]

---

106. ABS FMV, A 11 inv. j. 154, Greek political refugees in Czechoslovakia.
107. Tsivos, *Řecká emigrace*, 162.
108. Kryska, "Právo azylu," 146.
109. Compare Jan Rychlík, *Cestování do ciziny v habsburské monarchii a v Československu. Pasová, vízová a vystěhovalecká politika 1848–1989* [Traveling abroad in Habsburg monarchy and Czechoslovakia. Passport, visa and emigration policies, 1848-1989] (Prague: ÚSD AV ČR, 2007), 65-83.

In Greece, the democratization process that began after 1974 enabled individual refugees to repatriate. Czechoslovakia was supportive of their return, especially of entire families.[110] In July 1975, the Central Committee of the KSČ implied that all applications by the refugees from Greece would be positively resolved "unless there were serious objections."[111] But it was not until 1982 that the newly elected Greek socialist government guaranteed a right of repatriation to *ethnic* Greeks, who as a result of the civil war had become political refugees and lost their citizenship.[112] While recognizing as ethnically Greek anyone with at least one parent of Greek origin, the governmental decision effectively ruled out Greeks of Slavic (Macedonian) origin.[113] In 1983, the Greek government returned citizenship, regardless of repatriation status, automatically to all ethnic Greeks who had lost it based on the respective royal decrees, as well as their children, including those born of mixed marriages.[114] Ethnic Greeks could acquire citizenship through a simple assimilation process; however, Macedonians were forced to declare themselves ethnically Greek or prove their origin with a Greek birth certificate, which they often did not possess.[115] Facing greater obstacles to reclaiming confiscated property, Macedonians often opted to re-emigrate to Yugoslavia. These diverging trajectories of Greek and Macedonian refugees with the common Greek Civil War heritage during this final stage of repatriation, not only to Greece but also to Yugoslavia, represented a blow to the concept of socialist citizenship along with the ideals of social equality and internationalism.

---

110. NACR 1261/0 KSČ ÚV 02/1 Sv. 119, a.j. 118 Greek political emigration in Czechoslovakia.
111. NACR 1261/0 KSČ ÚV 02/4 Sv. 102, a.j. 162/2 [Resolution of the 162nd meeting of the Secretariat of the Central Committee of the KSČ of July 30, 1975].
112. Joint Ministerial Decision of the Ministers of Interior and Public Order no. 106841 of 29 December 1982 (Koini Ypourgiki Apofasi ton ypourgon Esoterikon kai Dimosias Taxis).
113. Eleni Paschaloudi and Stratos Dordanas, "Oi politikoi prosfyges kai i elliniki politeia, 1946-1989: Apo tin sterisi tis ithageneias ston epanapatrismo kai tin apokatastasi" [The political refugees and the Greek state, 1946-1989: From the revocation of citizenship to their repatriation and settlement], in *Praktika imeridas. Ellines politikoi prosfyges stin Anatoliki Evropi*, ed. Anna Karapanou (Athina: Idryma tis Voulis ton Ellinon, 2017), 70-71.
114. Tsekou, *Ellines politikoi prosfyges*, 200.
115. Králová and Tsivos, *Vyschly nám slzy*, 171-72.

Socialist Citizenship and National Belonging

The socialist citizenship that Czechoslovakia embraced in its post-1948 communist era was characterized by the dominance of social duties and rights over civil and political rights. The Czechoslovak emphasis on social rights was closely linked to the socialist understanding that citizenship represented not only a legal bond between citizen and society but also symbolized the belonging of individuals to the imagined community of all working peoples, who direct their joint efforts toward the higher aim of creating a "brave new world" of postwar socialism.

This redefinition of citizenship applied not only to Czechoslovak citizens but also to groups of noncitizens living on Czechoslovak soil: foreign nationals and stateless persons. For them, including the refugees from Greece, embracing communist doctrine and internationalism meant a shift from nationally to ideologically defined political loyalty, which constituted a precondition to obtaining "asylum," residency rights, and citizenship. Ethnicity or race, at least formally, no longer represented an obstacle to acceptance, replaced by class origin, commitment to building socialism, and political status. Those labeled political refugees, particularly former partisans, occupied the privileged position of meritorious comrades. At the same time, though, the absence of a clear delimitation of the term "refugee" and an independent authority to provide protection left refugees at the mercy of the communist leadership.

The provision of universal access to social rights based on political loyalty and internationalist solidarity reduced the practical importance of legal citizenship. For this reason, most civil war refugees declined to give up their Greek nationality despite their successful social integration, even if this meant being stateless for decades. Those who later opted for Czechoslovak citizenship often struggled to identify with it.[116] Social rights were a defining feature of socialist citizenship that filled many of the gaps left by statelessness. Yet they failed to provide refugees with an alternative to their lost sense of national belonging. Also, as most Eastern bloc countries gradually resigned from the utopian internationalist project and opened the way to growing nationalism, taking the form of nationally specific forms of communist rule, socialist citizenship was deprived of its appeal and its unifying power

---

116. Makris, *Děti vyděděnců*, 53; Králová and Tsivos, *Vyschly nám slzy*, 187-93.

that had transcended ethnic divisions within the transnational communist collective.

The inadequacy of social citizenship to meet the affective and material needs of refugees was, of course, connected with the overall collapse of the socialist project in 1989. State socialism was weighed down by the obvious discrepancies between its declared ideals and the everyday practices of "real socialism." Apathy and disenchantment were its fruits, for citizens and stateless alike. Looking at the more recent experience of the "refugee crisis" in Europe, neither material provision nor social security represents sufficient means for the successful integration of migrants. Their social inclusion may easily be in vain if not accompanied by their genuine (and not solely declarative) treatment as equal both in terms of social rights and political participation. Moreover, a sense of ideological belonging, although based on common values, does not seem to provide a sufficient unifying basis for social inclusion if a sense of national belonging is entirely missing.

Nikola Tohma is a postdoctoral research fellow at the Masaryk Institute and Archives of the Czech Academy of Sciences. She is a historian focusing on migration and refugeedom in Central and Southeast Europe. Her chapter was written as a part of the ERC Consolidator project "Unlikely Refuge? Refugees and Citizens in East-Central Europe in the 20th Century" under the European Union's Horizon 2020 research and innovation program (grant agreement No. 819461).

CHAPTER 6

Precarious Citizenship in Olivia Manning's *Balkan Trilogy*

Stanislava Dikova

Anglo-Irish writer Olivia Manning documented her experiences of flight and exile as a British subject across enemy-occupied territory during the Second World War in a trio of novels, known collectively as *The Balkan Trilogy*. The protagonists of this "postwar epic" are Guy and Harriet Pringle, a newly married couple, who, like their real-life counterparts, arrive in Romania on 3 September 1939, the day that Britain declared war on Germany.[1] Harriet joins her husband Guy, a character based on Manning's spouse R. D. 'Reggie' Smith, who is a British Council lecturer in English at the University of Bucharest to begin their married life. The novels chronicle the events from September 1939, including the assassination of Armand Călinescu, then Prime Minister of Romania, through the Balkan state's eventual alliance with Nazi Germany in November 1940, which necessitates Guy and Harriet's flight to allied Greece, to April 1941, when the German army reaches Athens. The trilogy ends as the Pringles and the rest of the British expatriate

---

1. Adam Piette, "World War II: Contested Europe," in *The Cambridge History of Twentieth-Century Literature*, ed. Laura Marcus and Peter Nicholls (Cambridge: Cambridge University Press, 2004), 431. Piette attributes the phrase to Alan Munton's study *English Fiction of the Second World War* (London: Faber & Faber, 1989).

community in the Greek capital make their way across the Mediterranean to Egypt.[2]

The three novels, *The Great Fortune*, *The Spoilt City*, and *Friends and Heroes*, written and published during the 1950s and 1960s, look back to the preceding decade from the political reality of Cold War London, carrying echoes of British political culture in this period. Post-1945 domestic political life was dominated by discussions about the future of the nation and the relationship between the state and its citizens. From a formal and largely legalistic category citizenship was transformed into a key component of wide-ranging political questions stretching from the function of the welfare state to issues pertaining to democratic participation, the rise of neoliberal economics, and immigration policy.[3] Recent historical interpretations have sought to emphasize the relational aspects of this process of conceptual and societal reconstruction. As Matthew Grant writes, citizens' understanding of themselves and their role in society during this period underwent significant transformation and acquired a more dynamic shape through "their interactions with other citizens, the state, and a whole panoply of institutions and organizations."[4] Ruth Lister's position that citizenship is "an expression of human agency in the political arena" and as such is a "fluid process" that "remains the object of political struggles" further emphasizes the role of individual agency and participation in this new framework.[5] The purely relational models however often risk obscuring the more insidious aspects of citizenship as an instrument for the consolidation of state power. Constantin Iordachi argues that citizenship is a form of state-building, which can be instrumentalized to enforce practices of governance and domination upon the populations

---

2. Manning wrote a follow up trilogy, known as *The Levant Trilogy*, documenting their time in Egypt and the Levant region, published between 1977 and 1980.

3. See for example, Glen O'Hara, *Governing Post-War Britain: the Paradoxes of Progress* (Basingstoke: Palgrave Macmillan, 2012); Lawrence Black, *Redefining British Politics: Culture, Consumption, Participation, 1954–1970* (Basingstoke: Palgrave Macmillan, 2010); Kathleen Paul, *Whitewashing Britain: Race and Citizenship in the Postwar Era* (Ithaca, NY: Cornell University Press, 1997); Randell Hansen, *Citizenship and Immigration in Postwar Britain: the Institutional Origins of a Multicultural Nation* (Oxford: Oxford University Press, 2000); James Hampshire, *Citizenship and Belonging: Immigration and the Politics of Demographic Governance in Postwar Britain* (Basingstoke: Palgrave Macmillan, 2005).

4. Matthew Grant, "Historicizing Citizenship in Post-War Britain," *The Historical Journal* 59, no. 4 (2016), 1190.

5. Ruth Lister, *Citizenship: Feminist Perspectives, Second Edition* (Basingstoke: Palgrave Macmillan, 2003), 37.

that fall within its purview.[6] Read in this way citizenship emerges as a threatening construct, which operates to protect state sovereignty by regulating human capital.

Much of postwar British literature was concerned with the complexities of the interactions between state and citizen. In Marina Mackay's view, the fiction of this period contributed to discussions of citizenship by placing heightened scrutiny on the "vertical relationships" between people and government, and offered responses increasingly "marked by skepticism, hostility, and resistance" towards the intrusion of the state in the lives of those who resided within its territory.[7] This orientation is not surprising in a period which saw the British government exercise "unprecedented control over its citizens' lives."[8] Postwar fiction often represented the state as "unaccountable" and "associated with the raw power of the institutions," exercised to curtail the rights of individual citizens.[9] A particular strand of this tradition includes writers such as Graham Greene, Malcolm Lowry, Edith Pargeter, Anthony Burgess, Anthony Powell, Paul Scott, and J. G. Farrell, who turned their attention to chronicling British "diplomatic eclipse and imperial decline," through the medium of post-imperial epic fiction, which gave them a chance to scrutinize the relationship between domestic policies and the positions Britain took on the international stage.[10]

Manning's historical fiction is loosely associated with this direction. The novels in *The Balkan Trilogy* explore Britain's changing geopolitical identity, while also exhibiting a deeper sense of distrust towards the machinery and principles of state organization as a whole. This disposition is partly connected with Manning's experience of having her own personal liberties compromised by state intervention, and partly with her political critique of the state's disregard for individual human suffering, which is why the biographical basis of the trilogy is so poignant and so effective. *The Balkan Trilogy* exposes the fundamental disbalance

---

6. Constantin Iordachi, *Liberalism, Constitutional Nationalism, and Minorities: The Making of Romanian Citizenship, c. 1750–1918* (Boston: Brill, 2019), 6; 8.

7. Marina Mackay, "Citizenship and the English Novel in 1945," in *Around 1945: Literature, Citizenship, Rights*, ed. Allan Hepburn (Montreal: McGill-Queen's University Press, 2016), 31–2.

8. Gill Plain, "Introduction," in *British Literature in Transition, 1940–1960: Postwar*, ed. Gill Plain (Cambridge: Cambridge University Press, 2018), 4.

9. Mackay, "Citizenship and the English Novel," 34.

10. Eve Patten, *Imperial Refugee: Olivia Manning's Fictions of War* (Cork: Cork University Press, 2011), 4.

at the heart of the relationship between state and citizen by portraying citizenship as an imaginary and easily corruptible form of security.

Michel Foucault highlights a similar tension in his discussion on the limits of government, which identifies two main philosophical approaches to this problem in European political thought: a revolutionary and a radical one.[11] The former, exemplified through Rousseau's writings and the legislators of the French Revolution, rests on principles of classical law. It aims to define the original rights that belong to every individual as the natural limits to sovereign power and then to clarify the conditions under which "a limitation or exchange of rights was accepted."[12] The radical approach, on the other hand, scrutinizes the matter from the position of governmental practice. Based on the English utilitarian tradition, it is concerned with the justification of specific governmental practices and technologies of power rather than with the formulation of ideal universal law and holds that the limits of government should be determined on the basis of "utility," not on individual rights. The nature of this utility is determined in correspondence with the interests of the "new economy of government."[13] As Foucault argues, one of the problems with the radical tradition is that it "separates the sphere of intervention of public authorities from that of the individual's independence," leaving the state impervious to accusations of infringement upon individual liberty.[14]

Manning's trilogy undermines the validity of this principle of state legitimacy in two specific ways: firstly, by questioning the capacity of state institutions to fulfil their basic functions and, secondly, by exposing citizenship, the political category which encapsulates the state-individual relation problem, as a precarious construct which deepens the disbalance of power in favor of the state. The novels are rich in examples of dysfunctional state organization, institutional failures, corrupt practices, lack of strategic thought and specialist knowledge, as well as sheer incompetence. This all combines to create an image of the state as a rickety construction, unable to meet its responsibilities to those who fall within its purview, while retaining an absolute power to determine their rights and living circumstances.

---

11. Michel Foucault, *The Birth of Biopolitics: Lectures at the Collège de France 1978–1979*, ed. Michel Senellart, trans. Graham Burchell (Basingstoke: Palgrave Macmillan, 2008), 39–40.
12. Foucault, *The Birth of Biopolitics*, 39.
13. Foucault, 41.
14. Foucault, 41.

This chapter focuses specifically on the second legitimacy crisis. In recent historical and legal literature, precarious citizenship has emerged as a composite concept, which seeks to illustrate the wide range of costs and impacts this condition can inflict on individual lives, from economic to emotional. Noora A. Lori defines precarious citizenship as "the structured uncertainty of being unable to secure citizenship rights."[15] Manning shows that this category can be extended to cover the experiences of those whose citizenship status has ceased to provide them with access to state protection. In territories where borders are frequently renegotiated and redrawn, the citizen becomes an abstract figure with little control over the basic parameters of individual existence, a disembodied instantiation of the "identity management infrastructures" operated by the state to enforce its boundaries.[16]

In their representation of people in flight, in situations of forced and voluntary migration, displacement, and statelessness, the novels in Manning's trilogy speak for persons, citizens and otherwise, disempowered and relentlessly bound by the power of the state. In doing so, they offer an account that focuses on lived human experiences, through which the category of citizenship in conflict and post-conflict zones is shown as particularly volatile and fragile. The following discussion is structured in three sections, each framed around a specific identity management tool used to reinforce the detrimental effects of existential insecurity incurred by experiences of precarious citizenship: identity documentation, citizenship status, and the promise of state protection.

Documents and Dislocations

The *Balkan Trilogy* project began in 1949 when Manning was commissioned to write a feature for the BBC Third Programme based on her wartime dislocation.[17] "A Year I Remember" closely follows the plot of

---

15. Noora A. Lori, "Statelessness, 'In-Between' Statuses, and Precarious Citizenship," in *The Oxford Handbook of Citizenship*, ed. Ayelet Shachar et al. (Oxford: Oxford University Press, 2017), 745–466.

16. Lori, "Statelessness," 473. In this connection, please see Laura Hilton's discussion of statelessness in Chapter 1, Dagmar Wernitznig's treatment of "para-citizenship" in Chapter 3, and Sarah Jacobson on "de-territorialized" citizenship in Chapter 11.

17. The commissioning memo for "A Year I Remember" dates from 16 June 1949. BBC/R/RCONT/RCONT1/24343—Manning, Olivia (Copyright file 1), BBC Written Archives Centre, Caversham, Reading, UK.

the published novels and documents Romania's changing attitudes towards the British, from protectors to enemies, under constant threat of invasion from either Germany or Russia. After the radio program, Manning seems to have laid the topic to rest while she completed four other novels, continued to work as a contributing scriptwriter for the BBC, and published literary reviews, mainly for the *Spectator*.[18] The idea of returning to their experiences of forced migration and turning them into a novel resurfaced in 1956, when it was suggested by Reggie, who pragmatically thought the timing might be good.[19] A potential publication could be scheduled to coincide with the twentieth anniversary of the start of the Second World War.

After a positive response from her publisher, she set to work on the text almost to the exclusion of all other professional obligations.[20] As Deirdre David writes, the political urgency of this moment, which amalgamated the Suez crisis and British imperial decline, the Hungarian Revolution and Cold War fears of invasion and nuclear attack, deepened the associations with the preceding decade and heightened the anxieties she was experiencing.[21] In this way the temporal distance between the two decades is bridged through a shared sense of insecurity around the future of the international world order, which places the individual in harm's way both within and beyond the borders of the nation-state.

The Great Fortune, the first novel in the trilogy, opens with a scene of geopolitical and human dislocation. Guy and Harriet are on the train to Bucharest, "Somewhere near Venice," when they witness the arrest of a German-speaking Jewish refugee in their carriage.[22] The man, having lost his documents is unable to prove his identity when prompted by the ticket inspector. Guy swiftly asks him what has been lost. "Everything. Everything. [. . .]," responds the man, who remains unnamed, "My pocket-book, my passport, my money, my identity card . . . My visa, my visa!"[23] The Pringles, who offer him a thousand-franc note, are

---

18. During this period, she adapted novels by Arnold Bennett, Elizabeth Gaskell, George Eliot, Ada Leverson, and Fanny Burney. BBC/R/RCONT/RCONT1/24343—Manning, Olivia (Copyright file 1); See also Deirdre David, *Olivia Manning: A Woman at War* (Oxford: Oxford University Press, 2013), 252.
19. David, *Olivia Manning*, 252-3.
20. David, 252.
21. David, 253.
22. Olivia Manning, *The Balkan Trilogy* (1960; London: Penguin, 1974), 9.
23. Manning, *The Balkan Trilogy*, 10.

left to wordlessly worry about the fate that awaits him, a human being who had declared only a page earlier that he was "a free man."[24]

Echoing Hannah Arendt's discussion in *The Origins of Totalitarianism*, Manning's description underlines the collective apathy and withdrawal of human feeling exhibited by the refugee's fellow passengers, the ticket inspector, and officials who come to escort him off the train, looking on "dumbly," with "detached interest."[25] The individual helplessness of the refugee is also on full display as he is led away by the guard, his face "expressionless."[26]

States use documents to make people "legible" as legal persons and this problem of legibility, as James Scott argues, is "a central problem in statecraft," due to its direct implications for the limits of government and the formation of national identities.[27] Documentation also legitimates the state's monopoly over the regulation of migration, interstate movement, border control, and eventual access to citizenship rights.[28] The interwar and postwar eras demonstrated the theoretical as well as practical short-sightedness of this system, which "presupposed mutually exclusive citizenries all of whom were distributed uniquely to one state or another," leaving members of minority communities across Europe exposed to prejudicial and discriminatory treatment.[29]

Manning's own text demonstrates a painful awareness of both the privilege granted by the Pringles' British passports and the burden on those unable to secure this all-important documentation. On the same train to Bucharest, another British expatriate, Prince Yakimov, appears on the train platform "carrying in one hand a crocodile dressing-case, in the other a British passport."[30] Prince Yakimov is a cosmopolitan figure of diminished grandeur, reduced to penury by the death of his partner Dolly and forced to flee country after country to escape the encroaching war and his mounting debts. Dressed in his signature sable-lined coat, which he claims was passed down to his family by the Russian Tzar,

---

24. Manning, *The Balkan Trilogy*, 10; 9.
25. Manning, *The Balkan Trilogy*, 10. See also Hannah Arendt, "The Decline of the Nation-State and the End of the Rights of Man," in *The Origins of Totalitarianism* (1951; New York: Meridian Books, 1958).
26. Lori, "Statelessness," 743; Manning, *The Balkan Trilogy*, 11.
27. James C. Scott, *Seeing Like a State: How Certain Schemes to Improve Human Condition Have Failed* (New Haven and London: Yale University Press, 1998), 2 qtd in Lori, "Statelessness," 744.
28. Lori, "Statelessness," 743.
29. John C. Torpey, *The Invention of the Passport: Surveillance, Citizenship and the State*, 2nd Edition (Cambridge: Cambridge University Press, 2018), 152.
30. Manning, *The Balkan Trilogy*, 13.

Yakimov comes from Yugoslavia and is initially accommodated easily with the assistance of the British legation. Through Yakimov's character Manning emphasizes the associated benefits which accompany the possession of the British passport, and the absurdity of grounding citizenship rights in exclusionary judgements around national belonging in the context of a rapidly developing post-imperial international world order. Introducing himself at a later point in the trilogy Yakimov confirms his Englishness as follows: "'Certainly I am. Typical Englishman, you might say. Mother Irish.' 'And your father?' 'Russian. White Russian, of course.'"[31] This example further evokes the history of population exchange which accompanied the British and wider European imperial projects, speaking directly to the postwar moment in which Manning was writing, where questions of belonging began to gather significant prominence against the backdrop of disintegrating empires.

In transposing these questions onto the political context of the Balkans, Manning's trilogy gains terrain and further critical perspective to confront the construction of belonging and exclusion she was observing in Britain in the 1960s, emphasizing the precarious nature of documentation and its obvious connections to ethnic, racial, and religious prejudice. The 1948 British Nationality Act had granted "every person" who is a citizen of the United Kingdom and Colonies, "the status of a British subject," enabling increased immigration from colonial territories.[32] The resulting social and political backlash found legal expression in the changes to the Commonwealth Immigrants Act made by Harold Wilson's Labour government in 1968, under increased pressure by conservatives.[33] Originally passed into law in 1962, the Act had already severed the relationship between citizenship and free movement to Britain from the empire. Holding a British nationality, evidenced by a passport, no longer meant holding citizenship and its associated protections in the eyes of the British state.[34] In this way, the construction of racialized

---

31. Manning, 718.

32. British Nationality Act 1948, UK Public General. Acts, 1948 Chapter 56 <https://www.legislation.gov.uk/ukpga/Geo6/11-12/56/enacted>

33. Sara Cosemans, "On Neoliberalism and Citizenship," in *History Workshop Online*, 3 May 2022 <https://www.historyworkshop.org.uk/on-neoliberalism-and-citizenship/> In this particular legal context, as Cosemans explains immigrants were separated into two groups, "United Kingdom belongers" and "non-belongers." The former applied to those "born, naturalized, or adopted in the United Kingdom or had at least one parent of grandparent in that category;" the latter became subject to immigration control and travel restrictions.

34. Sara Cosemans, "Modern Statelessness and the British Imperial Perspective. A Comment on Mira Siegelberg's Statelessness: A Modern History," *History of European Ideas* 47, no. 5 (2021): 805.

images of national identity, as Kathleen Paul puts it, officially began to outweigh "formal definitions of citizenship."[35]

"Protective Boundaries," Precarious Citizens

Manning returns to the apathy exhibited towards the plight of the refugee, encountered in the opening scene of *The Balkan Trilogy*, several times throughout the novels. We observe another example of collective apathy, when the first wave of Polish refugees following the Soviet invasion of Eastern Poland, begin to arrive in Bucharest.

> Here were parked a dozen or so of the Polish refugee cars that were still streaming down from the north. Some of the cars had been abandoned. From the others women and children, left while the men sought shelter, gazed out blankly. The well-dressed Rumanians, out to appreciate and be appreciated, looked affronted by these ruined faces that were too tired to care. [. . .] stories were already going round about the refugees; old anti-Polish stories remembered from the last war.[36]

The refugees themselves are not given a voice here, and the description conveys a sense of lifelessness, with women and children "gaz[ing] out blankly." Much like the "expressionless" face of the German refugee on the train, they appear stripped of dignity, rights, and recognition—a persistent, if clumsy, feature of Manning's portrayal of refugee groups and victims of violent conflict she observed but with whom she had little direct dealings.

She ascribes the psychology of disinterest to the predicament of refugees exhibited by the observers to national mythologies of exclusion and enmity connected to inter-state hostilities. In Manning's account, these state-manufactured mythologies loosen the connecting threads between human beings and defamiliarize them with each other's suffering, while also strengthening the position of the state itself as a guarantor of rights and protections. As Arendt writes in her analysis of communal complicity with acts of state aggression, "the seeming stability" of the surrounding structures "made each group forced out of its protective boundaries look like an unfortunate exception to an otherwise

---

35. Paul, *Whitewashing Britain*, 189. See also Nadine El-Enany, *(B)ordering Britain: Law, Race and Empire* (Manchester: Manchester University Press, 2020).
36. Manning, *The Balkan Trilogy*, 27–8.

sane and normal rule, and which filled with equal cynicism victims and observers of an apparently unjust and abnormal fate."[37] Though certainly unjust, the novels suggest, this fate is far from abnormal.

When Romanian refugees in turn begin to arrive in Bucharest on crowded trains following Hungary's annexation of Northern Transylvania several months later, they receive even less notice. Streaming into the capital during the interregnum between the King's forced abdication and the establishment of a fascist dictatorship, they receive neither support from their own state, nor assistance from their compatriots. Instead, they pass "their days standing dumbly before any large building where power might reside. Imagining that justice must eventually be brought out to them."[38] This description highlights the volatility of citizenship as a coherent category of political existence, even for those privileged enough to hold it. It also hints at the problem of political agency—the Romanians waiting for a benevolent dispensation from their government, Manning suggests, have relinquished their capacities as political agents capable of demanding more humane treatment, while also endowing the state with absolute control over their lives and those of their families. This of course is a prejudicial diagnosis based in part on Manning's pronounced dislike and distrust of Romanian cultural norms and attitudes. In the trilogy, she often describes Romanians as parochial, lazy, interested in gossip and scandal, steeped in traditional gender restrictions, untrustworthy, and cruel.[39] It is easy to recognize in these derogatory epithets the familiar orientalist tropes which have been used to construct the "circular, non-progressive arc of south-east European alterity" commonly associated with the Balkans, positioning the region as "Britain's most immediate civilizational other."[40]

---

37. Arendt, *The Origins of Totalitarianism*, 267–8.
38. Manning, *The Balkan Trilogy*, 466.
39. Some examples of this include instances occurring on pages 39, 105, 109, 143, 203, 303, 368. Andrew Hammond is the strongest critical voice to date who has made this point as part of his critique of British Balkanism, see Hammond, *British Literature and the Balkans: Themes and Contexts* (Amsterdam and New York: Rodopi, 2010), 235–7.
40. Hammond, *British Literature*, 11; 7–8. The anxiety associated with the ethnic "other" and racist theories of British supremacy and "way of life" were commonplace in this period and were often used as distraction tactics to explain away the dysfunctional structural mechanisms of state power, which were impinging on citizen's social and economic freedom. For a critical discussion see for example, Centre for Contemporary Cultural Studies, *Empire Strikes Back: Race and Racism in 70's Britain* (London and New York: Routledge, 1982) and Walter Rodney, *How Europe Underdeveloped Africa* (London: Bogle-L'Ouverture Publications and Tanzanian Publishing House, 1972). As Maria Todorova argues one of the aspects that drew most

The novel's description of ethnic Romanians, forcibly removed from their homes and left to suffer on the streets of their capital city is also connected to Manning's wider critique of inhumane practices of state consolidation facilitated through the citizenship paradigm. Romania's history of citizenship was marked by successive negotiations and re-negotiations of the status of several minority ethnic groups within its territories, including Greeks, Jews, Roma, Armenians, Muslims, and Dobrudjans, as well as the status of women and peasants, as part of the multi-religious and multi-ethnic legacy of the Ottoman empire. As Diana Dumitru notes, by the mid-1920s the influence of eugenicist discourses had gained traction in discussions of nationalism, which sought to re-establish the dominance of ethnic Romanians and the purity of Romanian blood, feared lost after the integration of the multiethnic regions of Transylvania, Bukovina, and Bessarabia within the nation-state's borders following the end of the First World War.[41] "The new nationalistic discourse," Dumitru writes, "openly promoting xenophobia and depicting minorities in contested territories as a menace to the territorial unity of the state, injected [. . .] new suspicions and fears."[42]

The overarching citizenship regime was built on the basis of a system of constitutional nationalism, designed to protect the economic and political interests of the "titular nation."[43] In different periods, minority groups such as the Jewish or Greek communities were subjected to discriminatory treatment and branded as representatives of cosmopolitan elites or instruments of foreign influence, whose purpose was to

---

persistent criticism and perpetuated increased promulgation of racialist discourse from Britain, and the West, more generally was, precisely the Balkans' ethnic diversity. See, *Imagining the Balkans* (Oxford: Oxford University Press, 2009), 128.

41. Diana Dumitru, *The State, Antisemitism, and Collaboration in the Holocaust: The Borderlands of Romania and the Soviet Union* (New York: Cambridge University Press, 2016), 54.

42. Dumitru, *The State*, 55. In his historical analysis, Iordachi also focuses explicitly on the relationship between the institutional formation of modern citizenship legislation in Romania and its political elites, 5-6. For a fictional account of this period, see Mikhail Sebastian's semi-authobiographical novel *De două mii de ani* (1934) / *For Two Thousand Years* (trans. Philip Ó Ceallaigh (London: Penguin Modern Classics, 2016).

43. Iordachi, *Liberalism*, 10. As Iordachi also notes up to 1918, the Romanian citizenship doctrine involved the following main features: "(1) conditions of naturalization, as well as civil right and duties, were inscribed in the Constitution; (2) admission to citizenship was placed under the control of parliament; (3) proclaiming Romania a 'Christian state,' the Constitution excluded all non-Christian inhabitants of the country from citizenship [. . .]; and (4) only Romanian citizens were allowed to own land and engage in certain liberal professions and activities."

undermine the integrity of the modern Romanian state.⁴⁴ Guy and Harriet cross into Romania when anti-minority and anti-Jewish sentiments were driving large-scale changes to the country's citizenship rules. In January 1938, the Romanian government revised existing criteria for citizenship, laid out in the 1923 Romanian constitution, and passed a law requiring all Jewish people who had received citizenship to reapply for it.⁴⁵ In 1940, Romania adopted equivalents to the Nuremberg Laws, forbidding Jewish-Christian marriages.⁴⁶ Manning's portrayal of the plight of native Romanians living in the contested Transylvania principality, who were effectively turned into refugees and were left with no protection by their own state, brings into sharp focus the precarious nature of citizenship and the illusory sense of safety it generates, even for majority ethnic groups. In some cases, the narrative suggests, the state is not a reliable source of protection *even* for those whose interests are encoded in its constitution.

Indirectly, Manning's own experience of state surveillance following her return to Britain at the end of the Second World War is an important factor in emphasizing the precarity of citizenship. Due to her husband's affiliation with the Communist Party of Great Britain, they were both subjected to government surveillance for nearly a decade.⁴⁷ It started in 1947, shortly after Reggie began working for the BBC, and ended in 1956, the year that Manning commenced writing *The Great Fortune*. MI6 agents actively infiltrated virtually every aspect of Reggie's and Olivia's professional, personal, and domestic lives. Their file contains reports by Reggie's BBC colleagues, copies of letters, observation notes from public events at which Olivia was present such as the Conference of Authors World Peace Appeal in 1954, and summaries of phone conversations.⁴⁸ In November of the same year, following the Soviet invasion of Czechoslovakia, Reggie formally resigned his

---

44. Iordachi, 11–12.
45. David, *Olivia Manning*, 82.
46. David, *Olivia Manning*, 82.
47. Their MI6 file held at the National Archives contains detailed notes on their doings and various reports gathered by the agents in charge from 1952 to 1956. See, "Reginald Donald SMITH and Olivia SMITH, alias Olivia MANNING," 01 Jan 1953-31 December 1955KV-2-2534, p. 1–63/ PF70065/V2, The National Archives, Kew, Richmond. It lists Manning herself as a subscribing member of the Party, though she has never admitted anything of the kind and this seems unlikely considering the anxiety she experienced due to Reggie's membership and her own broadly liberal political views.
48. See, The National Archives: KV-2-2534, p. 1–63/ PF70065/V2.

membership. Even after this was communicated to MI6, the agency continued to regard him as a security risk until at least February 1957.

Smith had been suspected of working to increase Soviet influence in Romania and the Middle East throughout the war, and the early years of his surveillance focused on his work with the British-Rumanian Friendship Association, formed in 1948 and known for its connections with the Communist Party. During the Cold War, communists in Britain were stigmatized "as archetypal bad citizens, attacked throughout society [...] inherently disloyal and dangerous."[49] Even the suspicion of communist affiliation was reason enough for the British government to turn against two of its legal citizens in search of evidence of a security breach, and in doing so denying them the basic human freedoms of privacy, belief, and association. The link between citizenship and belonging, as Manning illustrates both through her literary and biographical domains, is a slippery one and the power to sever it lies entirely in the hands of the state.

The Myth of State Benevolence

In addition to highlighting the precarity of citizenship, *The Balkan Trilogy* also develops a critique of the nation-state aimed specifically at the political assumption of its benevolence towards its citizens. Manning emphasizes the disempowering effects of state intervention on the lives of those residing within its borders, often exacerbated by the insecurities of violent conflict and inter-state political gambling and power plays. This tension gains further import in the context of the post- and inter-imperial territorial reorganization of the Balkans following the collapse of the Austro-Hungarian and Ottoman empires at the end of the First World War. The nation-state model, used for the ensuing reconstruction "aimed to reconcile majoritarian ethnic rule with guarantees of individual rights," a project whose failure had been signaled a century earlier through the Romanian constitution of 1866, which stipulated that non-Christians could not become citizens, effectively stripping large Jewish and Muslim minorities from any claims to citizenship.[50] In this complex multi-ethnic landscape, borders were

---

49. Grant, 'Historicizing Citizenship,' 1197. For an instructive discussion of the relationship between communist and anti-communist writers' influence on postwar political culture, see Matthew Taunton, *Red Britain: The Russian Revolution in Mid-Century Culture* (Oxford: Oxford University Press, 2019).

50. Mark Mazower, *The Balkans* (London: Weidenfeld & Nicholson, 2000), 105.

frequently challenged and redrawn as part of the political power struggles between a succession of emerging and *re*-emerging states fighting for sovereignty and the competing interests of vying imperial and post-imperial powers. Questions of citizenships were often resolved on the basis of an increasingly exclusionary practice of social control.

Manning questions the legitimacy of political systems incapable of reliably functioning in their citizens' interests and of protecting their basic rights. The Jewish banker, Drucker, who we meet in the first volume of *The Balkan Trilogy* as the father of one of Guy's students, Sasha, is one of the characters in the novel who represents this failure of justice most forcefully. Drucker is significant because his position in Romanian society and power within his own family was encapsulated in his Romanian citizenship. As Guy tells Harriet when they attend a lunch with the Druckers, "the brothers-in-law were all of different nationalities. Only Drucker held a Rumanian passport. It was evidence of Drucker's power in the country that the others—one German, one Austrian, and one Polish—had been granted *permis-de-séjour*. They existed in his shadow."[51] Drucker's social status is reinforced by his marriage to a young "Rumanian beauty," who further legitimizes his claim to integration.[52]

Soon after the fall of Paris, however, political favor in Romania begins to turn towards Germany and antisemitic fervor increases. Consequently, Drucker is arrested, his assets confiscated, and his family torn apart. He is accused of treason and placed in a holding cell "with low criminals and perverts," completely discredited by a show trial, and eventually convicted.[53] Engineered to distract from state failings related to the annexation of Transylvania and the resulting refugee wave, the trial is accompanied by media-created frenzy, with one of the newspapers proclaiming it, *"l'évenement social le plus important de l'été"* [the most important social event of the summer].[54] Stories and gossip of various kinds begin to circulate, which make Harriet realize "that among all this talk Drucker's own identity was lost. No one doubted the innocence of this friendless man, but that factor did not bear discussion. No one could help him. He was a victim of the times."[55] The next time Harriet sees him, on his way to a court hearing, Drucker is described "as an elderly stooping skeleton, a cripple who descended the steps by

---

51. Manning, *The Balkan Trilogy*, 97.
52. Manning, 99.
53. Manning, 156.
54. Manning, 381.
55. Manning, 381.

dropping the same foot each time and dragging the other."⁵⁶ His clothes are in tatters, he is kicked and beaten by the guards, robbed of a life and a future; he murmurs, "*Da, da*" [yes, yes], in zealous obedience" as he struggles to re-enter the van in which he will be transported.⁵⁷ There is a glimmer of recognition in Drucker's eyes when he sees Harriet, which reminds the reader of the shared history and humanity between the two characters, a memory of a past life.

Sasha, Drucker's young son, is sent to carry out his military service on the Bessarabian front, fighting against the invading Russian army. Following his father's arrest, he manages to escape and returns to Bucharest to discover what has happened to his family. Harriet is shocked by the contrast in his appearance: "when she saw him nine months before, [he] had been the well fed, well dressed son of a wealthy man. Now he smelled of the grave."⁵⁸ The Pringles hide him in their attic despite the danger of harboring an army deserter and the risks to their own safety. They grow close to Sasha and attempt to find a way to get him out of the country by obtaining a fake passport. But after a betrayal, their flat is raided and Sasha disappears without a trace.⁵⁹

The scenes of the novel, which describe the unfolding of the fascist "revolution" and Bucharest's transformation into an Iron Guard stronghold, are pervaded by a sense of precarity, which forges a deeper connection between Sasha and his hosts. Despite his harrowing account of the military camp and frontline warfare conditions he has witnessed, including the horrific loss of his closest friend, Sasha retains his boyish humor, sensitivity, and love of music.⁶⁰ While considering Sasha's perception of the political events occurring in front of his eyes, Harriet wonders what he makes of it.

> He certainly had not been disturbed. It probably never entered his head that events could jeopardise his protected position. As for the fate of Rumania, why should that mean anything to him? Although he had been born here, he was no more emotionally involved in the place than were the Pringles themselves. Reflecting

---

56. Manning, 417.
57. Manning, 417.
58. Manning, 319.
59. The trilogy briefly returns to Sasha, who re-emerges towards the end of the third novel in Athens, accompanied by an uncle, who has succeeded in getting him out of Romania. He believes that the Pringles have betrayed him and refuses to rekindle their close relationship, leaving Harriet pondering a sense of loss, see p. 859.
60. Manning, *The Balkan Trilogy*, 360.

on his English schoolboy slang that at once had placed and displaced him, she thought wherever he was, he would belong nowhere.[61]

This passage further illustrates the complexity of the state-citizen relationship as a source of life security and protection. In describing Sasha's position Manning seems to affirm a direct correlation between citizenship, national belonging, and the interests of a majority ethnic group. In Sonya Rose's analysis, formalizing the difference between citizenship and national identity opens the way precisely to the kind of exclusion on the basis of "ethnic" or "national" characteristics, suggested by Harriet's musings.[62] More precisely though, the text also seeks to represent the condition of precarious citizenship (and Manning seems to suggest that citizenship both as a legal status and practice is to some degree always precarious) as one of transcendental non-belonging, an idea which recurrently surfaces in conversations around human rights and frameworks of transnational protection, discussed in the postwar period.

Unlikely as it may seem, due to ideological divides in the context of Cold War politics, *The Balkan Trilogy* also highlights similarities between the approaches towards state consolidation taken by the Romanian and the British states respectively. Both were responding to external pressures on their sovereignty: the former was threatened by the territorial ambitions of surrounding nations and imperial powers, while the latter felt increasingly marginalized in the wake of its own disintegrating empire and vulnerability to Soviet infiltration.[63] Through this comparative historical framework, Manning's trio of novels capture

---

61. Manning, 465.

62. Sonya O. Rose, "Cultural Analysis and Moral Discourses: Episodes, Continuities and Transformations," in Victoria E. Bonnell and Lynn Hunt, eds., *Beyond the Cultural Turn* (Berkeley, CA: University of California Press, 1999), 217–39; see also Grant, "Historicizing Citizenship," 1196.

63. It has to be noted that a more careful comparison between Manning's representation of the British and the Romanian state is warranted but falls outside the scope of this paper, particularly in terms of the form of Cold War prejudice that dominated the way she characterizes the workings of the Balkan state. Whereas British failings in the trilogy are often explained simply through incompetence or lack of forward thinking, those of the Romanians seem connected to deeper sources of imagined or implied national and ethnic features. For a strong critique of Manning's Balkanism, see Andrew Hammond, "The Red Threat: Cold War Rhetoric and the British Novel," in Andrew Hammond, ed. *The Balkans and the West: Constructing the European Other* (Aldershot: Ashgate, 2004), 40–56; and for a more general overview of attitudes towards the Balkans in British literature, see Hammond's *British Literature and the Balkans*.

the transition between experiences of belonging and non-belonging, held in common by both societies on either side of the Second World War. Occurring at a time when "political rights and social citizenship were secure" and "self-evident" to many of those engaged with political debate and argument, Manning's account of their erosion offers an alternative narrative.[64]

In an influential 1954 paper, international historian Quincy Wright contends that the twentieth century brought into sharp focus the brewing conflict between modern states and their citizens. The "preoccupation with the sovereignty and independence of states," he writes, "induced a neglect of the rights of individuals. States [...] were free to deal with their nationals in their territory as they saw fit."[65] The Cold War exacerbated this conflict due to heightened demands of state consolidation in the name of security and protection from external threats posed by the opposing blocs. But as Wright suggests serious questions around legitimacy, the nature of liberal state organization, and the protection of individual autonomy remain unanswered.

Existential Insecurity

It is telling that the 1980s TV adaptation of Manning's novels into *The Fortunes of War* series starring Emma Thompson and Kenneth Branagh as Harriet and Guy, completely dispenses with the trilogy's political critiques. One of the reader's reports commissioned by the BBC to review the screenplay as part of their preparatory work laments the apparent excision of the entire political context of the work and its sole focus on character development as a great loss.[66] This decision to transform a novel of political critique of state power into a romance set against the backdrop of war-torn Europe is part of a larger pattern of the covert operational relationship between British institutions and the literature of the period.

As James Smith writes, during this time the British government and institutions actively participated in acts of political warfare, including

---

64. David Marquand, "Civil Republicans and liberal individualists: the Case of Britain," in Bryan S. Turner and Peter Hamilton, eds., *Citizenship: Critical Concepts* 1 (London, 1994), 241 qtd in Grant, "Historicizing Citizenship," 1205.

65. Quincy Wright, "Human Rights and Charter Revision," *The Annals of the American Academy of Political and Social Science* 296, The Futures of the United Nations Issues of Charter Revision (Nov, 1954): 46.

66. BBC Written Archives Centre—BBC/T/TVART/T48/403/1—Manning, Olivia.

the generation of propaganda, generally aimed either at damaging the enemy's morale or at sustaining Britain's own.[67] This act of creative obfuscation, undertaken by the BBC, further speaks to the difficulty of using cultural forms to think through the tension between individual human and social rights and the principles of control that underpin narratives of state power and sovereignty. Instead of confronting this tension productively and critically, postwar cultural institutions often eschewed it altogether; a failure, in a certain sense, that is both imaginative and political.[68]

Manning's *Balkan Trilogy*, in contrast confronted this tension head on, emphasizing the state's power in the regulation of all aspects of its citizens' lives. The novels describe the precarious realities of citizenship, which see individual human beings left at the mercy of state provision and intervention in the context of wider internal and geopolitical struggles. Manning takes special care to show how this existential insecurity affects both those often seen as most vulnerable to it such as refugees and stateless persons and those privileged enough to have secured citizenship status as members of majority ethnic groups.

The narrative explicitly interrogates the power of the state to render humanity and individual rights illegible with the stroke of a pen, by drawing a border or refusing a permit. The question of legibility, and through it the connection between the imaginative and the political realms, importantly also relates to the construction of the new international order and the publication of the Universal Declaration of Human Rights (UDHR), as Lyndsey Stonebridge and Joseph Slaughter have demonstrated. Drafters constructing the UDHR, they contend, "turned to the novel, particularly the European *Bildungsroman*, for a model of rights-bearing personhood."[69] This is not to say that Manning herself, or *The Balkan Trilogy* as a singular text, has sought to influence particular policy directions and state-making practices, though it certainly seeks to portray the real-life consequences of these larger structural processes.

---

67. James Smith, "Covert Legacies in Postwar British Fiction," in *British Literature in Transition, 1940–1960: Postwar*, ed. Gill Plain (Cambridge: Cambridge University Press, 2019), 338.

68. Lyndsey Stonebridge, *The Judicial Imagination: Writing after Nuremberg* (Edinburgh: Edinburgh University Press, 2011), 11.

69. Stonebridge, *The Judicial Imagination*, 11. See also Joseph Slaughter, *Human Rights, Inc.: The World Novel, Narrative, Form, and International Law* (New York: Fordham University Press, 2007).

What is clear, however, is that the three novels call for a revised relationship between nation-states and individual persons residing within and beyond their borders, with a renewed focus on the protection of rights. They also brand the restrictive practices developed by the postwar British state as corrosive to individual dignity and liberty, raising concerns around the limits of government power and the legitimacy of the nation-state's authority.

It is my hope that this chapter has been successful in showing that literary culture can enhance the scope and depth of existing historical approaches.[70] Citizenship studies is inherently and necessarily an interdisciplinary sphere of inquiry, which can and must be pursued along the vertical and temporal axes outlined in the Introduction to this volume to reflect the full complexity and dynamism of its subject. In addition to expanding the available repertoire of reference points and source materials, access to the literary imagination will provide historians of citizenship with an additional set of tools to navigate through "the complex proposition[s]" that citizenship as a concept presents.[71] Literary culture offers a space for reflection and experimentation, which combines the different forms of interaction between a more conceptual understanding of citizenship and an understanding of it as a lived experience, while preserving possibilities of "change and agency."[72]

It would be unfair to Manning's acute portrayal of the senseless suffering caused to many by inadequate forms of political organization embodied by the nation-state and its institutions to end on this almost optimistic methodological promise. *The Balkan Trilogy* finishes with the departure of a battered group of English expatriates leaving the Piraeus, the last safe harbor in Europe, to seek escape to a new continent: "They had crossed the Mediterranean and now, on the other side, they knew they were refugees. Still, they had a life—a depleted fortune, but a fortune."[73] This, on the last page of the novel, is the first instance of Harriet referring to herself and Guy as refugees, a change of status that underscores the universal condition of precarious citizenship, while also drawing attention to the diminishing value of human life in conditions of violent conflict and involuntary displacement.

---

70. See Iordachi, *Liberal Citizenship*, 21; 23.
71. Grant, *Historicizing Citizenship*, 1205.
72. Grant, 1205.
73. Manning, *The Balkan Trilogy*, 924.

Stanislava Dikova is a Postdoctoral Researcher and a Visiting Fellow at the University of Essex. Stanislava's research focuses on twentieth-century British fiction and political thought, with a special interest in women's writing relating to personal autonomy and state power. Her work is published in the *LSE Review of Books*, *The Modernist Review*, and *Feminist Modernist Studies*. She is also the co-editor of *Love and the Politics of Care* and *Love and the Politics of Intimacy*.

CHAPTER 7

The Francoist Conception of Citizenship in Postwar Spain

Carlos Domper Lasús

What happened to Spain? Any connoisseur of postwar European history could easily pose this question. Most works pay hardly any attention to the history of the two Iberian countries that continued to be ruled by right-wing dictatorships after the defeat of the Nazi army. At best, Franco's Spain is mentioned in passing, such as in Mark Mazower's description of the country as a sort of "hangover from a thankless past everybody wanted to forget."[1] Tony Judt provides one of the main explanations for this lack of interest. In his view, since 1989, historians have developed a teleological narrative of the post-1945 history of Europe. According to this perspective, after the defeat of Nazi Germany, the Old Continent learned the lessons of the past and headed toward unification in a post-national, conciliatory, and peaceful sphere, in which the long dictatorships' shadow vanished forever.[2] For their part, a significant number of Spanish scholars, especially those who have focused their research on the period after 1945, have practiced what might

---

1. This publication is part of the RYC2021 grant program funded by MCIN/AEI/10.13039/501100011033 and by the European Union "NextGenerationEU"/PRTR," where RYC2021-034912-I is my personal Ramón y Cajal grant reference.
Mark Mazower, *Dark Continent: Europe's Twentieth Century* (London: Penguin Books, 1998), 290.
2. Tony Judt, *Postwar: A History of Europe since 1945* (London: Pimlico, 2007), 5.

be termed reverse isolationism. That is, they have delved into the history of Franco's dictatorship based on its internal dynamics instead of trying to integrate it into broader European or transnational histories.

In contrast, this chapter contextualizes Franco's regime within one of the main political phenomena that took place in postwar Western Europe: the renegotiation of the concept of citizenship. As Rachel Chin and Samuel Clowes Huneke point out in the introduction to this volume, the political and social reconstruction that the European continent underwent after May 1945 led to a redefinition of what it meant to be a citizen and thus what it meant to belong to a state, a community, a nation, or an empire. In this vein, the chapter focuses on the Fuero de los Españoles—the Spanish Charter of Rights—the legal text that the regime passed to "guarantee" Spaniards a set of fundamental rights. It challenges traditional interpretations that view this document as merely a propagandistic instrument.[3] This analysis does not deny the charter's propagandistic character but rather aims to provide a deeper understanding of it by placing the charter in the framework of two intertwined processes. First, after the outbreak of the Cold War, Western European conservatives and far-right supporters, many of whom were anchored in a Christian legal tradition, began to reimagine their position within European affairs from a profoundly anticommunist position. Consequently, their conception of human rights looked back to a nineteenth-century conservative perspective.[4] Second, the Fuero overlapped with what Pepjin Corduwener calls the struggle to define the concept of democracy in postwar Western Europe. In other words, it was a time when different political actors in the liberated Western European countries began to reimagine and impose their ideas about what democracy meant.[5]

To do all this, I rely on different sources, from primary documents held at the Archive of the Spanish National Parliament to Spanish newspapers from the Francoist period and, above all, scholarly literature. Furthermore, through a peripheral but highly significant case such as

---

3. This legal text was published in *Boletín Oficial del Estado* (Official gazette of the state), July 18, 1945, 358–60. A monograph on the charter from a history of law perspective can be found in Enrique Álvarez Cora, *La constitución postiza. El nacimiento del Fuero de los Españoles* (Madrid: Biblioteca Nueva, 2010).

4. Marco Duranti, *The Conservative Human Rights Revolution: European Identity, Transnational Politics, and the Origins of the European Convention* (Oxford: Oxford University Press, 2017).

5. Pepjin Corduwener, *The Problem of Democracy in Postwar Europe: Political Actors and the Formation of the Postwar Model of Democracy in France, West Germany and Italy* (New York: Routledge, 2017).

that of Spain, I aim here to demonstrate the importance of considering the legacy of interwar counterrevolutionary movements to more fully understand the process of creating the category of "citizenship" within postwar Europe. Thus, in the following pages, as Courtman, Lashyn, and Kergomard do in their chapters, I approach this issue by drawing on legal/theoretical constructions of citizenship.

The chapter is divided into three parts. The first places Franco's regime in the context of postwar Western Europe. The second connects the Fuero de los Españoles to the main elements that characterized postwar European conservatism. The third shows the three different levels of representation to which Franco's organic citizenship gave access.

By contextualizing the law within these two postwar European processes, I seek to break down the wall that the main narratives of the postwar period have built between Spain and the rest of Western Europe. Exposing the links between Franco's regime and the European society that were (re)built out of the ashes of World War II under the supervision of the United States is essential to understanding how deep the legacy of counterrevolution was in post-1945 Europe. Contrary to the self-congratulatory narratives of European history after the Second World War, the following pages aim to show not only that antiliberalism did not disappear from European society but also that it played a role in the redefinition of the concept of citizenship during those years.

Undoubtedly, in postwar Europe, Franco's Spain was a minor power and clearly stigmatized by its obvious association with the regimes that had been defeated in 1945. Nonetheless, observing the process of political, social, and cultural reconstruction of the continent through the window offered by Franco's dictatorship offers a great advantage to historians. Specifically, it reveals a whole melting pot of individuals, ideas, and projects related to the world of the counterrevolution in the interwar period. In short, the chapter explores a set of actors and phenomena that was obscured by the blinding light that emanated from the triumph of liberal democracy from the mid-1950s onward.

A "Particular Democracy": Francoism and the Postwar International Order

After 1945, Francoism faced a complicated international situation. The Spanish regime, along with its Portuguese counterpart, was the sole survivor of a form of political organization based on the principles of a previous era. Such was the understanding of most of the representatives from more than forty countries who gathered in San Francisco (April 1945–June 1946) to create the United Nations. For this reason, not only did the United Nations General Assembly not invite a representative of the Spanish dictatorship, but it also adopted Resolution 39 on December 12, 1946, in regard specifically to this country. According to the resolution, the Francoist government had been imposed on the Spanish people by force with the help of the Axis Powers. Consequently, the Spanish regime had to be excluded from international organizations and conferences established by the UN.

Despite the aforementioned developments, Franco trusted in the continuity of his regime. He adapted as much as possible to the new postwar context but without yielding one iota of his power. On July 17, 1945, during his annual speech before the National Council of FET-JONS[6] (the Spanish single party), Franco was very clear in the presence of all those who, both inside and outside the country, were looking forward to changes in the regime. "All those who consider that Spain needs to import something from abroad," he claimed, "are wrong."[7] But he was aware of the need to adapt his dictatorship to the new circumstances. Franco himself, in the annual speech, put it this way: "As the good captain, we have to maintain the route of the ship, firmly adjusting the maneuver to the storms that can whip it."[8]

The Spanish dictator established a symbolic date to present the main measures with which his regime sought to convince the World War II noncommunist victors of its suitability to be part of the new international order. On July 18, the "Alzamiento Nacional" (National Uprising) day, Franco formed a new cabinet whose most striking change was the appointment of Alberto Martín Artajo, a well-known Catholic with pristine international connections, as minister of foreign affairs. Martín Artajo would be in charge of directing the key ministry in the process of Spanish adaptation to a new world dominated by those who had just defeated the regimes that had inspired (ideologically) and contributed (militarily) to the Spanish dictatorship's birth. To achieve this, the new minister based his strategy on Carrero Blanco's thesis.[9]

---

6. Falange Española Tradicionalista y de las Juntas de Ofensiva Nacional Sindicalista (Traditionalist Spanish Phalanx of the Councils of the National Syndicalist Offensive).
7. *ABC* 18 of July 1945: 32.
8. *ABC* 18 of July 1945: 34.
9. Admiral-General Luis Carrero Blanco was a Spanish navy officer and politician. A longtime confidant and right-hand man of Franco, he served as prime minister of the Francoist dictatorship and in various other high-ranking offices in the regime until his assassination in

According to this thesis, the significant ideological differences among the Allies would inevitably lead to a confrontation between the Soviet Union and the Western powers, making Spain a necessary ally for the latter because of its geostrategic importance. For this reason, the new minister developed a foreign policy that focused on underlining the regime's deep commitment to the defense of two increasingly important values in the United States and Western Europe: Catholicism and anticommunism.

Furthermore, Franco attempted to hide the dictatorial power of the Spanish single party with two key changes. First, he removed the ministerial rank of the *Secretaría general del movimiento* (general secretariat of the movement).[10] He also passed the control of the *vicesecretaría general de educación popular* (general vice-secretary of popular education), responsible for censorship, the press, and propaganda, from the Spanish single party to the Ministry of Education, headed by José Ibáñez Martín, a man whose Catholicism was beyond doubt. Second, two important laws were published in the *Boletín Oficial del Estado* (Official gazette of the state) on the same day: the Fuero de los Españoles and the Ley de Bases del Régimen Local (Local Governments Law).[11] Apart from these important laws, the Franco regime adopted two other measures that year. First, on September 11, the presidency of the government abolished the obligation of doing the fascist salute. Second, on October 22, the head of state promulgated the National Referendum Law, according to which certain laws should be decided in a national referendum in which all men over twenty-one and women over twenty-five would be enfranchised.[12]

The main purpose of adopting these measures was to demonstrate to the noncommunist states that Spain had a political regime comparable to those of parliamentary democracies, but underlining its peculiar character derived from the specificities of Spanish society and

---

a car bombing in December 1973. Javier Tusell, *Carrero. La eminencia gris del régimen de Franco* (Madrid: Temas de Hoy, 1993).

10. This office was the main administrative body of the single party. It was created in December 1937, and in August 1939 it acquired ministerial status. On this institution see Mercedes Peñalba, *La Secretaría General del Movimiento. Construcción, coordinación y estabilización del régimen franquista* (Madrid: Centro de Estudios Políticos y Constitucionales, 2015).

11. This legal text set up a new electoral mechanism through which henceforth councilmen would be elected.

12. A good summary in English of this policy of adaptation to the new international scenario developed by Franco's regime after 1945 can be found in José Luis Neila, "The Foreign Policy Administration of Franco's Spain: From Isolation to International Realignment, 1945–1957," in *Spain in an International Context, 1936–1959*, ed. Christian Leitz and David Dunthorn (Oxford: Berghahn Books, 1999), 277–98.

history. The concept of "peculiarity" is key here, because it enables us to connect the Francoist strategy to two texts that were fundamental to the process of political (re)construction in the post-1945 world: the Declaration on Liberated Europe and the Atlantic Charter. By means of the former, the United States, Great Britain, and the USSR offered financial help to liberated peoples. Yet according to point three in the latter text,[13] such aid was conditional on an unavoidable democratic requirement. Specifically, both the establishment of the new political order and the rebuilding of national economic life had to be achieved through processes that would enable the liberated peoples in question to create democratic institutions of their own choice.

In this sense, Franco regularly repeated the notion that "the forms, concepts, and nuances that have defined democracies over the years vary with the characters and political and economic circumstances of each people," and hence there were "as many democracies as countries."[14] In April 1945, *Arriba*, the flagship newspaper of the Spanish single-party press network, claimed that Spain had "a specific style of democracy capable of broad development without denaturalizing itself" and that Francoism was "one more of the twenty types of democracy registered by history and designed by political planners down to our own perilous times."[15] Consequently, as stipulated in the abovementioned documents, the peculiarities of Francoism had to be respected. Carrero Blanco put this clearly in July 1957 while defending the draft law on the legal regime of state administration in the Spanish legislature, the Cortes Españolas.[16] He stated that "we do not have to copy anyone. We respect the systems adopted by other peoples to rule their home, and we do not intend to impose our judgment on anyone, but, for this reason, we demand to be left alone."[17]

---

13. "They [the signatories] respect the right of all peoples to choose the form of government under which they will live; and they [the signatories] wish to see sovereign rights and self-government restored to those who have been forcibly deprived of them."

14. *Boletín Oficial de las Cortes Españolas* (Official gazette of the Spanish Cortes; hereinafter *BOCE*), May 14, 1946, 2980.

15. Quoted in Stanley Payne, *The Franco Regime: 1936–1975* (Madison: University of Wisconsin Press, 1987), 355.

16. This was the Francoist legislative chamber established in 1942. Its main function was the development and adoption of laws, but under a subsequent sanction reserved for Franco himself. That is, the Cortes was not intended as the repository of national sovereignty, since all sovereign power was concentrated in the dictator. On this institution see Miguel Ángel Giménez Martinez, *Las Cortes españolas en el régimen de Franco. Nacimiento, desarrollo y extinción de una cámara orgánica* (Madrid: Congreso de los Diputados, 2012).

17. *BOCE*, July 15, 1957, 11453.

How, then, did Franco's regime make the claim that Spain was indeed a democracy? As Franco explained in a speech delivered in Huelva in 1956, his concept of democracy implied "the real participation of men in the tasks of the state."[18] In order to be effective, such participation had to take place "through its natural organs of representation," that is, the family, the municipality, and the labor union, as Carrero stated during his 1957 intervention.[19] Therefore, Spain was not a liberal democracy along the lines of those gaining strength at that time in Western Europe. Indeed, as Franco contended in his 1956 discourse, "we repudiate that democracy."[20]

The Spanish dictator himself expressed clearly the central importance of Catholicism and antiliberalism in the Francoist conception of democracy. In a speech to the Cortes in 1946, he stated that it was "paradoxical to try to deny the title of democracy to a nation that lives under the principles of the Catholic faith, which permeates its laws of deep Christian spirit and organizes life taking into account the traditional activities of our nation. A nation that has its representative Cortes, elected by its municipalities, its labor unions, and its brotherhoods. A nation that has established the direct referendum of the Spaniards to decide on the problems of deep transcendence."[21]

"Organic democracy" was the Francoist version of corporatism, a system of political organization of society that the Roman Catholic Church strongly promoted from the late-nineteenth to the mid-twentieth centuries as a "third way" of social, political, and economic organization in the face of socialism and liberal capitalism.[22] Precisely for this reason, corporatism became a powerful political device against liberal democracy and permeated the authoritarian right and dictatorships during the interwar period.[23]

---

18. Here, the word "men" referred to human beings in general. It did not have a specifically male connotation.
19. *BOCE*, July 15, 1957, 11453.
20. *La Vanguardia*, April 25, 1956, 1.
21. *BOCE*, May 14, 1946, 2980–81.
22. The connection between political Catholicism and corporatism can be found in John Pollard, "Corporatism and Political Catholicism: The Impact of Catholic Corporatism in Inter-war Europe," in *Corporatism and Fascism: The Corporatist Wave in Europe*, ed. Antonio Costa Pinto (New York: Routledge, 2017), 42–59.
23. The relevance of organic representation for the European dictatorships of the interwar period is addressed in Antonio Costa Pinto, "Corporatism and 'Organic Representation' in European Dictatorships," in *Corporatism and Fascism: The Corporatist Wave in Europe*, ed. Antonio Costa Pinto (New York: Routledge, 2017), 3–41.

The Fuero de los Españoles and Postwar European Conservatism

The particular conception of democracy that the Francoist regime sought to develop necessarily had to be accompanied by an equally different conception of citizenship. Indeed, the concept of citizenship was taking on new meanings in Europe during these years, as the new states and the individuals living within them began to renegotiate their positions in society in terms of race, nationality, class, gender, and sexuality. The Francoist development of a new concept of citizenship did not take place in isolation. Actually, Francoism was no different from the other antiliberal regimes that came up in Europe after 1945. In fact, the countries that came under the control of the Soviet Union, and where the so-called people's democracy emerged, also developed alternative conceptions of citizenship, as can be seen in chapters by Weiser, Dobrowolska, and Tohma. Yet unlike what happened in most of Europe, the Fuero de los Españoles proposed a model of citizenship that did not result from negotiations between Spaniards and the state but rather from an agreement among the victors of the Spanish Civil War. Despite this, the new Francoist conception of citizenship was deeply connected to at least two of the main elements that characterized postwar European conservatism: the redefinition of the concept of human rights in a Christian and conservative direction and the reliance on corporatist theories as an alternative model for organizing society.

In what follows, I show the connection between the Fuero de los Españoles and these two aspects of European conservatism. I also aim to highlight the fact that conservatism became a political space in which Franco's dictatorship found ideological, political, and cultural ground compatible with some of its core values (Catholicism, anticommunism, and antiliberalism) and also where some people still looked to Francoism as a model from which to seek alternatives for the construction of the new European order, at least until the late 1950s. In distinguishing between Christian democracy and conservatism, I follow Ronald Irvin's distinction. He starts from the premise that Christian democracy is not a straightforward synonym for conservatism; rather, the organic links that most Christian democrats "have with organized labor and their clear-cut commitment to 'Christian principles,' 'democracy' and 'integration,' indicate that Christian Democracy is a distinctive political phenomenon, which should be categorized separately from traditional Conservatism."[24]

---

24. Ronald Irving, "Christian Democracy in Post-war Europe: Conservatism Writ-Large or Distinctive Political Phenomenon?," *West European Politics* 2, no. 1 (1979): 55.

The first of these characteristics of postwar European conservatism was the redefinition of the concept of human rights in a Christian and conservative direction. During the second half of the 1940s, most European countries adopted new constitutions that, in general, led to the implementation of different forms of social democracy.[25] Neither conservatives nor free-market advocates supported the dramatic increase in state power resulting from this expansion of state competencies. On the contrary, they often feared that the growing power of states ruled by majoritarian democracy would, as Friedrich von Hayek had noted in *The Road to Serfdom* (1944), lead to totalitarianism—that is, a form of government that eliminates all opposition parties, outlaws opposition to the state, and exercises an extremely high (if not total) degree of control over public and private life. Back then, however, conservatives could not win this battle at the national level because coalitions made up of socialists, communists, and Christian democrats enjoyed majoritarian popular support in most Western European countries.

Consequently, as Marco Duranti highlights, free marketers and conservatives worked hard to articulate a transnational opposition to the postwar interventionist consensus by promoting a transformation of the concept of human rights.[26] Their aim was to develop a concept of human rights that would emphasize the protection of individual rights and ignore, if not limit, those of a social nature that they directly related to the expansion of state power. This transformation grounded the concept in values stemming from Christian conservative social thought. In doing so, it created an intellectual and political space in which the main foundations underpinning the concept of citizenship developed by the Spanish dictatorship found at least two points of intersection: a recasting of conservative political language and the unfolding of an idea of European civilization based on Christian values.[27]

In regard to the former, throughout the second half of the 1940s, free marketers and conservatives reformulated old conservative political language, giving birth to a new political vocabulary of citizenship from which the Fuero de los Españoles drew. This new vocabulary established a clear distinction between individual rights and those of a social and economic nature. Individual rights related to political freedoms

---

25. Martin Conway, *Western Europe's Democratic Age: 1945–1968* (Princeton, NJ: Princeton University Press, 2020), and Corduwener, *Problem of Democracy*, 2017.

26. Duranti, *Conservative Human Rights Revolution*, 2017.

27. An approach to this question from the history of law perspective can be found in Alfons Aragoneses, "La libertad de la persona humana. El Fuero de los Españoles y la cultura de los derechos en la II postguerra," *História do Direito* 2 (2021): 131–48.

such as freedom of expression and conscience, and the right to private property, education, voting, and association. Conservatives, moreover, often rooted these rights in an imagined past. British Conservatives, for instance, argued that the origins of these rights lay in medieval charters such as the Magna Carta forced on King John in 1215.

Social and economic rights, on the other hand, were related to the redistribution of wealth and the creation of welfare states and ranged from the right to work to the right to get paid, housing, and social benefits. The UN's Universal Declaration of Human Rights, for example, included all these rights. But the European Movement (a postwar European organization that represented conservative opinion in Western Europe) adopted individual rights without mentioning social and economic rights. Conservatives argued that such rights augmented the state's power and thus potentially opened the door to totalitarianism.

The Fuero de los Españoles not only included both types of rights, albeit with significant limitations, but also showed this connection with the medieval charters.[28] In this vein, the text was named "Fuero" (a Spanish word that refers to the laws of the Middle Ages) and not "law," in order to disconnect it from the liberal tradition. Such a word came directly from traditional Catholic Spanish thought, which used the concept of "person" to refer to the insertion of the individual into society. The rights granted to Spaniards as "bearers of eternal values and members of a national unity" (Art. 1) were divided into two sections. Chapter I defined individual rights, which ranged from the right to honor (Art. 4), education (Art. 5), and participation in public functions (Arts. 10 and 11) to the right to express ideas (Art. 12), freedom of correspondence (Art. 13), inviolability of the home (Art. 15), assembly and association (Art. 16), and habeas corpus (Art. 18). Social and economic rights appeared in Chapter III and ranged from the right to work (Art. 24), to receive adequate remuneration (Art. 27), to social assistance and benefits (Art. 28) and access to housing and work tools (Art. 31). Yet Spaniards enjoyed these rights only on paper, because in practice the regime almost entirely restricted their exercise through at least three limitations. First, these provisions could not "undermine Spain's spiritual, national, and social unity." Second, they had to be ratified by pseudo-courts controlled by Franco. Finally, the validity of the articles

---

28. The antiliberal version of the concept of citizenship developed by the Franco regime differed in this respect from that of the communist regimes, which focused mainly on social rights, as Nikola Tohma points out in her chapter on Greek refugees in communist Czechoslovakia.

containing the principal individual rights (12, 13, 14, 15, 16, and 18) could be suspended unilaterally by the executive at any time.[29]

What was the point of enacting a bill of rights that could be suspended at any time? The answer to this question obliges us to recall that Francoism was the child of a period characterized by the rampant rise of antiliberalism and fascism. When that world disappeared after World War II, Franco's regime had no choice but to adapt to a completely different scenario dominated by liberals, democrats, and communists. But it was never willing to renounce its founding values. Given that its profound anticommunism and its staunch Catholicism were shared by many of those on the liberal side, Franco's foreign policy focused its efforts to seek support for postwar integration among the noncommunist victors of World War II around these two features. But from the point of view of the Spanish dictatorship, the fundamental premise for completing this integration process was that it should not endanger two essential elements. It could not challenge Franco's leadership or his regime's ability to impose itself on Spanish society, and it could not threaten the maintenance of a distance from liberal values. Liberalism was an ideology that, according to Franco's interpretation, had allowed communism to triumph, breaking the national, spiritual, and social unity of the Spanish nation and making civil war necessary to restore it. Franco himself expressed it very clearly when he stated in an October 1945 cabinet meeting that the regime's purpose was "to dress itself in the clothes of democracy without taking its risks."[30]

This revision of political language in line with postwar changes in European society was based on a Christian conception of rights. Indeed, on the basis of the idea of articulating transnational opposition to the postwar interventionist consensus, conservatives developed the idea of creating a European civilization on the bedrocks of Christianity. In this sense, many assumed that the different types of Christianity that existed in Western Europe were sufficiently compatible with one another to constitute a coherent cultural community. For them, Christianity had already demonstrated its universalist potential in the Middle Ages, when it had succeeded in "constructing a res publica Christiana against

---

29. See a detailed approach to the limitations on the rights granted by the Fuero de los Españoles in Marcelo Caprarella, "La ciudadanía secuestrada. La etapa franquista," in *De súbditos a ciudadanos. Una historia de la ciudadanía en España*, ed. Manuel Ledesma (Madrid: Centro de Estudios Políticos y Constitucionales, 2007), 311–41.

30. Quoted in Paul Preston, *Franco: A Biography* (New York: Basic Books, 1994), 546.

the disaggregating effects of feudalism and dynastic states as well as the danger of Islam."[31]

The Fuero de los Españoles was no stranger to the Christian conception on which European conservatism built its vision of European civilization and civil rights during the post–World War II period. Indeed, Article 6 stated categorically that Spain was a Catholic country and that the state would protect the practice of that religion. Moreover, none of the rights guaranteed by the Fuero could infringe on Catholic principles. Leopoldo Eijo Garay, the bishop of Madrid-Alcalá and member of the special commission appointed by the Spanish Cortes to analyze the draft of the Fuero de los Españoles sent to it by the head of state, expressed it clearly in one of the meetings of that commission. Resorting to the concept of "condemned propositions" coined by Pope Pius IX in his *Syllabus of Errors* of 1864,[32] the bishop of Madrid-Alcalá stated that "all these freedoms that are recognized in the Fuero de los Españoles would be condemned propositions insofar as they could be used for evil." Therefore, only "when they do not attack the spiritual or social unity, that is, when they cannot be used for the class struggle against the Catholic unity of the Homeland, only then are they not condemned propositions."[33]

This preeminence of Catholicism in a text of this nature was not only due to the profoundly Catholic character of the Franco regime, but also to the fact that Fernando María de Castiella was appointed as one of the law's principal drafters. This diplomat and professor of international law was a man of deep Catholic convictions and a member of the Asociación Católica Nacional de Propagandistas (National Catholic Association of Propagandists).[34] Having volunteered to fight in the División Azul (Blue Division),[35] he was appointed director of the

---

31. Duranti, *Conservative Human Rights Revolution*, 296–97.

32. According to the pope, these propositions were ideas and values that he deemed dangerous to the spiritual mission of the Roman Catholic Church. *The Syllabus of Errors* was a list of such ideas and values that were to be avoided by Catholics.

33. Spanish Parliament Archive, *Actas de la comisión especial del Fuero de los Españoles*, P-01-002346-0002-0007-005, 6–8.

34. The Catholic Association of Propagandists is a private association of Spanish Catholics that was founded in 1909 by the Jesuit priest Ángel Ayala. It aims to spread the Catholic faith and the apostolate by training and encouraging select minorities destined to direct the public life of society and the social and political action of Catholics, among whom they would play a unifying role. On the history of this association see José Luis Gutierrez García, *Historia de la Asociación Católica de Propagandistas* (Madrid: CEU, 2010).

35. This was a unit of volunteers from Francoist Spain within the Wehrmacht on the Eastern front during World War II. On this topic see Xosé-Manoel Nuñez Seixas, *The Spanish*

Servicio Exterior de Falange (Falange Foreign Service—the Spanish single-party foreign relations department) in 1942. Subsequently, in 1943, he was appointed director of the Instituto de Estudios Políticos (Institute of Political Studies).[36] After the Nazi defeat, Castiella abandoned his Germanophile positions and returned to Christian internationalism, which affected his influence on the Fuero de los Españoles. Based on his connections with the world of international Catholicism, Castiella aimed to gain for Franco's Spain a sympathetic understanding on the part of the ecclesiastical hierarchies and members of foreign Catholic associations.[37]

The second characteristic of the Francoist conception of rights that was deeply connected to postwar European conservatism was closely related to Catholicism: namely, the reliance on corporatist theories as an alternative model to liberalism and communism for organizing society. For postwar conservatives, the nineteenth-century distinction between liberty and democracy continued to be valid. Thus, they considered that voting rights could not be handed over to the masses since this endangered all other rights. In other words, for conservatives, championing political rights such as freedom of expression did not entail advocating that all citizens had the right to participate in free elections through universal suffrage. Authors such as Jouvenel brought to the postwar table theses that had been popular in the interwar conservative world, those of totalitarian democracy, according to which majoritarian democracy was the origin of totalitarianism.[38] According to this interpretation, the implementation of universal suffrage had engendered mob rule and undermined the rule of law, paving the way for absolute rule without judicial controls.

Considerations on the need to separate the granting of citizenship rights from universal suffrage also appeared within the special

---

Blue Division on the Eastern Front, 1941–1945: War, Occupation, Memory (Toronto: University of Toronto Press, 2022).

36. A Spanish public body for political studies related to the Falangist section of the Franco regime that shared some common points with the Italian fascist Istituto Nazionale di Cultura. After World War II, political Catholicism became more important in the ideology of the institute. During the Francoist dictatorship, it acted as an ideological instrument at the service of the regime. On this organization see Nicolás Sesma, *Antología de la Revista de Estudios Político* (Madrid: Centro de Estudios Políticos y Constitucionales, 2009).

37. Rosa Pardo, "Fernando María Castiella. Pasión política y vocación diplomática," *Historia Contemporánea* 15 (1996): 225–39.

38. On the work of Bertrand de Jouvenel and his influence on post-1945 Europe see Daniel Knegt, *Fascism, Liberalism and Europeanism in the Political Thought of Bertrand de Jouvenel and Alfred Fabre-Luce* (Amsterdam: Amsterdam University Press, 2017), 159–257.

commission of the Spanish Cortes entrusted with reviewing the draft of the Fuero de los Españoles. Thus, in one of its sessions, Raimundo Fernández Cuesta—who at that time was in charge of managing the Secretaría General del Movimiento—did not hesitate to state that the commission's mission was to prevent the drafting from giving rise to "a series of heresies within our Movement, among others, those of universal suffrage, a consequence of the French Revolution." In fact, as Esteban Bilbao, president of the commission, indicated, the objective was to prevent the text from having "a democratic sense in the bad sense of liberal democracy," that is to say, a sense that could lead to universal suffrage, parliamentarism, and political pluralism.[39]

In this context, corporatism emerged as one of the main alternatives to majoritarian liberal democracy among many European conservatives and far-right supporters. The foremost advocates of this model of representation belonged to neo-medieval currents of conservative Catholicism, which found a home in the European Union of Federalists[40] and, above all, in a French extreme right-wing organization with a great deal of weight therein, the Fédération. This organization sheltered former members of Action Française, such as Louis Salleron, and intellectuals who had collaborated with the Vichy regime, such as Bossot and Voirin. Generally, the Fédération promoted intermediate communities such as "families" or "professional organizations" to articulate the relationship between the state and the citizenry. This alternative was welcomed by both British business organizations, from which many of the United Europe Movement's funds came, and their French counterparts. Hendrik Brugmans, a Dutch citizen who was not a member of the Fédération but was president of the European Union of Federalists, also advocated for a corporatist organization of society. Thus, Brugmans called for the establishment of a States-General of Europe composed of eight corporatist groups, ranging from employees and employers to peasants and the middle classes, and from executives and professionals to groups of politicians, intellectuals, and religious

---

39. Spanish Parliament Archive, *Actas de la comisión especial del Fuero de los Españoles*, P-01-002346-0002-0007-002, 14 and 17.

40. An organization founded in December 1946 in Paris to promote a federalist vision of Europe based on anticommunism, antiparliamentarism, and corporatism. Alain Hick, "I. The European Union of Federalists (EUF)," in *Vol 4: Transnational Organizations of Political Parties and Pressure Groups in the Struggle for European Union, 1945–1950*, ed. Walter Lipgens and Wilfried Loth (Berlin: De Gruyter, 1991), 8–111; Knegt, *Fascism*, 213.

figures, consumer organizations, groups of politicians and judges, and youth movements.[41]

The origins of Catholic corporatist ideas are to be found in mid-to-late-nineteenth-century Catholic counterrevolutionary thought in Austria, France, and Germany, as a third way of conceiving political, social, and economic organization in opposition to both socialism and liberal capitalism. Specifically, the publication of Pope Leo XIII's encyclical *Rerum Novarum* marked the critical milestone in the development of Catholic social theory and activism on corporatism during the nineteenth century. Nonetheless, it was during the aftermath of World War I when, fueled by the release of Pius XI's 1931 encyclical *Quadragesimo Anno*, corporatist ideas became increasingly the vogue among younger Catholics frustrated with "parliamentary" political Catholicism and the limited success of Catholic parties against the threat of Bolshevism. Consequently, through the 1930s, corporatism became an extremely appealing proposal for the institutional hybridization of interwar dictatorships. In turn, they tended to create political institutions in which the function of corporatism was to give legitimacy to organic representation and to ensure the co-optation and control of sections of the elite and organized interests.

The Francoists built their model of representation and political participation on the previous existence of corporatist projects within Spain's conservative Catholic tradition. As in the rest of Europe, corporatist theories had been present in Spain since the nineteenth century and materialized in concrete political regimes during the interwar period. The first attempt to implement a corporatist regime in Spain occurred during the dictatorship of General Primo de Rivera (1923–1930). Eduardo Aunós, then minister of labor, created the Organización Corporativa Nacional (National Corporate Organization). Therein, employers and workers, under the presidency of a government representative, were to agree on the characteristics of labor relations in Spain. For Aunós, this organization was to be the prelude to the construction of a full corporate state, in which the labor corporations would eventually become the highest legislative body in the country. Three years later, corporatist representation was included in the preliminary draft of the Constitution of the Spanish Monarchy that was never approved, owing to the fall of the regime in January 1930. During the subsequent

---

41. Duranti, *Conservative Human Rights Revolution*, 257.

Second Republic, the Confederación Española de Derechas Autónomas (Spanish Confederation of Autonomous Rights, CEDA), the main Catholic conservative Spanish political force at the time, espoused the cause of Catholic corporatism as its own, although it was unsuccessful in implementing the idea. During those years, the fascist party, Falange Española, also adopted corporatist models. Indeed, point 6 of its Twenty-Six-Point Program outlined political representation as follows: "All Spanish people will participate ... through their family, municipal, and union function." This point would be included verbatim in Article 10 of the Fuero de los Españoles.

In this sense, the Fuero de los Españoles established that "all Spaniards have the right to participate in public functions of a representative nature, through the family, the municipality, and the labor union." The Francoist corporate system revolved around two pillars. On the one hand, the Cortes Españolas was composed of representatives of municipalities and provinces, labor unions, the government, and other institutions (including the army, the Catholic Church hierarchy, and civil corporations of the state). On the other, it introduced a corporatist electoral system that made it possible to elect the municipal councilmen (discussed in the last section of this chapter). This system attracted the attention of some international actors. For example, some Vatican circles concerned about the growing prominence of the Communist Party in post-1945 Italian political life viewed it with considerable sympathy, especially those surrounding Monsignor Alfredo Ottaviani, the powerful secretary of the Holy Office. For Ottaviani and his allies, the Spanish single-party corporatist structures offered a more attractive model for dealing with the dangerous threat of the powerful Italian Communist Party, as they allowed the Spanish dictatorship to implement a political participation system that prevented communist parties from participating in politics.[42] For his part, Brugmans, whose interest in models of corporatist representation has already been noted, traveled to Salazar's Portugal and Franco's Spain in early 1948 to establish contacts with the federalists of the two regimes. On his return, he wrote to the secretariat of the United Europe Federation in Geneva that "democracy" should not be a criterion for the selection of delegations to the Congress of Europe.[43]

---

42. Pollard, "Corporatism and Political Catholicism," 55.
43. Duranti, *Conservative Human Rights Revolution*, 257.

A Francoist Citizenship

The development of a concept of citizenship based on Catholic, anticommunist, and antiliberal values gave rise to corporatist mechanisms of political participation. Specifically, Article 10 of the Fuero de los Españoles established that "all Spaniards have the right to participate in public functions of a representative nature through the family, the municipality, and the union." Indeed, Franco's government published the law that rolled the mechanisms to make political participation possible into the same edition of the *Boletín Oficial del Estado* as contained the Fuero de los Españoles. Thus, Article 8 of the Ley de Régimen Local (Local System Law) established that Spaniards could elect the councilmen of their town councils, although never the mayors, through a very particular electoral mechanism. Likewise, a whole set of decrees later defined who had the right to participate in such elections.

The municipal elections set up by the Franco regime under the basis of the corporate principles of citizenship established by the Fuero de los Españoles were held for the first time in November 1948.[44] As mentioned above, these elections made it possible to elect some councilmen, although the mayors continued to be appointed by the Francoist authorities on a discretionary basis. The local government law divided the councilmen into three groups, and subsequent legislation established a specific electoral mechanism to elect those who would form part of each of the three. The first of these groups was formed by the councilmen who represented the families. This set of councilmen was directly elected by the so-called heads of families. Undoubtedly, this electoral mechanism allowed for a more significant number of people out of the three groups implemented to participate.[45] The second group comprised union representatives, that is, members of the Organización Sindical Española (Spanish Labor Union Organization—the regime's single union). In this case, the councilmen were elected indirectly by delegates who had previously been voted for by local members of the Francoist single union. The last of the groups had to represent the

---

44. On those voting see Carlos Domper Lasús, *Dictatorship and the Electoral Vote: Francoism and the Portuguese New State Regime in Comparative Perspective, 1945–1975* (Liverpool: Liverpool University Press, 2020).

45. Since this first group of elections had the largest electorate, the Franco regime tried to prevent a high abstention rate from being interpreted as the existence of opposition to its regime. Voting was therefore compulsory in the elections for this first group of councilors. Such a measure was also tried unsuccessfully in the Fourth French Republic, as Zoé Kergomard analyzes in this book.

interests of the municipality. However, the councilmen who would form part of this group were not chosen by electoral means. Instead, previously elected councilmen from the other two groups chose the municipality representatives in the town hall from among the names on a list that the civil governor had drawn up. Each municipal professionals' and property owners' organization had sent the names of several of its members to the civil governor so that he could choose those who would be definitively included on the list.

Given all that, who had the right to vote in these elections? And just who could exercise the citizenship established by the Fuero de los Españoles? Since the elections to choose the representative councilmen of the municipality were nothing more than a meeting at which the councilmen of the other two groups selected various people from a list provided by the civil governor, I will focus on the people who had the right to vote in the other two elections. Clearly, the elections for selecting the councilmen who represented the families allowed the highest number of people to vote. Specifically, they enfranchised each town's "heads of families" to vote. That is to say, they granted voting rights to all those who were responsible for the maintenance of a family unit, as long as they owned the home in which the family lived. Regarding the union elections, the number of people entitled to vote was much smaller than those who could vote to select the families' representatives. To be a delegate in such elections, it was necessary to meet three requisites. First, being affiliated with the Spanish Labor Union Organization was compulsory. Second, being head of a local union section was also mandatory (the union was divided into several branches such as metal, administration, food, and so on). Finally, being over twenty-five years of age was also a requirement.

Consequently, having a job was essential to vote in these elections, since it was impossible to maintain a family unit or join the Francoist union without being employed. It is essential to underline the fact that the Fuero del Trabajo (a sort of workers' rights charter), passed by the Franco dictatorship in March 1938, prohibited women from working. Therefore, women could not exercise the rights of political participation that emanated from the concept of citizenship established by the Fuero de los Españoles. Similarly, voting in both elections required not having been sentenced to lesser prison sentences. Accordingly, neither those who had supported the Republic during the civil war nor those who had been sentenced for sodomy—that is, gay men—were able to vote.

How did Spanish society receive the passing of the Fuero de los Españoles and the enactment of the citizens' rights it supposedly guaranteed? In truth, scholarship on the political attitudes of Spaniards toward Francoism has shown how ordinary people in Franco's Spain were depoliticized, or at least demobilized, until the mid-1960s.[46] The main concern of ordinary Spaniards had nothing to do with politics or international affairs. In the immediate aftermath of the civil war, most focused on getting by. In other words, their principal concerns were hunger, rationing, and other daily miseries. Later, as the dictatorship was consolidated and the Spanish economy grew, they sought better living conditions. Thus, for example, in a Spanish single-party report written in Valencia in November 1950, the provincial party official remarked that "Spaniards did not want more participation in politics, they just wanted lower prices, better wages, food, and access to a greater number of goods and services." These strategies helped the poor to survive the insensitivity of the state. Indeed, one could argue that they benefited from a regime that counted on conservatism and widespread passivity to carry out the projects that suited its interests.[47]

An Anti-liberal Conception of Citizenship

After May 1945, Europe underwent a reconstruction process that led to a (re)definition of core concepts for developing new political and legal systems. Different ideologies and political traditions began to struggle to define terms such as "democracy," "human rights," and "citizenship." In contrast to classical interpretations that link this phenomenon to the liberated societies of Western Europe and more recent works that show that it also took place in Eastern Europe, this chapter points out that this (re)definition also affected Franco's Spain.

In Franco's dictatorship, these attempts were related entirely to the main objective of its foreign policy after 1945, that of having Spain accepted as a valid international actor by the anticommunist victors of World War II. Thus, as happened in the case of the Eastern European dictatorships, Franco's Spain developed its conceptualization of the

---

46. Claudio Hernández Burgos, *Franquismo a ras de suelo. Zonas grises, apoyos sociales y actitudes durante la dictadura (1936–1976)* (Granada: Universidad de Granada, 2013), and Carlos Fuertes Muñoz, *Viviendo en dictadura: La evolución de las actitudes sociales hacia el franquismo* (Granada: Comares, 2017).

47. On this issue see Antonio Cazorla, *Fear and Progress: Ordinary Lives in Franco´s Spain, 1939–1975* (Oxford: John Wiley, 2009). The quote is on p. 26.

abovementioned political terms based on its own antiliberal cultural traditions. These traditions stemmed from nineteenth-century traditionalist conservative Catholicism in Spain. The Fuero de los Españoles was the legal text that made it possible to articulate this whole process of redefinition.

Indeed, the theoretical construction of the concept of Franco's citizenship that emerged from the Fuero was part of a foreign policy operation. Yet regardless of the success it may have had among European chancelleries, there is no doubt that such a definition had points in common and in many respects was consistent with the vision of citizenship and human rights defended by the most conservative sectors in Western European countries. In this sense, placing the Fuero de los Españoles in the European context allows us to illuminate a reality that has been neglected until recently: a legacy of fascism in post-1945 Europe. One of the main manifestations of this legacy was the existence of an authoritarian transnational European space made up of former fascist and Nazi militants as well as conservatives and Christian democrats close to conservatism, within which Francoism found a site of understanding and accommodation.

Carlos Domper Lasús is an assistant professor in the University of Zaragoza (Spain) History Department. He holds a PhD in political history, political science, and political theory from the Libera Università Internazionale degli Studi Sociali "Guido Carli" in Rome. He has been a visiting professor and researcher at various European, American, and Latin American universities. He is author of *Dictatorship and the Electoral Vote: Francoism and the Portuguese New State Regime in Comparative Perspective, 1945–1975* and *Combining Political History and Political Science: Towards a New Understanding of the Political.*

CHAPTER 8

Gender, Labor, and the Forging of Socialist Citizenship in East Germany

Rachel Weiser

On March 8, 1968, female factory laborers across the German Democratic Republic (GDR, or East Germany) celebrated International Women's Day with their workers' brigades. The East German government first introduced workers' brigades in the mid-1950s to nationalize industries more quickly and curb worker dissatisfaction. East Germany's governing party, the Socialist Unity Party of Germany (SED), hoped that brigades would increase productivity within factories and foster a more collective identity among workers. As part of the campaign, individual factories kept "brigade books" starting in 1959. Mandated by the East German state, these workplace diaries recorded factories' industrial, political, and cultural activities. The workers' uprising of 1953, the inefficiencies of the command economy, and the hemorrhaging of workers to the West caused state and factory officials to fret about the scarcity, reliability, and obedience of the labor force more broadly in the late 1950s.[1] For the regime, brigade books

---

1. Donna Harsch, *Revenge of the Domestic: Women, the Family, and Communism in the GDR* (Princeton, NJ: Princeton University Press, 2007), 6. For more economic history see Jeffrey Kopstein, *The Politics of Economic Decline in East Germany, 1945–1989* (Chapel Hill: University of North Carolina Press, 1997); André Steiner, *The Plans That Failed: An Economic History of the GDR* (New York: Berghahn Books, 2010); Peter C. Caldwell, *Dictatorship, State Planning, and Social Theory in the German Democratic Republic* (Cambridge: Cambridge University Press, 2003).

served to both increase surveillance and provide workers with a means to channel their discontent, especially after the Berlin Wall went up in 1961. Authors were encouraged to call out problems with people or in production. But, as this chapter will show, the practice of authoring brigade books came to mean much more to many female factory workers.

At a bridge-building factory in Schlabendorf, Elisabeth Schmidt wrote in her company's brigade book, as she had done daily throughout the late 1960s. As the book's author, she recorded various aspects of life in their factory, from production goals to quotas achieved. In one entry, Schmidt described the 1968 International Women's Day, noting that her factory manager "praised the success of the company, in which women in particular played a large part. This was followed by awards for us women who act as role models, who have understood how to work and learn as recommended by our socialist state. . . . I am particularly proud of this."[2] At a rail transport factory in Braunsbedra, Margarete Hellwig similarly reflected on the events of the 1968 International Women's Day and her own factory's female "role models." In her brigade book, Hellwig wrote, "The great achievements of our women are recognized, because they have played an essential part in building socialism in our country."[3]

These accounts from Schmidt and Hellwig are only two examples of the numerous women who recorded the lived experiences of female factory workers in brigade books. Authors had to submit their books to factory managers for review, meaning they no doubt included specific moments, phrases, and accomplishments the state would want to hear. Yet much of what women wrote was not necessarily politically expedient or strategic but showed a value for relationships and activities that extended beyond productivity. The practice of maintaining brigade books also shaped how many female workers made sense of their industrial labor and broader citizenship, as they wrote themselves and their colleagues into the socialist project daily. Simultaneously personal and state-sponsored, individual and collective, brigade books serve as an underutilized source for preserving the memories and experiences of female factory workers in particular. In addition, authors regularly included critical remarks in their brigade books, revealing the ways these workplace diaries developed into both a method through which women

---

2. Elisabeth Schmidt, "Phillip Müller Brigade," Brückenbetrieb Schlabendorf, *Brigadebuch* (Schlabendorf, Cottbus, 1968-1969), Wende Museum of the Cold War.

3. Margarete Hellwig, Brigade IV, Bahnhof Braunsbedra (Deutsche Reichsbahn), *Brigadebuch* (Braunsbedra, Halle, 1977), Wende Museum of the Cold War.

communicated their demands and frustrations directly with the state and the factory management and a discursive space for women to resist, critique, question, and celebrate the realities of women's wage labor and socialist citizenship in the GDR.

This chapter examines the intersection of gender, labor, and socialist citizenship in East Germany through the writings of female factory workers. Ideologically and politically, women's industrial labor was crucial for the regime. The contributions of women to the East German economy, however, were not simply rhetorical. By 1989, over 90 percent of women worked outside the home.[4] Yet this chapter moves beyond economics and the utility of women to the state, focusing instead on how factory work empowered women as socialist citizens and provided them a sense of accomplishment and purpose independent of child-rearing and the domestic sphere. Especially for those who had lived under the conservative gender norms of the Third Reich, it was important that women were no longer confined to the home. For many women, socialist citizenship in the GDR also meant gender equality through new professional opportunities, training programs, and supportive family policies. As a result, this chapter argues, participation in the factory served as both evidence of and a space in which to live out their full rights of East German citizenship. Brigade book entries in particular illustrate not only how women actively participated in the socialist state through wage labor, but also that it was through the factory that many women understood their roles and rights as socialist citizens.

As Nikola Tohma and Anna Dobrowolska explore in their contributions to this volume, work was key to constructing socialist societies in postwar Europe. In the GDR, laborers were essential ideologically, politically, and economically to building the "Workers' and Farmers' State."[5] Through its constitutions, policies, and official rhetoric, the East German state sought to develop worker-citizens, defining citizenship as participation in the socialist state and economy by guaranteeing all citizens' equal right to work and wages.[6] The SED emphasized the role of industrial production in particular in order to rebuild the

---

4. Gunnar Winkler, *Sozialreport DDR 1990: Daten und Fakten zur sozialen Lage in der DDR* (Stuttgart: Bonn Aktuell, 1990), 107; Josie McLellan, *Love in the Time of Communism: Intimacy and Sexuality in the GDR* (Cambridge: Cambridge University Press, 2011), 14.

5. Harsch, *Revenge of the Domestic*; Dorothee Wierling, "Work, Workers, and Politics in the German Democratic Republic," *International Labor and Working-Class History*, no. 50 (1996): 44–63.

6. Article 15, Constitution of the German Democratic Republic (1949).

country after the wreckage of the Second World War. In doing so, the SED established a kind of citizenship centered on the industrial sphere, specifically through the factory.[7]

The rights and duties of worker-citizens applied to women as well as men. Drawing on early socialist works—from Friedrich Engels and August Bebel to Clara Zetkin and Alexandra Kollontai—East German leaders insisted that women's equal participation in paid work was crucial to achieving gender equality more broadly.[8] Herbert Warnke, chairman of the national trade union representing all East German workers (Free German Trade Union Federation, or FDGB), for example, observed in 1952 that "the equality of women is rooted in her place in production."[9] In the party's eyes, gender equality in the socialist state started in the industrial factory. As a result, women's citizenship in the GDR was explicitly tied to their industrial labor.

The regime also couched women's wage labor as economically essential. Demographic changes caused by World War II and the casualties of millions of male soldiers had left the country with a disproportionately high female population, necessitating policies that integrated women into industry.[10] In order to accomplish both its ideological and economic goals, the SED implemented policies to codify new expectations of female worker-citizens. In 1949, the first East German constitution protected gender equality as well as women's equal right to work and wages.[11] Such constitutional guarantees primed workingwomen to have certain expectations about their labor and its connection to their rights as citizens. In the Third Reich, Nazi leaders had framed women's work as a temporary solution, especially during the war, insisting on the contingency of women's wage labor and the necessity of their domestic roles.[12] In the GDR, however, women were told, and guaranteed

---

7. While this chapter focuses on socialist citizenship as connected to wage labor, recent scholarship considers other important aspects of citizenship in East Germany. For more on the political and social function of elections and political parties in the GDR as more than simply propaganda, for example, see Ned Richardson-Little, *The Human Rights Dictatorship: Socialism, Global Solidarity and Revolution in East Germany* (Cambridge: Cambridge University Press, 2020).

8. Elizabeth Tobin and Jennifer Gibson, "East German Women's Work in the Transition from Nazism to Communism," *Central European History* 28, no. 3 (1995): 318.

9. Herbert Warnke quoted in Harsch, *Revenge of the Domestic*, 3.

10. Elizabeth Heineman, *What Difference Does a Husband Make? Women and Marital Status in Nazi and Postwar Germany* (Berkeley: University of California Press, 1999), 76, 177.

11. Article 7 and Article 15, Constitution of the German Democratic Republic (1949).

12. For more on mobilizing women's work for war in Nazi Germany see Leila Rupp, *Mobilizing Women for War: German and American War Propaganda, 1939–1945* (Princeton, NJ:

under law, that their work was of equal value and that their citizenship meant gender equality both in production and in socialist society.

The reality of women's work, however, often failed to match the rhetoric. Female factory workers endured lower wages, discrimination, and harassment. The labor market remained segregated, as women continued to work predominantly in lower-paid sectors of the economy, such as trade and light industry.[13] Meanwhile, heavy industry, considered high risk and therefore better paid, often excluded women. The SED, FDGB, and local factory leadership claimed to consider women's work important, but despite the constitutional guarantee of "equal pay for equal work," men were often given preference in hiring, even if candidates were equally qualified.[14] As a result, women experienced daily life in East German industry differently from their male colleagues. In her chapter on sex workers in Poland, Dobrowolska similarly explores the challenges to women's labor and promised emancipation under state socialism.

Scholars have extensively analyzed the role of women in the GDR, often highlighting how the socialist state failed its female citizens. The portrayal of women as passive victims of an authoritarian regime fits comfortably within a broader totalitarian model for understanding the GDR. Such scholarship focuses on the dictatorial rule of the one-party state, the omnipresence of the Stasi, and East German society as "shut down" and repressed.[15] Scholars have questioned the extent to which women specifically exercised agency under state socialism and criticized the characterization of socialist countries as "feminist."[16] These works contend that the GDR was a patriarchal regime that coerced,

---

Princeton University Press, 1978), and "'I Don't Call That *Volksgemeinschaft*': Women, Class and War in Nazi Germany," in *Women, War, and Revolution*, ed. Carol R. Berkin and Clara M. Lovett (New York: Holmes & Meier, 1980); Dörte Winkler, *Frauenarbeit im Dritten Reich* (Hamburg: Hoffman und Campe Verlag, 1977).

13. Harsch, *Revenge of the Domestic*, 254; Heineman, *What Difference Does a Husband Make?*, 182, 201–5.

14. Article 18, Constitution of the German Democratic Republic (1949); Heineman, *What Difference Does a Husband Make?*, 90, 182–86.

15. Sigrid Meuschel, *Legitimation und Parteiherrschaft: Zum Paradox von Stabilität und Revolution in der DDR 1945–1989* (Frankfurt am Main: Suhrkamp, 1992); Armin Mitter and Stefan Wolle, *Untergang auf Raten: Unbekannte Kapitel der DDR—Geschichte* (Munich: Bertelsmann, 1993). For more on debates about the GDR as totalitarian see Andrew Port, "The Banalities of East German Historiography," in *Becoming East German: Socialist Structures and Sensibilities after Hitler*, ed. Mary Fulbrook and Andrew Port (New York: Berghahn Books, 2013).

16. Nanette Funk, "A Very Tangled Knot: Official State Socialist Women's Organizations, Women's Agency and Feminism in Eastern European State Socialism," *European Journal of Women's Studies* 21, no. 4 (2014): 344–60.

misled, and used its female citizens.[17] Conversely, a growing number of scholars have engaged in feminist revisions of state socialism, arguing that socialist regimes actively supported their female citizens. Historians have argued that despite the authoritarian nature of socialist countries, much can be learned from the experiences of the Eastern bloc with regard to gender equity. Scholars have emphasized how many policies promoted social and cultural changes that enabled women to better balance their personal and professional lives compared to their counterparts in the West.[18]

By focusing on female experiences in the factory, this chapter navigates between these two schools of thought and argues that women could simultaneously embrace the emancipatory potential of socialist citizenship while challenging its contradictions and shortcomings.[19] Contrary to totalitarian models that cast women as victims of a regime that mandated backbreaking work, this chapter argues that female laborers not only contributed to the industrial sphere but also that factory work became an important part of their identity. The East German constitution guaranteed employment, but many female factory workers characterized their citizenship in the GDR as social and economic rights beyond their legal right to work: women owed the state their labor, and in return the state owed women gender equality in practice through professional opportunities, equitable policies, and social services.[20] Entries recorded in brigade books attest to the vertical dimension of citizenship and how the meaning of socialist citizenship in the GDR was not solely imposed but multidirectional, developed from both top down and bottom up.[21]

---

17. Kristen R. Ghodsee, "Untangling the Knot: A Response to Nanette Funk," *European Journal of Women's Studies* 22, no. 2 (2015): 248–52.

18. Kristen R. Ghodsee and Julia Mead, "What Has Socialism Ever Done for Women?," *Catalyst* 2, no. 2 (2018): 105; Francisca de Haan, "Ten Years After: Communism and Feminism Revisited," *Aspasia* 10, no. 1 (2016): 102–8.

19. Existing scholarship has suggested that many East Germans supported the creation of a socialist state but at the same time resisted or undermined (intentionally and unintentionally) aspects of the SED's agenda. Dolores L. Augustine, "The Power Question in GDR History," *German Studies Review* 34, no. 3 (2011): 633.

20. Kathleen Canning and Sonya O. Rose, "Introduction: Gender, Citizenship and Subjectivity; Some Historical and Theoretical Considerations," *Gender & History* 13, no. 3 (2001): 431–32.

21. *Making Sense of Dictatorship: Domination and Everyday Life in East Central Europe after 1945*, ed. Celia Donert, Ana Kladnik, and Martin Sabrow (New York: Central European Press, 2022).

At the same time, this chapter challenges solely positive portrayals of women living and working under state socialism. The relationship between the East German state and its female citizens was often contested, and workingwomen were not afraid to make their dissatisfaction with the East German government known. Factories in particular developed into spaces for women to voice their collective frustrations with the state for failing to deliver on their interpretation of their full rights as citizens. In this sense, citizenship meant a set of participatory rights and duties as well as claims on society and the state made by citizens.[22] Specifically, brigade book authors used the pages of their factory diaries to articulate problems directly to the state, such as the persistence of gender discrimination from both male colleagues and their own husbands. Brigade book authors also demanded solutions, such as training courses that would advance female laborers' careers and social services to ease women's domestic and maternal responsibilities.

Additionally, female laborers voiced their concerns and demands directly with various state organs through citizen petitions.[23] Citizen petitions were a regular feature of East Germans' everyday lives, and scholars estimate that at least two-thirds of all East German households submitted petitions between 1949 and 1989.[24] For the regime, petitions provided "valuable clues about the extent and nature of dissatisfaction with the SED's policies."[25] Meanwhile, ordinary citizens wrote petitions for a myriad of personal, political, and economic reasons, and the motivations among female factory workers varied as well. The fact that female laborers submitted citizen petitions voluntarily and frequently suggests that petitioners expected the state to listen to their concerns and rectify their problems. Brigade book entries and citizen petitions about industrial work illustrate that the factory served as

---

22. Kathleen Canning, "Class vs. Citizenship: Key Words in German Gender History," *Central European History* 37, no. 2 (2004): 226.
23. The right to petition was specific to neither Germany nor the twentieth century, and citizen petitions have both a rich history and an extensive historiography. Yet petitions held a "special place" within East German life, as citizens took full advantage of their constitutional right to petition. Article 3, Constitution of the German Democratic Republic (1949). For more on citizen petitions see Paul Betts, *Within Walls: Private Life in the German Democratic Republic* (Oxford: Oxford University Press, 2010); Felix Mühlberg, *Bürger, Bitten und Behörden: Geschichte der Eingabe in der DDR* (Berlin: Dietz Verlag, 2004); Jonathan Zatlin, *The Currency of Socialism: Money and Political Culture in East Germany* (Cambridge: Cambridge University Press, 2007); Mary Fulbrook, *The People's State: East German Society from Hitler to Honecker* (New Haven, CT: Yale University Press, 2005).
24. Zatlin, *Currency of Socialism*, 287, 293, 299; Betts, *Within Walls*; Fulbrook, *People's State*.
25. Zatlin, *Currency of Socialism*, 235.

a space for women not only to participate in but also to negotiate the terms of socialist citizenship in the GDR.

Finally, this chapter considers the gendered nature of industrial work—and socialist citizenship more broadly—in the GDR. Dobrowolska's chapter explores how citizenship remained gendered in postwar Poland despite socialism's claim to collapse gender as a social category. Theoretically, East German society and the factory specifically would be made up of class-conscious workers without distinguishing by gender. For this reason, workers' brigades were officially open to both men and women. The realities of gender discrimination, however, resulted in men and women remaining largely separate professionally. Additionally, while workers' brigades consisted of both male and female members, women dominated the authorship of the books and the activities recorded in them, as photos, rosters, and handwritten entries attest.[26] Many historians have examined brigades, but scholars have largely neglected their gendered dynamics.[27] This approach fails to recognize that men and women experienced brigades and industrial work differently.[28] Therefore, these books shed light on how women specifically described everyday life, industrial work, and socialist citizenship in East Germany.

Beyond a political status assigned to individuals by the state, citizenship can be understood as belonging to specific communities.[29] For example, Tohma, in her chapter on refugees from the Greek Civil War, explores how socialist citizenship in Czechoslovakia was defined as belonging to a community with shared ideals. Similarly, in all sectors of the East German economy, even male-dominated industries, women carved out space for female community within workers' brigades, and the relationships that developed often grew from a gendered sense of

---

26. The brigade books I examined for this chapter were all maintained by a female author. The female authorship of many brigade books suggests persistent gendered hierarchies in the factories and the perpetuation of the role of women as secretary.

27. Thomas Reichel, *Sozialistisch arbeiten, lernen und leben—Die Brigadebewegung in der DDR 1959–1989* (Cologne: Böhlau, 2011); Jörg Roesler, "Die Produktionsbrigaden in der Industrie der DDR. Zentrum der Arbeitswelt?," in *Sozialgeschichte der DDR*, ed. Hartmut Kaeble, Jürgen Kocka, and Hartmut Zwahr (Stuttgart: Klett-Cotta, 1994); Corey Ross, "Staging the East German 'Working Class': Representation and Class Identity in the 'Workers' State,'" in *Representing the German Nation: History and Identity in Twentieth-Century Germany*, ed. Mary Fulbrook and Martin Swales (Manchester: Manchester University Press, 2000).

28. Those that do address gender tend to focus on the male-dominated nature of workers' brigades. Till Großmann, for example, mentions women's brigades briefly, but primarily discusses male leaders. Till Großmann, "Moral Economies of Love and Labor in the GDR: Family Values and Work Ethics in Advice Columns, circa 1960," *Geschichte und Gesellschaft. Sonderheft* 26, no. 26 (2019): 218–19.

29. Canning and Rose, "Introduction: Gender, Citizenship and Subjectivity," 427.

solidarity rather than class comradeship. Brigade books and citizen petitions reveal how industrial factories developed into gendered spaces, which in turn served to transform women's status as worker-citizens into a broader conception of citizenship rooted in female community.

Problems Articulated

Female factory workers consistently used brigade books and citizen petitions to articulate problems women faced in East German industry. Specifically, authors complained about the persistence of discrimination and harassment from male colleagues and factory managers, especially regarding women's qualifications as skilled workers. Beyond women's legal right to work, East German leaders emphasized the importance of technical training for women to obtain advanced qualifications and gain experience in traditionally male-dominated occupations.[30] In 1963, for example, FDGB leader Warnke noted that "every factory leader must affirm the role of women as co-owners of the means of production.... Their promotion and development are urgently necessary, especially in industry."[31] In the revised 1968 Constitution, the advancement of women, "especially in professional qualifications," was explicitly designated a priority.[32] The East German state made extensive efforts throughout the 1960s and beyond to transform women into skilled workers through factory training programs, lecture series, and the obtaining of advanced technical degrees and skilled-worker certificates.[33] As a result, many brigade book authors and petitioners interpreted the constitutional guarantee of equal work and wages as extending to equal opportunities for training and advancement.

Although an increasing number of women had acquired vocational training and skilled-worker certificates by the late 1960s, gender discrimination persisted. Charlotte noted in a 1968 citizen petition to the FDGB, for example, that in her Dresden drilling and machines factory, "women are not fully respected by men, the opinion is still that women are far from understanding technology."[34] In 1963, Elke

---

30. Harsch, *Revenge of the Domestic*, 246.
31. Herbert Warnke quoted in Ursula Langspach-Steinhaußen, *Wie schreiben wie unser Brigadetagebuch?* (Berlin: Verlag Tribune, 1970), 50.
32. Article 20, Constitution of the German Democratic Republic (1968).
33. Heineman, *What Difference Does a Husband Make?*, 90.
34. The names of all petitioners have been changed to protect their privacy. Sächsisches Staatsarchiv—Hauptstaatsarchiv Dresden, 12465 FDGB-Bezirksvorstand Dresden, Nr. 0743.

similarly described numerous meetings scheduled to discuss the role of women in her Löbau factory. "Every time," she wrote, "not a single male official felt it necessary to take part in our deliberations.... Women themselves are left to solve women's problems."[35] Through citizen petitions, women marshaled the regime's language about women's participation in industry to criticize the gender inequality in their factories. Furthermore, both women went over the heads of their factory managers and wrote directly to the FDGB to call out the lack of respect from their male colleagues, demonstrating an expectation of gender equality as part of their broader rights as socialist citizens and laborers. Such accounts illustrate the obstacles women continued to face in production. Yet the persistence with which female factory workers submitted petitions directly to state organs about discrimination revealed how seriously women made claims about their understanding of socialist citizenship, insisting that women's equal right to work necessitated their equal treatment in the workplace.

Female laborers used their brigade books and citizen petitions to criticize not only their male colleagues but also their husbands. As they advanced in the workplace, women's skilled work often caused tension within the family. An author from a special vehicle factory in Berlin, for example, wrote about her peer, Colleague S., who wanted to attend courses for her engineering degree but met resistance from her husband because "he would have to pick up their three-year-old from day care [therefore] she could not attend the course."[36] Yet according to the author, the women in the brigade supported Colleague S. "against the will of her husband" because advanced qualifications were "beneficial to the entire society, not just a colleague studying for her own pleasure." This conflict, the author concluded, "is far too common among our female comrades and their backward husbands."[37]

The frustration over "backward husbands" illustrates women's understanding of the relationship between labor and socialist citizenship more broadly. Beyond their legal right to work, women expected the

---

35. Sächsisches Staatsarchiv—Hauptstaatsarchiv Dresden, 12465 FDGB-Bezirksvorstand Dresden, Nr. 1113.

36. Kollektiv Fertigungsmittel "Otto Von Guericke," VEB Spezialfahrzeugwerk, Direktionsbereich Technik, *Brigadebuch* (Adlershof, Berlin, 1986), Wende Museum of the Cold War. Brigade book authors used the prefix "Colleague" (*Kollegin*) instead of the traditional "Mrs." (*Frau*) when referring to female coworkers. While still using the feminine noun, the decision to use "Colleague" reveals how the egalitarian rhetoric of socialist citizenship extended even to forms of address in the East German factory.

37. Kollektiv Fertigungsmittel "Otto Von Guericke."

East German state to transform norms regarding women's wage labor, specifically male-female relationships both within and beyond the family. The author presented her resentment of "backward husbands" not as about women's dual roles as workers and homemakers but as about their husbands' continued expectation of normative gender roles that disregarded their wives' professional advancement and hindered something "beneficial to the entire society." In her description of Colleague S., the author framed technical training as an important means for women to contribute to the socialist state, as did the other female brigade members. Importantly, the author characterized her fellow brigade members as a community of workingwomen who validated one another "against the will" of their husbands. Brigade books capture how many female laborers made sense of their labor and citizenship through the lens of gender. Such accounts also reveal how female factory workers articulated support for the state's promise to liberate women from bourgeois domesticity and develop advanced technical skills while simultaneously communicating to state and factory leaders the challenges that workingwomen continued to face in the "Workers' and Farmers' State."

Solutions Demanded

Female factory workers used their brigade books and petitions not only to voice frustrations but also to propose solutions and promote their vision of what socialist citizenship should look like in practice. To do so, many women leveraged their authority as female laborers who actually worked in the factories, as well as female citizens who directly experienced the daily realities of gender discrimination, to instruct the state on what female worker-citizens needed. Specifically, authors demanded advanced technical training and social services to secure their broader rights of equal work, wages, and opportunities.

Brigade book authors regularly wrote about their participation in professional advancement, which many presented as essential in a socialist society that not only promised to protect women's equal right to work but also to train, promote, and advance them.[38] In 1961, for example, Edith Schmerse from an electronics factory in Berlin recorded

---

38. Augustine, "Power Question in GDR History," 643; Dolores L. Augustine, *Red Prometheus: Engineering and Dictatorship in East Germany, 1945–1990* (Cambridge, MA: MIT Press, 2007).

that technical training "will help to improve the achievements of women in all areas of life."[39] Schmerse characterized technical training as not only important for her own professional development and legal right to work but also as a solution to advancing the gender equality promised by socialist citizenship. She likely emphasized technical training to demonstrate her own commitment to industrial production to those factory leaders reading her brigade book. At the same time, she described training programs as key to the realization of her full rights as an East German worker-citizen and to women's development "in all areas of life" beyond the factory.

Other brigade book authors similarly presented advanced technical training as a solution to continued gender discrimination. In 1963, Colleague Grimm from a camera manufacturer in Dresden commented that the greatest obstacle to her career was her husband's objections.[40] After explaining her enrollment in advanced training courses, she wrote, "even more ideological work is needed for men, so that they see that it is also necessary for women to continue learning. I recommended that my husband, because I'm out and about a lot now, take a cooking course. He refused.... My husband also had the opinion, 'why are you working? I work and make plenty of money'."[41] Here, Grimm used her brigade book to communicate to factory managers the negative view of her professional advancement expressed by her own husband, who valued neither her time nor her newly gained expertise. Grimm presented the conflict, however, as more than a marital spat, but as a broader societal problem that required "even more ideological work" from the regime to change the ways men thought about women's productive labor. In her account, Grimm leveraged the regime's own rhetoric about female worker-citizens to demand it support women's professional training and school husbands on the value of their wives' industrial labor.

By recording the productive contributions of their brigades to the socialist economy, authors included specific content that factory leaders and state authorities would want to read about. At the same time, many female factory workers presented their professional accomplishments as contributing to a sense of gender solidarity, rather than class

---

39. Bundesarchiv Berlin-Lichterfelde, Stiftung Archiv der Parteien und Massenorganisationen der DDR (BArch-SAPMO), DY 34/14921.

40. Sächsisches Staatsarchiv—Hauptstaatsarchiv Dresden, 12465 FDGB-Bezirksvorstand Dresden, Nr. 1113.

41. Sächsisches Staatsarchiv—Hauptstaatsarchiv Dresden, 12465 FDGB-Bezirksvorstand Dresden, Nr. 1113.

consciousness. For example, Martina Hauke from a chemical factory in Leipzig wrote about her experience in a technical training program. "In a class of 35," Hauke recorded, "there were four male students and 31 female students. The girls quickly became friends."[42] Advanced technical training not only empowered individual women as socialist worker-citizens but also fostered gendered communities of solidarity and support. Authors used the pages of brigade books to celebrate one another's educational accomplishments, such as Margarete Hellwig from the rail transport factory in Braunsbedra, who included in one entry: "Three of our female colleagues are scheduled to pass their exams, then they will have all the prerequisites to obtain their skilled worker certificate. We wish them a lot of success in their work!"[43] Such entries reveal how many female factory workers framed their experience of labor and citizenship as both gendered and socialist, as technical training cultivated gender solidarity rooted in a shared commitment to productivist socialist principles and the emancipatory potential of women's wage labor.

Indeed, this gendered experience of labor was particularly evident in how female factory workers presented socialist competitions. Brigades entered competitions with one another for various criteria, such as the most productive or the most accident-free workplace. While some historians have argued that competitions simply served as a ritual of affirmation for the regime, brigade books suggest that socialist competition fostered a collective mentality among female brigade members.[44] In 1963, Charlotte Weichenhain from a textile factory in Zittau described the women in her brigade moving "from the 'I' and toward the 'we'" because of their participation in socialist competition.[45] Similarly, a brigade book author noted in 1972, "Of course, we don't have the opinion

---

42. Martina Hauke, Kollektiv DSF Forschungs-Planung, VEB Chemieanlagenbau Kombinat, *Tagebuch* (Leipzig, 1979–1982), Wende Museum of the Cold War.
43. Hellwig, Brigade IV, Bahnhof Braunsbedra (Deutsche Reichsbahn), *Brigadebuch*.
44. Modeled on the competitions within the Soviet Stakhanovite movement in the mid-1930s, socialist competition sought to further achieve production goals through the added incentive of competition. As a "voluntary-compulsory" activity, competitions took place between individuals, brigades, and state enterprises in the Soviet Union and other Eastern bloc states. In the GDR see Kopstein, *Politics of Economic Decline in East Germany*, 12; Jeanette Madarász, *Working in East Germany: Normality in a Socialist Dictatorship, 1961–79* (New York: Palgrave Macmillan, 2006); Ross, "Staging the East German 'Working Class,'" 166. For a transnational perspective see Katalin Miklóssy and Melanie Ilic, eds., *Competition in Socialist Society* (London: Routledge, 2014).
45. Sächsisches Staatsarchiv–Hauptstaatsarchiv Dresden, 12465 FDGB-Bezirksvorstand Dresden, Nr. 1113.

'this is not my job, I don't do it.' No! We are a collective and one person represents all the others."[46] Both authors included accounts of socialist competition intentionally, knowing their workplace diaries would be turned in and analyzed by factory leadership. Yet their entries also reveal that many workingwomen adopted the SED's goal for brigades to foster a collective identity among workers and framed that collective in gendered terms, as a community of women.

Despite the brigade movement's focus on class comradeship, the unintended consequence of such training programs and socialist competitions was that many women expressed pride in their accomplishments specifically as women. Elisabeth Schmidt, for instance, wrote in 1969, "The women of our factory have made our collective one of the most exemplary in bridge operations. We have already been honored twice in socialist competitions."[47] Likewise, when writing about the key to her factory's success in socialist competition, Anita Leicht explained, "It's because our collective consists almost entirely of women."[48] Many brigade members presented the socialist and the female as synonymous, whether they criticized gender discrimination within the collective by rallying together against male colleagues and factory managers or celebrated the accomplishments of women specifically in socialist competition. As the "Workers' and Farmers' State," the GDR staked its legitimacy in genderless class solidarity. While brigade books suggest that many female factory workers remained committed to the state's promise of gender equality, they also reveal the factory as a site of gendered solidarity that ultimately undermined the universality of the socialist project.

For many, the gendered nature of socialist citizenship in the GDR also played out in female laborers' struggle to balance their "double burden," the expectation of women to participate in full-time wage labor while simultaneously maintaining their primary role in the domestic sphere. Over the forty years of its existence, the East German state introduced various policies and initiatives aimed at enabling working mothers to commit fully to both roles. Despite the SED's claims, however, the party never entirely eliminated the "double burden." Furthermore, women's "double burden" was exacerbated by the continued expectation of traditional gender roles among most of the men in their

---

46. Kollektiv der Betriebsküche, VEB Burger Bekleidungswerke, *Brigadebuch*.
47. Schmidt, "Phillip Müller Brigade," *Brigadebuch*.
48. Anita Leicht, Analytik G59, Betribesdirektion Organische Spezialprodukte, VEB Chemische Werke Buna, *Brigadebuch* (Schkopau, 1977), Wende Museum of the Cold War.

lives. Thus, social services remained a key source of conflict and collaboration between the state and female citizens.

In the same way that women's participation in advanced training courses and socialist competition aimed to eradicate gender discrimination, female factory workers demanded social services to combat their "double burden." Social services became a crucial component of women's broader rights as worker-citizens in the GDR and had particular importance under state socialism more broadly.[49] Labor historians have argued that nonwage benefits served as a strategy by the state to "buy off" women.[50] But the consistent recording in brigade books and submission of citizen petitions from female factory workers suggest that many understood social services as an integral part of their rights as citizens. Female factory workers required more than just a constitutional guarantee of the right to work: the state needed to provide communal institutions such as day cares to enable their full-time labor. While training programs provided women with important opportunities for technical training and skills development, social services facilitated their participation in industry in the first place. In democratic societies, social citizenship is often considered partial and refers to a series of rights for those who are deprived of political rights.[51] For women in the GDR, however, social citizenship was not "secondary" but rather fundamental to affirming their political and legal rights to citizenship, specifically their constitutional guarantee to equal work and wages outside the home. The fact that women wrote directly to state organs demanding the improvement of social services reveals not only that women expected the state would deliver on its promises but also how women operated within the apparatus of the state to make their claims to citizenship heard.

Female factory workers regularly discussed women's "double burden" and the status of social services, especially child care. In a 1973 entry detailing her job search, for example, Anita Klein remembered "looking for a job for a long time where I could get day care as well."[52] After learning about the opportunities for career advancement and the

---

49. Shana Penn and Jill Massino, *Gender Politics and Everyday Life in State Socialist Eastern and Central Europe* (New York: Palgrave Macmillan, 2009), 2–3.

50. Harsch, *Revenge of the Domestic*, 49.

51. Canning, "Class vs. Citizenship," 240; Geoff Eley and Atina Grossmann, "Maternalism and Citizenship in Weimar Germany: The Gendered Politics of Welfare," *Central European History* 30, no. 1 (1997): 67–75.

52. Anita Klein, Kollektiv der Betriebsküche, VEB Burger Bekleidungswerke, *Brigadebuch* (Halle, Halle, 1970–1973), Wende Museum of the Cold War.

child care offered by a clothing factory in Halle, she wrote, "Finally, a job that promised both! I could not accept one that did not."[53] A job that "promised both" spoke to Klein's expectation of her ability to balance wage labor and motherhood in socialist society. While Klein heralded a job that provided employment and child care, she simultaneously used her brigade book to call out the limited availability of such services, as her use of "long time" and "finally" suggests a prolonged job search. While social services expanded in the 1970s owing to reforms advanced by Erich Honecker's government, they remained imperfect. Day cares increasingly became available, for instance, but wait lists were lengthy. As Klein's account suggests, the East German state consistently fell short on the promises made to women regarding the availability of communal institutions. Like the realities of gender discrimination in factories, the services aimed at easing women's "double burden" often failed to do so.[54] As a result, Klein used her brigade book to communicate directly to factory leaders about the continued difficulties she and other female worker-citizens faced.

Others used brigade books to more explicitly demand the state hold up its end of the bargain regarding social services. In 1987, an author from an automobile factory in Erfurt noted, "When moms go to work, our children need to be well looked after in nurseries and kindergartens. We must receive all possible care. . . . After all, we are working hard for the state!"[55] Her use of "must" illustrates the author's demand for social services, to "receive all possible care" in exchange for "working hard for the state." Both entries suggest how many female factory workers interpreted their broader rights as worker-citizens in the GDR: in exchange for their labor, the East German state needed to deliver on professional opportunities and communal institutions. For many workingwomen, socializing household tasks and child care was the fulfillment of socialism's promised gender equality by emancipating working mothers from domestic drudgery.

Many female factory workers directly connected social services to their broader rights as citizens in the GDR. In 1963, Erika Bergemann expressed her frustration at the inadequacies of social services, specifically the long wait times at communal laundries. She continued: "We need to take a very close look at the utilization of services . . . to

---

53. Klein, Kollektiv der Betriebsküche, VEB Burger Bekleidungswerke, *Brigadebuch*.
54. McLellan, *Love in the Time of Communism*, 72–74.
55. VEB Automobilwerkes, *Brigadebuch* (Eisenach, Erfurt, 1987), Wende Museum of the Cold War.

determine whether these services, intended for workingwomen, are actually being used by workingwomen. It is necessary to evaluate the extent to which workingwomen are taking advantage of institutions they have a right to."[56] Here, Bergemann not only criticized the realities of social services like laundry facilities but also demanded that factory and party leaders reevaluate such services to better serve East Germany's workingwomen. Communal institutions, Bergemann argued, were necessary for more than simply easing women's "double burden" but were in fact essential to building an equitable, just society for women. Specifically, Bergemann framed social services as something all workingwomen had a "right" to. In doing so, she demonstrated her familiarity with socialist conceptualizations of gender and equality, as well as her knowledge of the specific language the regime used to propagandize such principles. At the same time, she used her account to make demands and hold the regime accountable to its promises regarding women's "rights" as laborers and citizens.

The Emancipatory Promise of Socialist Citizenship

Following her entry on International Women's Day in 1968, Elisabeth Schmidt continued to write in her company's brigade book. She regularly recorded the industrial accomplishments of her fellow members, specifically "the women in our collective [who are] honored in socialist competitions."[57] In 1969, she reflected on the status of workingwomen and wrote that "it is clear to me that women play a real role in building the East German state, and it is clear that even more women need to take the path of qualification and further training in order to be employed in leading positions. But the worries and problems of our wives and mothers need to be addressed," she continued, "which still have an inhibiting effect on employment and studies. A lot still has to change."[58] Schmidt used her brigade book to demonstrate both her familiarity with the regime's economic priorities and what the rhetoric about women's emancipation through wage labor meant to her personally. Marshaling such concepts enabled Schmidt to communicate her own industrial accomplishments to the authorities reading her brigade book. At the same time, Schmidt asserted that she did not want to be

---

56. Sächsisches Staatsarchiv—Hauptstaatsarchiv Dresden, 12465 FDGB-Bezirksvorstand Dresden, Nr. 1113.
57. Schmidt, "Phillip Müller Brigade," *Brigadebuch*.
58. Schmidt, "Phillip Müller Brigade," Brückenbetrieb Schlabendorf, *Brigadebuch*.

"inhibited" in "employment." Furthermore, she expressed finding validation outside the home through "studies," "further training," "qualifications," and being "honored in socialist competitions."

Schmidt also used her brigade book entries as a means to criticize the regime, not only voicing her concern about the "worries and problems of our wives and mothers" but also stating clearly the need for those problems "to be addressed." In doing so, Schmidt reminded the regime of its promise to ease women's "double burden" through social services so that women could actually take courses and gain advanced technical training. Notably, after demanding that the concerns of working mothers be addressed, she concluded her entry with the assessment that "a lot still has to change." It was by acknowledging the shortcomings of the social reality for workingwomen that Schmidt affirmed her commitment to the socialist project. The possibility that a lot *could* change was essential to her conceptualization of socialist citizenship, and she used her brigade book to hold factory and state leaders accountable to that emancipatory vision for workingwomen as citizens of the GDR.

Rachel Weiser is an assistant professor in modern European history at Jacksonville State University. She received her PhD in history from Boston University in 2024. Rachel's research examines contested ideas of socialism through generations of working mothers in the German Democratic Republic from 1949 to 1989. More broadly, she is interested in the relationship between gender and dictatorship in modern European history.

CHAPTER 9

Compulsory Voting, Gender, and Race under the French Fourth Republic

Zoé Kergomard

"Abstention is always interpreted as an attitude that is hostile to the regime."[1] This perceived danger for postwar democracy in France served as a key argument for delegate Jacques Bardoux, a member of the small right-wing Peasant Party for Social Union (Parti paysan d'union sociale), when promoting his long-standing demand for compulsory voting in front of the Constituent Assembly charged with drawing up a new constitution in April 1946. Referencing the upcoming popular vote on the new constitution, which the press hoped would "ensure a future return to the normal exercise of democracy," he warned his colleagues: "If on June 2nd [1946], there were to be a large percentage of nonvoters, this phenomenon would be interpreted against the Republic."[2] Compulsory voting never achieved a parliamentary majority in France.[3] But by framing nonvoting as a potential threat

---

1. "Séance du 2 avril 1946," *Journal officiel de l'Assemblée nationale constituante* (*JOANC*), April 3, 1946. In the following, translations are from the author unless otherwise specified. I would like to thank the editors and contributors to this volume, my colleagues at the University of Jyväskylä, Yves Déloye, and my editor Paul Reeve for their helpful feedback on this text.
2. "Ce que disent les journaux," *La Croix*, February 22, 1946; "Séance du 2 avril 1946," *JOANC*, April 3, 1946.
3. Except for indirect elections to the upper house (the Senate under the Third Republic and the Council of the Republic under the Fourth Republic).

to the legitimacy of the new regime, Bardoux and his fellow proponents of compulsory voting asked key questions for postwar democracies and citizens: How should the new regime achieve both stability and democratic legitimacy? What roles should citizens play in decision-making processes? Was voting in particular, as a key democratic ritual, a "civic duty" for citizens, and if so, should it become mandatory? More broadly, which practices made the ideal postwar citizen?

Looking beyond the nonadvent of compulsory voting in postwar France, this chapter takes the recurrent debates on the subject during the Fourth Republic as a case study to analyze the renegotiation of citizenship "from above" and "from below" in the context of the reconstruction of democracy after the Second World War and the collaborationist Vichy regime. I thereby build on and extend scholarship historicizing the complex institutionalization of voting procedures and practices that unfolded in parallel to the (limited and nonlinear) extension of voting rights in the newly emerging nation-states in the nineteenth century.[4] In this vein, instead of taking for granted the centrality of voting rights and practices in dominant representations of citizenship and democracy, my aim is to question their importance in relation to other practices and rights shaping various modes of relating to society and to the state over time.[5]

Furthermore, as Rachel Chin and Samuel Huneke develop in their introduction, compulsory voting crystallizes two related tensions within the ideals, norms, and practices of citizenship at the center of this book. First, compulsory voting highlights an ever-changing (im)balance between the rights and duties associated with being a citizen and acting as one, through which citizenship can simultaneously or alternatively deploy an emancipatory and/or disciplinary potential.[6] Scholars have usually explained the repeated rejection of compulsory voting in France since the Third Republic in comparison with other countries as the result of an emerging republican, individualistic concord on (male) universal suffrage as a fundamental right against the attempts of conservatives and later center-right republicans to

---

4. For a review see Zoé Kergomard, "Moments of Democratic Evaluation? Literature Review on the History of Elections and Election Campaigns in Western Europe from the Nineteenth to the Twenty-First Century," *Archiv Für Sozialgeschichte* 60 (2020): 485–512.

5. Engin F. Isin, "Theorizing Acts of Citizenship," in *Acts of Citizenship*, ed. Engin F. Isin and Greg M. Nielsen (London: Palgrave Macmillan, 2008), 15–43.

6. See Ruth Lister et al., *Gendering Citizenship in Western Europe: New Challenges for Citizenship Research in a Cross-National Context* (Bristol: Policy, 2007).

"organize"—that is, constrain—mass democracy via compulsory voting in particular. Instead of sanctions for nonvoters, Yves Déloye suggests that the priority of republican elites had been to rationalize voting procedures and to educate and emancipate citizens so as to turn them into rational, autonomous, and disciplined voters, freed from their social ties in the voting booth while also conscientious of their "civic duties."[7] But the partly emancipatory, partly disciplinary techniques of "social orthopedics," from republican catechisms to the ritualization of secret voting in the voting booth, did not magically create the ideal, autonomous yet dutiful citizen that elites wished for.[8] Nonvoting reemerged regularly as a "problem" for representative democracies seeking to ensure the legitimacy of elections, not least in Western postwar democracies operating under a "constrained" ideal of democracy that aimed at governmental stability and limited popular participation.[9] Against this backdrop, postwar elites and intellectuals debated across the Atlantic whether nonvoting was a lesser evil compared to the fascist experiences of mass mobilization, or a form of democratic "apathy" that potentially threatened the legitimacy, and hence the stability, of the new regimes.[10]

In postwar France in particular, such debates on nonvoting and the subsequent consideration of compulsory voting as a possible solution also exemplify a second tension within citizenship: one between processes of inclusion and exclusion, because they collided with newly redrawn boundaries of the demos across both gender and race lines. After decades of suffragist struggles, French women were finally enfranchised in 1944 by France's provisional government. Their arrival onto the political scene as voting citizens, candidates, and politicians destabilized the gendered separation of spheres and roles and the

---

7. Yves Déloye, "Chronique d'une allergie républicaine au vote obligatoire (XIXe–XXe siècles)," in *Le vote obligatoire: Débats, enjeux et défis*, ed. Anissa Amjahad, Jean-Michel de Waele, and Michel Hastings (Paris: Economica, 2011), 69–88; for a transnational conceptual history of compulsory voting see Anthoula Malkopoulou, *The History of Compulsory Voting in Europe: Democracy's Duty?* (New York: Routledge, 2014).

8. Alain Garrigou, *Le vote et la vertu: Comment les français sont devenus électeurs* (Paris: Presses de la Fondation nationale des sciences politiques, 1992), 277; about the limits of politization processes, Michel Offerlé, "Capacités politiques et politisations: Faire voter et voter, XIXe–XXe siècles," (1) and (2), *Genèses* 67, no. 2 (2007): 131–49, and 68, no. 3 (2007): 145–60.

9. Jan-Werner Müller, *Contesting Democracy: Political Ideas in Twentieth-Century Europe* (repr.; New Haven, CT: Yale University Press, 2013); Martin Conway, *Western Europe's Democratic Age: 1945–1968* (Princeton, NJ: Princeton University Press, 2020).

10. Guy Paltieli, "Between Realism and Relevance: Apathy and Political Theory 1950–1970," *Global Intellectual History* 8, no. 1 (July 22, 2021): 1–22.

long-standing androcentric representation of the autonomous, rational "citizen-soldier."[11] Indeed, the ideal of voter autonomy had long served to legitimize the exclusion or marginalization of voters deemed too dependent on others, beginning with women, who had been under the legal authority of their husbands (or fathers) since Napoléon's 1804 Civil Code. As Silyane Larcher has shown, the prerequisites of "independence" and "freedom" for electoral capacity also served as a downplayed form of racialization in debates over the enfranchisement of newly freed slaves in 1848.[12] This both gendered and more or less overtly racist framing of electoral capacity was also repeatedly invoked during the Third Republic against the claim to citizenship, or simply to voting rights, for colonized "subjects." As Emily Fransee discusses in this book, such arguments still stood in the way of political equality for men and even more for women throughout the empire, even if parallel discussions to the introduction of female suffrage led to the recognition of their citizenship in 1946. Compulsory voting thus also provides us with a lens through which to study the renegotiation of citizenship norms and ideals in connection with profound transformations of gendered and racialized social and political hierarchies.

To assess discussions on compulsory voting, I analyze parliamentary debates and their coverage in the press, first to map the various positioning of parties on the issue, and then to retrace the concepts and arguments used to (de)legitimize compulsory voting. Because parliamentary debates, especially in France, often use abstract language, for instance by invoking an impersonal "citizen" in the masculine form, I also examine debates in the press, within parties, social movements, and the administration.[13] These wider debates shed light on the practical questions raised by compulsory voting and the political strategies of

---

11. Anne-Sarah Bouglé-Moalic, *Le vote des françaises. Cent ans de débats 1848–1944* (Rennes: Presses universitaires de Rennes, 2012); Luc Capdevila, "Le mythe du guerrier et la construction sociale d'un 'éternel masculin' après la guerre," *Revue française de psychanalyse* 62, no. 2 (1998): 607.

12. Silyane Larcher, *L'autre citoyen: L'idéal républicain et les Antilles après l'esclavage* (Paris: Armand Colin, 2014).

13. The chapter draws particularly on debates and reports relating to compulsory voting found in the archives of the Ministry of the Interior at the Archives Nationales (AN) and of the Socialist Parliamentary Group (GPS) and the right-wing deputy Édouard Barrachin (EBA), who developed an expertise on electoral reforms, both at the Sciences Po Archives (SPA). To account for the diverse (and unstable) press landscape of the period, the press corpus combines articles from press clippings collected by the Library of Sciences Po; articles on compulsory voting accessible through digitized collections (*Le Monde*; various newspapers on the *Gallica* collection); and articles collected by actors themselves on the issue.

more or less powerful actors for and against it, including their electoral calculations as to which parts of the electorate they really wanted to see at the voting booth. Looking beyond these power relations, I show that the abstract language of parliamentary debates contributed to the invisibilization of (noncommunist) female activists and women's organizations who pushed for compulsory voting in the aim of mobilizing (noncommunist) women as a new powerful electoral force. Because the debate focused on mainland France, it was also mostly disconnected from the still-contested issue of voting rights overseas, revealing the persistent otherness of overseas voters (particularly when categorized as indigenous) for French political elites.

Shifting Alliances, Electoral Calculations, and Unforeseen Barriers

The failure to introduce compulsory voting under the Fourth Republic happened despite a series of attempts by political actors—mostly but not exclusively from parties of the right and center-right—to push for this idea throughout the period. Their perseverance reflects their recurring hopes of obtaining a majority in a context of quickly evolving political fronts and recurrent debates on voting rights and electoral law. Their projects stood partly in continuity with earlier discussions of electoral reforms (compulsory voting and plural voting, sometimes together with female suffrage) as almost magical solutions to regenerate a discredited Republic—and indeed the demos itself.[14] At the end of the war, the possibility of making voting compulsory arose again among center- and right-wing politicians hopeful for a "new Republic" but also more broadly in Resistance circles.[15] This context of general renewal

---

14. Such calls came from the heterogeneous discourse of "state reform" in the early 1930, building on a (partly authoritarian) critique of republican institutions, Nicolas Roussellier, "La contestation du modèle républicain dans les années 30: La réforme de l'État," in *Le modèle républicain*, ed. Serge Berstein and Odile Rudelle (Paris: Presses Universitaires de France, 1992), 319-35. But compulsory voting was also discussed more broadly within departmental assemblies, and even within the progressive Human Rights League, "Voeux des conseils généraux," AN F/1cII/195; Emmanuel Naquet, "La LDH, les droits de l'homme et le politique," in *Matériaux pour l'histoire de notre temps* 72, no. 1 (2003): 17-27. About the conjunction of compulsory voting and female suffrage, Bouglé-Moalic, *Le vote des françaises*.

15. Nicolas Roussellier, "Rénover la République?," in *Le moment PRL: Le Parti républicain de la liberté, 1946-1951*, ed. Sylvie Guillaume et al. (Rennes: Presses universitaires de Rennes, 2019), 75-82; Philippe Viannay, Jean-Daniel Jurgensen, and Robert Salmon, *Cahiers de Défense de la France* ([Paris], 1944), 45; André Bendjebbar, *Libérations rêvées, libérations vécues: 1940-1945* (Paris: Hachette, 1994), 51.

opened up opportunities for long-standing proponents of compulsory voting to push for this idea, such as Bardoux and conservative old-timer Joseph Denais for the Republican Party for Freedom (RPF / Parti républicain de la liberté, PRL).

Revealing the openness of the issue, the right-wing origin of these first initiatives initially did not prevent other politicians from supporting the idea. In the constitutional commission of the first Constitutional Assembly in late 1945, it even obtained majority support, owing to the support of delegates from the Christian democratic Popular Republican Movement (Mouvement républicain populaire, MRP) but also the French Section of the Workers' International (SFIO, which would later become the Socialist Party), while Communists frontally opposed this "undemocratic" project.[16] While compulsory voting was not a central part of the constitutional debate, it was from then on a live enough possibility to be discussed in the dynamic postwar press.[17] For some journalists, compulsory voting was no longer the "reactionary" project it had been during the Third Republic, while others noted it caused a "lively emotion in public opinion."[18] But the balance of forces shifted in February 1946 and the idea was dropped, when the SFIO's parliamentary group as a whole decided to withdraw its support, officially mentioning the alleged unpopularity of compulsory voting, but in fact as part of a larger deal with the Communists.[19] In contrast, a comparable configuration had led in March 1946 to the introduction of a weakened form of compulsory voting (with only symbolic sanctions meant to shame nonvoters) in the new Italian constitution as part of negotiations between

---

16. Maurice Kriegel-Valrimont, Première assemblée constituante. Commission de la Constitution, "Séance du 6 décembre 1945," AN C//15287. The vote was decided by twenty-seven votes for and fourteen against.

17. About the two constitutional processes and their later problematization see Jenny Raflik, *La république moderne. La IVe République (1946–1958)* (Paris: Seuil, 2018), 49–74; Emmanuel Cartier and Michel Verpeaux, eds., *La Constitution du 27 octobre 1946 : Nouveaux regards sur les mythes d'une Constitution "mal-aimée"* (Paris: mare & martin, 2018).

18. "Le vote obligatoire," *Concorde: Hebdomadaire Républicain, Politique et Littéraire*, December 15, 1945; Jean-Maurice Hermann, "Vote obligatoire et statut des partis," *Ambiance*, December 26, 1945.

19. This time, compulsory voting was rejected with twenty-three votes (seventeen for), Première assemblée constituante. Commission de la Constitution, "Séance du 20 février 1946," AN C//15287. The vote was decided by twenty-seven votes for and fourteen against. About the deal with the Communists see Jean Paul Scot, "1944–1947. État, institutions et luttes de classes," *Cahiers d'histoire de l'Institut Maurice Thorez* 8, no. 6 (1974): 125–26.

Communists and Christian Democrats, a process that was discussed in the French press.[20]

In later years, Cold War logic would only strengthen these alternating left/right and Communist/non-Communist divides on the issue. This weakened its chances in Parliament but also heightened its momentum, as it became seen as an electoral tool to weaken the French Communist Party (PCF), which consistently opposed it throughout the period as being a "reactionary" and "antidemocratic" measure fueled by the "fear of voters."[21] Countering "extremists" by urging "moderates" to vote had long been an argument of conservative and centrist actors in favor of compulsory voting.[22] Now, proponents of compulsory voting aimed specifically to counter the "communist peril" in the voting booth through compulsory voting—a strategy that they rarely expressed in Parliament but casually discussed within parties and in the media.[23] In the absence of clear statistics on the social and political stratification of nonvoting at the time, politicians and journalists shared the impression that the noncommunist middle classes were more prone to nonvoting than followers of the "Communist Church," in a context where only the Catholic Church seemed able to compete with the mass mobilizing power of the PCF.[24]

Despite this early opposition, the difficulties of the young Fourth Republic gave proponents of compulsory voting several windows of opportunity to bring their idea forward and argue for its necessity. After the first constitutional project was rejected in a popular vote in June 1946, compulsory voting was again discussed—but rejected with a tight majority—for the second proposed constitution submitted to

---

20. Nonvoters' names would be officialized, a sanction sometimes suggested in French projects, but usually in conjunction with fees: "L'adoption du vote obligatoire menace de provoquer une crise en Italie," *Le Monde*, March 2, 1946; see Anna Rossi-Doria, *Diventare cittadine: Il voto delle donne in Italia* (Florence: Giunti, 1996), 46; Howard McGaw Smyth, "Italy: From Fascism to the Republic (1943–1946)," *Western Political Quarterly* 1, no. 3 (1948): 220.

21. See in the party's journal *L'Humanité*, "Veut-on imiter le Portugal?," December 8, 1945; "Le vote obligatoire: Une violation de la démocratie," October 30, 1950.

22. Malkopoulou, *History of Compulsory Voting*, 34.

23. "La Réconciliation française s'inquiète de l'accroissement du péril communiste," *Le Monde*, May 25, 1953; Vincent Auriol, *Mon septennat, 1947–1954* (Gallimard, 1970), 300.

24. Rémy Roure, "Voter, voter bien," *Le Monde*, June 15, 1951. The first political science studies on nonvoting were still debating this question: François Goguel, "Géographie du référendum et des élections de mai-juin 1946," *Esprit* (1940-), no. 124 (7) (1946): 27–54; Mattei Dogan and Jacques Narbonne, "L'abstentionnisme électoral en France," *Revue française de science politique* 4, no. 1 (1954): 5–26.

referendum in October 1946.²⁵ But echoing Bardoux and others' interpretation of turnout as a mark of legitimacy, voices in the conservative press described the comparatively lower turnout rates for this second referendum (67.62 percent compared to 79.63 percent for the first referendum) as a "deadly threat," and Gaullists characterized it as a bad sign for the young regime, whose parliamentary architecture they opposed.²⁶ In later years, with unstable governments not least due to the strength of the two main opposition forces (Gaullists and Communists, who both left the government in 1947), electoral law generally, and the voting system in particular, remained contentious topics. Each new debate on electoral law presented an opportunity for its proponents to push for compulsory voting, in a context in which turnout rates had become increasingly politicized. After the fall of his cabinet in February 1955, the radical prime minister Pierre Mendès-France himself campaigned on promises to solve the "crisis of democracy" and suggested measures to "moralize" both politicians and citizens, including compulsory voting as a way for the latter to reclaim democracy.²⁷

But despite these shifting alliances and prominent endorsements, compulsory voting raised practical problems that became barriers to its introduction. How could nonvoting be sanctioned when electoral registration itself was not compulsory and absentee voting options limited? In such a moment of disruption, many citizens were still on the move in mainland France and throughout the colonial empire, because of consequences of the war, rural exodus, and labor migration. Although compulsory voting did not make it into the eclectic electoral reform of 1951, an amendment was passed to make registration compulsory for citizens in mainland France and in overseas departments. But without any form of control or sanction, it remained a dead letter.²⁸ In later years, a significant part of the constituency in mainland France

---

25. 274 against, 269 for, with some abstentions. "Séance du 3 septembre 1946," *JOANC*, September 4, 1946.

26. Robert Pimienta, "Les chroniques de l'"Ordre.' Vers le vote obligatoire," *L'Ordre*, October 19, 1946; Alain Garrigou, *La politique en France de 1940 à nos jours* (Paris: La Découverte, 2017), 101.

27. Pierre Rosanvallon, "Pierre Mendès France et la 'démocratie généralisée,'" in *Pierre Mendès France et la démocratie locale: Actes du Colloque du Conseil Général de l'Eure*, ed. Dominique Franche and Yves Léonard (Rennes: Presses universitaires de Rennes, 2015), 23-30. Compulsory voting was also favored with similar arguments by the Club Jean Moulin, close to Mendès France: see Philippe Reclus, *La République impatiente ou le club des Jacobins (1951–1958)* (Paris: Éditions de la Sorbonne, 1987), 65-76.

28. "Séance du 21 mars 1951," *JOAN*, March 22, 1951; electoral law of May 9, 1951.

remained unregistered—according to official statistics, about 8.5 percent of male citizens, and 19.9 percent of female citizens, in 1954.[29] Reports within the Ministry of the Interior evaluating the possibility of compulsory voting thus discussed several possibilities for making registration automatic but concluded that it would only overload the already complex process of establishing and revising the electoral roll. It might even affect French citizens' relations with the state, as establishing a citizens' register, as in other European countries, would require citizens to declare their residence.[30] In November 1955, as the National Assembly discussed and even accepted a new amendment for compulsory voting in a first reading, the minister of the interior, Maurice Bourgès-Maunoury (Radical Socialist Party), immediately declared it inapplicable, and it never made it into law.[31] Yet the press announced the eventuality of compulsory voting for the upcoming January 1956 general elections, a perspective that observers linked to the peak of 2.2 million new registrations and the lowest abstention rate since 1945 (17.2 percent).[32] Even without legal obligation to vote, the debates on compulsory voting still impacted electoral rules, with the new obligation of registration, and citizens' voting practices.

Voting as Duty or Freedom

In addition to the electoral calculations and practical issues discussed above, recurring debates on compulsory voting led politicians and journalists to put forward competing ideals and concepts of democracy and citizenship in a context of postwar democratic refoundation that was increasingly marked by Cold War antagonisms.[33] Proponents of compulsory voting presented nonvoting as a "threat" that would bias "popular representation" and hence sovereignty.[34] Only compulsory voting, they argued, would allow "true universal suffrage" or even

---

29. "Note sur la proposition de loi tendant à remédier à l'abstentionnisme et à instituer le vote obligatoire," July 13, 1955, AN F/1cII/195.

30. "Lettre du préfet de la Seine au Bureau des Affaires Politiques, Ministère de l'Intérieur," March 24, 1954, AN F/1cII/195.

31. "Séance du 15 novembre 1955," *JOAN*, November 16, 1955.

32. François Goguel, "Les élections françaises du 2 janvier 1956," *Revue française de science politique* 6, no. 1 (1956): 5–17.

33. On the contestedness of "democracy" after 1945 see Martin Conway, "Democracy in Western Europe after 1945," in *Democracy in Modern Europe: A Conceptual History*, ed. Jussi Kurunmäki, Jeppe Nevers, and Henk te Velde (New York: Berghahn Books, 2018), 231–56.

34. Louis Marin, "Séance du 3 septembre 1946," *JOANC*, September 4, 1946.

"a total vote."³⁵ This argumentation followed a line of "republican organicism" from earlier debates, insisting on "responsibilities" toward the community—thus reframing long-standing elitist and/or paternalistic understandings of voting as an exclusive "capacity," or at least a "function," and less as a "right."³⁶ The advent of female suffrage made the direct expression of such an antiegalitarian line of thought impossible, but compulsory voting advocates' dislike of universal suffrage as an individual right remained visible, particularly as they also endorsed familial suffrage as a way to give large families (originally only fathers, but now also mothers) a larger electoral voice. In contrast to compulsory voting, plans for familial suffrage seemed to be doomed after the war, as endorsement by the Vichy regime was a political stain on the proposal.³⁷ The view that compulsory voting was "reactionary" was less well established, but these ideological genealogies made it particularly easy for its opponents—from the Communists to civil servants in the Ministry of the Interior—to oppose compulsory voting on the grounds of "the French temperament," the "republican tradition," or even "the French traditions of freedom" without much further explanation.³⁸

"Freedom" itself was a much-contested concept in this debate, to the point that SFIO deputy and law rapporteur Jean Biondi explained the constitutional commission's rejection of compulsory voting in April 1946 "on the same grounds as its proponents . . . : freedom."³⁹ To plead in favor of compulsory voting, PRL delegate Marcel Rupied had tried to distinguish between "licentiousness" and "freedom [exercised]

---

35. Joseph Denais, "Proposition de résolution tendant à inviter le gouvernement à instituer le vote obligatoire, séance du 7 juin 1945," June 8, 1945, Documents de l'Assemblée consultative provisoire (DACP); Janine Alexandre-Debray (Gaulliste), "Séance du 17 mars 1953," *Journal officiel du Conseil de Paris (JOCP)*, December 31, 1953.

36. Malkopoulou, *History of Compulsory Voting*, 114–36. On the development of a legal doctrine in that vein, Yves Déloye, "La peur du grand nombre: La 'science électorale' contre la démocratie représentative dans la France de la IIIᵉ République (1890–1930)," in *La République à l'épreuve des peurs: De la Révolution à nos jours*, ed. Lisa Bogani, Julien Bouchet, Philippe Bourdin, and Jean-Claude Caron (Rennes: Presses universitaires de Rennes, 2018), 137–48.

37. Édouard Bonnefous and Jean-Baptiste Duroselle, *L'année politique, économique, sociale et diplomatique en France* (Paris: Éditions du Grand Siècle, 1946), 73. See Jean-Yves Le Naour, *La famille doit voter: Le suffrage familial contre le vote individuel* (Paris: Hachette, 2005); Margaret Cook Andersen, "French Settlers, Familial Suffrage, and Citizenship in 1920s Tunisia," *Journal of Family History* 37, no. 2 (2012): 213–31.

38. "Lettre du préfet de la Seine au Bureau des Affaires Politiques, Ministère de l'Intérieur," March 24, 1954, AN F/1cII/195; Albert Ouzoulias (PCF), "Séance du 17 mars 1953," *JOCP*, December 31, 1953; "Note d'information sur la proposition de loi déposée le 5 mai 1950 tendant à établir le vote obligatoire . . .," [1950], AN F/1cII/195.

39. "Séance du 2 avril 1946," *JOANC*, April 3, 1946.

within the bounds of common sense, honesty and legality."[40] But opponents could easily mock this particular understanding of freedom by referring to threatened sanctions on nonvoters, thus rejecting any notion of a positive liberty (responsibility in collective government) while reaffirming a negative understanding of the concept (need for protection from the state).[41] In the same debate, Communist deputy Albert Petit mocked the proposal of Bardoux and others to increase the suggested financial fee after a second repeat offense: "And after the third repeat offense, we shoot them!" His party colleague Charles Benoist added "in the name of freedom!"[42]

While some politicians or journalists favorable to the idea discussed compulsory voting as a tool for a "true democracy" or a "militant democracy," opponents drew comparisons with nondemocratic countermodels to delegitimize the idea.[43] Compulsory voting would be "audaciously tyrannical" or could lead "toward a regime that will look a lot like fascism," a reference used in particular by Communist actors who claimed to be the ones defending "democracy."[44] But the most effective rhetorical weapons against compulsory voting proved to be the terms "totalitarian"/"totalitarianism," which had circulated among French Catholics to make sense of both fascism and communism during the 1930s, and were now helping to coalesce an anticommunist front.[45] Shortly after the Communist coup in Czechoslovakia in 1948, former Resistant Rémy Roure, who was close to the anticommunist and Christian left, opposed compulsory voting in *Le Monde*, finding it "dangerous at a time of multiplying obligations in countries of 'totalitarian democracy' (if one can use this absurd term), which eventually lead to the prohibition of choice. Have we not just learned that in Czechoslovakia

---

40. "Séance du 2 avril 1946."
41. On the contemporary discussion of compulsory freedom as a positive liberty see Malkopoulou, *History of Compulsory Voting*, 17–48.
42. Malkopoulou, 17–48.
43. Jean Cayeux (SFIO), "Séance du 2 avril 1946," *JOANC*, April 3, 1946; Jean Texcier, "Grandeur et servitude de la démocratie," *Clartés: L'hebdomadaire de combat pour la Résistance et la démocratie*, January 4, 1946.
44. Maurice Nau, "La commission fait marche arrière," *L'Aurore: Organe de la Résistance Républicaine*, February 21, 1946; Joseph Barsalou, "L'organisation des pouvoirs," *Libération*, December 16, 1945; "Résolution de l'Union des syndicats ouvriers de la Marne," *La Champagne*, January 16, 1946.
45. James Chappel, "The Catholic Origins of Totalitarianism Theory in Interwar Europe," *Modern Intellectual History* 8, no. 3 (November 2011): 561–90; Kevin Duong, "'Does Democracy End in Terror?' Transformations of Antitotalitarianism in Postwar France," *Modern Intellectual History* 14, no. 2 (August 2017): 537–63.

there will be massive and compulsory voting, with music, with 'bonuses for unanimity' and open ballots? This is how 100 percent majorities are achieved and how dictatorships are established."[46]

Although compulsory voting had been introduced in Czechoslovakia long before Communist rule (1920), references to this case, and more generally to controlled elections and turnout rates nearing 100 percent in other Communist countries, helped both to stigmatize compulsory voting in France and to qualify the characterization of nonvoting as a problem in the first place. In reaction, compulsory voting proponents pointed to examples in countries considered "Western" and "democratic," such as the Netherlands, Italy, and especially Belgium—the common inspiration in France since its introduction of compulsory voting in 1893.[47] "Can one reasonably pretend that our Belgian friends are not democrats and don't respect the rights of the individual?" asked SFIO deputy Pierre Métayer in 1955.[48] Ironically, although the proponents of compulsory voting actually meant to fight communism in France, the strength of the antitotalitarian argument weakened the chances of compulsory voting. This disconnect between political positions and arguments created confusion—and sparked derision among other parties—whenever the Communists were the ones opposing compulsory voting as an "infringement on the freedom of citizens."[49]

Despite disagreements on "freedom," "democracy," or the palatability of sanctions, most participants in the debate shared an understanding of voting as a duty. Proponents of compulsory voting, especially from right-wing positions, traditionally emphasized the view of voting as "not only a right, but also a duty," referring to republican notions of "virtue."[50] For the Socialist delegate Jean Cayeux, it was more a logical act of balancing rights and duties, just like the "obligation to pay taxes" went along with the "right of citizenship."[51] But even opponents of compulsory voting, in Parliament or in the press, also saw voting as a "civic duty."[52] Conversely, nonvoting was commonly framed as a

---

46. Rémy Roure, "Élections," *Le Monde*, May 24, 1948.
47. Déloye, "Chronique d'une allergie républicaine."
48. Pierre Métayer, "Pour défendre la démocratie, instituons le vote obligatoire," *Le redressement économique*, June 1955, SPA EBA 17.
49. André Mercier (PCF), "Séance du 15 novembre 1955," *JOAN*, November 16, 1955.
50. Denais, "Proposition de résolution," June 8, 1945, DACP; Bardoux, "Séance du 2 avril 1946," *JOANC*, April 3, 1946.
51. Jean Cayeux, "Séance du 2 avril 1946."
52. Roure, "Voter, voter bien."

transgression ("faute") or even a "mortal sin."[53] The option to abstain for political reasons, sometimes framed as "combative nonvoting" ("abstentionnisme de combat"), featured only marginally in this discussion, for instance in the case of anarchists or Communists protesting government policies after their exclusion from government.[54] Facing an unsatisfying slate of candidates, proponents of compulsory voting commonly invoked the option to cast a blank vote, presenting this option as the civic-minded, responsible counterpart to shameful nonvoting.[55] But this framing ignored the possibility of boycotting elections or referenda out of principle, even out of a sense of "duty."[56] Debates often invoked the stereotype of a citizen "going fishing on Sundays" instead of voting as a way to depoliticize and stigmatize nonvoting as irresponsible behavior.[57] This use of that phrase actually reversed its earlier, subversive use by anarchist writer Octave Mirbeau in his critique of elections.[58] But paradoxically, the common framing of nonvoting as a passive and nonpolitical act actually weakened the argument that it might threaten the regime's legitimacy.

The insistence on voting as a duty thereby went together with the reaffirmation of androcentric representations of citizenship linked to fears of devirilization in postwar France.[59] The figure of the "lazy" nonvoter as an irresponsible fisherman targeted not just any citizen, but a stereotypical average French man with a "rebellious spirit."[60] Parliamentary debates and media reports mostly referred to an abstract "citizen" or "voter" in the masculine form, a wording that invoked a male citizen by default, and more rarely to "the male or female voter" ("l'électeur ou l'électrice"). Deputies, journalists and civil servants discussing compulsory voting drew parallels with other, androcentric

---

53. Denais, "Proposition de résolution," June 8, 1945, DACP; Roure, "Voter, voter bien"; see also Denis Barbet, "Quand les mots de l'abstention parlent des maux de la démocratie," *Mots. Les langages du politique*, no. 83 (2007): 53–67.

54. Jean Biondi (SFIO), "Séance du 2 avril 1946," *JOANC*, April 3, 1946; Jean Cristofol (PCF), "Séance du 21 mars 1951," *JOAN*, March 22, 1951

55. About the link between compulsory voting and the demand to recognize blank votes in France, Jérémie Moualek, "À la recherche des 'voix perdues': Contribution à une sociologie des usages pluriels du vote blanc et nul," unpublished PhD thesis (Paris: Université Paris-Saclay, 2018), 90-91.

56. Cristofol, "Séance du 21 mars 1951."

57. Métayer, "Pour défendre la démocratie."

58. Octave Mirbeau, *La grève des électeurs. Suivi de prélude* (1902; Paris: Éditions du Boucher, 2002), 12.

59. Capdevila, "Le mythe du guerrier."

60. Yves Florenne, "La fête des urnes," *Le Monde*, April 26, 1955; "Note sur le vote obligatoire," June 24, 1958, AN F/1cII/195.

dimensions of citizenship that also implied a responsibility or duty to act, as opposed to female passivity: the paterfamilias's management of family property, or the duty to "defend the fatherland," following the older ideal of the "citizen-soldier."[61] Nonvoting was therefore often condemned as a "civic desertion" by citizens betraying their fatherland, which echoed particularly strongly at the conjunction of Second World War sufferings and the ongoing wars of decolonization.[62] Indeed, in the words of fifty-year-old SFIO deputy Pierre Métayer, this concerned particularly "our young fellow citizens [who, unlike us] no longer feel the intrinsic value of the right to vote, won at the price of so many sacrifices by our elders. They do not understand very well what was long considered the attainment of a veritable new dignity for the humblest among us: that of citizen, true proof of equality between human beings at least in one dimension."[63]

Despite the concept's ultimate rejection, the debate on compulsory voting thus served to reaffirm an androcentric and duty-centered ideal of citizenship for younger generations.

Compulsory Voting and Women's Political Agency

The stereotypical Frenchman invoked by journalists and politicians notwithstanding, (non-Communist) female organizations and party sections also advocated compulsory voting with women in mind, in a context of intense competition to mobilize women for the first postwar elections in 1945 and 1946.[64] Already in 1945, the proposal was in the platforms of older and newer conservative organizations, such as the Catholic Civic and Social Women's Union (Union féminine civique et sociale, UFCS), the Free French Women (a short-lived right-wing group of women members of the Resistance, who also advocated for familial suffrage), and the women's section of the Republican Federation,

---

61. Jean Ravail, "Note pour M. le ministre: Le système du vote obligatoire," [1950], AN F/1cII/195; Ferdinand Mazuez (SFIO), "Séance du 15 novembre 1955," *JOAN*, November 16, 1955.

62. Marcel Rupied (PLR), "Séance du 2 avril 1946," *JOANC*, April 3, 1946.

63. Pierre Métayer, "Pour défendre la démocratie, instituons le vote obligatoire." Here again, the masculine form "les hommes," common in French until now ("les droits de l'homme"), refers to a universal category yet also suggests men are particularly meant.

64. Bruno Denoyelle, "Des corps en élections. Au rebours des universaux de la citoyenneté: Les premiers votes des femmes (1945-1946)," *Genèses* 31, no. 1 (1998): 76–98; William Guéraiche, *Les femmes et la République: Essai sur la répartition du pouvoir de 1943 à 1979* (Paris: Les Éditions de l'Atelier / Éditions ouvrières, 1999).

led by Henriette Denais, the wife of Joseph Denais.[65] Compared to parliamentary debates, there was little debate in the newspapers of these organizations on the boundaries of "freedom" for female voters, such was their overall insistence on voting as a "duty" for female citizens—an ever-present term in their calls for women's mobilization. Following the older essentialist, complementarian legitimation of female suffrage, they justified women's participation in politics based not simply on their rights as citizens but on their merits as participants in the war effort and, now that the war was over, as mothers or wives.[66] In an interview in the newspaper of the conservative National Women's Union (Union nationale des femmes, UNF), the Free French Women thus admitted that women "do have a great deal of knowledge to gain in order to attain the necessary competency," but their "new spirit and intact ideal" could help them bring "moderation" in French politics—and, implicitly, weaken the Communists.[67]

Compulsory voting gained further traction among non-Communist women's organizations as their hopes to unite women as a new political force were disappointed. As in other countries, the introduction of female suffrage did not instantly undo the century-long exclusion of women from democratic political life. Female political activists remained at the margins of political parties of all orientations and struggled to get women elected. Furthermore, turnout rates soon showed signs of a gender gap in participation, which, like early polls and studies, were read as a sign of uninterest in politics.[68] To secure women's participation and hence their potential power in French politics, the successors of the suffragist organizations, such as the French Union of Female Voters (Union française des électrices, UFE) also started lobbying for compulsory voting in 1951, partnering with the UNF. They contacted the press and high-ranking male parliamentarians in non-Communist parties, regardless of whether they were already pushing

---

65. Union féminine civique et sociale, ed., La *Vie politique et les femmes* (Paris: Éditions Spes, 1945); "Les femmes et les partis politiques," *Revue des électrices*, September 1, 1945.

66. Éric Alary and Dominique Veillon, "L'après-guerre des femmes 1947, un tournant?," in *L'année 1947*, ed. Serge Bernstein and Pierre Milza (Paris: Presses de Sciences Po, 1999), 487–508; Sylvie Chaperon, "Le creux de la vague: Mouvements féminins et féminismes 1945-1970" (doctoral thesis, European University Institute, 1996).

67. "Les femmes et les partis politiques."

68. Bonnefous and Duroselle, *L'année politique*, 121. This question gave way to larger, more nuanced studies later on; see Maurice Duverger, *La participation des femmes à la vie politique* (Paris: UNESCO, 1955).

for compulsory voting.[69] This mode of action was helped by their connections with these men but also revealed their difficulties advocating directly for such a measure in Parliament, with so few elected women.

Both the continuing gender segregation of politics and the abstract language of party and parliamentary work make it difficult to assess the influence of this advocacy work on the various proposals pushed forward by (overwhelmingly male) politicians after 1946. These politicians did not mention either their contacts with female activists or women as a target group. Among the few female politicians endorsing a proposal for compulsory voting, MRP deputy Germaine Peyrolles, an erstwhile member of the Resistance and a member of the UFCS, did not speak during the parliamentary debate on the topic.[70] When the Gaullist Janine Alexandre-Debray defended a resolution in favor of compulsory voting at the Paris municipal council in 1953, her highly philosophical speech on the necessity of "virtue" for democracy only referred to an abstract citizen in the male form.[71] The discursive rules of parliamentary work themselves thus obscured women as a potential target group for compulsory voting—further contributing to rendering women's activism invisible. But by advocating for compulsory voting in the aim of fully including women in politics, female activists added a new argument in its favor: it could be a tool to correct long-standing political inequalities—an egalitarian argument that since then took precedence over duty-based reasonings in contemporary debates.[72]

The objective of women's political inclusion did not make compulsory voting a left-wing project. Instead, it revealed divergent understandings of female citizenship among women's organizations, whose relations were strained by the Cold War in any case. Still, women's newspapers on the left (such as the UFF's *Femmes françaises* and the SFIO women's section's *Femmes socialistes*) showcased a broader understanding of female participation in politics and society, from parties themselves to the various like-minded organizations and social work. The notion of voting as a duty was noticeably less present here than in the newspapers of the Catholic UFCS, for instance, or those of the

---

69. Edmée de la Rochefoucauld, "La réforme électorale," *Revue des électrices*, April 1, 1951; "À la Commission du Suffrage Universel," *Revue des électrices*, April 1, 1953.

70. Chaperon, "Le creux de la vague," 754.

71. "Séance du 17 mars 1953," *JOCP*, December 31, 1953.

72. See, for instance, in French political science Michel Hastings, "Les fantômes du vote obligatoire," in *Mélanges en l'honneur du Professeur Jean Rossetto*, ed. Pascal Jan, Pierre Mouzet, and Véronique Tellier-Cayrol (Paris: LGDJ, 2016), 291–301. About this argumentative shift see Malkopoulou, *History of Compulsory Voting*.

successor organizations of the suffragist movement—whose fight for gender equality still mostly centered on participation in institutional politics.[73] Early on, *Femmes françaises* dismissed compulsory voting with a general left-wing line of argument. It would "smell more like fascism than democracy," wrote the teacher, labor union, and secularist activist Jacqueline Marchand in 1946.[74] Left-wing activists later also more specifically criticized the UFE's advocacy of compulsory voting in the name of all women. In the small "women's" section of the left-wing newspaper *Libération* called "For You Mesdames," the journalist and future UFF vice president Andrée Marty-Cabgras mocked the new alliance of the UFE with male politicians like Paul Giaccobi—who, not long before, had opposed female suffrage. She denied other women's organizations' legitimacy to speak in the name of all women, and proposed another understanding of "freedom" and "obligation" as seen from less privileged positions:

> Perhaps it would be useful for [Giaccobi] to know the opinion of the millions of women workers in factories, offices, housewives who, less privileged than others, less free too, do not intend to be bound by the obligation to vote. But how can all these women make their voices heard? . . . Let them think about it, in any case, from now on, because the moment is approaching when it will be possible, [and] necessary, for the female opinion to be expressed. And it can carry a great deal of weight.[75]

Speaking in the name of these "less privileged," "less free" women, Marty-Cabgras thus presented compulsory voting as a privilege of those free enough to choose to limit their own freedoms. But in indirectly reminding her readers ("them") of the upcoming elections, she nonetheless shared with the UFE and other women's organizations the hope of making French women count through their electoral participation.

The boundaries of women's political agency, autonomy, and freedom were thus central both in the mobilization for and against compulsory voting and in discussions within women's organizations over

---

73. "Congrès national. 'Les femmes et leurs responsabilités civiques,'" *Notre journal*, March 1951.

74. Jacqueline Marchand, "Pour 350000fr. de constitution S.V.P. . . ," *Femmes françaises*, January 18, 1946.

75. Andrée Marty-Capgras, "Si toutes les femmes du monde . . . ," *Libération*, February 9, 1951.

the ideals of citizenship for women. As during the decades of suffragist struggles, female activists moved between a pragmatic understanding of voting as a tool (possibly among other tools) to achieve broader rights for women, and as a fundamental right in itself, a symbolic milestone on the road to equality. Nowhere were these questions more urgent than for women's rights activists overseas, who fought against different forms of discrimination, at the intersection of gender, race, and class. In Martinique, Guadeloupe, Guyane, and Réunion, which in 1946 became French departments of equal status to those of mainland France, women's rights activists forcefully demanded equal social rights with women in mainland France.[76] Urging women to the voting booth was one action among others in a repertoire of ways to mobilize women in that aim. But for the *négritude* thinker and activist Paulette Nardal, linked to the Catholic UFCS, voting also had a highly symbolic dimension for women in Martinique, marking their equal status both with men and with women all over the "nation." Without endorsing compulsory voting, Nardal still called nonvoting a "social sin" in her newspaper *La femme dans la cité* in 1946, calling on the women of Martinique to seize their voting rights as a new form of power: "You are not aware of your own worth. You do not count yourself as important to the nation.... However, it is above all especially on that day, the day of the election, that you become the equal of man. It is on that day, with all class distinctions abolished, that you, like every woman, will inform the nation of your autonomous will."[77]

Nardal thus opened another understanding of voting as an empowering duty for the women of Martinique, a performance of their power and of their rights as full citizens.

The "Other" Voter Overseas

The implicit focus of parliamentarians on men in mainland France also largely disconnected the debate on compulsory voting from the still-unsettled issue of voting rights and practices overseas. From 1946

---

76. Clara Palmiste, "Le vote féminin et la transformation des colonies françaises d'Amérique en départements en 1946," *Nuevo Mundo Mundos Nuevos*, June 2014, https://journals.openedition.org/nuevomundo/66842; Myriam Paris, "Un féminisme anticolonial: l'Union des femmes de La Réunion (1946-1981)," *Mouvements* 91, no. 3 (2017): 141-49.

77. Pauline Nardal, "Abstention, crime social," *Femme dans la cité*, November 1946; translation by Tracy Denean Sharpley-Whiting in Paulette Nardal, *Beyond Negritude: Essays from Woman in the City* (Albany, NY: SUNY Press, 2014), 73-77.

onward, suffrage was universal throughout the French Union, in theory. In practice, it remained highly unequal across race and gender lines because of discriminatory voting systems.[78] These persistent inequalities, and the impression that these elections were just a façade hiding the lack of local sovereignty, led independence movements from Cameroon to Algeria to use election boycotts as a confrontational action, thereby denying any legitimacy to French electoral institutions.[79] Even when previously colonized "subjects" could vote and wished to do so—with their own diverse motivations—electoral registration itself remained an administrative challenge and a focus of political disputes.[80]

Compulsory voting was rarely discussed with regard to French Union territories, although electoral rights and participation were key questions for their political future. The Assembly of the French Union, which quickly proved itself to be no more than a consultative body, focused on voting rights themselves and never discussed compulsory voting. In the National Assembly, even in its overseas commission and in political parties, the few nonwhite politicians representing colonized populations struggled to be heard.[81] In one instance, Yacine Diallo, a deputy from Guinea, opposed compulsory voting during a meeting of the socialist parliamentary group on the simple grounds that "distances and transport barriers would make compulsory voting inapplicable" in his district.[82] He found support from his colleague Jacques Bianchini from Corsica, who mentioned similar issues, but their opposition was not discussed further, and the socialist group remained

---

78. Frederic Cooper, *Citizenship between Empire and Nation: Remaking France and French Africa, 1945-1960* (Princeton, NJ: Princeton University Press, 2014). See the chapter by Emily Lord Fransee in this book.

79. Marc Michel, "Une décolonisation confisquée? Perspectives sur la décolonisation du Cameroun sous tutelle de la France 1955-1960," *Outre-Mers. Revue d'histoire* 86, no. 324 (1999): 229-58; Bernard Droz, "L'élection législative du 30 novembre 1958 en Algérie," *Outre-Mers. Revue d'histoire* 95, no. 358 (2008): 29-44.

80. On elections overseas see Laurent Jalabert, Bertrand Joly, and Jacques Weber, eds., *Les élections législatives et sénatoriales outre-mer (1848–1981)* (Paris: Les Indes savantes, 2010); about voting practices in Senegal, Juliette Ruaud, "À la lisière du vote. Socio-histoire de l'institution électorale dans le Sénégal colonial (années 1840-1960)," unpublished PhD diss. (Bordeaux and Laval: Université de Bordeaux; Université Laval, 2021); about registration issues, Séverine Awenengo Dalberto, "La première carte d'identité d'Afrique occidentale française (1946-1960)," *Annales. Histoire, Sciences Sociales* 75, no. 1 (November 2, 2020): 113-51.

81. Marc Michel, "L'empire colonial dans les débats parlementaires," in *L'année 1947*, ed. Serge Bernstein and Pierre Milza (Paris: Presses de Sciences Po, 1999), 189-217; Emily Marker, "Obscuring Race: Franco-African Conversations about Colonial Reform and Racism after World War II and the Making of Colorblind France, 1945-1950," *French Politics, Culture & Society* 33, no. 3 (2015): 1-23.

82. "Séance du 7 novembre 1950," SPA GPS 1.

divided on the question. A heated discussion in the National Assembly on November 15, 1955, which led to the provisional adoption of compulsory voting, was preceded and followed by interventions from nonwhite overseas deputies contesting the remaining barriers to participation in their territories, again revealing a major disconnect in these debates between the metropole and the colonial territories. With little reaction from their colleagues, Hamadoun Dicko (Soudan, SFIO) challenged the double college system in the name of the Assembly of the French Union, while Mohamed Salah Bendjelloul (Algeria, Gaullist) asked about provisions for Algerians working in mainland France to vote.[83]

Civil servants' reports on compulsory voting, despite their more practical orientation, were also noticeably discreet, and ill at ease, on the relevance of this proposal for the overseas territories. A 1955 report from the Ministry of the Interior did mention barriers to the introduction of compulsory voting overseas (including the overseas departments), but for different reasons than in mainland France, where registration seemed to be the main issue: "In Algeria, for the second college, in overseas departments and in the territories of the French Union, where there remains a portion of the electorate that is illiterate or ignorant of the French language, the rigorous application of compulsory voting might, perhaps, be premature; and one can question the appropriateness of the sanctions planned to accompany compulsory voting."[84]

An exemption to compulsory voting would thus be justified for overseas voters, with the notable exception of the Algerian first college (overwhelmingly "Europeans"). The main issue raised by the report, then, was that this exemption might infringe on "equality before the law," as sanctions would only fall on citizens in mainland France and "Europeans" in Algeria—although electoral law was already highly discriminatory in the French Union, beginning with the double college system. Notably, this reversal of the principle of "equality" was also a common rhetorical strategy used by politicians in mainland France to downplay evidence of racist discrimination at a time when explicit racist speech was becoming increasingly unacceptable.[85] In this instance, the report resorted to the argument long used to justify the "temporal

---

83. "Séance du 15 novembre 1955," *JOAN*, November 16, 1955.
84. "Note sur la proposition de loi."
85. Marker, "Obscuring Race."

deferral" of rights extensions in the colonies: that certain electoral innovations were "premature" for overseas (nonwhite) voters—except for "Europeans" in Algeria.[86] The reasons given merged earlier, class-based arguments about capacity and autonomy used against extensions of suffrage with a downplayed form of racialization that was recurrent in French political discourse. While in 1848 some mainland politicians had deemed former slaves "not free enough" to be enfranchised, in this instance colonized peoples were in a sense not free enough for the notion of holding them accountable for nonvoting to even be considered.[87] The problem of "freedom" discussed in Parliament and in the press with regard to compulsory voting thus applied neither to women nor to colonized populations.[88]

New Solutions for an Old Problem?

Twelve years after the June 1946 constitutional referendum, the Fourth Republic fell with the military coup of May 1958 in Algiers. Its most ardent critic, Charles de Gaulle, agreed to return as prime minister if he could design a new constitution. In September 1958, the referendum for the Constitution of the Fifth Republic, in which all citizens of the French Union (including Algerian women) were entitled to participate equally, was supposed to put an end to the perpetual crisis of the Fourth Republic and help find a way out of the "events" in Algeria. In this context, various political actors, particularly on the right, again discussed and proposed compulsory voting as a way to secure the legitimacy of the new regime.[89] Addressing the discussion, the press agency *Index* noted the difficulties of enforcing compulsory voting overseas, where electoral participation "is traditionally weaker than in the metropole" and where "difficult communications" would make compulsory voting with sanctions "scarcely conceivable."[90] Here again, the issue mentioned was that of "creating discrimination between the metropole and overseas," if the obligation to vote were to apply only

---

86. Gary Wilder, *The French Imperial Nation-State: Negritude and Colonial Humanism between the Two World Wars* (Chicago: University of Chicago Press, 2020), 118.
87. Larcher, *L'autre citoyen*.
88. Tyler Stovall, *White Freedom: The Racial History of an Idea* (Princeton, NJ: Princeton University Press, 2021).
89. Marcel Gabilly, "Un principe à inscrire dans la constitution: Le vote obligatoire," *Le Figaro*, June 28, 1958; Jules Romains, "Pour le vote obligatoire," *L'Aurore*, July 11, 1958.
90. "Le vote obligatoire sera-t-il institué à l'occasion du prochain référendum?," *Index*, July 5, 1958, SPA EBA 17.

in mainland France (the agency report did not specify the status of the overseas departments). In the end, the consultative constitutional committee left it to a future electoral law to possibly introduce compulsory voting.[91] Publicly, the new minister of the interior, Émile Pelletier, a former prefect, questioned "whether it would fully be adapted to our psychology."[92] While he left open the option of enforcing it in the next legislative elections, this type of culturalist argumentation confirmed the circular narrative that compulsory voting was not, never had been, and never would be right for France. In fact, the minister's administrative notes on the issue rather insisted on the practical issues of controlling nonvoting and enforcing sanctions, only wondering in passing about the potential reactions of "an already highly diversified electorate in its consistency and its tendencies: metropole—overseas departments—Algeria—overseas territories—French citizens abroad."[93]

Not unlike in 1946, however, electoral turnout mattered a great deal to the new government, this time in mainland France and overseas. Pelletier's services loosened deadlines for electoral registration, extended postal voting to new categories, and established options for French citizens abroad to vote for the first time, as well as for groups affected by decolonization and the Algerian war: "Europeans" repatriated from Morocco and Tunisia, Algerians currently residing in mainland France, and soldiers. Like Third and Fourth Republic elites, then, the government preferred to act on voting conditions rather than introducing compulsory voting. It also invested in a new mass-media communications policy geared directly toward promoting electoral participation, recycling old messages such as "Vote yes, vote no, but vote," or "Abstention = Desertion."[94]

While voting was recommended from above, it remained voluntary—but it was not "free" everywhere. In Algeria, while pro-independence forces called for a boycott of the referendum and threatened with reprisals those Algerians who participated, French authorities, together with the army, aimed to ensure high turnout (and a high level of support for the new constitution). Their efforts particularly targeted Algerian women, whose social and political rights had become a political weapon in the war. Posters and slogans stated that "You don't have the

---

91. Comité national chargé de la publication des travaux préparatoires des institutions de la Ve République, *Documents pour servir à l'histoire de l'élaboration de la Constitution du 4 octobre 1958*, vol. 2 (Paris: La Documentation française, 1988), 127–28.
92. "Près de 44 millions d'électeurs sont inscrits," *Le Monde*, September 19, 1958.
93. "Note au ministre de l'intérieur," October 6, 1958, AN F/1cII/560.
94. "Votez oui votez non mais votez," 1958, *La contemporaine*, AFF33426.

right not to vote" and presented voting as a sign of "submission to the laws of the Republic that protect women," articulating a disciplinary understanding of political citizenship as a protection from the alleged private subordination of Algerian women.[95] Contrary to 1946, the high turnout and support for the proposed constitution in the referendum (80.63 percent turnout, 82.60 percent "yes" overall, apart from French Guinea) were (momentarily) celebrated as a sign of allegiance to the French Republic and to de Gaulle. The French press eagerly circulated pictures of Algerian women wearing Islamic headscarves at the voting booth.[96]

While proponents of compulsory voting during the Fourth Republic had thus not attained their objective, the debates that they initiated contributed to cementing a gendered and racialized understanding of the ideal citizen as simultaneously autonomous and conscious of "his" civic duties. This focus invisibilized other claims to, and configurations of, citizenship more closely related to female and nonwhite citizens. Instead of a supposedly "non-French" system of compulsory voting, the young Fifth Republic cemented its legitimacy through a focus on elections and referenda, and through subsequent offensive communication campaigns mocking the by-then infamous stereotypical Frenchman who went fishing instead of voting.[97]

Zoé Kergomard is senior lecturer at the University of Zurich. She received her PhD in contemporary history from the University of Fribourg in 2018.

---

95. Diane Sambron, *Femmes musulmanes: Guerre d'Algérie 1954–1962* (Paris: Éditions Autrement, 2007), 43–72.
96. "Raz de marée 'oui,'" *L'Union*, September 29, 1958.
97. "Le péché par négligence: L'abstention," *Les actualités françaises*, ORTF, March 28, 1962, http://www.ina.fr/video/AFE85009451. On these campaigns see Zoé Kergomard, "Dépolitiser au risque de repolitiser l'abstention? Les faux-semblants des campagnes gaullistes d'appel au vote (1958–1969)," *Mots. Les langages du politique* 134 (2024): 21–38.

CHAPTER 10

Commercial Sex, Gender, and Citizenship in Postwar Poland

Anna Dobrowolska

"Women in the Polish People's Republic have equal rights with men in all spheres of public, political, economic, social and cultural life" proclaimed the 1952 Polish constitution.[1] According to Communist propaganda, all citizens, regardless of their gender, could and should participate equally in the building of a new, socialist society. As the country emerged from the rubble of war and entered the path of Soviet-style industrialization, citizenship came to be redefined to serve the Communist project's needs. Most importantly, labor became central in these new visions of citizenship, as both men and women were expected to join hands to reconstruct a nation ravaged by war. Women in particular were encouraged to enter new industries and pursue professional education. Equally important was reproductive labor, as the state encouraged both male and female citizens to produce healthy babies to rebuild the nation and consolidate its newly acquired ethnic unity. In the early postwar years several measures were put in place to encourage reproduction, including pronatalist propaganda, a strict ban on abortion, and a campaign against venereal diseases, seen as one of the main threats to the biopolitical reconstruction of the nation.

---

1. Article 66, Constitution of the Polish People's Republic (1952), http://libr.sejm.gov.pl/tek01/txt/kpol/e1952a-spis.html (March 10, 2023).

At the very center of these discourses, this chapter argues, was prostitution, viewed as a threat to both the reconstruction of the nation and the construction of a new socialist society. As the commercial sex market epitomized the capitalist economy, "bourgeois" morality, and the inherent inequality between men and women, it is hardly surprising that it was difficult to reconcile the existence of such a market with the construction of a new socialist society. Because authorities perceived paid sex to be foreign to socialist morality, they took several steps to curtail the sex industry. In the early postwar years several ideas were proposed, including criminalization of clients and the so-called resocialization of women in special facilities. Sex workers were forced to leave the profession. Those who refused to do so were charged with the crime of "work avoidance" and sent to labor camps. It was not until the mid-1950s that the post-Stalinist thaw would enable more public discussions of prostitution to take place. Ironically, in the post-Stalinist years, prostitution would become a handy metaphor for all the ills and wrongdoings of the early Communist period.

Examining the place of sex workers in Communist Poland helps to highlight just how fragile the foundations of women's emancipation under communism really were. The boundaries of gendered citizenship were demarcated by a woman's participation in the labor force, her class position, and reproductive capacity, as well as sexual conduct. An imputed opposition between "decent women" and "prostitutes" informed understandings of gendered citizenship among both state officials and the broader public. By taking a closer look at attempts to police female sexuality, this chapter therefore reflects on the contentious nature of women's citizenship in the first decade of state socialism. Drawing on police documents, press publications, and expert discourse, as well as poetry, it demonstrates how the figure of the prostitute—symbolized most famously in the "rubble woman" who sold sex in the ruins—played a crucial role in the debates on gendered citizenship in the early postwar years.

Yet, while accusations of sexual misconduct became central to defining the boundaries of women's participation in the public sphere, toward the end of the 1950s, women's erotic capital grew increasingly important in the discussions of socialist modernity. The images of "kittens," that is, sexually attractive young women who appeared on the covers of many magazines, attest to this remarkable, albeit at times paradoxical, transformation of state-socialist gendered citizenship. By tracing the ambiguities and tensions surrounding women's sexual agency and erotic appeal this chapter contextualizes the debates on women's emancipation in the 1950s beyond the usual binary of backlash and progress to argue that visions of gendered citizenship were very much in flux in the first postwar decade. Rather than focusing on a single dimension of women's lives, this chapter puts labor, homemaking, and sex in conversation with one another in order to highlight the variety of social, political, and sexual expectations women faced in 1950s Poland.

Women's Double Burden and the Question of Emancipation

Did communism emancipate women? What was the impact of socialist regimes on the transformations of sexuality and gender in postwar Europe? Did women—in the words of Kristen Ghodsee—have better sex under socialism?[2] These questions have recently become central in the scholarship on gender under state socialism. While the previous historiography perceived any state intervention into private life as oppressive, in recent years feminist scholars have pointed out how Communist interventions into the private sphere transformed women's social position in East Central Europe, especially in the early postwar years. As Małgorzata Fidelis pointed out, "The Stalinist system offered women a set of multiple, yet limited, identities: women could be workers, mothers, wives, labor heroines, or political activists."[3]

The recent research on women's political activism under socialism has provoked debates about the limits of individual agency under authoritarian regimes. For scholars such as Ghodsee or Magdalena Grabowska, official women's organizations like the Committee of the Bulgarian Women's Movement or the Polish League of Women provide a starting point from which to analyze the role played by socialist activists in global debates on women's rights as well as to uncover forgotten genealogies of Eastern European feminist movements.[4] Nanette Funk

---

2. Kristen Ghodsee, *Why Women Have Better Sex under Socialism: And Other Arguments for Economic Independence* (London: Bodley Head, 2018).

3. Małgorzata Fidelis, "Equality through Protection: The Politics of Women's Employment in Postwar Poland," *Slavic Review* 63, no. 2 (2004): 301–24, 303.

4. Kristen Ghodsee, *Second World, Second Sex: Socialist Women's Activism and Global Solidarity during the Cold War* (Durham, NC: Duke University Press, 2018); Magdalena Grabowska, *Zerwana genealogia, Działalność społeczna i polityczna kobiet po 1945 roku a współczesny polski ruch kobiecy* (Warsaw: Wydawnictwo Naukowe Scholar, 2018); Magdalena Grabowska, "Bits of Freedom: Demystifying Women's Activism under State Socialism in Poland and Georgia," *Feminist Studies* 43, no. 1 (2017): 141–68. See also Basia A Nowak, "Constant Conversations: Agitators in the League of Women in Poland during the Stalinist Period," *Feminist Studies* 31, no. 3

has famously criticized such research as "revisionist," claiming that the only agency women had under communism was "passive," often harmful for "true" women's causes, and that the state curtailed attempts to behave proactively.[5] That is, Funk seems to argue that feminist actions by definition need to be liberal and centered on individual self-actualization rather than the collective good. But as Ghodsee points out in her response to Funk, this version is just one of many possible definitions of feminism. According to the revisionist scholars, only by expanding our definition of feminism to include non-Western experiences can we fully understand the Communist project's impact on women's social positions and political movements in the Eastern bloc.[6]

The notion that individual agency has to be understood in a broader socioeconomic context has particularly influenced research on women's labor force participation under state socialism. As Rachel Weiser argues in her contribution to this volume, once Communists seized power across Eastern and Central Europe, labor became central to redefining citizenship and gender roles. In the attempt to quickly expand the labor force numbers for the purposes of large-scale industrialization projects, women were encouraged to enter the labor market, often in professions previously perceived as unfeminine, such as miners and tractor drivers.[7] Propaganda posters featured images of strong labor heroines working for peace and for the development of their fatherland. These policies had an impact: by 1954, women constituted 33 percent of Poland's labor force.[8] Yet official declarations of gender equality turned out to be superficial in other ways. Even in the Stalinist period, women were seldom promoted to managerial and skilled positions, and work conditions on the shop floor remained grueling, making it even more burdensome for women to reconcile paid work with unpaid labor at home.[9] In recent scholarship, the so-called double burden of women's

---

(2005): 488–518; Barbara A. Nowak, "Serving Women and the State: The League of Women in Communist Poland" (PhD diss., Ohio State University, 2004).

5. Nanette Funk, "A Very Tangled Knot: Official State Socialist Women's Organizations, Women's Agency and Feminism in Eastern European State Socialism," *European Journal of Women's Studies* 21, no. 4 (2014): 344–60.

6. Kristen Ghodsee, "Untangling the Knot: A Response to Nanette Funk," *European Journal of Women's Studies* 22, no. 2 (2015): 248–52.

7. Małgorzata Fidelis, *Women, Communism, and Industrialization in Postwar Poland* (Cambridge: Cambridge University Press, 2010).

8. Katherine Lebow, *Unfinished Utopia: Nowa Huta, Stalinism, and Polish Society, 1949–56* (Ithaca, NY: Cornell University Press, 2013), 98.

9. Fidelis, *Women, Communism, and Industrialization*, 77–81.

productive and reproductive labor has been held up as an example of the inherent limitations of socialism's emancipatory aims.[10]

Women's newly acquired role in production did not mean that reproduction became any less important to the Communist authorities. On the contrary, as Barbara Klich-Kluczewska and Mie Nakachi both underscore, the postwar Communist governments were deeply concerned with "making up for the losses of war" and "replacing the dead." Women's reproductive capacities thus became central to the process of the postwar reconstruction.[11] Polish authorities, concerned with population growth, encouraged women to have many children. They awarded mothers with ten or more children a Cross of Merit modeled after the Soviet Mother Heroine titles.[12] The state also upheld the prewar penal code, which criminalized abortions, thereby forcing thousands of women to seek unsafe, clandestine procedures. Other pronatalist policies included the expansion of institutionalized medical care for mothers and newborns, especially in the rural areas, as well as a countrywide campaign against venereal diseases (so-called Akcja W) launched in 1948. As Marcin Kacprzak, a doctor and social reformer, claimed, "The protection of the biological value of the Nation must come first among our most urgent priorities."[13] Not unlike in the West, in the immediate postwar years the government viewed women as the key to rebuilding a nation ravaged by war. In Eastern Europe, however, these pronatalist policies were combined with a strong emphasis on women's labor, which to some extent mitigated the degree to which the postwar reproductive policies pushed women back into the domestic sphere.

Even though many of the Stalinist-era family policies were quite conservative compared to earlier revolutionary efforts at gender equality, the postwar legal interventions substantially altered the private lives of women in East Central Europe.[14] New Communist legal codes put

---

10. See, for instance, Paulina Bren, "Women on the Verge of Desire: Women, Work, and Consumption in Socialist Czechoslovakia," in *Pleasures in Socialism*, ed. David Crowley and Susan E. Reid (Evanston, IL: Northwestern University Press, 2010), 177–96. For more on the "double burden" see Rachel Weiser's chapter in this volume.

11. Barbara Klich-Kluczewska, "Making Up for the Losses of War: Reproduction Politics in Post-war Poland," in *Women and Men at War: A Gender Perspective on World War II and Its Aftermath in Central and Eastern Europe*, ed. Maren Röger and Ruth Leiserowitz (Osnabrück, Germany: Fibre Verlag, 2012), 308–29; Mie Nakachi, *Replacing the Dead: The Politics of Reproduction in the Postwar Soviet Union* (New York: Oxford University Press, 2021).

12. Klich-Kluczewska, "Making Up for the Losses of War," 316.

13. Marcin Kacprzak, "Słowo wstępne," *Opiekun Społeczny*, no. 1–3 (1948): 5.

14. See Wendy Z. Goldman, *Women, the State and Revolution: Soviet Family Policy and Social Life, 1917–1936* (Cambridge: Cambridge University Press, 1993).

an end to discrimination against children born out of wedlock and (at least on paper) offered support to single mothers.[15] In Poland, the legalization of divorce in 1946 meant that, for the first time in Polish history, marriage became a secular rather than religious institution, based on equality and respect.[16] Likewise, in Czechoslovakia, sexologists announced a departure from the bourgeois models of marriage and highlighted that, as Kateřina Lišková argues, "socialist marriage was to be based on mutual affection, not economic constraints."[17] In the popular press, men were encouraged to participate in household chores and take up more active roles as husbands and fathers.[18] Although all these legal and discursive developments did not always easily translate into everyday practice, the impact of state socialism on transforming the discourses surrounding gender and the family should not be underestimated.

Most recently, scholars have become interested in the role that sexuality played in these social transformations of the early Communist period. As Lišková has pointed out, sexuality "was far from an insignificant private matter" for socialist states.[19] Contrary to Cold War stereotypes, Eastern Europe did not lag behind the West when it came to redefining sexual morality.[20] In the late 1950s, after a period of postwar pronatalism, Communist governments in the region adopted more liberal approaches toward reproduction, legalizing abortion and promoting family planning long before the Western "sexual revolution" gained momentum. As sex became increasingly important in the lives of

---

15. Ulf Brunnbauer, "'The Most Natural Function of Women': Ambiguous Party Policies and Female Experiences in Socialist Bulgaria," in *Gender Politics and Everyday Life in State Socialist Eastern and Central Europe*, ed. Shana Penn and Jill Massino (New York: Palgrave Macmillan, 2009), 77-96. See also Barbara Klich-Kluczewska, *Family, Taboo and Communism in Poland, 1956-1989*, trans. Soren A. Gauger (Berlin: Peter Lang, 2021).

16. Barbara Łobodzinska, "Divorce in Poland: Its Legislation, Distribution and Social Context," *Journal of Marriage and the Family* 45, no. 4 (1983): 927-42.

17. Kateřina Lišková, "Sex under Socialism: From Emancipation of Women to Normalized Families in Czechoslovakia," *Sexualities* 19, no. 1-2 (2016): 211-35, 217.

18. See, for instance, Jill Massino, "Something Old, Something New: Marital Roles and Relations in State Socialist Romania," *Journal of Women's History* 22, no. 1 (2010): 34-60.

19. Kateřina Lišková, *Sexual Liberation, Socialist Style: Communist Czechoslovakia and the Science of Desire, 1945-1989* (New York: Cambridge University Press, 2018), 31.

20. Kristen Ghodsee and Kateřina Lisková, "Bumbling Idiots or Evil Masterminds? Challenging Cold War Stereotypes about Women, Sexuality and State Socialism," *Filozofija i Drustvo* 27, no. 3 (2016): 489-503. See also Agnieszka Kościańska, *Gender, Pleasure, and Violence: The Construction of Expert Knowledge of Sexuality in Poland*, trans. Marta Rozmysłowicz (Bloomington: Indiana University Press, 2020).

socialist citizens, the state supported the development of institutionalized sexology and large-scale publications of sexological advice.[21]

Most important, however, these public discussions of sexuality under state socialism were rarely ever only about sex. Armed with examples of sexual misconduct and immorality, journalists and experts engaged in heated debates over the definition of socialist modernity and the role of the state in enforcing normative values. Not surprisingly in this context, prostitution functioned as a particularly potent social metaphor. As Barbara Havelková observes in the Czechoslovak case, discussions of social dangers connected with paid sex played a role in upholding gendered norms of behavior for all women, not only sex workers.[22] Similarly in Poland, the debates on commercial sex affected the position of all women.

Rachel Chin and Samuel Huneke note in the introduction to this volume that "citizenship is not mere theory" but also social practice. In the vertical dimension of understanding citizenship they put forward, citizenship becomes a product of complex multilevel negotiations between different social actors. Studying the debates over "prostitution" in 1950s Poland reveals how these negotiations took place in contexts that, at first glance, had nothing to do with formal, legal frameworks of citizenship. As this chapter explores, in the postwar period the discussions of sex workers' misconduct contributed to delineating the boundaries of acceptable gender performances in the public sphere. In particular, they affected the ways in which women's position as socialist citizens became defined in relation to their productive, reproductive, and erotic capital. In the profound political and economic transition of the postwar decades, citizenship and its gendered aspects became a highly negotiated practice. Contrary to the early postwar pronouncements of gender equality and the centrality of labor in the socialist citizenship project, after 1956 the state retreated from the revolutionary policies, seeing the "Polish road to socialism" in the reestablishment of traditional gender roles.

---

21. Kościańska, *Gender, Pleasure, and Violence*; Agnieszka Kościańska, "Beyond Viagra: Sex Therapy in Poland," *Sociologický Časopis / Czech Sociological Review* 50, no. 6 (2014): 919-38, https://doi.org/10.13060/00380288.2014.50.6.148.

22. Barbara Havelková, "Blaming All Women: On Regulation of Prostitution in State Socialist Czechoslovakia," *Oxford Journal of Legal Studies* 36, no. 1 (2016): 191.

Against "Bourgeois Habits"

Before 1939, the market for commercial sex in Poland had been regulated to some extent by the authorities. Although brothels were formally illegal, the state acknowledged the fact that prostitution existed and needed to be controlled for public health reasons. Women who sold sex had to carry special identity documents, the so-called black books (*czarne książeczki*), and undergo regular venereal examinations.[23] In 1925, the government created special units of the women's police to combat pimping and human trafficking, but the market continued to grow despite policewomen's best efforts.[24] Social reformers campaigned for abolition of prostitution, yet to no avail. It was not until after the Second World War that the new regime challenged the interwar legislation and policing methods and implemented new strategies aimed at curbing the market of commercial sex.

Labor integration and social rights were seen as key to the process of constructing socialist citizenship in postwar East Central Europe, as Nikola Tohma highlights in her contribution to this volume. The early postwar policies on commercial sex were largely inspired by Marxist theories, which claimed that there should be no prostitution in a socialist economy, since the economic exploitation of working-class women would be abolished.[25] In a society where everyone would have a job and social security, there would be no need to sell sex. Therefore, from very early on, the authorities targeted prostitution as a residue of bourgeois morality. "Professional debauchery [*nierząd zawodowy*] . . . is one of the most disgusting forms of exploitation . . . and is a remnant of the vanishing capitalist system," wrote the commander of the Citizens' Militia (Milicja Obywatelska, henceforth MO)[26] in a 1948 executive order, setting the stage for a new institutional approach toward sex work.[27] Black books were abolished, and women who wanted to leave the profession were to be offered help from state institutions. "Hostels for working

---

23. Krzysztof Kloc, "Prostytucja w Krakowie międzywojennym 1918–1939," *Klio—Czasopismo poświęcone dziejom Polski i powszechnym* 31, no. 4 (2014): 87–129.

24. David Petruccelli, "Pimps, Prostitutes and Policewomen: The Polish Women Police and the International Campaign against the Traffic in Women and Children between the World Wars," *Contemporary European History* 24, no. 3 (2015): 333–50.

25. Jacquilyn Weeks, "Un-/Re-productive Maternal Labor: Marxist Feminism and Chapter Fifteen of Marx's *Capital*," *Rethinking Marxism* 23, no. 1 (2011): 31–40, https://doi.org/10.1080/08935696.2011.536327.

26. Citizens' Militia was the state-socialist police force.

27. Archiwum Główne Policji (Main Police Archive) 4/14 B, Tymczasowa instrukcja o obowiązkach Milicji Obywatelskiej w walce z nierządem, 90.

women" were installed to offer accommodation and integrate women into the labor market.

But this reeducation project was far from voluntary. Women who refused to comply were labeled "persistent prostitutes" and persecuted. The Stalinist period in Poland began in 1948, as the Communist Party unified its political power, getting rid of the opposition and imposing strict control over all spheres of social and economic life. This control was achieved through state violence and strict policing of certain social groups, including sex workers. As the socialist state understood citizenship primarily in connection to one's productivity in the labor force, those who refused to work had to be punished. In a manner similar to the examples of psychiatric ward patients in postwar Vienna, as analyzed by Dagmar Wernitznig in this volume, strange-looking and improperly behaving women were deemed to be a threat to the stability of the new political system. In Poland in the early 1950s, women charged with "debauchery" were sentenced to a labor camp and banned from entering larger cities such as Warsaw.[28] The behavior of those who stayed in the hostels also came under scrutiny, and any attempts to assert their agency within these institutions, for example through rebelling against the hostels' staff or even owning makeup products, were labeled "abnormal" or "pathological."[29]

The unofficial number of women registered as "prostitutes" in police documents seemed to confirm that socialism had achieved success in limiting the scale of sex work. In 1949, the MO reported that the number of women who "engaged in debauchery" dropped from 2,168 in January to 1,605 in August. In July 1950, the official estimates were as low as 1,162 women registered countrywide.[30] In 1952, Poland ratified the United Nations Convention for the Suppression of the Traffic in Persons and of the Exploitation of the Prostitution of Others, which state propaganda heralded as the final step in eradicating sexual

---

28. Archiwum Akt Nowych (Archive of Modern Records in Warsaw, henceforth AAN), Komisja Specjalna do Walki z Nadużyciami i Szkodnictwem Gospodarczym, 2/170/0/4/3189, Wniosek o rozpoznanie sprawy w trybie postępowania przed Komisją Specjalną, Warsaw, March 17, 1953, 44.

29. AAN, Najwyższa Izba Kontroli (henceforth NIK), 2/356/0/5.4/1343, AAN, NIK, 2/356/0/5.4/1343, Sprawozdanie nr 148/52/pf, Bydgoszcz, February 91952, 59.

30. AAN, Komitet Centralny Polskiej Zjednoczonej Partii Robotniczej (henceforth KC PZPR), 2/1354/0/237/VII t. 2679, Raport sytuacyjny KG MO za miesiąc sierpień 1949 r. Ściśle tajne, 138-39; AAN, KC PZPR, 2/1354/0/237/VII t. 2680, Raport sytuacyjny KG MO za miesiąc lipiec 1950 r. Ściśle tajne, 118.

commerce by the new regime.[31] Yet such political actions had little to do with the lived reality, and public opinion would soon target this issue.

On paper, the authorities maintained a strict antiprostitution policy. A Polish refugee interviewed by Radio Free Europe (RFE) in Munich claimed, "The Polish police raid streets and nightclubs and arrest all women suspected of prostitution. She who cannot produce a labor certificate or prove that she is a housewife is subjected to a medical visit and sent to forced labor camps."[32] Yet already in the 1950s, the persistence of sexual commerce led some commentators to conclude that the situation was possible thanks to the cooperation between sex workers and MO officers. The police forces were rumored to benefit from confidential information provided by sex workers. In 1954, another refugee interviewed by RFE testified, "Although prostitution does not exist on paper, everyone in Gdynia knows that there is a certain category of girls that are tolerated, or even supported by the police."[33]

As these sources suggest, despite propagandistic proclamations to the contrary, the existence of sexual commerce under state socialism became a "public secret" that everyone knew about but no one dared to discuss openly. Moreover, if only indirectly, the sources reveal how the gendered definitions of citizenship affected approaches toward women who sold sex in the early postwar years, casting them as "others" not only because they transgressed sexual boundaries but also as both unproductive and unreproductive members of the socialist society. Debates on the place of prostitution in the newly founded socialist society would soon become a central feature of the post-Stalinist thaw. While the sole fact of discussing matters previously deemed to be taboo certainly provided a sense of liberation and became a symbol of the thaw, debates on prostitution also revealed several anxieties surrounding the impact of the Stalinist project on gender roles and family lives.

---

31. Barbara Klich-Kluczewska, "Unzüchtiger Realsozialismus. Prostitution in der Volksrepublik Polen," *Osteuropa* 56, no. 6 (2006): 308. For more on the convention see Sonja Dolinsek and Philippa Hetherington, "Socialist Internationalism and Decolonizing Moralities in the UN Anti-trafficking Regime, 1947–1954," *Journal of the History of International Law* 21, no. 2 (2019): 212–38.

32. Open Society Archives at Central European University, Budapest (hereafter OSA), "Prostitution in Poland," October 16, 1952, HU OSA 300-1-2-26806; Records of Radio Free Europe / Radio Liberty Research Institute: General Records: Information Items, http://hdl.handle.net/10891/osa:637c42bf-cf09-4de1-9920-37e5a1f9b8ca.

33. OSA, "Various Information from Poland," September 20, 1954, HU OSA 300-1-2-50508; Records of Radio Free Europe / Radio Liberty Research Institute: General Records: Information Items, http://hdl.handle.net/10891/osa:5549999e-633d-47b8-976c-e4c7dd0ec310.

Gendering Socialist Morality

Stalin died in 1953, and some liberalization of political life in the bloc followed soon thereafter. Yet it was not until February 1956 and Khrushchev's famous secret speech that the thaw reached its full scale. In Poland the political turmoil was magnified by the death of Boleslaw Bierut, the Communist Party leader, on March 12, 1956, in Moscow, and workers' protests in Poznań in June. The period of Stalinist terror had ended, which enabled a significant political reconfiguration, with Władysław Gomułka, himself a victim of Stalinist purges, assuming power as the leader of the party in October of that year. In his political program, called the "Polish road to socialism," Gomułka reasserted the importance of national identity in building the socialist state. The cultural and political thaw lasted between 1956 and 1957.

Commercial sex featured prominently in discussions of Stalinism and its impact on Polish morality. In February 1955, an anonymous individual wrote a letter to the magazine *Chłopska droga* (Peasant path) in response to a recent radio broadcast about prostitution in Warsaw. The author connected the problem with immorality observed in Nowa Huta (New steelworks), a factory town near Cracow planned as an exemplary socialist settlement. The letter complained that young people arriving in Nowa Huta without proper guidance from their parents and political organizations lacked morals. Women—the author underlined—could easily be led astray by observing the promiscuous behavior of prostitutes who frequented bars there. The author of the letter—most likely of a working-class background, judging from the writing style—stressed that youth were the future of the country and that Nowa Huta was everyone's responsibility. "We need to . . . call the entire nation to fight for socialist morality," the letter concluded.[34]

Even though the letter was probably never published and survives only in the Ministry of Justice's archival files, the nation nonetheless heard the call to action. A few months later, the influential poet Adam Ważyk published his seminal *Poem for Adults*, symbolically inaugurating a period of post-Stalinist thaw in literature and culture.[35] The poem drew on strikingly similar observations as the above-quoted letter, describing Nowa Huta as a place where "fifteen-year-old whores walk

---

34. AAN, Ministry of Justice, 2/285/0/4.1/1825, List czytelnika "Chłopskich dróg" nt. prostytucji, February 24, 1955, 1–3.

35. Marci Shore, "Some Words for Grown-Up Marxists: 'A Poem for Adults' and the Revolt from Within," *Polish Review* 42, no. 2 (1997): 131–54.

down the planks to the basement" and promiscuous women throw their aborted fetuses into the Vistula River. Ważyk aimed to disclose the ills and wrongdoings of the Communist utopia.[36] Thanks to him, "prostitution," together with other "social pathologies" such as alcoholism and hooliganism, became a prominent metaphor for the failure of early Communist modernization.

Ważyk's poem was soon followed by a report from Nowa Huta written by Ryszard Kapuściński (who later became one of Poland's greatest nonfiction authors) and published in the Communist youth magazine *Sztandar Młodych* (Youth banner).[37] Following in Ważyk's footsteps, Kapuściński focused on how communism had failed the working class in Nowa Huta, fostering unlivable conditions and betraying the trust that young people had placed in the Communist project. Lack of moral guidance resulted in the proliferation of prostitution and venereal diseases, especially among young women. In particular, Kapuściński lamented shortages of housing and cruel regulations in hostels that provided accommodation only to single laborers in same-sex dormitories, thus preventing young people from enjoying married life. For Kapuściński—as for many other authors of that period—happy private life equaled a nuclear, heteronormative family, in which a woman was able to realize her "natural" calling of motherhood.

Ważyk's and Kapuściński's writings have often been interpreted literally, as evidence of promiscuity in Nowa Huta and of the scale of prostitution in the mid-1950s. I propose instead to read these texts as examples of how the figure of the prostitute could be weaponized to reimagine socialist citizenship and women's social position in general. It is hardly a coincidence that Ważyk, Kapuściński, and the earlier letter from a reader of *Chłopska droga* take up the same tropes, focusing on the proliferation of prostitution in Nowa Huta and its degrading effect on "decent women" in order to convey their concern with the state of socialist morality. Despite official declarations of gender equality, these texts share an inherently gendered vision of how socialist citizens should organize their intimate lives.

Without question, Nowa Huta was a social experiment. It was an exemplary socialist city planned to counterbalance the influence of nearby Cracow, which was the symbolic center of Polish conservatism

---

36. Lebow, *Unfinished Utopia*, 97–123.
37. Ryszard Kapuściński, "To też jest prawda o Nowej Hucie," *Sztandar Młodych*, no. 234 (1955): 2.

and a living reminder of pre-1945 social order. Often compared by historians to the Soviet city of Magnitogorsk, Nowa Huta was supposed to be the birthplace of the new Polish working class.[38] Thus, anything that happened there could easily become a metaphor for the state of Polish socialism, especially in the heated sociopolitical discussions of the mid-1950s. As Katherine Lebow has pointed out, women who came to Nowa Huta longed for independence, adventure, job stability, and higher living standards, just as much as men did.[39] Yet while Nowa Huta's men were rarely portrayed as problematic, except for discussions of hooliganism, women's paid labor and presence in the public sphere came under close scrutiny during the post-Stalinist thaw. By focusing on scandalous examples of juvenile prostitution and venereal infections, commentators painted a picture of Nowa Huta's women as sexual deviants and victims of forced industrialization. By suggesting that women belonged at home in their supposedly natural roles as mothers and housewives, these commentators redrew the boundaries of socialist citizenship, arguing that the most important way in which women could participate in building the socialist project was through reproductive rather than productive labor.

In these discussions the Stalinist period was portrayed as a time of "unnatural" experiments with the gender order. Consequently, as the country entered the "Polish road to socialism," women's reproductive capacities and sexual respectability became important lenses through which gendered citizenship was reimagined after 1956.[40] These categories' boundaries were, however, purposefully blurred. While in the Stalinist period authorities maintained that women were perfectly capable of combining their responsibilities as industrial workers and mothers, after 1953 many women were forced out of professions such as mining and transportation under the pretense that these occupations were harmful to their reproductive health.[41] As any woman could potentially become a mother, their participation in the labor force had to conform to narrow definitions of well-being.

Similarly, allegations of prostitution were often extended to all women who asserted more agency in their intimate lives. For example,

---

38. Stephen Kotkin, *Magnetic Mountain: Stalinism as a Civilization* (Berkeley: University of California Press, 1995).

39. Lebow, *Unfinished Utopia*, 101.

40. Dobrochna Kałwa, "Post-Stalinist Backlash in Poland | Backlash Post-Stalinien en Pologne," *Clio: Histoire, Femmes et Sociétés* 41, no. 1 (2015): 151–60.

41. Fidelis, *Women, Communism, and Industrialization*, 203–37.

in 1955, the Nowa Huta MO reported that 10 percent of female hostel inhabitants were either "prostitutes" or "half-prostitutes."[42] Judging from other MO documents, the latter term may have denoted women for whom paid sex was a supplementary, rather than the main, source of income.[43] In reality, however, any woman who had extramarital sexual relations could be labeled a half-prostitute. The improbably high numbers of "half-prostitutes" in MO reports thus suggest a general relaxation of sexual mores among single women in Nowa Huta rather than an expansion of its market for commercial sex. For the general public, though, these reports served as a point of departure to discuss the problematic presence of independent women in the public sphere.

Public Women, Public Sphere

The 1957 documentary *Paragraf zero* (Article zero) offers a powerful visual manifestation of how the discourses of prostitution intertwined with more general concerns over women's sexual agency and negotiated boundaries between the public and private spheres. The film opens with evening scenes from the streets of Warsaw. As cars and pedestrians rush through the city center, we get a sense of a lively and modern city life. Single, attractive women sit in a café. But this quaint picture is quickly disrupted. "Look closely," emphasizes the narrator; "people come to this café not only to attend social meetings and engage in conversations. They come here with other issues in mind."[44] The camera follows a woman in high heels as she leaves the café through a dense curtain. Although nothing is yet said openly, the message is very clear: it is suspicious for single women to spend time alone in such places.

The next scene leaves even less room for speculation. "It's 11 p.m.," explains the voiceover; "we are again on the street." As the camera follows a single woman walking around a street corner, the narrator explains that prostitution had been abolished by postwar legislation. "We are not only modern, but also subtle," continues the commentary. "Of course, every woman can walk alone at night. Have casual relationships. Have her own 'guardian.'" As we learn seconds later, in a scene of sexual assault, walking alone at night can lead to very unpleasant

---

42. Lebow, *Unfinished Utopia*, 120.
43. Archiwum Instytutu Pamięci Narodowej (Institute for National Remembrance Archive), Ka 410/37, Pismo Komendanta MO w Katowicach dot. kobiet uprawiających nierząd, July 23, 1951, 60.
44. *Paragraf zero*, dir. Włodzimierz Borowik (Wytwórnia Filmów Dokumentalnych, 1957).

consequences. Once young women step on this path, there is little that can be done to save them from becoming "rubble women" (*gruzinki*), selling sex on the postwar ruins of Polish cities. As this excerpt reveals, the filmmakers not only criticize the insufficient policing of prostitution by the state, but foremostly challenge the visions of socialist modernity marked by gender equality and new roles assumed by women in the public sphere.

Paragraf zero became an iconic visual representation of public concerns over prostitution and sexual morality during the post-Stalinist thaw. The documentary not only demonstrates how prostitution could become a metaphor of the state of socialist society in general but also reveals tensions surrounding young women's sexual agency. The café scene points to new practices of sociability in mixed-gender settings. As the first generation raised after the war was entering adulthood, public opinion grew increasingly concerned with their attitudes toward consumption, how they spent free time, and their intimate relationships.[45] Young people (especially women) seemed to take socialist expressions of gender equality seriously, expecting equal access to education, work, entertainment, and also intimacy. According to Hanna Malewska's research from the late 1950s, over 40 percent of women had their first sexual experiences before the age of eighteen.[46] It was these new practices of intimacy that often shocked older generations and provoked questions about the true meaning of socialist morality in Poland.

In his 1960 pamphlet *Sodom and Gomorrah?* the writer and educator Salomon Łastik observed that contemporary Polish society had witnessed "a move toward greater sexual freedom. Women demand their rights, don't want to suffer silently with their husbands who often treat them like objects. . . . Many young women don't care if it's allowed or not to have sexual intercourse before getting married. But let's not trade freedom for promiscuity."[47] While Łastik observed many worrisome transgressions of public morality and repeatedly warned that "the way from promiscuity to prostitution is not very long" and that sexual initiation at a young age could be very harmful to a girl's mental health, his response to the problem was not to simply return to

---

45. Małgorzata Fidelis, *Imagining the World from behind the Iron Curtain: Youth and the Global Sixties in Poland* (New York: Oxford University Press, 2022), 14–38.

46. Hanna Malewska, *Kulturowe i psychospołeczne determinanty życia seksualnego* (Warsaw: Państwowe Wydawnictwo Naukowe, 1967).

47. Salomon Łastik, *Czy Sodoma i Gomora: Na tematy obyczajowe* (Lodz: Wydawnictwo Łódzkie, 1961), 105.

the previous frameworks of "bourgeois morality."[48] Rather, he called for a close reevaluation of how socialist morality was understood and translated into educational practice. While acknowledging the need "to denounce every instance of sexual excess, having nothing in common either with true feelings, or love, or human dignity," he also stressed the necessity of a gender-specific approach toward moral education.[49] Men had to learn to respect their female partners, but women needed to acknowledge their "lofty" role as potential mothers. Only in this way, Łastik concluded, would it be possible to build "the most humanistic morality—socialist morality."[50]

Unlike in Western Europe, where, as Emily Lord Fransee and Zoé Kergomard argue in their contributions to this volume, voting rights stood at the center of the political project and affected its gendered character, in nonliberal people's democracies of East Central Europe women's political agency was largely shaped by other factors.[51] The discussions of prostitution reveal how important sexuality was in defining the rights and responsibilities of socialist citizens. The attempts at redefining socialist morality were thus fueled by many, often contradictory, values. While writers such as Łastik acknowledged the principles of gender equality embedded in the socialist project, they were often troubled by their real-life consequences. Women's emancipation was to be applauded as long as it conformed to the narrow boundaries of socialist citizenship, built around an axis of productive and reproductive labor. Any attempt to transgress these boundaries by, for instance, assuming a more independent position in the public sphere, taking up skilled professions, or asserting one's sexual agency endangered socialism's very core. As the country embarked on the "Polish road to socialism," heteronormative masculinity occupied an increasingly central role in the visions of socialist citizenship, with women assigned passive roles rather than active participation in the political project.

The Paradoxes of Post-1956 Morality

The late 1950s saw an unparalleled scale of public debates about prostitution. Had we only taken into account discussions of transactional

---

48. Łastik, 104.
49. Łastik, 118.
50. Łastik, 120.
51. On nonliberal visions of citizenship see also Carlos Domper Lasús's chapter in this volume.

sex, we could arrive at the conclusion that erotica had been erased from the public sphere and that post-Stalinism was characterized by a retreat into traditional gender norms and restrictive visions of sexuality. While condemnations of prostitution and concerns over youth morality certainly formed a vital part of the public debates, this period also witnessed a remarkable explosion of public interest in sexual imagery and eroticized representations of women's bodies. Paradoxical as it may seem, perhaps it is exactly this combination of sexual openness and conservativism that provides the key to understanding the transformation of women's citizenship in the 1950s.

In February 1957, the satirical weekly *Karuzela* published a caricature titled "Parliamentary striptease" on its cover.[52] In it, an attractive woman named "Prawda" (Truth) takes off pieces of clothing with code names such as "professional secrecy," "secret," and "top secret." The subtitle reads, "The truth is undressing herself in the eyes of the nation"—a clear reference to political discussions spurred by the thaw of 1956.[53] Yet apart from referring to the period's political climate, the image also reveals the surprising role played by eroticized female bodies, striptease in particular, in the Polish political imaginary of the late 1950s. While in discussions of prostitution journalists and experts claimed that commercial sex was foreign to socialism and needed to be counteracted by the state, other kinds of sexualized performances received much less scrutiny. The year 1957, for instance, saw the first striptease show at the Warsaw student club Stodoła (the Barn), and soon such forms of entertainment entered the programs of state-owned entertainment companies.[54] Women's erotic qualities became important measures of social modernity and symbolized Polish aspiration to Western lifestyles.

Most remarkably, images of "kittens" (*kociaki*) became a visual manifestation of political and social de-Stalinization. The term had its origins in the Stalinist period and at first denoted female partners of "bikini boys" (*bikiniarze*). These were members of the youth counterculture fascinated with the West and famous for their ties depicting a

---

52. Stanisław Gratkowski [Ibis], "Sejmowy Strip-Tease," *Karuzela*, February 27, 1957, 1.

53. More on Poland in 1956 see Paweł Machcewicz, *Rebellious Satellite: Poland, 1956* (Washington, DC: Woodrow Wilson Center, 2009).

54. Archiwum Państwowe w Warszawie (State Archives in Warsaw), Warsaw Entertainment Enterprise (Stołeczna Estrada w Warszawie), 72/3325/0/3.1/10, Protokół nr 1, April 20, 1965, 86, 88.

scantily clad woman.⁵⁵ Their girlfriends—"kittens"—followed Western fashion, occupied themselves with their appearances, and sought entertainment rather than fulfillment as factory workers. While such behavior was criticized in the propaganda of the early 1950s, it experienced a revival after the cultural constraints of the Stalinist period were lifted. As Małgorzata Fidelis and Katarzyna Stańczak-Wiślicz point out, contrary to the Stalinist role models of female high-productivity workers, "kittens" became the ultimate symbol of womanhood after the thaw. They symbolized a return to the "natural" order, in which women would be defined by their traditional gender roles and erotic appeal to men.⁵⁶

The sexual thaw of 1956-1957 manifested itself in a constant assessment of women's beauty and sexual appeal. There is hardly a better illustration of this process than the sudden revival of Miss Polonia beauty pageants, organized in 1957 in Sopot and in 1958 in Warsaw.⁵⁷ Images of attractive young women flooded the pages of popular newspapers. After 1957, *Przekrój* started publishing "kitten crosswords," with a photograph of an attractive woman in the center.⁵⁸ Many magazines regularly used similar photographs on their covers in an effort to raise their readerships.⁵⁹ Popular magazines also organized photographic contests, such as "the most beautiful student smile" (*Po prostu*, 1955) or "beautiful girls to the screen" (*Film*, 1958), suggesting that the most meaningful way in which a young woman could participate in public life was through being an object of the male gaze.⁶⁰

This voyeuristic fascination with women's bodies clearly dominates the documentary *Sopot 1957*, which reported on social and cultural transformations of the post-Stalinist years, focusing on the city of Sopot, a holiday resort on the Baltic Sea and an important cultural center. As the camera observes female vacationers in skimpy swimming suits, the commentary clearly suggests the voyeuristic purpose of the images: "Sopot is famous for its beautiful views [the camera shows a young sunbather rubbing her body with a towel]. What a landscape! [the camera

---

55. Lebow, *Unfinished Utopia*, 142–45.
56. Katarzyna Stańczak-Wiślicz et al., *Kobiety w Polsce 1945–1989. Nowoczesność, równouprawnienie, komunizm* (Cracow: Universitas, 2020), 424–25.
57. Jerzy Kochanowski, *Rewolucja międzypaździernikowa: Polska 1956–1957* (Cracow: Społeczny Instytut Wydawniczy Znak, 2017), 72–77.
58. See, for example, "Krzyżówka z kociakiem," *Przekrój*, June 14, 1959, 22; Iwona Kurz, *Twarze w tłumie: Wizerunki bohaterów wyobraźni zbiorowej w kulturze polskiej lat 1955–1969* (Izabelin: Świat Literacki, 2005), 133.
59. Kochanowski, *Rewolucja międzypaździernikowa*, 68.
60. Fidelis, "Are You a Modern Girl?," 176; Stańczak-Wiślicz et al., *Kobiety w Polsce*, 428–30.

FIGURE 10.1 A local beauty pageant, 1959.
Source: National Digital Archives (Narodowe Archiwum Cyfrowe), Wojskowa Agencja Fotograficzna, 3/39/0/-/6986-1.

zooms in on a woman brushing her hair]. What a location! [a close-up shows a woman sunbathing in a deck chair]. Young researchers are conducting studies in the field of leg-ology [the camera zooms in on young men looking at the legs of women who pass by]."[61]

The male gaze is certainly key to understanding the thaw discussions of sexuality. Once censorship was relaxed, female bodies quickly became objects to be looked upon and rated according to sex appeal. Paradoxically, while sex workers were scrutinized and pathologized for exercising sexual agency, popular culture increasingly objectified female bodies for the purposes of male entertainment. Sexual agency was reserved for heterosexual men, who benefited most from the

---

61. *Sopot 1957*, dir. Jerzy Hoffman and Edward Skórzyński (Wytwórnia Filmów Dokumentalnych, 1957).

FIGURE 10.2 Entrant in a local beauty pageant, 1959.
Source: National Digital Archives (Narodowe Archiwum Cyfrowe), Wojskowa Agencja Fotograficzna, 3/39/0/-/6986-1.

liberalization of discourses of sexuality of the thaw period. Women, for their part, faced new and often contradictory social expectations.

Between 1956 and 1957 Poland thus witnessed a notable relaxation of visual discourse, in which women's sexuality played an important role. As the figure of the labor heroine faded into the past, new expectations toward women's participation in public life arose. Women were now expected to be aesthetically pleasing, to follow the latest fashions, to participate in new forms of socializing in cafés, restaurants, and at dances. Simultaneously, the state still expected women to pursue an education and wage labor, even if in less ideologized occupations than a few years before. Moreover, reproduction did not disappear from the picture. On the contrary, as the abortion law was liberalized in April 1956 and the state endorsed the activities of the Society for Conscious Motherhood (a family planning NGO), women's reproductive decisions were now discussed more than ever. But it was no longer the number of babies born that most concerned experts. Instead, public discussion increasingly shifted toward helping female citizens plan their families. In the gendered discourse of contraception and reproduction, it was predominantly women who were responsible for obtaining expert advice about planned parenthood, persuading their partners to use contraceptives, and arranging their family lives in a rational way.[62] Hence, the double burden of the Stalinist period slowly transformed into a triple burden, casting women in the simultaneous and demanding roles of housewives, laborers, and eroticized "kittens."

Anna Dobrowolska is a historian of modern Poland whose research focuses on the history of sexuality under state socialism. She is a postdoctoral researcher at the University of Warsaw and a Visiting Max Weber Fellow at the European University Institute in Florence. She holds a PhD in history from the University of Oxford. She is author of *Zawodowe dziewczyny. Prostytucja i praca seksualna w PRL* (Professional girls. Prostitution and sex work in state-socialist Poland), which is the first full account of the history of commercial sex in postwar Poland.

---

62. Agata Ignaciuk, "No Man's Land? Gendering Contraception in Family Planning Advice Literature in State-Socialist Poland (1950s–1980s)," *Social History of Medicine* 33, no. 4 (2020): 1327–49.

CHAPTER 11

Southern Italian Migrants and Contested Social Rights in 1970s Italy and West Germany

Sarah Jacobson

In its January 1973 newsletter, the Italian-based Unione Inquilini (Tenants' union) ran a provocative article titled "None of Us Chose to Emigrate." The Unione Inquilini was an organization that formed in the late 1960s to address rampant housing shortages and high rent prices in northern Italy and subsequently migrated into West Germany. These housing issues especially impacted the hundreds of thousands of migrants from Southern Italy who had moved north to fill labor needs, only to find inadequate and unaffordable housing awaiting them. The January 1973 newsletter highlighted the efforts of tenants to "self-reduce" their rents in Milan, Turin, and elsewhere in Italy—a broad-based movement to pay no more than 10 percent of one's wages in rent irrespective of amounts stipulated in rent contracts. The editors then discussed similar housing protest actions by Italian migrants in Frankfurt am Main, West Germany, using a building that was slated for demolition as an example. Although it had previously housed four German families for a total of 500 DM (German marks), the same building had now been rented room by room to migrants for a total of 10,000 DM. The authors proclaimed, "To the *padroni* [owners], we are not men and women who emigrate. They just want our labor. For this reason, there are no houses for immigrants, no schools for our children." "Migrant workers refuse to pay these prices,

245

or to leave these houses!" they declared.[1] In a few sentences, this newsletter encapsulated the transnational evolution of collective protest among Southern Italian migrants as they pushed for affordable housing in their new communities in the long 1970s.

This chapter focuses on Southern Italian migrants' participation in housing occupations to offer a comparative study of how discursive definitions of citizenship shifted in two different postwar European states. As the other contributions in this volume highlight, the postwar decades were a time of great transnational movement as people rebuilt lives, economies, and governing systems. The frequent lack of congruence between ethnic/national identity and the parameters of nationally bound citizenship meant that many individuals challenged previous categorizations and understandings of citizenship. In this vein, this chapter analyzes how Southern Italian migrants contested who and how one qualified for the benefits of the welfare state—or raised questions of deservingness and belonging. More particularly, the study evaluates how migrants pushed for housing assistance in the industrial centers of Turin and Frankfurt am Main in the late 1960s and early 1970s. By comparing Italian migrants' experiences both within and outside their nation-state, this chapter highlights one of the main threads spanning this volume. It questions the traditional linkage between citizenship and national identities to show how Southern Italian migrants were treated as second-class citizens both within and outside their nation of origin and how they sought to expand localized social rights in their new environments.

The chapter argues that migrant demands for adequate and affordable housing in the 1960s and 1970s symbolized more than just a social need. Rather, migrant participation in housing occupations—and residents' and officials' responses to migrants' housing claims—also illustrated contested understandings of citizenship, social rights, and community building. By comparing the experiences of Southern Italian migrants in two locations, the chapter highlights how social and economic rights began to be de-territorialized and linked to the individual person rather than expressly to the nation-state.[2] Given the

---

1. "Nessuno di noi ha scelto di emigrare," and "Chi ha paura di chi?," *Il giornale dell'Unione Inquilini*, January 1973. All translations are the author's own.

2. Karim Fertikh, "From Territorialized Rights to Personalized International Rights? The Making of the European Convention on the Social Security of Migrant Workers (1957)," in *Marginalized Groups, Inequalities and the Post-war Welfare State: Whose Welfare?*, ed. Monika Baár and Paul van Trigt (New York: Routledge, 2020), 29–48.

historical moment the chapter examines, it is little surprise that migrants and their advocates used the language of human rights and/or basic needs—coupled with shared understandings of common humanity—to advance their claim to housing as one based on individual entitlement rather than nationality. As historian Samuel Moyn points out, the 1970s witnessed two powerful "waves" of human rights and basic needs discourses that created a powerful tool for social movements. This combined momentum allowed marginalized groups—such as Southern Italian migrants—to paint their claims as entirely in line with an individualized right to "an absolute minimum of essential goods and services," even as this embrace of sufficiency undermined earlier visions of greater political and economic parity stemming from the Global South.[3]

The impetus for this chapter draws from the framework of Geoff Eley's and Jan Palmowski's seminal 2008 volume *Citizenship and National Identity in Twentieth-Century Germany*.[4] By decoupling citizenship from the nation-state, Eley, Palmowski, and other scholars pointed to the value of investigating how citizenship is contingent, contested, relational, and indeterminate. They demonstrated how citizenship can serve as an analytical tool for understanding how communities are built and how boundaries of inclusion and exclusion are continually drawn and redrawn. Though the contributions in Eley and Palmowski's edited volume focused specifically on the German context, their reflections on citizenship as a category that is constantly "under construction" have broader implications beyond the boundaries of one nation-state.[5] After all, other contributions in this volume—such as Tohma's examination of the status of Greek refugees in the Eastern bloc (chapter 5) or Hilton's and Courtman's evaluations of displaced persons in Western Europe (chapters 1 and 4)—show how "forms of citizenship and national belonging do not always map straightforwardly or comfortably onto one another."[6]

Comparing Southern Italian migrants' housing claims in Turin in Italy and Frankfurt am Main in the former Federal Republic of Germany

---

3. Samuel Moyn, *Not Enough: Human Rights in an Unequal World* (Cambridge, MA: Belknap Press of Harvard University Press, 2019), 130.
4. Geoff Eley and Jan Palmowski, eds., *Citizenship and National Identity in Twentieth-Century Germany* (Stanford, CA: Stanford University Press, 2008).
5. Geoff Eley, "Some General Thoughts on Citizenship in Germany," in Eley and Palmowski, *Citizenship and National Identity*, 237–38.
6. Geoff Eley and Jan Palmowski, "Citizenship and National Identity in Twentieth-Century Germany," in Eley and Palmowski, *Citizenship and National Identity*, 13.

(FRG) makes sense for four reasons. First, both cities experienced a significant increase in industry and migrant worker populations during the postwar economic miracle. This growth was largely due to labor recruitment efforts facilitated by federal officials and labor union representatives combined with the private business interests of corporations such as the automobile manufacturers and construction companies. Second, Turin and Frankfurt lend themselves to comparison based on national historic parallels. Though one must be cautious in conflating the particularities of such histories, both Italy and Germany unified late in comparison with other Western European nation-states. As such, earlier definitions of citizenship and political participation had largely been determined at regional or local levels. Moreover, both states experienced highly centralized regimes during the Second World War that conflated citizenship with exclusionary parameters of national belonging. In response to their respective fascisms and in the context of the Cold War, leaders within both postwar republics employed antifascist and democratic tenets to redetermine what it meant for someone to be a full member of the community. This strategy created space for more contestation and claims-making than in previous decades.

Third and most important, comparing Southern Italian migrants who were formal citizens in one city and legal outsiders in another underscores the mutability of national identity in administering the protections of citizenship via the welfare state. If one examines their actions and the outcomes of their protests, it is undoubtedly significant that Southern Italians advocated for adequate housing both within and outside their nation-state. But what is rather more remarkable is that the language and modes of protest—in addition to public and state responses—are surprisingly similar in both cities, irrespective of formal citizenship status or national identity. Finally, this chapter emphasizes migrant housing issues in two urban contexts because many dimensions of citizenship are experienced at the local (interpersonal) level, rather than the national level. In other words, individuals' ability to access the rights and protections of citizenship is usually determined, as Adelheid von Saldern points out, "through the local arena, for instance, in their dealings with state bureaucracies."[7] The localized and administrative nature of citizenship rights is amply highlighted in this volume—as manifested by actors such as the Viennese medics

---

7. Adelheid von Saldern, "Citizenship in Twentieth-Century German History: Chances and Challenges of a Concept," in Eley and Palmowski, *Citizenship and National Identity*, 201.

who determined female refugee patients' citizenship status discussed by Wernitznig in chapter 3, or the IRO or West German officials who handled the refugees', DPs', and stateless persons' citizenship applications that Hilton and Courtman investigate in chapters 1 and 4 respectively. In terms of this case study, Southern Italian migrants frequently directed housing appeals to local leaders, and it was those local leaders who decided to make state aid or housing available to migrants through local bureaucratic channels.

Localized interactions over housing consequently demonstrate how citizenship is a social practice—or a "constantly evolving set of actions, beliefs, and decisions," in the words of this book's editors in the introduction. In this case, these social practices emerged from exchanges between migrants, other citizens, and social and state organizations. To illustrate these interpersonal exchanges, the chapter relies on archival sources, news reports, and several interviews that I conducted with migrant participants in housing protests. I contacted one of the interviewees after discovering the book he wrote about his experiences as a Unione Inquilini leader and housing occupier in Frankfurt. Other interview opportunities arose after networking with various associations or individuals still involved with social housing assistance who maintained contact with former occupiers. As sources, these interviews corroborate or complicate narratives gleaned from archival sources and newspaper articles published at the time. They are especially significant as there are not many materials left by migrants themselves—most print sources are closely tied to more vocal political activist groups. In addition, I utilize newspaper coverage to offer a rich account of the interaction between migrant occupiers and other members of the public.

As a way to organize this chapter, I rely on Kathleen Canning's concept of "participatory citizenship." More specifically, I borrow the defining characteristics of Canning's term to illustrate how Southern Italian migrants (1) articulated claims, (2) engaged in contest, and (3) made their own meanings of citizenship.[8] Following this schema, the first portion of this chapter briefly analyzes how Southern Italian migrants articulated their claims to housing through flyers distributed to neighbors and commentary within news media. The second section will turn from discourse to action, examining housing occupations to understand how migrants highlighted their precarious living conditions

---

8. Kathleen Canning, "Reflections on the Vocabulary of Citizenship in Twentieth-Century Germany," in Eley and Palmowski, *Citizenship and National Identity*, 216.

and demanded access to state welfare. Finally, the chapter concludes with an analysis of local responses to migrant protests.

This examination of residents' and state responses to migrant housing activism demonstrates that migrants did not make new meanings of citizenship entirely on their own. This was a dialogic process whereby definitions of what it meant to be a community member entitled to state protection shifted through public discourse. Through the lens of housing, this chapter thus contends that in the postwar era, citizenship (and the associated protection of a welfare state) was continually constructed and renegotiated. To use the vertical dimension of citizenship introduced in this volume, this repositioning of rights and definitions most often occurred through everyday interactions on societal rungs within ladders that stretched within and beyond the strict geographic bounds of the nation-state.

Articulating Claims

The areas of Southern Italy and the islands of Sardinia and Sicily have long been regions of emigration owing to long-standing socioeconomic disparities with the wealthier north. Factors such as lower levels of industrialization, a reliance on agricultural production, and high birth rates meant that many working-age individuals left the region in search of better opportunities.[9] In contrast, many industrial centers in northern Italy and West Germany experienced significant increases in production demands during the postwar economic boom. As a result, many Southern Italian migrants either used official recruitment channels or found their own way to factories in need of labor. In 1955, labor union and government representatives signed the Treaty of Rome, which facilitated the movement of Italian workers to industrial centers of West Germany. They were known as "guest workers" in Germany, as their stay was intended to be temporary. West Germany signed similar labor agreements with Turkey, Greece, Portugal, Spain, and the former Yugoslavia in subsequent years. Italians constituted the largest group of migrants in West Germany from the mid-1950s until 1970, numbering 573,600 in total.[10] By 1971, one in every seven Frankfurt residents

---

9. See Guido Pescosolido, "Italy's Southern Question: Long-standing Thorny Issues and Current Problems," *Journal of Modern Italian Studies* 24, no. 3 (2019): 441–55.

10. Rita Chin, *The Guest Worker Question in Postwar Germany* (Cambridge: Cambridge University Press, 2007), 62. Italians would be overtaken by Turkish workers the very next year, with the Turkish population rising to 652,800 in 1971.

came from outside the FRG.¹¹ In addition, northern Italian corporations such as Fiat even sent special trains—called "sun trains"—to bring additional laborers to the "industrial triangle" of northern Italy. Between 1958 and 1963, more than 1.3 million southerners migrated to northern Italy.¹² This influx of migrants contributed significantly to Turin's population growth, which grew from 720,000 inhabitants in 1951 to over 1.8 million in 1971.¹³

For migrants in the 1960s and 1970s, urban renewal plans exacerbated challenges they already faced in finding housing. In both Turin and Frankfurt, city planners used the destruction of city centers during the war as an impetus for reconstructing previously run-down areas into revitalized business, commercial, and luxury housing districts. As speculators bought up areas that had once provided low-income housing, Southern Italian migrants' circumstances only worsened as they confronted rental discrimination. Signs reading "No foreigners allowed" in Frankfurt mirrored those in Turin that stated "We do not rent to southerners."¹⁴ As a result of these compounding factors, migrants frequently lived in cramped apartments while generally paying higher prices in rent than long-term residents.¹⁵ One Italian migrant in West Germany, for instance, paid 400 DM for a single room for himself and his seven children, while sharing one toilet with twenty-two other people.¹⁶ Only 9 percent of West Germans paid such a high rent—the majority of native-born renters paid less than 350 DM for entire

---

11. "Mehr Ausländer als je zuvor," *Frankfurter Rundschau*, April 6, 1971.

12. Turin Museum, "L'immigrazione a Torino dal dopoguerra agli anni settanta," https://www.museotorino.it/view/s/bdd983a0cb2e4c06912b6539e0d1cee7#.

13. Città di Torino—Direzione Servizi Civici—Settore Stattistica e Toponomastica, "I numeri dell'immigrazione Italiana a Torino, 1910-2011" (Città di Torino, 2011), 28, https://www.ilmattinodifoggia.it/userUpload/immigraziane_torino_2011.pdf.

14. Northern Italians historically considered Southern Italians to be inferior, evoking stereotypes that centered on aspects such as family size, superstition, health and hygiene, literacy rates, and work habits. For reference see Iain Chambers, "The 'Southern Question'... Again," in *The Routledge Handbook of Contemporary Italy: History, Politics, Society*, ed. Andrea Mammone, Ercole Giap Parini, and Giuseppe A. Veltri (London: Routledge, 2015). See also John Dickie, *Darkest Italy: The Nation and Stereotypes of the Mezzogiorno, 1860-1900* (New York: St. Martin's, 1999); and Aliza S. Wong, *Race and the Nation in Liberal Italy, 1861-1911: Meridionalism, Empire, and Diaspora* (New York: Palgrave Macmillan, 2006).

15. For a comprehensive study on migrant housing disparities in Frankfurt am Main see Maria Borris, *Ausländische Arbeiter in einer Großstadt: Eine empirische Untersuchung am Beispiel Frankfurt* (Frankfurt am Main: Europäische Verlagsanstalt, 1973).

16. Dokumentationszentrum und Museum über die Migration in Deutschland e.V. (DOMiD—Cologne), *Damals... 'Herzlich Willkommen!'; Die ersten Gastarbeiter in Bayern*, VHS, dir. Sybille Krafft (Munich: Bayerischer Rundfunk, 1994), video: DV 0123.

apartments, and 56 percent paid less than 200 DM total.[17] Across the border, the lack of housing availability in Turin meant that some Southern Italian migrants repurposed army barracks on the urban fringes where open sewage ditches caused illness and even death.[18]

Whether on their own or in concert with other disadvantaged residents, Southern Italian migrants in the two cities invoked the language of rights and/or basic needs to articulate housing claims and to challenge their precarious living situations. They perceived these rights to be predicated on their common humanity, regardless of national boundaries or administrative limits.[19] In addition to such universalizing language, migrants and the journalists who reported on their actions frequently gendered migrants' claims to rights. They relied heavily on women's and children's voices to emphasize traditional notions of home and family—or what they had in common with long-term residents rather than what made them different.

The contention that social rights stem from a wider (and international) system of values is important in understanding the larger process by which some rights began to be de-territorialized when massive numbers of individuals crossed geographic borders in postwar decades. The devastating impact of the Second World War and the widespread violation of basic rights gave rise to broad perceptions about indisputable human rights that were attached to the individual, no matter their location or circumstances. For instance, Article 25 of the 1948 Universal Declaration of Human Rights stated than individuals were entitled to "a standard of living adequate for the health and well-being of themselves and of their family, including food, clothing, housing and medical care and social services."[20] It was not until later decades, however, that minoritized populations and others would effectively tap into the language of human rights to assert claims to the individual rights detailed within the document, as the declaration's

---

17. Borris, *Ausländische Arbeiter*, 152.

18. "Sgombero alle Vallette delle due case occupate," *La Stampa*, February 13, 1973.

19. For an investigation of how Southern Italian migrants' housing claims scaled up to debates over human rights and social integration in the European Parliament see Sarah Jacobson, "Guaranteeing Human Rights? Italian 'Gastarbeiter:innen' and Housing Activism in 1960s and 1970s West Germany," *Journal of Contemporary History* (FirstView), https://doi.org/10.1177/00220094241247066.

20. "Universal Declaration of Human Rights," United Nations, https://www.un.org/en/about-us/universal-declaration-of-human-rights. Masculine pronouns have been changed to gender-neutral.

original intent was to redeem conservative lawmakers' visions of national communities.[21]

At the national level, neither the West German or Italian constitution guaranteed a right to adequate housing, although the "assurance of suitable living quarters" was explicitly mentioned in labor agreements signed between West Germany and Italy in the 1950s.[22] Italian migrant housing occupiers instead referred to adequate and affordable housing as a basic right tied to their humanity when asserting their claim to decent housing in the early 1970s, irrespective of their national identity or citizenship status. Take, for instance, a flyer written by a group of female Southern Italian migrants for their neighbors in the Westend neighborhood of Frankfurt in 1972. They addressed the letter to "German Women, Colleagues, and Neighbors." While explaining why they participated in rent strikes and housing occupations, the migrant women proclaimed, "We do not want to just work here like crazy; we have the right to live decently like all human beings. However, one cannot live decently if one has to pay four to five hundred marks [DM] for a damp room from the meager wages we earn. We need clean, proper housing—not the hovels they lease to us foreigners. We need enough space to be able to live together with the whole family ... [rather than being] crammed into one or two tiny rooms."[23] Significantly, these authors associated a right to housing with being "human beings." And a mere roof overhead was not sufficient. They demanded housing that was "clean," "proper," and had adequate space. While they were not formally West German citizens, Southern Italian migrants claimed a deterritorialized or universal right, appealing to working German women who also had to contend with lack of affordable rent and scarcity of food and clothing. In other words, it was common household challenges and a sense of common humanity that the protesters invoked when confronting the injustice of their housing conditions.

While referring to themselves as "human beings," Italian migrants in Frankfurt also compared their living conditions to that of animals to highlight their meager living conditions. In a 1971 street demonstration in Frankfurt, representatives from the Unione Inquilini joined

---

21. Moyn, *Not Enough*, 44.

22. Ulrich Herbert, *A History of Foreign Labor in Germany, 1880–1980: Seasonal Workers, Forced Laborers, Guest Workers*, trans. William Templer (Ann Arbor: University of Michigan Press, 1990), 206.

23. Institut für Stadtgeschichte (IfS–Frankfurt am Main), Collection: Ortsgeschichte. 1972: Hausbesetzungen, file: S3/A 10.210.

FIGURE 11.1 Children participate in a 1971 demonstration against high rent prices and unsanitary living conditions in Frankfurt. Photo by Ullrich Winkler for the *Frankfurter Rundschau*. Institute für Stadtgeschichte Frankfurt am Main (IfS), ISG FFM S6b-38 Nr. 1274.

with children who held signs protesting the amount of rent they paid for run-down apartments (figure 11.1). Reporters snapped pictures of the signs written in German, Italian, and Turkish that read, "We are not sheep but human beings, which is why we refuse to pay the rents the owners ask from us that amount to highway robbery." The demonstrators claimed that housing was a "right" and that they would not pay one more cent in rent until they received decent housing that amounted to 10 percent of their wages. The positioning of children alongside such stark rhetoric served to personalize the claims, creating an association of the conditions and price with the impact on the socially vulnerable.

In contrast to those in Frankfurt, Southern Italian migrants within Italy were, as official Italian citizens, theoretically able to more directly criticize what they viewed as the failures of the welfare state. In practice, however, these internal migrants often faced similar levels of ostracism, born of biases embedded in cultural differences between the north and the south. Just as Southern Italian women in Frankfurt appealed to other women by tapping into gendered sympathies of motherhood and the home, migrants in northern Italy used similar paradigms to place their appeals in the sphere of morality to illuminate disparities in the welfare system. They likewise took their protests to local authorities and the local press, showing how the administration of social rights was bound to local agencies.

The most drastic examples of marshaling emotional appeal and traditional conceptions of home centered on the death of a child. In multiple instances in northern Italy in the early 1970s, public attention was caught up in news reports that portrayed such a tragedy as symbolic of the supposed failure of the welfare state to provide an adequate standard of living. In 1971, for instance, a baby died as a result of heart and lung conditions he developed in connection with living in dilapidated housing in Milan. His family had participated in a housing occupation, and during the eviction they had to stand outside in the rain—circumstances that doctors believed exacerbated the child's already weak heart and lungs. Journalists from the Italian Communist Party–affiliated newspaper *L'Unità* trumpeted the father's claim that inadequate housing led to his son's death. Having emigrated from Southern Italy, the father lamented that his son, Massimiliano Ferretti, died "because we were denied the right to a dry room, because they ignored my application for public housing for years."[24] A poem published in one of Unione Inquilini's newsletters mapped the death of Massimiliano onto the larger issue of basic or human rights:

> Everyone who opens their eyes to the light
> has the right to life, the right to the beautiful
> the right to the ugly—HAS THE RIGHT TO EVERYTHING!
> A safe home, affection, care,
> a job, bread, joy for everyone.
> your little heart . . . asked
> your fragile body . . . asked
> but you died before achieving it![25]

Here, too, the poem's author associated a safe home with human rights embodied at birth. In the wake of public outcry over the baby's death, the mayor of Milan agreed to make two hundred apartments available to those who had occupied the house alongside the Ferrettis, including Massimiliano's family. In so doing, city administrators partially acknowledged that housing was a fundamental human right.

Three years later, thirteen hundred individuals took part in a housing occupation on Strada delle Cacce in Turin. Here, too, a young child tragically died from a respiratory illness connected to the lack of

---

24. "Tragica morte di un bimbo coinvolto nello sgombero di una casa occupata," *L'Unità*, June 9, 1971.
25. "A Massimiliano F.: Vittima degli stenti e dell'ingiustizia sociale," *Il giornale dell'Unione Inquilini*, July-August 1971.

heating in the buildings.[26] To protest her death, occupiers took over Turin's city hall. One of the city's representatives, Diego Novelli, recalled that "at the end of the courtyard they placed a fake coffin covered with plastic flowers: the allusion to the death . . . of a girl from a family who illegally occupied an accommodation without any services, heating and even glass . . . was evident."[27] In both cases, occupiers used moral connotations about death and the innocence of the vulnerable (children) to lend weight to their claim that current housing policies were unjust. Plainly put: they associated the right to life with the right to proper housing.

Migrant protests in northern Italy and the language of migrant women in Frankfurt emphasized a similar theme—that their actions were not simply about matters of comfort but rather that basic housing was necessary to sustain life. In each case, the very fact of being human served as justification enough for the right to decent housing. This argument differed markedly from political rhetoric or legislation that tied the rights and protections of citizenship to national identity. Moreover, migrants and reporters frequently focused on women's and children's experiences to create a connection with other residents while circumventing other legal or political arguments. In essence, rather than wedding traditional notions of home and family to the nation-state—as had been particularly emphasized in the former fascist states—migrants instead turned gendered conceptions of family relations on their head to frame a denationalized conception of citizenship. They thus tied a basic standard of living to the family unit on the premise of universal basic or social rights.

Engaging in Contest

Even when Southern Italian migrants were not speaking with reporters or insisting on more equitable housing practices, they engaged in "participatory citizenship" through other actions, most visibly through housing occupations. Taking over apartments to which they had no legal claim, Southern Italian migrants and other occupiers disputed the constructed boundary between public and private as they made an

---

26. "Un episodio della 'guerra dei poveri' nel quartiere Mirafiori," *La Stampa*, September 28, 1974.

27. Piero Giordanino, *Diego Novelli: Lettere al sindaco* (Turin: Società editrice internazionale, 1979), 7.

embodied claim to the right of housing.[28] They highlighted how the welfare state mechanisms that supposedly guaranteed a basic standard of living were failing and needed to be expanded. And they grounded their demands in familiar tropes of providing basic needs for one's family. As they did so, migrants asserted that they deserved the same rights as other community members based on their common humanity.

Reflecting different national housing approaches, migrant participation in housing occupations varied in Frankfurt and in Turin. West German social housing prioritized rent subsidies for those in need of aid, whereas the Italian strategy focused on large-scale public housing construction. In Frankfurt, Italian migrants thus took over private housing, such as those in Leipziger Strasse and in Friesengasse. In contrast, protesters in Turin focused on public housing, such as when six hundred families took over a large, public complex just north of the city in Falchera Nuova. In both cities, the occupations rejected local housing practices, contested inequitable rental prices, and called into question what it meant for migrants to belong in their new communities.

Of the roughly two dozen occupations in Frankfurt in the early 1970s, Italian migrants initiated those on Leipziger Strasse and Friesengasse. Both were located in the Westend neighborhood that was experiencing a large share of speculation and gentrification. Most participants in these occupations had previously lived at Bettinastrasse 35, in which sixty-two Italians shared accommodations with "cockroaches, rats, mice, [and] cracked plaster falling from the ceiling."[29] In reaction to such dismal living conditions, four Italian migrant families decided to occupy Leipziger Strasse 3 in the spring of 1973. Although the building was in good condition, it had been kept empty for years. The Unione Inquilini speculated that the bank that owned it wished to tear it down to make space for a new high-rise.[30] The Italian migrant occupiers were quickly supported by other groups, such as the Unione Inquilini and the Jusos, the youth faction of the Social Democratic Party whose members were generally more politically progressive. Together, the occupiers and their supporters formed a human chain to "defend" the

---

28. For more theoretical reflections on this type of protest see Judith Butler, *Notes toward a Performative Theory of Assembly* (Cambridge, MA: Harvard University Press, 2015).
29. amantine, *Gender und Häuserkampf* (Münster: UNRAST, 2011), 17.
30. "Pagine dell'emigrante," *Il giornale dell'Unione Inquilini*, June 1973; Giuseppe Zambon, *Francoforte è il nostro futuro. Emigrazione e lotta per la casa in Germania* (Milan: Nova Cultura Editrice, 1978), 93. Giuseppe Zambon was one of the founders of the Unione Inquilini in Milan and moved the organization into Frankfurt when he received a call for help from an Italian migrant living in West Germany.

occupation and successfully prevented forced eviction. In addition, one of the Unione Inquilini leaders recalled that a representative from the Italian consulate "who was a bit on the [political] left" promised the Italian migrants decent housing.[31] Not only did their actions criticize rampant speculation on real estate, but Italian migrants also used embodied protest to insist on a right to adequate housing as community members, regardless of their country of origin and the risk of legal action. In this case, many community members and even an Italian state representative supported their actions.

Fellow residents of Bettinastrasse followed suit just a few months later when promises of housing from the city's head of social services fell through. On September 3, 1973, Italian migrants hauled mattresses and other necessities to Friesengasse 5 and 7 to signal their impatience with administrative channels. News reporters once again portrayed the impact of poor housing conditions on children when outlining the occupiers' motivations for taking over Friesengasse 5-7. For instance, one article by the politically conservative *Frankfurter Allgemeine Zeitung* related that one Italian father was forced to send his children back to Italy because of unsafe and unhygienic conditions within their Bettinastrasse apartment: namely water that continually ran down the walls.[32] A newspaper more sympathetic to the political left, the *Frankfurter Rundschau*, reported one of the female Italian occupiers saying, "We couldn't live one more day in Bettinastrasse. When I prepared my husband's breakfast in the evening, the rats had already eaten it by morning."[33] Regardless of their political positions, both newspapers invoked relatable images of home and family. Journalists couched Italian migrants' actions within a wider system of values that included a basic standard of living, especially for families. Explanations for occupying were not limited to journalists' rhetoric. Italians took objects and domestic necessities with them to the occupation. By doing so, the migrants signaled their rationale very clearly—they acted out of a need to procure living spaces adequate for their needs. By criticizing state apparatuses, they also engaged in contest to protest the lack of social assistance as marginalized community members.

In Italy the following year, one of the largest housing occupations in Western Europe occurred in Turin. Nearly six hundred families took

---

31. Giuseppe Z., interview with the author, Frankfurt, June 20, 2018.
32. "Friesengasse 7 wieder besetzt," *Frankfurter Allgemeine Zeitung*, November 9, 1973.
33. "Italiener besetzten Häuser in der Friesengasse," *Frankfurter Rundschau*, September 3, 1973.

over public housing buildings in the Falchera neighborhood in the northernmost outskirts of the city. Occupiers faced significant challenges during the first few weeks of the occupation. First, they had to travel a great distance to arrive; only one public transit line served the area. Second, because the apartments were not finished, none of the utilities had been turned on, meaning that the occupiers had to rely on the fire hydrant for water.[34] Third, because of a lack of services, occupiers had to establish their own food market and schools for the children. Finally, there was a great amount of tension between occupiers and those who had been assigned apartments within the Falchera complex. Many of the assignees were also of low socioeconomic status and had been waiting for years for a social housing assignment. In some cases, the assignees joined in with the occupiers, whereas in other cases disagreement led to verbal or physical conflict.[35]

Within the Falchera housing complex and on the streets of Turin, protest (by the occupiers) and counterprotest (by assignees) galvanized public opinion and sparked discussions within the city council. Many reporters took to labeling the conflict a "war between the poor."[36] At the same time, the tension highlighted the failure of the Italian social state to protect low-income residents, especially regional migrants newly arrived in their communities. The process of assigning public housing was widely known to be one of "clientelism"—one had to have an inside connection to receive an apartment. This strategy ignited sweeping accusations of corruption and inequality.[37]

When journalists asked the occupiers why they took over the new Falchera complex, many participants referred to unsatisfactory or unsafe conditions in their previous accommodations. One woman attributed her decision to take action to the rats that shared her apartment (they "resembled rabbits") and the fact that her children continually fell ill.[38] What's more, the migrants' identity as Southern Italians

---

34. Archivio Storico della Città (ASdC—Turin), Local Publication: Mario Alba, Amilcare De Leo, and Umberto Grassi, eds., "L'altra storia. Vent'anni dopo: Falchera Nuova," 52.
35. Alba, De Leo, and Grassi, "L'altra storia," 64-65.
36. One example is "L'invasione si estende a tutti i quartieri della città," *La Stampa*, October 23, 1974, which incorporates "invasion" into the title as well. The concept was so charged it also featured in city council meetings, such as that on October 21, 1974. See ASdC, Collection: Consiglio Comunale—Sessioni Straordinari, October 21, 1974.
37. Fulvio Conti and Gianni Silei, *Breve storia dello stato sociale* (Rome: Carocci editore, 2005), 194.
38. Archivio Storico della Nuova Sinistra "Marco Pezzi" (*MP*—Bologna), Collection: A. Ricci, file: 002,18, "800 alloggi occupati a Torino," *Avanguardia operaia* 4 (October 13, 1974): 8-9.

frequently played a role in their decision to occupy. Carmella, for example, cared for both her wheelchair-bound husband and two children. At first, she had refused to leave her former apartment in the city center, hanging from her balcony banners that read "House occupied to protest evictions!" as many neighboring tenants were either forced out or offered monetary incentives to leave. She related in an interview that she trusted the man who persuaded her to occupy an apartment in the Falchera because he was Sicilian like her.[39] In the ensuing months of the Falchera occupation, participants selected a committee that included a mixture of occupiers and assignees to negotiate with the city administration. In the course of their discussions, committee members highlighted the precarity of living conditions for migrants and other low-income individuals while criticizing disparities within the public housing system—thus pointing to a gap between the safety net supposedly guaranteed by the welfare state and the reality on the ground.

In both Turin and Frankfurt, Italian migrants risked legal action in order to get what they felt entitled to—proper housing. Though formal citizens in one location and not another, they forced conversations about who was entitled to, and which entities were responsible for, guaranteeing a basic standard of living. Though public reaction was mixed, journalists and migrants themselves emphasized women's and children's voices to highlight commonalities between occupiers and fellow residents. Doing so built bridges across class and social lines to underscore that migrants had human needs to which others could relate. Between the act of occupying and reports on their efforts, questions about citizenship or community membership and state aid came forcefully and visibly into the public sphere.

Making Their Own Meanings of Citizenship

Just as neighbors in both cities diverged in their responses to the occupations, city administrations were often divided over how to respond to migrant occupiers' actions. Internal discussions usually fell along political lines, though most government representatives recognized widescale housing needs in both Turin and Frankfurt. By taking over local living spaces and asserting their "human" right to housing, migrants placed responsibility for social aid at the community level. Municipal reactions to migrant protest demonstrations were thus at the forefront

---

39. Carmella S., interview with the author, Turin, January 27, 2018.

of negotiating what it meant to be a community member, catalyzing reevaluations of the rights, responsibilities, and locations of citizenship.[40]

The mixed response to Italian migrant occupiers in Frankfurt illustrated the Social Democrat–led government's indecision of how to respond to housing occupations. While the Social Democrats portrayed themselves as a party sympathetic to the plight of workers, they also found themselves embroiled in increasing concerns over internal security with the rise of domestic terrorism.[41] Two of the leaders of the RAF (Rote Armee Fraktion, or Red Army Faction), for instance, had previously been active in Frankfurt, where they had set fire to a large department store in 1968. In this political climate, the chief of police Knut Müller at times construed student-led housing occupations as "hotbed[s] of political crime" where "the climate of terror is bred."[42] This characterization often differed from official responses to other housing occupations that city leaders recognized as being conducted out of social need. Once migrant occupiers repelled eviction efforts in Leipziger Strasse 3 in May 1973, for instance, city officials agreed to work with the Italian consulate to let some of the families temporarily live on the premises, while promising housing to other Italian migrants in Bettinastrasse within three months. Frankfurt's same police chief reportedly told journalists, "We couldn't just haul women and children out of the house," while explaining that it was better if the building came under the jurisdiction of the local housing authority.[43] This reaction was markedly different from his comments about occupations being potentially seditious acts. Initially, then, it seemed that the city administration was willing to prioritize social need, even though non-German residents had violated trespassing laws.

---

40. The demonstrations enacted by migrant occupiers closely resemble the efforts of other minoritized groups to convince local state officials and residents that they were a significant minority whose concerns deserved attention. For a parallel conversation on LGBTQ+ demonstrations in the 1970s see chap. 6 in Samuel Clowes Huneke, *States of Liberation: Gay Men between Dictatorship and Democracy in Cold War Germany* (Toronto: University of Toronto Press, 2022).

41. Andreas Baader and Gudrun Ensslin, who set fire to two department stores in Frankfurt in 1968, later helped form the left-wing terrorist group the Red Army Faction. In addition to these events, Frankfurt had frequently been the site of clashes between police and students and other political activists in the late 1960s. For an overview of the internal tension between democracy and terrorism see Karrin Hanshew, *Terror and Democracy in West Germany* (Cambridge: Cambridge University Press, 2012).

42. "Nach dem Straßenschlacht in Frankfurt: SPD-Radikale wollen Polizei-Chef abschießen," *Abendpost*, March 30, 1973.

43. "'Geduld hat sich gelohnt,'" *Frankfurter Rundschau*, May 21, 1973.

Yet it was the failure to live up to promises of adequate housing that led to Italian migrants' ensuing occupation in Friesengasse in September 1973. Here the official response was much less sympathetic. About one week after Friesengasse's initial occupation, the police posted notices outside the buildings informing the Italians that they were violating the law. Invoking both the 1965 Foreigner Act and agreements within the European Economic Community, the notice informed the migrants that they were responsible for providing adequate housing for themselves and their families "from their own means." It further warned that if they did not "immediately remedy the current illegal situation," they could be subject to "eviction and deportation."[44] Here the difference in legal status was paramount to the administration's definition of citizenship, as migrant occupiers were clearly coded as foreigners. Though race was never explicitly invoked here and elsewhere, the word "foreigner" often served as a stand-in for drawing lines of difference that could be construed along the parameters of race. Despite this threat of deportation, though, city leadership eventually worked with the landlord to allow two of the families to stay in the apartments for four months.[45] In addition, the director of social services once again promised all the Italian migrants within Bettinastrasse 35 that they would procure housing for them within three months.[46]

In contrast to the situation in Frankfurt, city officials in Turin had a much larger number of occupiers to deal with. Despite vehement opposition from Christian Democrat representatives, the mayor appointed a committee tasked with housing the occupiers in late fall of 1974. The mayor ended up invoking a nineteenth-century law that allowed local government to requisition private housing that was not inhabited.[47] Under his leadership, the administration finally came to a formal agreement with representatives from the Falchera and other occupations throughout the city on November 26, 1974. As part of the agreement, city and occupier-appointed representatives categorized occupiers by

---

44. IfS, Collection: Wohnraumkonflikte; Untersuchungen zu Arbeitsplatzsituationen im polit, Kontext, file: V 183/14.

45. There is no evidence that Italian migrants were deported because of their participation in occupations. There are instances, though, of officials refusing to renew migrants' residence permits when there was proof they had participated in parallel demonstrations such as marches or rent strikes.

46. "Nur zwei Familien konnten bleiben," *Frankfurter Neue Presse*, September 3, 1973.

47. The precedent was established after a large earthquake displaced residents of the city of Naples in the 1800s. Naturally its invocation drew opposition from a variety of other political leaders. ASdC, Collection: Consiglio Comunale—Sessioni Straordinari, June 3, 1974.

need—a basis from which they would establish a timeline for finding accommodations. The final count consisted of the following:

Group A (368 households)—most urgent need
Group B (325 households)—to be relocated within three months
Group C (180 households)—to be relocated by the end of the year
Group D—those who did not qualify for state assistance[48]

In early 1975, however, the city administration seemed to back out of its agreement. Occupiers renewed their protests, causing disruptions to traffic when they took over city administrative offices.

Seven months into the occupation, in June 1975, Turin's leadership shifted from a Christian Democrat-dominated coalition to a government headed by the Italian Communist Party. The incoming mayor, Diego Novelli, signed a new agreement with occupiers. Many participants in the Falchera occupation believed that their protest actions had played a significant role in the election; one former occupier, Gilberto A., said in an interview that the occupations were "the impetus for Novelli in winning the election."[49] Though the implementation of the deal orchestrated by Novelli ran into some challenges, most occupiers did receive housing by the end of 1975. In this case, local administration stepped in where the regional and national public housing entities had failed. This example illustrates how the welfare state was administered locally. One shift in leadership at the city level meant that the process for receiving state housing aid changed for over eight hundred households.

The responses of local leadership in both Turin and Frankfurt marked significant changes in considering who was responsible for the social well-being of city residents, even if those in need of aid were not longtime inhabitants or full citizens. In the case of Turin, migrants' status as Italian nationals did not necessarily guarantee equitable access to the welfare state until they forcibly advocated for social rights; city officials went against the regionally administered public housing authority when the national housing strategy failed to offer an adequate safety net to all citizens. In a similar vein, Frankfurt's city administration

---

48. ASdC, Collection: Ass. Problemi della casa: Relazione sullo stato delle occupazioni, "Assessorato ai Problemi della Casa Edilizia Pubblica e Privata." This report is also confirmed by an interview I conducted with one of the committee members: Gilberto A., interview with the author, Turin, December 14, 2017.

49. Gilberto A. interview.

made housing aid available to new arrivals, although Italians in the FRG were not formal West German citizens. By articulating housing claims both verbally and physically, Southern Italian migrants in both areas challenged commonplace ideas of who deserved state aid. In the process, they redefined the parameters of citizenship. The relational process of disputing housing claims thus illustrates how some rights and protections began to be more closely related to participatory citizenship on the local level, rather than strictly tied to national identity.

The repercussions of migrants' actions and localized state responses also had longer ramifications on political-legal processes of administering social protections. For instance, the year when Southern Italian migrants protested poor living conditions in Frankfurt (1973) was the same year in which Frankfurt's Housing Office made 350 apartments available to "foreign workers" through participation in a federal government social housing program. In 1974, that number increased to 800, and the local administration anticipated allocating 1,300 apartments in 1975.[50] A year after the Falchera occupation was resolved (1976), Turin's mayor Novelli pointed to the need for federal solutions to Italy's housing crisis, indicating that Turin's remedy was only a bandage for larger issues in administering housing aid and protection. It would take two more years, but the Italian Parliament finally passed the Fair Rent Act in 1978. Some of the stipulations included a minimum rental contract at a price calculated according to the real estate value, enhanced protections against eviction, and a streamlined process for obtaining rent subsidies.[51] As a result, migrants not only forged their own meanings of citizenship at the local level but influenced recalibrations of citizenship rights on national and international levels as well.

Contesting Social Rights

Examining migrant housing activism in Italy and West Germany illuminates how two formerly authoritarian states, still rebuilding from the destruction of World War II, grappled with the meanings and protections of citizenship in postwar decades. At a time of significant economic growth and when the welfare state was perceived to be in its golden years, the lack of adequate and affordable housing for migrants

---

50. Ernst Karpf, *Eine Stadt und ihre Einwanderer: 700 Jahre Migrationsgeschichte in Frankfurt am Main* (Frankfurt: Campus Verlag, 2013), 323, footnote 160.

51. *La Gazzetta Ufficiale*, n. 211, L. 27 luglio 1978, n. 392, Disciplina delle locazioni di immobili urbani.

in industrial centers highlighted the inadequacy of national welfare systems to care for the workers fueling the economic miracle.[52] Southern Italian migrants pointed out disparities by articulating housing claims in terms of basic rights. They engaged in contest by visibly taking over apartments, catalyzing conversations in the public sphere about rights and community membership. The ways that fellow residents and city administrations responded to their claims redefined who qualified for and how one received state housing aid. Both the language of migrant protests and the outcomes of their actions thus illuminate a broader transition to the de-territorialization of social rights. By engaging with their communities through participatory citizenship via discourse and action—and the at least partial recognition of their housing claims by local authorities—migrant housing protests in the 1970s help illustrate how citizenship is not a static relationship, rather one continually negotiated and renegotiated between different stakeholders.

Housing continues to be one of the most pressing problems for migrants and other socioeconomically disadvantaged individuals today. The COVID-19 pandemic exacerbated long-standing housing issues of availability, discrimination, inequality, and aid. According to a June 2022 report by the Europe Housing Forum, affordable housing makes up only 3 percent of Germany's housing market.[53] In September 2022, over one thousand people, the majority of whom were non-Italian, applied for ten subsidized apartments in Turin.[54] Despite housing being firmly entrenched as a basic human right, there are no robust international systems for guaranteeing adequate and affordable housing, even for EU members after the codification of a European citizenship in 1992 (the history of which Lashyn traces in the following chapter). Yet the case of Southern Italian migrants in Frankfurt and Turin in the 1970s shows how quickly questions of housing aid and who can access state assistance can change. The solutions may just need to be co-constructed locally—on the streets, within neighborhoods, in city offices, and, of course, at home.

---

52. Hartmut Kaelble, *A Social History of Europe, 1945–200: Recovery and Transformation after Two World Wars*, trans. Liesel Tarquini (New York: Berghahn Books, 2013), chap. 10, "The Welfare State," 250–70.

53. Europe Housing Forum, "Affordable Housing Statistics across Western Europe," June 7, 2022, https://europehousingforum.eu/affordable-housing-statistics-across-western-europe/.

54. Paolo Coccorese, "In coda per un alloggio da 300 euro al mese: Mille domande per dieci appartamenti Atc," *Corriere della Sera*, September 30, 2022, https://torino.corriere.it/cronaca/22_settembre_29/coda-un-alloggio-300-euro-mese-mille-domande-dieci-appartamenti-atc-cabe8d3e-4026-11ed-815f-9b7904035c1c.shtml#.

SARAH JACOBSON

Sarah Jacobson is a Visiting Assistant Professor in European History at Albion College. After being awarded a PhD in history from Michigan State University in 2021, she was a lecturer at the University of Tennessee, Knoxville, and a postdoctoral fellow at the Leibniz Institute for European History (Mainz, Germany) and in the Berlin Program for Advanced German and European Studies at Freie Universität. Her research interests center on migration, urban history, and social movements.

CHAPTER 12

The Emergence of European Citizenship
Serhii Lashyn

In 2020, there were more than thirteen million citizens of European Union (EU) countries who resided in a member state of which they were not a national.[1] Working, studying, joining their spouses, or simply enjoying life in a place they liked—all these people took advantage of their right to free movement guaranteed by their "fundamental status" as European citizens.[2] Today, European citizenship, by which I mean a status common to nationals of member states rooted in EU primary law, is a tangible reality that shapes the daily lives of millions of people. How did European citizenship emerge, and what preceded it? This chapter traces the historical roots of one of the cornerstone concepts of contemporary EU law.

Locating those roots is not an easy task. On the one hand, European citizenship was only formally introduced in 1992, in the Treaty of Maastricht signed by Germany, Italy, France, Belgium, the Netherlands, Luxembourg, Denmark, Greece, Ireland, Portugal, Spain, and the

---

1. Directorate-General Justice and Consumers, *EU Citizenship Report 2020: Empowering Citizens and Protecting Their Rights* (2020), 3.
2. *Rudy Grzelczyk v Centre public d'aide sociale d'Ottignies-Louvain-la-Neuve* [2001] Case C-184/99 ECLI:EU:C:2001:458, 2001 European Court Reports 6193, para. 31.

United Kingdom.[3] Strictly speaking, then, it is a relatively new legal phenomenon for the European project. On the other hand, fervid proponents might find its origins as far back as in antiquity, as did Cornelis Berckhouwer, a liberal Dutch politician and former president of the European Parliament—the legislative body of the EU and its predecessor, the European Economic Community—which is composed of members elected by the nationals of member states every five years through direct universal suffrage. Speaking in the Parliament in 1977, Berckhouwer contended that it was "necessary to make all Community nationals into European citizens, just as in the year 212, Emperor Caracalla conferred citizenship on all inhabitants of the empire."[4]

While it would be an overstatement to see the origins of European citizenship in such distant epochs, it did develop over the course of the twentieth century, long before it was formalized in 1992. Tracing its evolution highlights the unprecedented turns that citizenship took in postwar Europe to transcend borders and overcome the limits of the nation-state.

This chapter follows the temporal dimension set out by Chin and Huneke in the introduction to this volume and tracks the appearance of the idea of European citizenship through documents related to European integration, including political speeches, manifestos, declarations, reports, publications, records of discussions, treaties, and working documents from before, during, and after World War II. The formation of European citizenship took decades and, because of its role in the European project, occurred mostly in the aftermath of World War II. The sources reveal that the concept of European citizenship arose in wildly different contexts and was elucidated by a variety of people. In Huneke and Chin's terminology, the vertical dimension of European citizenship made the idea emerge as the sum of many contributions from different actors. The concept of European citizenship was constructed in a multilevel discourse that crossed borders and could not be contained to one particular discipline. How this idea was reiterated and gradually elaborated in these diverse settings, I argue, reveals important new facets of the phenomenon of European citizenship.

First, there was no single or dominant idea of European citizenship. Over the decades, it took different forms. Moreover, because of its vertical dimension, there was no uniform understanding of citizenship as

---

3. Treaty on European Union [1992] (OJ C191/1).
4. Euroforum—Europe Day by Day, No. 42/77 (1977), Annex 2, 2.

such in the context of European integration, as different politicians filled the notion of European citizenship with divergent meanings. Some invoked it as a symbolic gesture, while others imagined it as a fully fledged legal status akin to national citizenship. As a consequence, the idea of European citizenship was shaped inconsistently and had no clear scope before it was finally formalized in 1992.

Second, when discussed as a legal concept, European citizenship was construed as more than just a symbol of integration. European politicians and lawyers often imagined it filled with de-territorialized rights and duties, while also encompassing an equally de-territorialized social component. Despite its many forms and fluctuating definitions, European citizenship was thus frequently thought of as a meaningful status of its holders, not merely as an honorary title for the nationals of member states.

Third, European citizenship was not only designed for the benefit of its holders. It encompassed an important external dimension, which demonstrated the unity of member states and their citizens to the outside world. Nowadays, European citizenship is relevant primarily inside the Union, with the narrow exception of consular protection abroad.[5] But its external dimension played an important formative role, as a means of demonstrating the bloc's political unity, when the concept of European citizenship was being debated, but before its formal introduction.

Finally, certain problems facing European citizenship today began to take form before the Maastricht Treaty. These include limitations caused by the applicability of Union law only in the presence of a cross-border dispute and the consequential exclusion of wholly internal matters from its purview, the adverse effects of tying European citizenship to nationality, the elitism of the European ideal as embodied in European citizenship, and the commodification of European citizens.

This chapter will undertake a detailed analysis of each of these four points. It first offers a brief overview of the scholarship on the history of European citizenship. In the main section, I analyze a selection of some of the most important sources to mention the idea of European citizenship, contextualizing these documents in the broader history of the concept. Some conclusions follow.

---

5. Directive 2015/637 of April 20, 2015, on the coordination and cooperation measures to facilitate consular protection for unrepresented citizens of the Union in third countries and repealing Decision 95/553/EC (OJ L106/1).

The Prehistory of European Citizenship

European citizenship continues to receive extensive attention in the literature, above all in legal scholarship, but also in sociology, philosophy, political science, and history. This steady interest stems in part from the significance of European citizenship within EU law, as well as the ways that more general questions of European integration are reflected in it. In the legal scholarship in particular, historical investigations into European citizenship serve as context, setting the stage for substantial legal research on the concept or its parts.[6] There is, however, some research dedicated solely to the analysis of the historical evolution of European citizenship.[7] This chapter builds on these works, while departing from them in two important ways. First, it looks further back than many of these works, finding the roots of European citizenship in the prewar era. Second, I approach the development of European citizenship in a conceptually distinct fashion, treating it primarily as a legal category while also acknowledging its relevance for other disciplines.

---

6. Armin von Bogdandy and Felix Arndt, "European Citizenship," in *Max Planck Encyclopedia of Public International Law* (Oxford: Oxford University Press, 2011); Stefan Kadelbach, "Union Citizenship," in *Principles of European Constitutional Law*, ed. Armin von Bogdandy and Jürgen Bast, 2nd ed. (London: Bloomsbury, 2009); Dimitry Kochenov and Richard Plender, "EU Citizenship: From an Incipient Form to an Incipient Substance? The Discovery of the Treaty Text," *European Law Review* 37 (2012): 373-75; Patricia Mindus, *European Citizenship after Brexit: Freedom of Movement and Rights of Residence* (Cham, Switzerland: Palgrave Macmillan, 2017), https://doi.org/10.1007/978-3-319-51774-2; Hanneke van Eijken, *EU Citizenship and the Constitutionalisation of the European Union* (Amsterdam: Europa Law, 2015), 12-15; Anthony James Venables, *Piecing Together Europe's Citizenship: Searching for Cinderella* (Baden-Baden: Nomos, 2016), 45-50, https://doi.org/10.5771/9783845274836.

7. Pietro Costa, "From National to European Citizenship: A Historical Comparison," in *Lineages of European Citizenship*, ed. Richard Bellamy, Dario Castiglione, and Emilio Santoro (London: Palgrave Macmillan, 2004), https://doi.org/10.1057/9780230522442_11; Gerard Delanty, "European Citizenship: A Critical Assessment," *Citizenship Studies* 11, no. 1 (2007): 63-72, https://doi.org/10.1080/13621020601099872; Jan van der Harst, Gerhard Hoogers, and Gerrit Voerman, eds., *European Citizenship in Perspective: History, Politics and Law* (Cheltenham, UK: Edward Elgar, 2018); Espen Daniel Hagen Olsen, "The Origins of European Citizenship in the First Two Decades of European Integration," *Journal of European Public Policy* 15, no. 1 (2008): 40-57, https://doi.org/10.1080/13501760701702157; Willem Maas, "The Evolution of EU Citizenship," in *Making History: European Integration and Institutional Change at Fifty*, ed. Sophie Meunier and Kathleen R. McNamara (Oxford University Press, 2007); Willem Maas, *Creating European Citizens* (Lanham, MD: Rowman & Littlefield, 2007); Willem Maas, "European Union Citizenship in Retrospect and Prospect," in *Routledge Handbook of Global Citizenship Studies* (London: Routledge, 2013), https://doi.org/10.4324/9780203102015.ch36; Stefanie Pukallus, *Representations of European Citizenship since 1951* (London: Palgrave Macmillan, 2016); Antje Wiener, *European Citizenship Practice: Building Institutions of a Non-state* (London: Routledge, 1999);

Much of the literature shares the 1951 Treaty of Paris as its point of departure.[8] Some scholars pick up later, such as Antje Wiener, who begins with the 1974 Paris summit, or Dimitry Kochenov and Richard Plender, who trace the roots of European citizenship back to the 1970s.[9] The choice of 1951 is understandable. The Treaty of Paris marks the beginning of the institutionalization of European integration. Yet, as this chapter demonstrates, the idea of European citizenship was present in public discourse not only before 1951 and during World War II, but also in the interwar period. Approaching European citizenship as a concept that transcends its legal existence, this chapter argues that the roots of European citizenship lie in the decades preceding the 1951 Treaty of Paris.

There is a great diversity in how researchers approach this subject matter, both methodologically and conceptually. Some focus on its political dimensions, such as Antje Wiener, Willem Maas, and Gerard Delanty.[10] Others, among them Dimitry Kochenov, Richard Plender, and Espen Olsen, emphasize the legal category that embodies European citizenship.[11] Finally, there are commentators who pick a distinct lens through which they examine European citizenship. For instance, Stefanie Pukallus traces different understandings of European citizenship that she frames as its representations by the European Commission, the executive institution of the EU and its predecessors, in the public discourse, while Pietro Costa compares the development of national citizenship with European citizenship from the angle of constructing a collective identity.[12]

While building on the selection of sources in the existing literature, which rightly link modern European citizenship status with the freedom of movement laid down at the early stages of European integration, this chapter understands European citizenship as, above all, a legal concept embedded in the political, cultural, and social realities

---

8. Maas, "Evolution of EU Citizenship," 234; Maas, *Creating European Citizens*, 11–12; Pukallus, *Representations of European Citizenship*, 39–67; Olsen, "Origins of European Citizenship," 41–45. An exception is one of the publications authored by Willem Maas, which goes to as early as 1943: see Maas, "European Union Citizenship."

9. Wiener, *European Citizenship Practice*, 63–73; Kochenov and Plender, "EU Citizenship," 374.

10. Wiener, *European Citizenship Practice*; Maas, "Evolution of EU Citizenship"; Maas, "European Union Citizenship"; Delanty, "European Citizenship."

11. Kochenov and Plender, "EU Citizenship"; Olsen, "Origins of European Citizenship."

12. Pukallus, *Representations of European Citizenship*; Pietro Costa, "From National to European Citizenship," 207–26.

surrounding it. On a broader note, this chapter looks at European citizenship as a trailblazer in the transcendence of national borders. It seeks to demonstrate how citizenship became thought of as something not constrained to nation-states in the specific context of European integration following World War II. As the other contributions to this volume demonstrate, the postwar period caused tectonic shifts in popular understandings of citizenship, its perception and value, as well as its legal mechanics. The emergence of European citizenship was a part of these wider processes.

In addition to the historiography on European citizenship, there is a breadth of legal scholarship covering its many facets that frequently includes a historical overview of the subject matter.[13] Moreover, European citizenship is habitually included in general reference works on EU law.[14] Also, a vital contribution to the development of European citizenship as a legal status within Union law has been made by the Court of Justice of the European Union (CJEU) by means of producing an extensive body of relevant case law. The only and the highest judicial body in the structure of the EU, the CJEU is responsible for adjudicating cases that involve EU law and for interpreting that law. Finally, one has to pay some attention to the vast scholarship on global citizenship

---

13. Matthew James Elsmore and Peter Starup, "Union Citizenship—Background, Jurisprudence, and Perspective: The Past, Present, and Future of Law and Policy," *Yearbook of European Law* 26, no. 1 (2007): 57–113, https://doi.org/10.1093/yel/26.1.57; Pavlos Eleftheriadis, "The Content of European Citizenship," *German Law Journal* 15, no. 5 (2014): 777–96, https://doi.org/10.1017/S2071832200019143; Francis Geoffrey Jacobs, "Citizenship of the European Union—a Legal Analysis," *European Law Journal* 13, no. 5 (2007): 591–610, https://doi.org/10.1111/j.1468-0386.2007.00385.x; Dimitry Kochenov, "The Essence of EU Citizenship Emerging from the Last Ten Years of Academic Debate: Beyond the Cherry Blossoms and the Moon?," *International and Comparative Law Quarterly* 62, no. 1 (2013): 97–136, https://doi.org/10.1017/S0020589312000589; Joe McMahon, Adam Cygan, and Erika Szyszczak, "EU Citizenship," *International and Comparative Law Quarterly* 55, no. 4 (2006): 977–82, https://doi.org/10.1093/iclq/lei139; Ulrich Klaus Preuß, "Problems of a Concept of European Citizenship," *European Law Journal* 1, no. 3 (1995): 267–81, https://doi.org/10.1111/j.1468-0386.1995.tb00032.x; Christoph Schönberger, "European Citizenship as Federal Citizenship: Some Citizenship Lessons of Comparative Federalism," *European Review of Public Law* 19, no. 1 (2007): 61–81; Jo Shaw, "The Interpretation of European Union Citizenship," *Modern Law Review* 61, no. 3 (1998): 293–317, https://doi.org/10.1111/1468-2230.00145; Niamh Nic Shuibhne, "EU Citizenship after Lisbon," in *The European Union after the Treaty of Lisbon*, ed. Diamond Ashiagbor, Nicola Countouris, and Ioannis Lianos (Cambridge: Cambridge University Press, 2012), https://doi.org/10.1017/CBO9781139084338.006.

14. Fabian Amtenbrink and Hans Vedder, *European Union Law: A Textbook* (Eleven International, 2021), 385–416; Paul Philip Craig and Gráinne de Búrca, *EU Law: Text, Cases, and Materials* (Oxford University Press, 2011), 819–53; John Fairhurst, *Law of the European Union*, 11th ed. (New York: Pearson, 2016), 323–70; Alina Kaczorowska-Ireland, *European Union Law*, 4th ed. (London: Routledge, 2016), 657–710.

that looks into the transformation of citizenship in the increasingly global world from various disciplinary and interdisciplinary standpoints.[15] Building on these diverse bodies of scholarship, this chapter offers an account of the earliest traces of European citizenship as a legal concept that continues to shape the political and social realities of the European project.

European Citizenship before and during World War II

Some of the earliest ideas of European citizenship can be found in the work of the Pan-European Union in the years before World War II. Also known as the Pan-European Movement, it was founded in 1922 by politician and philosopher Richard Coudenhove-Kalergi in the aftermath of the devastations of World War I.[16] Of mixed Austrian-Japanese descent, Coudenhove-Kalergi came from a noble family and is now widely regarded as one of the pioneers of European integration.[17] While a fervent proponent of European integration, Coudenhove-Kalergi was not affiliated with a particular political group or party. Instead, he called for European unity as an antidote to what he identified as three major threats to Europe's existence: intra-European war, the Russian military threat, and economic ruin.[18]

In 1930, Coudenhove-Kalergi proposed a constitutional document for a European Federation of States, the Pan-European Pact. The pact was ambitious. It included a common defense clause similar to that now part of the North Atlantic Treaty.[19] Significantly, Article 5 of the

---

15. Kwame Anthony Appiah, "Global Citizenship," *Fordham Law Review* 75, no. 5 (2007): 2375–92; Linda Bosniak, "Citizenship Denationalized," *Indiana Journal of Global Legal Studies* 7, no. 2 (2000): 447–509; Lynn Dobson, *Supranational Citizenship* (Manchester: Manchester University Press, 2006); Yasemin Nuhoğlu Soysal, *Limits of Citizenship: Migrants and Postnational Membership in Europe* (Chicago: University of Chicago Press, 1994).

16. Patricia Wiedemer, "The Idea behind Coudenhove-Kalergi's Pan-European Union," *History of European Ideas* 16, no. 4–6 (1993): 827–33, https://doi.org/10.1016/0191-6599(93)90229-J.

17. Martyn Bond, *Hitler's Cosmopolitan Bastard: Count Richard Coudenhove-Kalergi and His Vision of Europe* (McGill-Queen's University Press, 2021); Michael Thöndl, "Richard Nikolaus Graf Coudenhove-Kalergi, Die 'Paneuropa-Union' und der Faschismus 1923-1938," *Quellen und Forschungen aus italienischen Archiven und Bibliotheken* 98, no. 1 (March 18, 2019): 326–70, https://doi.org/10.1515/qfiab-2018-0015.

18. Richard Nikolaus Coudenhove-Kalergi, "Das Paneuropäische Manifest," in Rolf Hellmut Foerster, "Die Idee Europa 1300-1946: Quellen zur Geschichte der politischen Einigung," DTV 1963, 226–36 (1923).

19. Richard Nikolaus Coudenhove-Kalergi, "Paneuropäischer Pakt." in Christian Pernhorst, "Das paneuropäische Verfassungsmodell des Grafen Richard N. Coudenhove-Kalergi" (1930: Baden-Baden: Nomos 2008), 113–49.

pact provided that "all citizens of the European Federation of States are at the same time European citizens."[20] In Coudenhove-Kalergi's model, European citizenship was construed as one of the means of building a federation, hence as federal citizenship.

Moreover, the pact constructed European citizenship with meaningful content. It provided that "all European citizens enjoy economic equality in the tropical colonies of European States in Africa."[21] The privileges associated with European citizenship thus drew on European colonial rule in Africa, making it an explicitly colonial enterprise. Colonial European citizenship, aimed at pooling the exploitation of different parts of Africa by different European powers, contrasts with modern, predominantly postcolonial approaches to European citizenship. At the same time, the pact illustrates that this early idea of European citizenship was filled with rights and duties.

In September 1939, after the outbreak of World War II, the United Kingdom and France floated plans that proposed a federal union of the two nations.[22] In June 1940, Jean Monnet, later a founding father of what would become the European Union, suggested to the British prime minister Winston Churchill what he called a "partnership" between the two countries, which would include "the same parliament, one state, one citizenship."[23] Faced with the German army's rapid advance into metropolitan France, Churchill agreed and proposed the idea of a "Franco-British Union" to his cabinet.[24] In the midst of war, Monnet and Churchill thus envisaged one citizenship under a Franco-British superstate as a way of counteracting the Nazi threat. In fact, Churchill's cabinet even issued a formal declaration calling for an "indissoluble union" of the two countries, announcing that "every citizen of France will enjoy immediately citizenship of Great Britain, every British subject will become a citizen of France."[25] While signifying the early seeds of citizenship's transcendence of national borders in Europe, these plans were ultimately received skeptically by French and

---

20. Coudenhove-Kalergi, "Paneuropäischer Pakt."
21. Coudenhove-Kalergi, "Paneuropäischer Pakt."
22. John Pinder, "European Community and Nation-State: A Case for a Neo-federalism?," *International Affairs* 62, no. 1 (1986): 41.
23. Edwin Newman, "Monnet on Political Unity," *European Community*, no. 134 (1970): 16; Pinder, "European Community and Nation-State," 41.
24. Newman, "Monnet on Political Unity," 16.
25. Avi Shlaim, "Prelude to Downfall: The British Offer of Union to France, June 1940," *Journal of Contemporary History* 9, no. 3 (1974): 50, https://doi.org/10.1177/002200947400900302.

British policymakers at the time and construed as a "highly symbolic" gesture in light of France's imminent fall.[26]

Postwar Developments

The end of World War II created a unique environment for overhauling laws and setting up entirely new legal systems, both on the national and international levels. The immediate postwar period offered an opportunity for the large-scale revision of rules and legal concepts, including citizenship. One of the reasons for this shift was how the Nazi dictatorship had employed citizenship laws and policies as instruments of racial discrimination. Courtman sheds light on these practices at the beginning of his study of the postwar naturalization policy of West Germany in this volume. A reconstruction of citizenship as a legal category was further warranted by the large numbers of stateless people who struggled because of their status, as Hilton and Tohma explore in their respective chapters. The revision of citizenship as a legal concept also took place in Franco's Spain, something that Lasús details in his chapter. At the European level, citizenship was likewise to be redefined and reimagined as a part of the efforts to unite European nations.

Several years after the Allied Powers' victory in World War II, Churchill proposed "a Europe where men of every country will think as much of being a European as of belonging to their native land, and that without losing any of their love and loyalty of their birthplace."[27] Stefanie Pukallus identifies this appeal as one of the roots of contemporary European citizenship.[28] Indeed, Churchill saw the future of Europe without borders, where everyone could travel freely and say, "I am a citizen of this country too."[29] Churchill seemed to envision a common status for Europeans that would legally enable freedom of movement. Moreover, Churchill made this statement to support the idea of a united Europe in the context of the impending formalization of the European project. Of course, by this point, Churchill had lost the 1945 general election

---

26. Rachel Chin, *War of Words: Britain, France and Discourses of Empire during the Second World War* (Cambridge: Cambridge University Press, 2022), 35.
27. Winston Churchill, "Speech at the European Rally in Amsterdam" (1948), in Winston Churchill, *Europe Unite: Speeches 1947 and 1948*, ed. Randolph Churchill (London: Cassell, 1950), https://doi.org/10.5040/9781472581778.
28. Pukallus, *Representations of European Citizenship*, 39.
29. Churchill, "Speech at the European Rally."

to the British Labor Party led by Clement Attlee, and his views on the future of Europe held rather less sway.

Churchill was less sympathetic toward a strictly federal model for united Europe. Such a model, which supposed establishing a federation of European states, thereby merging them into one country, indeed was proposed by other political thinkers of that epoch. Particularly, it was suggested by the European Parliamentary Union (EPU), an informal association of members of national parliaments of different European countries. The EPU was founded after World War II by Coudenhove-Kalergi, who during the war had been persecuted by the Nazis. After the Austrian Anschluss, he had fled to Czechoslovakia, then to France and, after the occupation of France, to the United States of America. The EPU aimed to propose a draft constitution for Europe, and it advocated for a federalist model in the form of a United States of Europe.[30] The federation would feature, in its view, "European citizenship based on a declaration of the rights of man and a European Court of Justice."[31] Unlike Churchill, the European Parliamentary Union championed a federal solution for uniting Europe. Its proposal was, in essence, a continuation of Coudenhove-Kalergi's prewar efforts.

Around the same time, the European Movement proposed a less ambitious model. An association of thinkers and politicians united by their shared federal vision for Europe, the movement has counted among its affiliates Churchill, West German chancellor Konrad Adenauer, Italian deputy Altiero Spinelli, Belgian prime minister Paul-Henri Spaak, French president François Mitterrand, and British philosopher Bertrand Russell. Their vision for Europe also included "a Common Citizenship, without loss of original nationality."[32] This suggestion was made in the context of the movement's proposal for a nonfederal Europe. It aligns closely to the contemporary realities of European citizenship, in which national citizenship exists alongside European citizenship.

The proposals drafted by both the European Parliamentary Union and the European Movement influenced the beginnings of the

---

30. Heribert Gisch, "The European Parliamentary Union (EPU)," in *Transnational Organizations of Political Parties and Pressure Groups in the Struggle for European Union, 1945–1950*, ed. Walter Lipgens and Wilfried Loth (Berlin: De Gruyter, 1991), 157, https://doi.org/10.1515/9783110892260-005.

31. Gisch, 159.

32. Alan Hick, "The 'European Movement,'" in *Transnational Organizations of Political Parties and Pressure Groups in the Struggle for European Union, 1945–1950*, ed. Walter Lipgens and Wilfried Loth (Berlin: De Gruyter, 1991), 337, https://doi.org/10.1515/9783110892260-008.

European project, as prominent politicians of that epoch actively took part in both groups. Whereas Coudenhove-Kalergi's model would have superseded national citizenship with a supranational European citizenship, the European Movement's vision retained the basic structure of national citizenship, which perhaps helps explain its long-term success.

In the 1950 Schuman Declaration, in which the French foreign minister Robert Schuman called for a coal and steel union between France and West Germany, there are two specific mentions of a European federation.[33] As Pukallus notes, Schuman suggested the plan at the dawn of the Cold War and was partially motivated by suspicion of a rearmed and reindustrialized West Germany.[34] While it made no explicit mention of common citizenship, the Declaration implied a common status for nationals of member states as it envisaged the free movement of workers in the coal and steel industries later realized in the Treaty of Paris.

Finally, in 1950, Konrad Adenauer, West Germany's first chancellor, expressed support for a broader unification of West Germany and France, one that would merge the two countries' citizenships.[35] While this proposal was not well received in France, it offered a clear indication of West Germany's support for Schuman's plan.[36] Indeed, Adenauer's suggestion signified a growing political unity between the two countries that still serves as the bedrock of European integration. Although it was more of a political statement than a specific plan, the fact that this kind of rhetoric was voiced in the public discourse paved the way for more specific discussions later.

These mentions of common citizenship—both direct and implied—suggest two conclusions. First, the idea of European citizenship popped up relatively frequently in discussions of European integration in the early postwar years. Coming from politicians and thinkers of different nationalities, taking place in various countries and in different settings, these early models of European integration included shared citizenship. Second, citizenship was included in both federal and nonfederal models. While citizenship is a logical component of any federal state, the

---

33. Robert Schuman, "The Schuman Declaration" (1950), in *Theories of Federalism: A Reader*, ed. Dimitrios Karmis and Wayne Norman (Palgrave Macmillan, 2005), https://doi.org/10.1007/978-1-137-05549-1.

34. Pukallus, *Representations of European Citizenship*, 39–40.

35. Berend, *History of European Integration*, 73.

36. Berend, 73.

inclusion of citizenship in nonfederal models was an unexpected turn, given that these plans did not anticipate the creation of a superstate.

The Treaty of Paris and the Treaty of Rome

The Treaty of Paris, signed by the Netherlands, Belgium, Luxembourg, France, Italy, and West Germany on April 18, 1951, created the European Coal and Steel Community (ECSC), which would, decades later, become the EU.[37] As Huneke and Chin note in the introduction to this volume, the postwar context made the prevention of another disastrous military conflict the key reason for launching the project of European unification. While the treaty did not introduce shared citizenship in a formal sense, it explicitly prohibited discrimination based on nationality in the coal and steel industry and thereby introduced mobility for workers in those sectors.[38] As Maas and Pukallus both observe, free movement was introduced out of economic pragmatism and was pushed particularly by Italy, which sought to simplify movement of its workforce to richer countries.[39] In this volume, Jacobson offers an insightful investigation into how the migration of Southern Italian migrants into Germany and northern Italy triggered a shift in the citizenship discourse amid the shortage of affordable housing. In the European legal context, mobility of workers and nondiscrimination became intrinsically linked. Unrestricted movement allowed workers to move freely across the member states, while prohibition of discrimination precluded employers from refusing to hire the workers based on their nationality. One does not make sense without the other. These components, which are today united in the legal concept of European citizenship, originated in the Treaty of Paris.

The Treaty of Paris also added a social element. The signatories undertook "to ensure that social security arrangements do not inhibit labor mobility."[40] That is, the treaty provided for cooperation between the member states in the domain of social security in order to realize worker mobility. This provision illustrates the very early inclusion of a social dimension within European freedom of movement by means of legally de-territorializing social claims and entitlements. After the

---

37. Treaty Establishing the European Coal and Steel Community 1951 (UNTS 261/140).
38. Treaty Establishing the European Coal and Steel Community, art. 69(1).
39. Maas, *Creating European Citizens*, 14–15; Pukallus, *Representations of European Citizenship*, 45.
40. Treaty Establishing the European Coal and Steel Community, art. 69(4).

Treaty of Paris, for the workers in the coal and steel industry, nationality no longer mattered for the narrow purposes of employment. Because nationality still mattered for other purposes, this freedom of employment was not a fully fledged European citizenship but rather an early sign of its later emergence. Indeed, the success of labor mobility in the coal and steel industry inspired politicians to broaden that mobility to other industries in the 1957 Treaty of Rome, which established the European Economic Community (EEC).[41]

Today, European citizenship is associated with four specific rights: the right to mobility, the right to participate in elections to the European Parliament, the right to enjoy consular protection of other member states, and the right to petition EU institutions.[42] While these last three rights are used in only specific political contexts, the right to free movement is a popular part of most European citizens' daily lives. As a result, it is also heavily regulated by the secondary law.[43] This is why, as Maas contends, free movement can be called the "most notable component" of European citizenship status.[44]

Thus, based on the fact that free movement was first introduced for some industries in the Treaty of Paris and was subsequently extended to all industries in the Treaty of Rome, the legal core of the most important right of European citizenship was laid down already in the 1950s, decades before formal European Union citizenship came into being.

Toward a Political Union

Following the ratification of the Treaty of Paris, European citizenship began to expand from the domain of workers' mobility to the field of political participation. While this evolution took decades, it too first appeared in the early 1950s. In 1953, for example, an unnamed representative in the Constitutional Committee of the European Political Community proposed citizenship in the context of a federal or confederal community.[45] Later in 1960, before becoming president

---

41. Maas, *Creating European Citizens*, 17–18.
42. Consolidated version of the Treaty on the Functioning of the European Union (OJ C326/47), art. 20(2)(a).
43. Directive 2004/38/EC of April 29, 2004, on the right of citizens of the Union and their family members to move and reside freely within the territory of the Member States (OJ L158/77).
44. Maas, "Evolution of EU Citizenship," 232.
45. Report of the Constitutional Committee–Ad Hoc Assembly Instructed to Work Out a Draft Treaty Setting Up a European Political Community, Session of January 1953 (1953).

of the European Parliament, Italian politician Gaetano Martino observed, "European consciousness is gaining ground among the peoples and will gain still more ground when it can be translated into concrete action."[46] Martino spoke against labeling the emerging union of European countries as a supranational union and instead termed it federal.[47] In Martino's view, this federalist vision of Europe included "conferring dual citizenship on Europeans."[48] That is, he envisioned national and European citizenship existing simultaneously.

Another prominent proponent of European citizenship at that time was Lionello Levi Sandri, commissioner for social affairs in the first-ever European Commission—the EEC's executive organ—led by Walter Hallstein. In 1961, for instance, at a social policy round table, Levi Sandri stated, "The free movement of workers could be considered as the first aspect of a European citizenship."[49] In a plenary session of the Commission held in 1962, he again spoke on the matter of regulating the free movement of workers. In his view, "free movement of workers was not only a means of bringing together the factors of production more effectively; it was the first outward sign of a European citizenship."[50] Later that year, Levi Sandri also noted in the Parliament that the freedom of movement should not be considered a means of tackling the problem of unemployment in some parts of the Community "but would have to be achieved in any case because it amounted to a first step towards an official recognition of a common European citizenship."[51] These remarks, made while discussing social security for migrant workers and the harmonization of member states' social policies, underscore how economic mobility slowly evolved into a common idea of European citizenship imbued with social prerogatives and political rights.

A few years later, in 1966, Levi Sandri observed that the European labor market "is contributing to the creation of a spirit of European citizenship among our peoples."[52] Whereas Levi Sandri spoke of the

---

46. Seventh Joint Meeting of the Members of the Consultative Assembly of the Council of Europe and the Members of the European Parliamentary Assembly: Official Report of Debates (1960), 25. For an overview see "Council of Europe," *International Organization* 14, no. 4 (1960): 676–78, https://doi.org/10.1017/S0020818300010456.
47. Seventh Joint Meeting of the Members, 25.
48. Seventh Joint Meeting of the Members, 25.
49. *Bulletin of the European Economic Community*, no. 11 (1961): 51–52.
50. *Bulletin of the European Economic Community*, no. 1 (1962): 75.
51. *Bulletin of the European Economic Community*, no. 8 (1962): 61.
52. Lionello Levi Sandri, "Social Policy in the Common Market 1958–65," European Community Information Service (1966).

first signs of common citizenship in 1962, by 1966 he was discussing how the labor markets were stimulating the emergence of the spirit of such citizenship. The Commission shared his perception. In 1967, it called the free movement of workers "the beginnings of European citizenship."[53]

At this point, European citizenship became a regular component of the debates about European integration and, particularly, the free movement of workers. The next stage involved more frequent suggestions to introduce European citizenship status as a formal concept in the Community's primary law. Those proposals were articulated much earlier than the Maastricht Treaty and can be traced back to when the negotiations for a political union began.[54]

The idea of European citizenship resurfaced in 1962 during discussions on the Draft Treaty for the Establishment of a Political Union. The introductory and explanatory report produced by a committee tasked with studying the draft treaty and led by the French politician Christian Fouchet indicates that the German representatives pressed for citizenship to be included.[55] They did so because citizenship would have been "a corollary to the unification of laws, which is one of the aims of the European Union," and because citizenship would allow the Community "to express, through outward symbols, the common membership of the States and peoples of the Union."[56] That is, it would speed up the process of unification, both inward and outward. While the suggestion was positively received, representatives decided against an express inclusion of common citizenship in the treaty text.[57] The reason for this decision remains unclear. Records only show that "it appeared preferable that [European citizenship] should not figure expressly in the Treaty and that the question should be reviewed by the Council at a later stage."[58] Introducing European citizenship at that time was, perhaps, considered a bold move that, although desirable, was ahead of its time.

Above all else, these discussions underscore that European citizenship as a formal legal concept was on the table in the earliest phases of

---

53. Information Memo P-41/68, Commission of the European Communities–Spokesman's Groupe (1968).
54. *Towards Political Union: A Selection of Documents with a Foreword by Mr. Emilio Battista* (General Directorate of Parliamentary Documentation and Information, 1964).
55. The report is reproduced in *Towards Political Union*, 36.
56. *Towards Political Union*, 36.
57. *Towards Political Union*, 36.
58. *Towards Political Union*, 36.

modern-day European integration. Thirty years before the Maastricht Treaty, European citizenship was mooted at the highest levels. Second, the position of the German delegation during these negotiations reveals that one of the main functions of European citizenship was actually to demonstrate the bloc's political unity abroad. This outer dimension of European citizenship is almost absent in modern scholarship, as European citizenship status today has real meaning only inside the EU.

Although the draft treaty failed and European citizenship was not introduced as a legal concept, its external dimension remained on Europe's political agenda. In 1967, for instance, Italian politician Mario Pedini spoke in the European Parliament about the necessity of strengthening the Community and thus making it more attractive for nonmember European countries. In order to do so, those countries would have to perceive the European Community as a kind of "state" in which "they may share with full rights of citizenship."[59] That is, Pedini too subscribed to the view that European citizenship would have a distinctive outer dimension. It would become a feature that would make the Community attractive to other states, underscoring Europe's political unity and perhaps contributing to the Community's growth.

While some celebrated the emerging European citizenship during this period, a certain discontent with the realities of the Community also persisted. In 1965, for instance, the Merger Treaty combined the executive institutions of Euroatom, ECSC, and EEC, leading to a Commission reshuffle. A few years later, the journalist Margot Lyon critiqued the inner functionality of the Commission, its linguistic and national composition. Pointing out the dominance of French language within the Commission, she also highlighted the Community's innate elitism, accessible only to those with excellent educations and high foreign language proficiency.[60] Lyon concluded, "The best Eurocrats feel themselves to be, not stateless technocrats, but charter members of Europe, the first holders of 'European' citizenship."[61] This observation points to disenchantment with the distant ideal of a united Europe that many Europeans experienced then and continue to feel today. In

---

59. *Fourteenth Joint Meeting of the Members of the Consultative Assembly of the Council of Europe and the Members of the European Parliament—Official Report of Debates* (1967).

60. Margot Lyon, "Reshuffling the Eurocrats," *European Community*, no. 111 (1968): 10–11.

61. Lyon, 11.

Lyon's sardonic view, the very concept of European citizenship embodies this disenchantment, a luxury available only to a select few.

Indeed, as we have seen, European citizenship was always tied to European commerce and, over time, did become its own kind of luxury good. In 1969, for example, Commissioner Guido Colonna di Paliano, an Italian diplomat, observed that freedom of establishment and freedom to supply services were "basic personal rights attaching to future citizenship of an economic Europe."[62] This was, perhaps, one of the first seeds of the modern-day "commodification" of EU citizens that places citizens' mobility on par with other market freedoms (goods, services, and capital) and subjects their freedom of movement to the condition of economic activity or self-sufficiency.[63] At the same time, migration inside the Community driven by economic reasons was conducive to bringing social claims, such as those made by Southern Italian workers who are the focus of Jacobson's contribution to this volume. The mobility of European workers blurred the boundaries of national social systems and caused some de-territorialization of social rights, later embodied in the legal concept of modern-day EU citizenship.

In 1972, during the first summit after the Community's first enlargement, which encompassed the UK, Denmark, and Ireland, the Italian prime minister Giulio Andreotti proposed formally establishing European citizenship.[64] He suggested that it would supplement the citizenship currently possessed by the "inhabitants" of member states.[65] It is significant that Andreotti spoke of inhabitants, not citizens, because recently some commentators have suggested making it possible to acquire European citizenship after a period of residence in the EU, thereby removing the requirement that European citizens must hold a member state's citizenship.[66] What is now considered a rather

---

62. *Bulletin of the European Communities* 2, no. 8 (1969): 158.
63. Mark van Ostaijen, Ursula Reeger, and Karin Zelano, "The Commodification of Mobile Workers in Europe—a Comparative Perspective on Capital and Labour in Austria, the Netherlands and Sweden," *Comparative Migration Studies* 5, no. 1 (2017): 1-22, https://doi.org/10.1186/s40878-017-0048-0.
64. "The First Summit Conference of the Enlarged Community (II)," *Bulletin of the European Communities* 5, no. 11 (1972): 46.
65. "First Summit Conference of the Enlarged Community (II)."
66. Rainer Bauböck, "The Three Levels of Citizenship in the European Union," *Phenomenology and Mind* 8 (2015): 73, https://doi.org/10.13128/PHE_MI-17735; Theodora Kostakopoulou, "Ideas, Norms and European Citizenship: Explaining Institutional Change," *Modern Law Review* 68, no. 2 (2005): 242-43, https://doi.org/10.1111/j.1468-2230.2005.00536.x; Jacqueline Bhabha, "'Get Back to Where You Once Belonged': Identity, Citizenship, and Exclusion in Europe," *Human Rights Quarterly* 20, no. 3 (1998): 605, https://doi.org/10.1353/

radical reformist idea was actually conceived of twenty years before the formal introduction of European citizenship.

Furthermore, Andreotti suggested filling European citizenship with meaningful political content. Specifically, he indicated that European citizenship should permit the "exercise [of] some political rights, such as that of participating in communal elections."[67] This part of Andreotti's vision is now a reality—the Treaty on the Functioning of the EU guarantees the right of European citizens to vote and stand as candidates in local elections, even if they are not citizens of the state in which they reside.[68] As Fransee's study of women's suffrage and Kergomard's investigation into the idea of compulsory voting demonstrate, voting rights are of particular importance for the construction of a citizenship regime. The inclusion of this element in the idea of European citizenship contributed substantially to its later emergence as a legal status.

In 1974, at a Community summit, state leaders agreed to establish a working group tasked with looking into "the possibility of establishing a passport union and, in anticipation of this, the introduction of a uniform passport."[69] The passport union was expected to include "stage-by-stage harmonization of legislation affecting aliens and . . . the abolition of passport control within the Community."[70] Their ambitions went even further, and it was agreed that another working group would study "the conditions and the timing under which the citizens of the nine member states could be given special rights as members of the Community."[71] This decision marked a significant step toward common European citizenship. These decisions not only paved the way for uniform passports and the abolition of passport checks but also envisaged harmonization of laws and, most importantly, the bestowal of certain common rights on the nationals of the member states.

The Commission was subsequently tasked with reporting on the prospects of the implementation of these policies. The following

---

hrq.1998.0023; Randall Hansen, "A European Citizenship or a Europe of Citizens? Third Country Nationals in the EU," *Journal of Ethnic and Migration Studies* 24, no. 4 (1998): 754–55, https://doi.org/10.1080/1369183X.1998.9976664.

67. "First Summit Conference of the Enlarged Community (II)," 46.

68. Consolidated version of the Treaty on the Functioning of the European Union, art. 20(2)(b).

69. Communiqué of European Community "Summit" Meeting–Background Note No. 27/1974 (1974), para. 10.

70. Communiqué of European Community "Summit" Meeting–Background Note, para. 10.

71. Communiqué of European Community "Summit" Meeting–Background Note, para. 11.

year, it observed that the creation of a passport union and abolition of border checks "would gradually give non-member countries the feeling that here were the beginnings of Community citizenship."[72] Nevertheless, the Commission also noted that European citizenship did not yet exist.[73] It also insisted that the Parliament would have to be elected directly by universal suffrage in order to make citizenship a reality. Such a direct election indeed took place four years later.[74] By this point, European citizenship was thought of as a politically meaningful status, one that would put "Community nationals on the same footing as the nationals of the host country with regard to political rights."[75] Later, the Commission stated, "On the road towards European Union," it is "participating in the progressive creation of a European citizenship."[76]

In 1975, a further step was taken toward common citizenship when the Belgian prime minister Leo Tindemans presented a report to the European Council.[77] Outlining a vision for transforming the Communities into a European Union, Tindemans insisted, "European Union is not a matter only for the States or the Governments: it concerns the European citizen as well."[78] He thereby called for "a citizen's Europe"—an expression that was first introduced by the Commission in the early 1970s and which is now firmly a part of the EU's political lexicon.[79] The report manifested a new turn in the emergence of European citizenship, bringing the project closer to the individual. In European integration, Tindemans saw something that went far beyond economic collaboration. Rather, the European project would involve the "rapprochement of peoples who wish to go forward together, adapting their

---

72. "Towards European Citizenship: Implementation of Point 10 of the Final Communiqué Issued at the European Summit Held in Paris on 9 and 10 December 1974," *Bulletin of the European Communities*, Supplement 7/75, 1975, 15.

73. "Towards European Citizenship: Implementation of Point 10," 16.

74. Maas also notes the significance of the direct election for the democratic process in Europe, which ultimately led to the formalization of European citizenship. Maas, *Creating European Citizens*, 34.

75. "Towards European Citizenship: Implementation of Point 11 of the Final Communiqué Issued at the European Summit Held in Paris on 9 and 10 December 1974," *Bulletin of the European Communities*, Supplement 5/75, 1975, 28.

76. "The Protection of Fundamental Rights as Community Law Is Created and Developed," COM(76) 37, *Bulletin of the European Communities*, Supplement 5/76, 1976, 14.

77. Leo Tindemans, *European Union: Report by Mr Leo Tindemans, Prime Minister of Belgium, to the European Council* (*Bulletin of the European Communities*, Supplement 1/76, 1976).

78. *Bulletin of the European Communities*, no. 12 (1975).

79. Tindemans, *European Union: Report by Mr Leo Tindemans*, 26; Pukallus, *Representations of European Citizenship*, 96.

activity to the changing conditions in the world while preserving those values which are their common heritage."[80] This ambitious report was met with mixed reactions, as not all member states were excited by the prospect of integrating foreign nationals.[81]

The report was also notable because Tindemans suggested that the Union should protect citizens' rights and should make European unity perceptible in the daily lives of Europeans.[82] Regarding the former, Tindemans proposed strengthening the protection of civil and consumer rights, while offering more advanced protection of the environment.[83] As to the latter, Tindemans referred to fostering student mobility and media collaboration and paid special attention to the free movement of persons (all persons, not just workers). He maintained that "the day that Europeans can move about within the Union, can communicate among themselves and when necessary receive medical care without national frontiers adding to the problems of distance, European Union will become for them a discernible reality."[84] Tindemans's report marks a further deviation from earlier models of common citizenship that were based chiefly on the free movement of workers. Including all Europeans within the ambit of shared citizenship, Tindemans suggested bringing European institutions closer to citizens rather than the other way around.

Although these conversations took place at an elite level, by the 1970s the idea of European citizenship enjoyed widespread support from citizens of Community countries. The 1976 edition of Eurobarometer, the public opinion survey regularly conducted by the Commission, reported that, among the nationals of the member states, "seven out of ten are in favour of European citizenship."[85] It is, of course, not entirely clear what form of European citizenship enjoyed such support. The Eurobarometer specifically mentioned only the so-called European passport.[86] Nevertheless, later opinion polls confirmed that the public continued to support European citizenship.

In 1983, an analysis of the past decade's surveys concluded that "the idea of European citizenship has not only permeated all strata of the

---

80. Tindemans, *European Union: Report by Mr Leo Tindemans*, 26.
81. Maas, *Creating European Citizens*, 32.
82. Tindemans, *European Union: Report by Mr Leo Tindemans*, 26
83. Tindemans, 26–27.
84. Tindemans, 27–28.
85. *Euroforum—Europe Day by Day* no. 1/76 (1976).
86. *Euroforum—Europe Day by Day* no. 1/76 (1976).

population, but has also taken deeper root than sound common sense might lead one to think."[87] Strikingly, this analysis of public opinion suggested that the growing feeling of European citizenship involved an outer dimension. The polls found that a sense of common citizenship had made Europeans "more open towards, and less suspicious of, other nations."[88] They were "gradually coming to acquire a feeling of European citizenship, with all that implies for their attitudes to the world geopolitical structure."[89] European citizenship was thus seen as contributing to Europeans' realization of their place in the global political arena.

Around 1976, European politicians started to speak of European citizenship as if it were already present.[90] One of the first recordings of this change in language can be found in one of the speeches given by George Thomson, a British politician who served as the European commissioner for regional policy. Thomson pointed to how various Community policies, regarding consumer protection, social welfare, and the environment, benefited citizens directly and were thus imbuing citizenship with political meaning. Thomson enthusiastically asked, "Is there in fact already as such a European citizenship? I believe such a citizenship is coming into existence. Lawyers have long been aware of this."[91] Referring to the emerging legal status that nationals of all member states enjoyed, Thomson indicated that they needed further formalization. More than fifteen years before the Maastricht Treaty, he referenced European citizenship as something that already existed or, at least, would soon come into existence.

These discussions of European citizenship did have some important limitations. The concepts of European citizenship and of citizenship as such in the supranational context were not always the same as understood today. European citizenship was often, although not always, understood quite loosely. Many proponents of shared European citizenship did not think of it in the same way that they perceived national citizenship. Rather they often understood it as a form of idealistic attachment or as a symbolic means of political participation.

---

87. Division IX/C/11—Coordination and Preparation of Publications, *Europe as Seen by Europeans: Ten Years of European Polling 1973–1983* (1983), 12.
88. *Europe as Seen by Europeans*, 28.
89. *Europe as Seen by Europeans*, 28.
90. Pukallus, *Representations of European Citizenship*, 96; Wiener, *European Citizenship Practice*, 65–66.
91. George Thomson, *Address to the European Building Societies Congress* (1976), 20.

Politicians often spoke of European citizenship flippantly, absent details of implementation. In contrast, commissioners and other officials were usually modest in their expectations and focused on specific steps that might foster European citizenship, whatever was meant by it. These politicians and bureaucrats were not unaware of this lack of agreement about what European citizenship meant. Take, for example, Hector Riviérez, a French member of European Parliament from the European Progressive Democrats. In 1978, during a discussion of Mario Scelba's report on the implementation of the 1974 Paris Communiqué, Riviérez pointed out that the communiqué actually spoke of the citizens of the member states, not of the Community.[92] He also expressed his concerns over the precise meaning of the special rights to be granted to all Community citizens. Notably, this uncertainty persists today in the form of doubts about the exact meaning of the expression "the substance of the rights" used by the CJEU in its famous 2011 *Ruiz Zambrano* decision.[93] In that case, the CJEU ruled that Union law prohibits measures by national authorities that deprive EU citizens of the genuine enjoyment of the substance of rights associated with their European citizenship status.[94] While articulating this prohibition clearly, the court left obscure the precise content of those rights and their substance.

Another connection with modern-day uncertainties over European citizenship is how Riviérez was wary of the Community's choice against the development of European citizenship as a legal concept independent of member state nationality. It meant that the Community bodies could intervene to protect the rights granted to Community citizens only when Community law is broken.[95] This concern persists today with regard to the wholly internal rule that limits the scope of European citizenship.[96]

Citizenship as a Legal Concept

Political discussions and philosophical discourse began to converge in the 1980s, when politicians proposed European citizenship as a legal

---

92. European Parliament, *Proceedings of the Round Table on "Special Rights and a Charter of the Rights of the Citizens of the European Community" and Related Documents*, 1979, 108.
93. *Gerardo Ruiz Zambrano v Office national de l'emploi (ONEm)* [2011] Case C-34/09 ECLI:EU:C:2011:124, 2011 European Court Reports 1232, para. 42.
94. *Gerardo Ruiz Zambrano v Office national de l'emploi*.
95. *Gerardo Ruiz Zambrano v Office national de l'emploi*.
96. Serhii Lashyn, "The Aporia of EU Citizenship," *Liverpool Law Review* 42, no. 3 (2021): 361–77, https://doi.org/10.1007/s10991-021-09279-y.

concept enshrined in law. At that time, single citizenship was discussed as a legal status in great detail, focusing on the specific rights that such status would entail. This is particularly evidenced in the reports produced by the Italian politician Guido Gonella on the Commission's memo on the issue of accession to the European Convention on Human Rights and by another Italian politician, Pietro Adonnino, for the ad hoc Committee on a People's Europe.[97] European citizenship was often spoken of as if it were already present or agreed upon. As commissioner Frans Andriessen observed in 1984, "Union citizens would enjoy dual citizenship—citizenship of their own State and citizenship of the Union."[98] In 1987, the Commission had already stated that "332 million Europeans have a new citizenship: one that in no way supplants their national citizenship, but supplements it," meaning that European citizenship enhances the national citizenship of the member states without replacing it.[99]

An attempt to introduce European citizenship as a legal concept took place in the Draft Treaty Establishing the European Union authored by Altiero Spinelli and adopted by the European Parliament in 1984.[100] The draft treaty provided that "the citizens of the Member States shall *ipso facto* be citizens of the Union."[101] Although the draft treaty did not enter into force because it was not ratified, the inclusion of citizenship in its text was quite important for furthering political discussion on European citizenship, as Maas observes.[102]

Just a year before the Maastricht Treaty was ratified, Italian member of the European Parliament Rosaria Bindi submitted a report. She framed this report in the larger context of the crisis of the nation-state caused by rising globalization.[103] She believed that the understanding

---

97. "Report from the Ad Hoc Committee on a People's Europe," *Bulletin of the European Communities* 3-1985; "Report Drawn Up on Behalf of the Legal Affairs Committee on the Memorandum from the Commission of the European Communities on the Accession of the European Communities to the Convention for the Protection of Human Rights and Fundamental Freedoms" (Doc. 160/79–COM(79) 210 Final) Document 1-547/82, PE 74.231/Fin (European Parliament Working Documents 1982-1983, 1982).
98. "The Future Development of a Political European Union," address given by Mr. Franciscus Henricus Johannes Joseph Andriessen (1984), 10.
99. *New Rights for the Citizens of Europe*, European File 11/87, June–July 1987, EU Commission brochure, 3.
100. Maas, *Creating European Citizens*, 35.
101. Draft Treaty Establishing the European Union, OJ C77/33 (1984), art. 3.
102. Maas, *Creating European Citizens*, 35–36.
103. Rosaria Bindi, *Interim Report of the Committee on Institutional Affairs on Union Citizenship*, European Parliament Document A3-0139/91, May 23, 1991.

of citizens as subjects was obsolete and the very concept of citizenship should be connected to fundamental rights and democratic participation.[104] In light of the threats to human rights that the dominance of the citizenship of nation-states may pose, Bindi saw the EU as a unique opportunity for "overcoming these limits and resolving problems, with which the individual State is now ill-equipped to deal."[105] Essentially, Bindi saw the constitutional momentum of the European project as a unique opportunity to remedy the many shortcomings of national citizenship regimes by means of creating a supranational citizenship.

At the same time, Bindi was cautious about attaching European citizenship to the nationality of member states. Doing so would give nation-states a grip on European citizenship, thereby negating the added value it might create. Among such problems, she pointed to "the decision by a Member State to make the acquisition of its own citizenship too easy, at least from the point of view of the other Member States."[106] This is exactly what happened in 2020 when the Commission launched infringement procedures against Cyprus and Malta because of their investment citizenship schemes, which effectively allowed the purchase of citizenship by wealthy individuals.

The Undetermined Future of European Citizenship

To further European integration and to achieve the "ever closer union among the peoples of Europe," a common citizenship category had to be established.[107] Its emergence was not, however, predestined. The notion of European citizenship took diverse forms and changed over time.

For legal scholars, the historical analysis above sheds light on the concept of European citizenship found now in the primary law of the Union. Sometimes confusing, limited, and elusive constructs of European citizenship as a legal concept could be better understood in the context of its historical evolution. It is also illuminating for legal researchers—often preoccupied with refining terminology or with normative, if not scholastic, analysis of legal categories—to appreciate just how fluid and divergent the discussion of European citizenship that preceded its formal birth really was.

---

104. Bindi, *Interim Report*.
105. Bindi, 9.
106. Bindi, 11.
107. Treaty on European Union [1992] (OJ C191/1), art. 1.

For historians, the nonlinear development of European citizenship provides a vivid example of the tectonic transformations that citizenship underwent in postwar Europe in the course of what Lasús calls in his contribution "the renegotiation of the concept of citizenship." The transcendence of national borders and departure from understanding citizenship as the exclusive domain of nation-states occurred in a time of rebuilding following the Second World War. Remarkably, the journey of European citizenship from a vague, idealist, and symbolic idea to a fully fledged legal reality happened within one generation and accompanied the political debates surrounding the uniting of Europe.

Now a functioning concept of EU law for more than thirty years, European citizenship is far from a done deal. Among other concerns, its social component remains a hotly debated political issue. The problem of democratic deficit that European citizenship was supposed to resolve remains on the Union's agenda. The future of European citizenship is as undefined and undetermined as its past.

Serhii Lashyn is a doctoral candidate at Universität Hamburg. He teaches as an adjunct lecturer at Universität Hamburg and Europa-Kolleg Hamburg. Previously he served as a Young European Ambassador within EU NEIGHBOURS East, worked at a law firm, graduated with an LLM degree with distinction from Central European University, and was a recipient of the Academic Scholarship of the President of Ukraine during his bachelor's studies at Yaroslav Mudryi National Law University.

Index

Page references in *italics* indicate illustrations.

abortion, 224, 228, 229, 243–244
Adenauer, Konrad, 277
Adorno, Theodor, 89
Africa: colonialism and, 274; France and, 49, 51, 52; suffrage, 52–57
Algeria, 47, 49, 54, 107n69, 220, 221, 222–223
Andreotti, Giulio, 283–284
anticommunism, 120–121, 135, 167, 211. *See also* communism
antiliberalism, 169, 170, 172n28, 173, 181–182
antisemitism, 156
Archimède, Gerty, 58
archives, 15–16, 28–29, 87, 164, 249
Arendt, Hannah, 2, 3, 26n6, 28, 149, 151–152
Aryan descent, 79, 92
Association of French Union Women from Overseas and the Metropole (AFUW), 46–47
asylum, 118, 128–134, 139, 141
Atlantic Charter, 168
Austria, 74, 83. *See also* Vienna (Austria)

Balkan Trilogy (Manning), 20, 76; dislocation in, 148–149, 151–152, 154, 156–158; documentation in, 149–150; origins, 147–148; state in, 146–147, 155, 156, 160–161; TV adaptation, 159
Bardoux, Jacques, 201, 202, 208
Basic Law, 86–87, 93–94, 105, 107–109, 111
beauty pageants, 241, *242*, *243*
belonging, 2, 30, 159, 246
Beneš, Edvard, 126
benevolence, 155–159
Berckhouwer, Cornelis, 268

Bergemann, Erika, 198–199
Berlin Wall, 184
Bindi, Rosaria, 289–290
biological racism, 102–103, 113
black books, 231
Bloch, Marc, 18–19
Bolshevism, 177
borders, 147, 155–156, 272
Braverman, Suella, 2
Brecht, Bertolt, 31
brigade books: generally, 183–185; career advancement in, 193–194; factory work in, 189–190, 191, 197, 199–200; men criticized in, 192; quotes from, 195–196; the state and, 198; verticality of citizenship in, 188
Britain: communism in, 154, 155; elections, 275–276; Europe and, 274, 275–276; geopolitical identity postwar, 145, 161; Romania and, 148, 152, 158; welfare state, 5–6
British Nationality Act (1948), 150
Brubaker, Rogers, 9
Bundesministerium des Innern (Federal Ministry of the Interior), 95–98, 101, 103–107, 108, 110

Călinescu, Armand, 143
Cameroon, 53–54
Camp XV, 75
Canning, Kathleen, 3, 8, 9, 28n14, 29, 249
Care and Maintenance files (CM/1), 36–37
Carrero Blanco, Luis, 166–167, 168, 169
Castiella, Fernando María de, 174–175
Catholicism, 167, 169, 172, 173–175, 177–178, 182, 207
Chad, 49

294 INDEX

Chamisso, Adelbert von, 30
Charter of Rights (Spain, Fuero de los Españoles), 22
children: childcare, 198; deaths, 254–256; murders, 76, 77, 78; in protests, *254*; race and, 89–90; as refugees, 116, 130, 131
Chinese people, 109
Christianity: Catholicism (*see* Catholicism); citizenship and, 155, 262; conservatism, 170–171; democratic movements, 206, 262–263; law and, 164, 173–174; marriage with Jews, 154; Orthodoxy, 121
Churchill, Winston, 274, 275
citizen petitions, 189–190, 191, 192, 193, 197
citizens, 1, 79, 158, 216
citizenship: definitions, 3–10, 49, 151; antiliberalism and, 172n28, 181–182; aspirational citizenship, 27, 44; Christianity and, 155, 262; citizenship studies, 161; common citizenship, 277, 281, 285, 287; Czechoslovakia and (*see* Czechoslovakia—citizenship and); dual citizenship, 135; formal citizenship (*see* formal citizenship); under Francoism, 179–181; gender and, 54, 69–70, 190, 195, 196; Germany and (*see* Germany—citizenship and); ideologies of, 126–127; Jewish people and, 155; labor and, 224, 227; law and (*see* law—citizenship and); legal citizenship, 118, 134–140, 141; losing, 32, 35, 103–104, *122*, 126, 134; models of, 170; Muslim people and, 155; vs. nationality, 29; nation-state and, 8–9, 247; Nazism and, 21, 101–102; para-citizenship (Wernitznig), 15–16, 67–74; participatory citizenship, 8, 249, 256; post-war rebuilding and, 65–66; precarious citizenship, 158; race and, 54, 112; redefinitions, 141, 144, 145, 153–154, 155, 260–264; Romania and, 153n44; scholarship on, 6, 8–9, 21; social citizenship, 8, 17, 134–140; socialism and, 136–137, 138–139, 142, 185–186; socialist citizenship (*see* socialist citizenship); as social practice, 230, 249; Spain and, 170, 179–181; as state-building, 144–145; temporality and, 10, 18–20, 23–24; verticality of, 10, 16–18, 49, 67, 188, 250, 268–269; voting and, 63; women and, 66–68, 69–70
Cold War, 35, 68, 72, 81–82
collect, 16, 245–246
collectivity, 196, 246
colonialism, 48, 52–57, 127, 218–219, 220–222, 274
commodification, 283
Commonwealth Immigrants Act, 150
communism, 116, 117; anticommunism, 135; in Britain, 154, 155; in Czechoslovakia, 141, 211–212; in France, 207; in Greece, 120; in Italy, 263; law and, 228–229; in Poland, 225, 232; resistance to, 120; sexuality and, 229–230; sex work and, 233, 234; women and, 225, 226–230
compulsory voting: generally, 201–203, 204–205, 222, 223; in French territories, 219–220; support for, 206–209, 212, 213; views on, 210–214; women and, 214–218
comradeship, 196
constitutional nationalism, 153
constitutions: European constitution (draft), 276; French constitution, 201, 221; housing and, 253; Polish constitution, 224; Romanian constitution, 155; social democracy and, 171; women and, 191
corporatism, 169, 175, 176, 177–178
Cosemans, Sara, 150n34
Costa, Pietro, 271
Coudenhove-Kalergi, Richard, 273–274, 276
Cournarie, Pierre, 56
Court of Justice of the European Union (CJEU), 272, 288
COVID-19 pandemic, 265
Czechoslovakia: asylum in, 128–129, 139, 141; citizenship and, 27, 118, 132, 134–140, *135*, 141, 190; communism in, 117, 141, 211–212; Germans in, 125; Hungarians in, 125, 125n38; postwar, 125; sex work and, 230; Soviet invasion, 154; statelessness in, 131, 132–133, 138
—Greek refugees in: generally, 116–117; bureaucracy and, 132–133; communist solidarity, 123–125; lives of, 40, 115–116, 130–131; naturalization and, 97, 135–136,

INDEX

139–140; reception, 126–127; social rights, 137–138, 141

Declaration on Liberated Europe, 168
de Gaulle, Charles, 49, 221, 223
Déloye, Yves, 203
democracy, 164, 165–169, 170, 201–202, 203–204, 206–207, 208
denazification, 72, 79, 80, 83
deportations, 73
deterritorialization, 252, 269, 278, 283
displaced persons (DPs): archival traces of, 28–29; emotional lives of, 17, 25, 39; in Germany, 11–12, 99, 100; Jewish persons, 32–35; repatriation, 27, 34; statistics on, 36–37, 39
divorce, 229
documentation, 130, 149. *See also* passports
Duranti, Marco, 171

Eastern Europe, 91, 97, 98–103, 106, 113, 123, 229
Éboué, Félix, 49, 61
Eijo Garay, Leopoldo, 174
elections, 57–59, 179, 180, 213, 214. *See also* voting
electroconvulsive therapy (ECT), 72, 81
Eley, Geoff, 247
Emde, Silke von der, 29, 39n66
empire, 4, 49
encumbered *(belastete)* citizens, 79
enfranchisement, 13
Epstein, Anne, 38
espionage, 81–82
ethno-nationalism, 91
eugenics, 65–66, 153
Eurobarometers, 286–287
Europe: Britain and, 274, 275–276; citizenship and, 18, 267–275, 277–278, 279–282, 283–289, 290–291; groups within, 176–177; integration, 12; labor and, 280–281; laws and, 270–271, 272–273, 288, 289; voting rights, 284
European Coal and Steel Community, 12, 278
European Economic Community (EEC), 279
European Movement, 172, 276–277
European Parliamentary Union (EPU), 276–277
European Union, 7, 270–271, 272–273, 285–286, 289
expatriation, 161

family: gender and, 74, 78, 236; Stalinist policies, 228–229; structures, 235
Fanon, Frantz, 89
fascism, 12, 22
Federal Ministry of the Interior (BMI), 95–98, 101, 103–107, 108, 110
Fehrenbach, Heide, 89–90
Felman, Shoshana, 64
female suffrage, 50, 51, 52–57, 63, 203, 210, 218
feminism, on communism, 226–227
feminist movements, 13
fiction, postwar, 145
Fidelis, Małgorzata, 226, 241
Fitzpatrick, Sheila, 35n45
formal citizenship: as exclusive, 9; in Italy, 16, 248, 260; laws and, 8; protections from, 26; socialism and, 136; in Spain, 22; in West Germany, 16
Foucault, Michel, 146
France: Africa and, 49; Algeria and, 49; anticommunism in, 211; citizenship and, 5, 20, 21–22, 107n69; communism in, 207; democracy in, 201–202, 203–204, 208; empire and, 49, 50, 51, 60, 63; European citizenship and, 274; naturalization guidelines, 88; racism and elections and, 220–221; suffrage in (generally), 219; unification, 277; Vichy regime, 46, 49, 50, 55, 56, 176, 210; women and, 46–47. *See also* compulsory voting
Francoism: generally, 163–164, 165, 178, 181–182; citizenship and, 170, 179–181; democracy and, 170; political changes under, 167–169; postwar international order and, 165–169; rights and, 172–173, 175
freedom, 210, 212, 217, 221, 283
French Revolution, 146, 176
FRG. *See* Germany, West
Fuchs, Rachel, 38
Fuero de los Españoles, 170–178, 179, 181, 182
Fukuyama, Francis, 2
Funk, Nanette, 226–227

gay and lesbian liberationism, 13
gay men, 180
GDR. *See* Germany, East
gender: citizenship and, 54, 69–70, 190, 195, 196; conformity and, 67; family

INDEX

gender (*continued*)
and, 74, 78, 236; gender equality, 185, 186, 192, 194, 238, 239; labor and, 190, 191–193, 195; morality and, 234–237; statelessness and, 38, 40–41, 43–44; work as gendered, 190
General Hospital (Vienna), 65–66, 67, 70, 71–72
German language, 70–71
Germany: displaced persons (DPs), 11–12, 99, 100; identity, 85; statelessness in, 34
—citizenship and: Czechoslovakia and, 27, 97, 125; displaced persons (DP) and, 37; expansions of, 6; marriage and, 99, 100–101, 103–104; noncitizenship and, 33; race and, 92, 96, 105–106, 107–109, 111–112; requirements, 20
Germany, East, 108–109; citizenship and, 185; scholarship on, 187–188; women and, 186–187, 189, 190–191, 193, 197, 198–199
Germany, West: Basic Law, 86–87, 93–94, 105, 107–109, 111; industry and, 277; Italian migrants in, 250–252, 257–258, 261, 264, 278; labor and, 250–251; race and, 88, 90, 105–111, 262; unification, 277
—housing and: Italian migrants claims generally, 16, 247–248, 257–258, 260; laws, 262–263; living conditions, 253–254; rent prices, 251–252; shortages, 245
—naturalization in, 93–105; generally, 19–20, 36; applications, 87–88; legal aspects, 22, 110–111; race and, 91, 106–107
Ghodsee, Kristen, 226, 227
Giacobbi, Paul, 50–51, 56, 57
Gomułka, Władysław, 234
government, limits of, 146
Greece: citizenship and, 19, 117, 119, 121–123, *122*; communism in, 120; as nationality, 133, 139, 141; refugees and, 17, 97; repatriation, 140. *See also* Czechoslovakia—Greek refugees in
Greece Civil War: citizenship and, 140, 190; documentation and, 130; labor integration and, 119; refugees from, 27, 115, 121, 126, 127. *See also* Czechoslovakia—Greek refugees in

Grenier, Fernand, 50, 51
Großmann, Till, 190n28
Guadeloupe, 58
Guiana, 58

Havelková, Barbara, 230
Hayek, Friedrich von, 171
Heimann, Lotte Grünfeld, 33
historiography on race, 88, 90
Holborn, Louise, 37
homelessness, 11, 131
homophile groups, 13
hospitals. *See* women—psychiatric hospitalizations
housing; deaths and, 255–256; housing shortages, 235, 245–246; Italy and, 16, 245–246, 247–248, 249, 251, 253, 255–257; Poland and, 235; protests and, 256, 258–261; race and, 262; rent prices, 254, *254*, 264; as a right, 254, 260, 264–265; Turin and, 258–259; West Germany and (*see* Germany, West—housing and)
housing shortages, 245–246
human rights, 171, 247, 252–253, 254–256
Hungarian people: in Czechoslovakia, 125, 125n38
Hungarian Revolution, 148

identitarian movements, 5
illness, 75
imagined community, 135–136
Immigration Act (1924), 32
India, women's voting rights, 57, 59–60
integration, 269
International Refugee Organization (IRO), 11, 27, 35, 36–37, 38–39, 40, 41, 43–44
International Tracing Service (ITS) Digital Archive, 29
intersectionality, 9, 21, 27–28, 42
investment citizenship schemes, 290
Iordachi, Constantin, 144–145, 153n43
Irvin, Ronald, 170
Italy: citizenship and, 42; communism in, 263; democracy in, 206–207; free movement, 278; housing and, 16, 245–246, 247–248, 249, 251, 253, 255–256; protests in, 256; Southern Italy, 250, 254; unions in, 245

Jewish people: antisemitism towards, 156; citizenship and, 92–93, 111–112,

INDEX 297

155; denationalization, 32, 33, 85–86; marriage with Christians, 154
Judt, Tony, 163

Kapuściński, Ryszard, 235
Karadzos, Georgios, 130, 136
Kerno, Ivan, 32
Klich-Kluczewska, Barbara, 228
Kostopoulos, Tasos, 121

labor: citizenship and, 224, 227; Europe and, 280–281; gender and, 190, 191–193, 195; labor camps, 225; labor integration, 118–119; reproductive labor, 224, 228, 243; West Germany and, 250–251; of women (*see* women—labor of); workers' brigades, 183–184, 190, 195
Larcher, Silyane, 204
Łastik, Salomon, 238–239
law: Christianity and, 164, 173–174; classical law, 146; colonialism and, 48; communism and, 228–229; Europe and, 270–271, 272–273, 288, 289; in Spain, 167–168, 174, 179
—citizenship and: BMI commission, 109–110; European citizenship, 281–282, 288–290; frameworks, 7; naturalization applications, 87–88, 93, 94, 101–102; race and, 90, 91, 92
League of Nations Mandate, 53
Lebow, Katherine, 236
Lechner, Hans, 110
leftist resistance, 120
legal citizenship, 118, 134–140, 141
Leo XIII, 177
Léro, Jeanne, 57
Levi Sandri, Lionello, 280–281
Lišková, Kateřina, 229
Lister, Ruth, 144
Lori, Noora A., 147
Lyon, Margot, 282–283

Maas, Willem, 16, 278, 279
Maastricht Treaty (1992), 18, 267–268, 269, 281, 287
Macedonian people, 140
Madagascar, 52, 58
Makris, Praxitelis, 130–131; *Děti vyděděnců*, 115
Manning, Olivia, 154. See also *Balkan Trilogy* (Manning)

marriage: citizenship and, 40–41, 99, 100, 103–104; documentation, 132; Jewish-Christian marriages, 154; marriage and, 100; mixed marriages, 135; models of, 229; women and, 40–41, 99, 103–104
Marshall, T. H., 6–7, 8, 9, 17, 137
Martín Artajo, Alberto, 166
Martinique, 58
Martino, Gaetano, 280
Marxism, 231
Mazower, Mark, 163
Mekas, Jonas, 25
men: gaze of, 242–243; male suffrage, 47, 63; in Poland, 236
Merger Treaty, 282
migrants vs. refugees, 30
Mirbeau, Octave, 213
Monnet, Jean, 274
morality, 234–237, 239–244
Mosler, Hermann, 106, 108
mothering, 77–78
Moyn, Samuel, 44, 247
multiculturalism, failures of, 2
Muslim people, 54, 55, 155

Nakachi, Mie, 228
Napoleonic Civil Code, 69
Nardal, Paulette, 218
national belonging, 141–142
National Constituent Assembly (NCA), 59, 60–61, 62
nationalism: constitutional nationalism, 153; ethno-nationalism, 91
nationality: vs. citizenship, 29; Greek nationality, 133, 139, 141; losing, 32, 35, 103–104, *122*, 126, 134; passports and, 150
National Socialist German Workers' Party (NSDAP), 85
national sovereignty, 168n16
nation-state, 4, 8–9, 247
naturalization: denaturalization, 126, 168; in France, 88; in Prussia, 91–92; race and, 109; in West Germany (*see* Germany, West—naturalization in); World War II and, 101–102
Nazism: attitudes toward, 134; Austria and, 65; Camp XV, 73; citizenship and, 21, 101–102; denazification, 72, 79, 80, 83; femininity and domesticity under, 79; labor and, 43; legal proceedings, 12; literature

INDEX

Nazism (*continued*)
    about, 30; Romania and, 143; sex work and, 71; support for, 105
    —race and: children, 89–90; classification by race, 92n24; legislation, 85–86, 89–90, 91, 102, 113–114, 275; *Volk,* 93
newspapers, 216
nonvoting: generally, 203, 222; colonized people and, 221; compulsory voting and, 209; political stratification of, 207; views on, 212–213, 214, 218
North Atlantic Treaty, 273
Nowa Huta (Poland), 234–236, 237

Orthodoxy, 121
otherness, 68, 152n41

Palmowski, Jan, 247
Pan-European Union, 273–274
Paragraf zero (documentary), 237–238
paranoia, 81
participatory citizenship, 8, 249, 256
passports, 31, 139, 149, 150–151, 157, 284–285. *See also* documentation
Paul, Kathleen, 151
Peasant Party for Social Union, 201
peculiarity, as term, 168
Pius IX, 174
Pius XI, 177
Poland, 100, 119; citizenship and, 41; communism in, 225, 232; conservatism, 235–236; housing and, 235; men in, 236; refugees in, 124; sexuality (regulation of), 15–16; sexuality and, 240–241; sex work and, 230, 231–232, 235, 242–243; socialism and, 234, 236; women and, 224, 225, 227
policing, 71, 131, 132, 231, 233, 261
postwar fiction, 145
Prak, Maarten, 4
precarious citizenship, 158
prisoners of war, 98–99, 102
progress, teleology of, 6–7
propaganda, 160, 174n34, 227
prostitution. *See* sex work
protests: housing and, 256, 258–261; in Italy, 256
psychiatry, 15, 22. *See also* women—psychiatric hospitalizations
Pukallus, Stefanie, 271, 275, 277, 278

race: citizenship and, 54, 112; historiography on, 88, 90; housing and, 262; law and, 105; naturalization and, 109; Nazism and (*see* Nazism—race and); West Germany and, 105–111, 262
racism: biological racism, 102–103, 113; Eastern Europeans and, 91, 98–103, 106, 113; France elections and, 220–221; state racism, 112
Rasse, as term, 89–90, 105, 106, 109, 113
Red Army, 64, 66, 261
Refugee Convention (1951), 2, 129, 131–132
refugees: in *Balkan Trilogy,* 149, 151; children as, 116, 130, 131; definitions, 141; vs. migrants, 30; politicization of, 128; residency rights, 136; statelessness of, 131, 132–133. *See also* Czechoslovakia—Greek refugees in
repatriation, 28, 34, 40, 122, 123, 140
reproductive labor, 224, 228, 243
Réunion, 53
rights: in Czechoslovakia, 141; of European citizenship, 279; experience of, 138; housing, 254, 264–265; language of, 252; social rights, 137, 141, 252, 264–265; of women, 197
right to petition, 189n23
Riviérez, Hector, 288
Romania: in *Balkan Trilogy,* 143, 148, 152–153, 154, 156; Britain and, 148, 152, 158; citizenship and, 153n44; constitution, 155; Nazism and, 143; Soviet Union and, 154–155
Rose, Sonya O., 3, 28n14, 29, 158
Rousseau, Jean-Jacques, 4n13, 146

Schäfer, Hans, 110
Schama, Simon, 4
Scheffler, Erna, 105, 107–109
Scheuner, Ulrich, 107, 109
Schönwälder, Karen, 90n17
Schuman Declaration, 277
Scotland, 7
Scott, James, 149
Senegal, 54, 55, 59
sexual assault, 66
sexual citizenship, 8, 13

sexuality, 15–16, 229–230, 238–239, 240–241
sex work: communism and, 233, 234; Czechoslovakia and, 230; in *Paragraf zero*, 237–238; perceptions of, 239–240; Poland and, 230, 231–232, 235, 242–243; regulation of, 71; as threat, 225; violence and, 237–238; women registered as, 232; World War II and, 231
Shoah Foundation, 29
Smith, James, 159–160
Smith, Mark B., 137
social citizenship, 8, 17, 134–140
socialism: citizenship and, 136–137, 138–139, 142, 185–186; competition within, 195; Eastern Europe and, 123; in Guadeloupe, 58–59; Poland and, 234, 236; scholarship on, 187–188; women under, 189
socialist citizenship: in East Germany, 185; emancipatory promise of, 199–200; gender equality and, 194; national belonging and, 141–142
Socialist Unity Party of Germany (SED), 183, 186, 187
social services, 198–199
solidarity, 135, 195
Somers, Margaret, 8
sovereignty, 168n16
Soviet Union, 123, 124, 137, 154–155, 167
Spain: citizenship and, 22, 170, 179–181; Civil War, 170; corporatism, 177–178; as democracy, 169, 170; laws in, 167–168, 174, 179; postwar history, 163; Soviet Union and, 167. *See also* Francoism
Staatsvolk, 112; *Volk* and, 85–86, 93, 111
Stalin, Joseph, 234. *See also* communism
Stańczak-Wiślicz, Katarzyna, 241
state: vs. citizens, 158; legitimacy of, 146–147, 149; regulative power, 160; state benevolence, 155–159; state reform, 205n14
statelessness: age and, 39, 78; in Czechoslovakia, 131, 132–133, 138, 139; declaring, 32, 33–34; disloyalty and, 119–128; emotions of, 119; feelings of, 25–27, 30–31, 44; gender and, 38, 40–41, 43–44;

proving, 37; of refugees, 131, 132–133; repatriation and, 28, 34, 40; women and, 70, 73, 76
state racism, 112
Štiks, Igor, 137, 138
Suez crisis, 148
suffrage: female suffrage, 50, 51, 52–57, 63, 203, 210, 218; in France (generally), 219; male suffrage, 47, 63; universal suffrage, 268
suicide, 75, 76, 77n45

teleology, 6–7, 163
temporality and citizenship, 10, 18–20, 23–24
Third Reich, 75, 79, 80, 93, 112, 185, 186
Thomson, George, 287
Tilly, Charles, 3, 9
Tindemans, Leo, 285–286
totalitarianism, 26n6, 171
Transylvania, 152, 153, 154, 156
trauma, 66
Treaty of Maastricht. *See* Maastricht Treaty (1992)
Treaty of Paris, 271, 278–279
Treaty of Rome, 279
Trump, Donald, 2
truth, 240
Türcksin, Christian, 101n54
Turin, 258–260, 265

Ubangi-Shari, 46
Ukraine, 35, 43
Ule, Carl Hermann, 108
Unione Inquilini, 245, 249, 253–254, 257, 258
United Nations, founding, 12, 166
United Nations Relief and Rehabilitation Administration (UNRRA), 11, 27
United States: Europe (intervention in), 123; immigration quotas, 32; voting rights, 7
United States Holocaust Memorial Museum (USHMM), 28–29
Universal Declaration of Human Rights, 12, 17, 160, 172, 252–253
universal suffrage, 268

Vasiljević, Jelena, 134
Vialle, Jane, 46–47

Vichy regime, 46, 49, 50, 55, 56, 176, 210
Vienna (Austria), 22, 65–68; canals, 82; citizenship and, 67; division of city, 64–65; espionage in, 81–82; immigration and, 64, 68–69; Nazism and, 65
Volk, 108; *Staatsvolk* and, 85–86, 93, 111
voting: citizenship and, 63; under colonialism, 52–57, 218–219, 220–222; compulsory voting (*see* compulsory voting); as duty, 213, 216–217, 222–223; freedom and, 209–214; nonvoting (*see* nonvoting); registration, 61. *See also* elections
voting rights, 7, 21–22; employment and, 180; European citizens, 284; gay men, 180; as gendered, 48; women and, 51, 57–58, 62–63, 180, 215

war, 66, 222
Ważyk, Adam, 234–235
wealth, distribution of, 172
Weichenhain, Charlotte, 195
welfare, 5–6, 137, 172, 246, 248, 255, 257
women: agency of, 214–218, 225–227, 238, 239; citizenship and, 27, 30, 40–41, 66–68, 69–70; communism and, 225, 226–230; East Germany and, 186–187, 189, 190–191, 193, 197, 198–199; elected, 58; family (role in), 74; gendered expectations, 38, 43, 236, 243; as passive, 214; perceptions of, 59; Poland and, 224, 225, 227; reconstruction post-war, 1; representations of, 240–242, *242*, *243*; rights of, 13, 105; sexuality, 15–16, 238; sex work (*see* sex work); under socialism, 189; statelessness and, 38, 70, 73, 76; in Vienna, 66, 71; voting rights and, 51, 57–58, 62–63, 180, 215
—labor of: discrimination, 191–193; double burden and, 197–199; in East Germany, 186–188; International Women's Day, 183, 184; prohibited from working, 180; socialism and, 119, 185, 194–195, 227, 241
—psychiatric hospitalizations: generally, 66, 68; experiences, 67, 69, 70–72, 75–77, 80, 81; pathologies, 73–74
workers: worker-citizens, 185–186; workers' brigades, 183–184, 190, 195
World War I, 26, 95, 155, 273
World War II: anticommunism and, 120; citizenship and, 10, 273–278; democracy and, 202, 205–206; destruction and, 1; displaced persons and, 100; documents around, 268; labor postwar, 186; naturalization and, 101–102; postwar history, 165, 166; reconstruction and, 1, 168; rights and, 252; sex work and, 231
Wright, Quincy, 159

Yugoslavia, 134, 137, 140, 150

www.ingramcontent.com/pod-product-compliance
Lightning Source LLC
Chambersburg PA
CBHW021850230426
43671CB00006B/329